D0850115

Sociobiology and
Human Politics

Sociobiology and Human Politics

WITHDRAWN

Edited by
Elliott White
Temple University

LexingtonBooks
D.C. Heath and Company
Lexington, Massachusetts
Toronto

GN
36 .9
.S 13

Library of Congress Cataloging in Publication Data

Main entry under title:
Sociobiology and human politics.

Includes index.
1. Sociobiology—Addresses, essays, lectures. 2. Political sociology—Addresses, essays, lectures.
I. White, Elliott. II. Title: Human politics.
GN365.9.S613   304   79-6016
ISBN 0-669-03602-1   AACR2

Copyright © 1981 by D.C. Heath and Company

All rights reserved. No part of this publication may be reproduced or transmitted in any form or by any means, electronic or mechanical, including photocopy, recording, or any information storage or retrieval system, without permission in writing from the publisher.

Published simultaneously in Canada

Printed in the United States of America

International Standard Book Number: 0-669-03602-1

Library of Congress Catalog Card Number: 79-6016

Contents

Acknowledgments

I wish to thank the stalwart typists of the Word Processing Center in the College of Liberal Arts at Temple University for preparing most of this manuscript for publication. I especially want to thank Ms. Betty Seidman, the graduate secretary in the Department of Political Science, for her invaluable and invariably competent assistance. The editors at Lexington Books, especially Carolyn Yoder, also rendered helpful advice. Not least, I cannot forget the patient encouragement of my wife, Arleen.

Excerpts from the following publications have been reprinted with the permission of the authors and publishers.

Mary Jane West Eberhard, "The Evolution of Social Behavior by Kin Selection," *Quarterly Review of Biology* 50 (1975):30.

Mary Jane West Eberhard, "Born: Sociobiology," *Quarterly Review of Biology* 51 (1976):89-92.

Ilan Eshel, "On the Neighbor Effect and the Evolution of Altruistic Traits," *Theoretical Population Biology* 3 (1972):258-277.

William D. Hamilton, "Innate Social Aptitudes of Man: An Approach from Evolutionary Genetics," in *Biosocial Anthropology*, edited by Robin Fox (New York: John Wiley and Sons, Inc., and London: Malaby Press Ltd., 1975).

John Hartung, "Natural Selection and the Inheritance of Wealth," *Current Anthropology* 17 (December 1976):612-613 (Chicago: University of Chicago Press).

Richard Lewontin, *The Genetic Basis of Evolutionary Change* (New York: Columbia University Press, 1974).

Matilda White Riley, "Aging, Social Change, and the Power of Ideas," *Generations, Daedalus* (Fall 1978).

Robert Trivers, "The Evolution of Reciprocal Altruism," *Quarterly Review of Biology* (1971):35-36, 45-47, 47-54.

Robert Trivers, "Parent-Offspring Conflict," *American Society of Zoologists* 14 (1974):257-259, 259-260, 262.

S.L. Washburn, "Human Behavior and the Behavior of Other Animals," *American Psychologist* 33 (March 1978):412.

Sewall Wright, "Evolution and Genetics of Populations," in *Variability within and among Natural Populations* (Chicago: University of Chicago Press, 1978), vol. 4, pp. 23, 53, 452, 453, 462, 463.

Introduction

This book grew out of a symposium on sociobiology and politics held on April 11, 1977, at Temple University. Robert Trivers, then of Harvard University, delivered the featured paper on "sociobiology and politics," surely one of the first attempts to link the two fields. Professor Trivers was joined by three discussants: Marvin Bressler from Princeton University, Albert Somit from the State University of New York at Buffalo, and Glendon Schubert from the University of Hawaii. In considering the publication of the proceedings, however, I saw no reason to exclude other prominent political scientists who had become interested in the relationship between biology and politics. As a result, Roger Masters, Hiram Caton, and Fred Willhoite also accepted invitations to prepare chapters for the book. In addition, noted ethologist William Etkin, who attended the symposium, agreed to contribute. All the chapters, then, were prepared especially for the book.

Chapter 1 by Robert Trivers forms the centerpiece for the collection. Professor Trivers begins by describing sociobiology in clear, authoritative terms. He then brings within the focus of the social sciences two of his most seminal and pioneering contributions to sociobiological thought: his theories of reciprocal altruism and of parent-offspring conflict—theories laden with political implications, which nevertheless have never been considered in the study of politics. Finally, Professor Trivers reveals his understanding of the political ramifications of his own and other sociobiological writings.

The following two chapters, by William Etkin and by Hiram Caton, critically assess those aspects of sociobiological theory that relate to political and social science. Professor Etkin points to such factors as ecological variation and change, learning, and the human "capacity for foresight and planning" as important qualifications for any narrow sociobiological theoretical perspectives. Professor Caton also calls attention to the huge gap between genes and traits, between our genetic endowment and our behavioral potential—a gap that is not adequately accounted for in a strict sociobiological analysis.

Roger Masters argues in chapter 4 that even if factors emphasized in sociobiological theory do affect animal behavior, they do so as influences and not as sole determinants; there are, in short, many other factors to consider. Professors Masters and Caton both consider sociobiological theory within the broader context of Western political philosophy, pointing to those strands that contemporary sociobiology implicitly continues.

In chapter 5 Albert Somit focuses on "the nature of human nature" as treated within modern political philosophy, listing the major issues raised within this tradition and suggesting how contemporary sociobiology relates to them. Chapter 6 by Marvin Bressler treats the ideological and politically explosive issues generated by sociobiological analysis, or at least by some responses to it, and indicates how legitimate concerns may be exploited to justify scientifically repressive attitudes. In chapter 7, Glendon Schubert, following a far-reaching critique of sociobiological principles, proceeds in an equally far-ranging survey to suggest ways in which some of these principles might relate to various aspects of political science.

In the concluding two chapters, two of Trivers's most original and politically sensitive ideas are studied in relation to politics. In chapter 8 Fred Willhoite applies the concept of reciprocal altruism to political science, noting in his discussion the relevance of other concepts such as *rank* and *envy*. Finally, in chapter 9 I relate Trivers's theory of parent-offspring conflict to political socialization, linking at the same time evolutionary theory as more broadly conceived.

It occurs to me, as editor of this book, to say something about the possible implications of sociobiology—and perhaps of the life sciences more generally—to the process of scientific inquiry. I would also like to venture an unscientific prediction as to how the future course of political science might be influenced by the emerging developments in the life sciences. (The reader unversed in sociobiological theory might wish to read the first section of chapter 1 by Trivers before continuing here.)

A field called the "sociobiology of science," if one ever should emerge, would suggest that scientists, like everyone else, think and act so as to maximize the successful propagation of their genes. Accordingly, even outwardly cooperative gestures—such as citations of or praise for a colleague's work—reduce to calculated attempts to further one's own work. In other words, a scientist cites another's work in order to have the compliment returned. In the absence of such calculated cooperative effort, scholars and scientists will, like everyone else, pursue their own (genetically defined) interests exclusively. Speaking for myself, how can I possibly claim that my role as editor and as contributor to this book was not undertaken without consideration of its impact on my professional advancement, and therefore on my own personal advancement and—as inclusive-fitness theory would have it—that of my family.

Whatever the motivation, it is clear that the various chapters of this book are highly individual. If that individuality is entirely reducible to a genetically defined self-interest, then any objectivity—and, of course, pretense to objectivity—is shattered. Human reason becomes a hoax and a self-delusion, as does science itself and sociobiology along with it. Joseph Losco, in his doctoral dissertation, "Understanding Altruism: An Inquiry into various Perspectives of Altruism, Concentrating on the Contribution of Sociobiology" (Temple University, 1980) cites Robert Trivers's disparaging remark on the powers of reason (in his foreword to Richard Dawkins's *The Selfish Gene*) to the effect that, "the conventional view that natural selection favors ever more accurate images of the world must be a very naive view of mental evolution." Losco goes on to observe: "In light of such humbling thoughts, it is surprising that sociobiologists make such exaggerated claims for their own theoretical framework which, we must conclude, is likewise a reflection of their own neurophysiological processes."

Of course, it is possible that sociobiologists and their dim view of human reason are entirely right, although it would remain to be explained why genetic interests leading to impartial insights are theirs alone. Yet it is difficult for me, as editor of this collection, to believe that in each chapter the ideas being proposed, discussed, and criticized do not have a meaning and significance on their own terms that cannot be reduced to a genetic (or for that matter, environmental) level. Perhaps that is my own delusion, but to believe otherwise is to cast doubt on the validity and objectivity of any scientific enterprise. (Granted, this is why such delusions may be necessary, assuming all scientific endeavor to be somehow adaptive.)

The fact that scholars and scientists differ and disagree, as they surely do in this book, might be presented as an argument for a relativistic position, whether historically or sociobiologically based. Yet the alternative to an egalitarian relativism wherein each individual's "truth" is merely that and no more might encompass the idea of a hierarchy wherein some individuals, by virtue of greater ability and experience, are more apt than others to envision the truth. Everyone may be fallible, but some are more fallible than others. We all recognize that the science of medicine is imperfect, but we still wish to consult the best doctor around.

Trivers implicitly recognizes this principle of hierarchy at one point in his discussion of parent-offspring conflict. He observes that conflict may exist even when parents and their offspring share the same interest—in which case parents, by virtue of their greater experience, will see things differently and, presumably, with greater wisdom than do their offspring.

In the case of humans, this possibility takes on an added dimension with what Etkin refers to as our unique "capacity for foresight and planning." If contemporary neurobiology should establish a scientific basis for such a capacity, as I believe it may well do (my paper at the 1979 American Political Science Association meeting on "Sociobiology, Neurobiology and Political Socialization" elaborates this contention), then human neurobiology will move to the forefront in the explanation of human behavior and hence of science as well. In both *Sociobiology* and *On Human Nature*, Edward Wilson leaves this possibility open, making clear that for him sociobiology is only half, albeit an extremely critical half, of an emerging "behavioral biology" that includes, as its other half, neurophysiology. As the latter term—as used by Wilson—implies, the study of the brain may stress a materialistic, genetically reductionistic view that will turn out to be generally compatible with the sociobiological perspective now taken by Wilson, Trivers, and others. If, however, the future course of neurobiology happens to be more independent and perhaps more mentalistic, then behavioral biology—as a union and ultimately a synthesis of neurobiology and sociobiology—will also develop more independently of contemporary sociobiology, with the latter also undergoing qualification on its own terms with the passage of time.

To venture a further unscientific speculation, I believe that such an emergent behavioral biology will be brought to bear on science itself. The "behavioral biology of science" will acknowledge the profound human genetic variability that characterizes human populations and therefore the scientific community itself; it will acknowledge individual differences in background and experience as well as in intellect; and it will, finally, accept the possibility that the hypotheses, concepts, and findings that characterize the process of scientific inquiry exist and are subject to validation on their own terms, irreducible to a merely genetic or environmentalist level.

I will make one final unscientific prediction. Such a developing behavioral biology should also form the basis for what Gunther Stent in *The Coming of the Golden Age* calls a "classical paradigm" for political and social science. Up to now political and social science have had no consistent approach. The current behavioral umbrella has suffered from divisive splits in the past and is now, in any case, in the process of being overturned by the increasingly strong winds emanating from the life sciences. Thus I believe that what Stephen Toulmin has called the "would-be discipline" of the social sciences is now being replaced with its classical paradigm. This development, following Stent, means that the general concepts that increasingly will guide future inquiry and will themselves find a fuller validation at differing levels of explanation are presented and explicated for the first time in a systematic fashion. In classical genetics at the turn of the century, the concept of the gene both guided future reseach and came itself to be understood on the level of molecular biology, whereupon genetics entered a new phase in its development as a field.

I will not speculate here on the course of political and social science following their classical era, because I believe that we will not transcend our new status until both sociobiology and neurobiology—both of them also fledging fields—are ready to transcend theirs. And the prospect for their doing so before the passage of generations or even centuries seems to be slight.

The beginning of a classical era for political and social science seems, in any event, to provide quite enough excitement and challenge to last for several generations. Naturally I would like to think of this book as one small step on the road to an elaboration of a classical paradigm for political science. Even if the book contains much in the way of criticism of sociobiological theory, that fact hardly negates the whole of its approach. As Roger Masters concluded his chapter, "It is already clear" [that sociobiological theory] can be of incalculable importance in improving our understanding of human behavior—provided, of course, that its acceptance rests on a balanced understanding of other factors in evolution."

1

Sociobiology and Politics

Robert Trivers

I should say at the very outset that despite some recent efforts at remedial education, I still know virtually nothing about political science. The connections in this chapter between sociobiology, so called, and the social sciences will mainly be drawn with reference to anthropology and psychology. I will start by describing what the recent work in sociobiology is about; then I will focus on reciprocal relations, parent-offspring relations, and deceit and self-deception, emphasizing the new ways in which we view these subjects when we see them in terms of natural selection. Finally, to be true to the "politics" in the title of this chapter, I will discuss the political attacks on sociobiology and the political implications of sociobiology.

Basic Concepts in Sociobiology

To go back to the beginning—which for an evolutionary biologist means Darwin—in 1859 we were given a scientific theory of creation. Until then, the central problem in biology was to explain the unique attributes of living creatures. Living creatures, as opposed to inanimate objects, appear to display a purpose, or purposive behavior. They act as if they are trying to do something. Two questions naturally arise. What are living creatures trying to do, and how did it come about that they are trying to do something?

A Theory of Creation and a Theory of Meaning

Darwin's theory of evolution through natural selection supplied the answers to both questions. By showing how living creatures were created (that is, how they evolved), he showed what they were created to do. He argued that the special attributes of living creatures had come about by means of a process of natural selection repeating itself generation after generation and

Ed. Note: This chapter is based on the talk by Robert Trivers at the Conference on Sociobiology and Politics held at Temple University in Philadelphia on April 11, 1977. It is also supplemented by material from his forthcoming volume on the *Principles of Social Evolution* (Cambridge, Mass.: Harvard University Press), as well as by material from his classic articles on "The Evolution of Reciprocal Evolution" (1971) and "Parent-Offspring Conflict" (1974).

now having gone on, we believe, for about 4 billion years here on earth. Natural selection simply refers to the fact that in nature some individuals leave more surviving offspring than others and that, therefore, the genetic traits, the inheritable traits, of those who are leaving more surviving offspring tend to dominate in future generations.

Another way of putting this is as follows. Imagine that genes are constantly mutating and appearing in natural populations. Some are adversely associated with reproductive success; that is, they decrease the number of surviving offspring of those bearing these genes and thereby decrease the number of surviving copies of themselves. Some genes are neutral, and some increase reproductive success. It is the ones that *increase* reproductive success that tend to be woven together by natural selection.

Once this is stated, the answer to the second question emerges by inspection, namely, organisms are assumed to be attempting to maximize their own reproductive success, where reproductive success is defined as surviving offspring measured at some appropriate time in the future. An individual that leaves more surviving offspring than another is said to be more *fit*. In the context of natural selection, fitness does *not* refer to health, strength, or vigor; it refers only to individual reproductive success and is always demonstrated after the fact. That is, even in the classical theory one cannot in principle say whether one individual is more fit than another until both are dead and their offspring have been counted. If the poor leave more surviving offspring than the rich, then they are, by definition, more fit. To say that the poor are *less* fit than the rich, because they have already lost out in competition for resources (that is, because they are poor), and that therefore the rich should do nothing to ameliorate the condition of the poor since this would interfere with the operation of natural selection (and therefore nature's plan) is nonsense, but clever nonsense which, as one would predict (if people speak to further their own reproductive interests), is spoken more often by rich people than by the poor. To make the point once again: statements about fitness make no assertions whatever about the desirability, moral worth, intellectual cleverness, or any other trait of an individual organism other than its reproductive success; but human beings are expected to argue with each other about the desirability, moral worth, and intellectual cleverness of individual humans in order to advance the reproductive interests of the arguers.

The *function* of a genetic trait refers to the way in which the trait in the past (and probably in the present, although not necessarily) increased the reproductive success of those bearing the trait relative to those without it. In the context of natural selection it is incorrect, and sometimes badly incorrect, to say that the function of a trait is that, in one way or another, it helps the *species* to survive. This is irrelevant to whether a trait is favored by natural selection. Indeed, it is likely that some widespread traits, such as 50:50 sex ratios at conception (Fisher 1958) and male-male competition, including aggression and associated aggressive structures (Trivers 1972), sometimes hurt the species' chance of surviving, but exist nevertheless because individuals possessing such traits outreproduce those without them.

In the context of nonsocial traits, the belief that a given trait (such as a kneecap) has been evolved to benefit the species is merely incorrect; the belief leads to no fundamental misunderstanding of the kneecap, since one assumes that the kneecap benefits the species by furthering the survival of the individuals who make up the species. But in the case of social traits, the distinction is crucial because one can imagine a trait that benefits one individual while harming another or, conversely, one that harms the individual possessing it but benefits another. It makes all the difference in the world whether you believe that I am beating you up for the greater good of mankind or whether you believe that I am beating you up to further my own ends (ultimately, reproductive). I believe that it is possible to see the social world almost exactly upside down by convincing oneself that social traits evolve for the benefit of others.

It is no wonder that Darwin's theory at once provoked a deep response from within his culture. Christianity, especially, felt itself under attack. Its own theory of creation seemed rather sketchy when compared to Darwin's, and it lacked any developmental principle or logic beyond the statement that that which was created was good. By contrast, the concept of natural selection is a creative principle. Natural selection continually recreates and evolves life. In religious terms, God created this living world by natural selection and recreates it in every generation by natural selection. If that which is created is good, then natural selection is good.

One might think that the religious would have delighted at the discovery of so important a creative principle and would have moved to explore its implications. Instead, an attack was launched on many fronts against the very *fact* of evolution; and this inevitably diverted attention from the deeper discovery, namely, the actual mechanism by which change was effected. Once it was clear that the pre-Darwinian tradition of species-advantage thinking continued unabated within biology, Christianity as well as other elements in society was able to admit to the *facts* of evolution without risking any of its deeper preconceptions. This must be a common pattern in human history, whereby a concept is transmuted and rendered impotent (natural selection favors what is good for the species) in order to retain older patterns of thought. Thus is progress impeded. Darwin's work became a minor update to the first few pages of Genesis, and nothing more, when in reality Darwin had discovered the exact, ongoing way in which organic creation is achieved.

The Species-Advantage, Group-Selection Fallacy

Several times in his writings Darwin explicitly recognized that natural selection does not favor traits that are good for the species, for the population, or for the group. It does not favor attributes beneficial to any unit larger than the individual. Nevertheless, after the transient production of Social Darwinism, virtually all biologists settled down to the comfortable belief that natural selection favored what was good for the species. One can find that view expressed even today within biology, and until the 1960s it was virtually the only view expressed. There was no knowledge that Darwin himself did not believe this and that it could not be demonstrated from his work. In the 1960s two things happened. First, there was a wholesale return to natural selection as Darwin understood it. Second, Darwin's natural selection was combined with Mendel's genetics so as to give a more precise and general definition of an individual's self-interest (Hamilton 1964).

There were several reasons for the return to Darwin's concept of natural selection, but perhaps the most important was a book by V.C. Wynne-Edwards (1962) that took the group-advantage interpretation to a logical extreme and forced the confrontation out into the open. Wynne-Edwards argued that animals had evolved a wide range of devices for regulating their own populations, devices involving altruistic reproductive restraint by numerous individuals. That is, individuals were imagined to restrict their own reproduction well below what they were capable of in order to prevent overpopulation and eventual group extinction. In response to this theory, evidence was gathered on some key points. For example, are birds really reproducing as fast as they can in nature, or are they, as Wynne-Edwards argued, often withholding reproduction in order to keep the larger population from going extinct? The evidence gathered seemed to give an unequivocal answer, namely, that birds were reproducing as quickly as they could. Herring gulls, for example, normally produce a clutch of two or three eggs and only very infrequently (about 1 in 1,000 times) lay four eggs. If one gives a herring gull an extra egg or an extra little chick when its clutch is hatching, it ends up raising fewer surviving offspring than if it had started out with only three. This is because it is unable to meet the demands of the larger clutch, so that there is sufficiently higher mortality among the chicks to offset the initial advantage of beginning with four.

Thus the first thing that happened in the 1960s was a return to individual natural selection, with individual reproductive success as the criterion that selection was presumed to be maximizing. The difference this change made can be illustrated by describing one example as it was seen by the two alternative viewpoints, one based on the concept of individual advantage and the other on advantage to the group. The example is infanticide in langur monkeys, the deliberate murder of infants by adult males under conditions that are now reasonably well understood. Langur monkeys run around in groups of about ten to twenty adult females and their young, with whom is typically associated a single adult male. There also exist some large all-male groups, members of which occasionally try to displace the adult male associated with a group of adult females. When such a displacement is successful—that is, when a new male has come into the group—he starts to murder the very young. In particular, he tries to kill infants up to about six months of age, but shows a preference for the very youngest. In addition, he kills infants that are born during the next six months. Shortly after they are born, he murders them.

The initial interpretation of this behavior was a typical example of species- or population-benefit reasoning. It ran, "Well, this is really a population regulation device. The male responds to density by killing off youngsters so as to keep the population from eating itself out of house and home, at which point *everyone* would starve to death. So, better to exercise this kind of prudential restraint." But the facts do not fit this view. For example, why does the male kill only infants under six months of age? These infants are vulnerable to mortality anyway, and have low reproductive value (potential contribution to future generations). In order to regulate population, it would be better to direct one's murder against older individuals—juveniles, or, preferably, young adult females. In addition, the male only kills newborns during the first six months after his takeover, yet he may be associated with the group for as many as five years; thus the infanticide is tied to times of power takeover, which have not been shown to correlate correctly with fluctuations in density. There is, therefore, no clear way in which density is interacting with male behavior so as to regulate itself. Infanticide *is* more commonly reported at high densities, but this is apparently because takeovers are then more frequent (Hrdy 1979). Finally, mothers and other adult females resist strenuously; it is not clear, from a species-advantage viewpoint, why individuals should resist so intensively what is good for the species.

These same facts, however, easily fit an interpretation based on individual advantage. The male did not father the offspring he kills, and if he is distantly related to the male he is displacing—as seen typically to be the case—then he is distantly related to the offspring that he kills. So the cost to the male is trivial, whereas he enjoys an almost immediate benefit in reproductive success. By killing a suckling infant, the male brings its mother more quickly into reproductive readiness. This is because females who are nursing infants are not ovulating. They are not ready to produce their next offspring. By killing off their infants, the male saves himself, so to speak, that amount of female effort that would have been expended on unrelated offspring. Females who lose infants come into estrus within days of the loss.

After infants are seven or eight months old, they are weaned and no longer inhibit maternal reproduction. It is logical, therefore, for a male to direct his murderous impulses only against those who are still nursing. The male's preference for the very young is also explicable, since these are the ones that will require the greatest investment before their mothers are freed to breed again. Finally, the gestation period is seven months in langurs. If a male kills infants born during the six months succeeding his takeover, he will not kill any of his own but, rather, will continue to kill infants fathered by the previous male.

As for the mothers, one would expect them to resist the male's behavior. Their own reproductive success is not improved by having their children killed. The children's reproductive success is likewise adversely affected, so one would expect natural selection to favor countermaneuvers by the adult females and their young, several of which have now been decribed. Adult females may band together to resist the assault. Typically, older females, often related to the mother, intervene and try to protect the infant from the male, sometimes successfully. Mothers with infants of about four or five months of age will sometimes separate themselves from the group and travel on the periphery, where they are presumably more vulnerable to predation but less vulnerable to infanticide. Langur infants tend, in general, to avoid adult males, even their fathers, which contrasts sharply with the behavior of species such as baboons in which infanticide is unreported.

Finally, Hrdy (1978) has discovered a possible counterstrategy that shows nicely how a conflict of interest may generate deceit. She describes a case where a female came into estrus, that is, sexual receptivity, associated with ovulation, while the old male was still in the troop. She mated frequently with this male. A month later she did not come into estrus, which is one indication that she was pregnant; and within two months she had begun to show specific changes in coloration of her perineal region that correlate with pregnancy. Thus she was pregnant, by Hrdy's criteria. When she was two months pregnant, the old male was ousted by a new male. Within a week of this takeover, the female came into estrus again (or pseudoestrus, since Hrdy did not believe the female was then ovulating). In any case, the female looked as if she was in estrus, she was sexually receptive, and she copulated numerous times with the new male. Five months later—not seven months later—she gave birth to an offspring who was not attacked by the new male. Hrdy suggests that the pseudoestrus confused the male about his own paternity and thus protected the newborn.

In summary, let me emphasize two points. First, in group- or species-advantage thinking, one individual's self-interest is typically elevated to that of the entire group. In this example, the adult male's self-interest has been elevated to that of the species. It is even given a new name; what he is concerned about is population regulation, something that is beneficial to all.

The individual with the power to get away with murder becomes a bene-factor, a patron to the weak and foolish. Elevating the self-interest of the powerful to that of the species tends to make the behavior of the powerful appear justified. This must be one of the reasons for the popularity of species-advantage reasoning.

A related feature of such reasoning is that it tends to distract attention from the self-interest of the subordinate actors. No one analyzes how selection acts on them. Thus counterstrategies are overlooked, and resistance tends to be minimized. Conflict is overlooked or explained away as serving some larger function. Those who took up the cry against sociobiology because it appeared to slight the interests of the oppressed failed to appreciate that the foundations of sociobiology have precisely the opposite effect: they call attention to the self-interest of all subordinated actors.

Categories of Social Behavior

It is natural to define categories of social behavior by reference to natural selection, that is, by specifying how behavior affects the reproductive success of individuals involved in social encounters.

We begin with the simplest social situation: one individual (called the *actor*) performs a behavior that affects a second individual (called the *recipient*). Ignoring behavior that has no effect on the reproductive success of the actor (or, separately, on that of the recipient), there can be only four categories: (1) actor receives a benefit but inflicts a cost on the recipient (*selfish*), (2) actor suffers a cost but confers a benefit (*altruistic*), (3) actor and recipient receive benefits (*cooperative*), and (4) actor and recipient both receive costs (*spiteful*). These behaviors are summarized diagrammatically as follows:

Actor	*Recipient*	
B	C	selfish
C	B	altruistic
B_1	B_2	cooperative
C_1	C_2	spiteful

Selfish and cooperative behavior both find natural homes within evolutionary theory; in each case, the actor enjoys a benefit so that genes in the actor for inducing such behavior should become more numerous. Cooperative traits are also favored by selection acting on the other individual, but the spread of selfish traits may be opposed by selection acting on the recipient. Altruistic and spiteful behavior pose a problem for evolutionary theory, because in each case the actor suffers a cost. Spiteful behavior appears to be very rare in nature, but altruistic behavior is surprisingly common. If there exist genes that predispose an individual to act altruistically, then such genes ought to appear *less* frequently in subsequent generations because they appear less frequently in the offspring of the altruist.

One possible way that such altruistic genes can be selected is by return benefit, where this is larger than the initial cost. [*Ed. note*: Trivers has dealt with this important subject in his classic paper, ''The Evolution of Reciprocal Altruism'' (1971), from which several sections will be reprinted shortly to amplify the preceding reference and to relate it directly to human behavior.]

Hamilton's Kinship Theory

A second way that altruistic behavior can be selected is via kinship. Hamilton (1964) showed how this could happen and, in so doing, gave us a new and more general measure of an individual's self-interest. Consider the case in which the recipient of an altruistic act is related to the actor. There is some chance that genes located in the actor are also found in the recipient, by direct descent from a common ancestor. Thus, if the benefit given is large enough when compared to the cost suffered, then the gene or genes for altruism may enjoy a net benefit. To give the argument a quantitative form, we need only specify the probability that a relative has a gene that is found in the actor. Call this probability *degree of relatedness*, or *r*. Degree of relatedness is simple to calculate in diploid species like our own (those in which each individual has two sets of chromosomes). Bear in mind two statements that are approximately true: each individual gets half its genes from each parent, and each parent passes on only half of its genes to each offspring. With these results, *r*s can be calculated. For example, assuming no inbreeding, let us calculate one's *r* to one's half-siblings, related through one's mother. If one has a gene, there is a half chance that one got it from one's mother. If she had it, there is a half chance that she passed it to one's sibling. So *r* to one's half-sibling is $1/2 \times 1/2 = 1/4$. As long as the benefit one is giving the sibling is more than four times the cost, the genes will show a net benefit since the gene appears in the recipient only one-quarter of the time, whereas it always appears in the actor.

If one is related through both one's parents, *r* is $1/4 + 1/4 = 1/2$, so the benefit for altruistic behavior directed toward full siblings need be merely twice as great as the cost, in order for natural selection to favor it. One is related to cousins by one-eighth, so the benefit has to be greater than eight times the cost. The general rule is that altruism will be favored whenever benefit times *r* is greater than cost, or $Br > C$.

According to John Maynard Smith, who tells the story, this particular argument was summarized by J.B.S. Haldane ten years earlier in a bar.

During an evening of drinking, someone asked Haldane whether—after a lifetime studying evolution—he would still be willing to give up his life to save his brother. He replied, "No, but for two brothers or eight cousins." That expresses exactly the quantitative relationship that is supposed to hold under kinship theory. The less related one is, the more one has to aid the recipient if one's genes are to show a net benefit.

So Hamilton coined the term *inclusive fitness*. Fitness is a synonym for reproductive success. Inclusive fitness, then, is a measure of an individual's effects on the abundance of its own genes. It consists of an individual's personal reproductive success plus the effects that individual has on other relatives devalued by the degrees of relatedness to these relatives. *Natural selection favors the traits of individuals who maximize their own inclusive fitness.*

Reciprocal Altruism

The model presented here is designed to show how certain classes of behavior conveniently denoted as "altruistic" (or "reciprocally altruistic") can be selected for even when the recipient is so distantly related to the organism performing the altruistic act that kin selection can be ruled out.[1] The model will apply, for example, to altruistic behavior between members of different species. It will be argued that under certain conditions natural selection favors these altruistic behaviors because in the long run they benefit the organism performing them.

The Model

One human being saving another who is not closely related, and who is about to drown, is an instance of altruism.[2] Assume that the chance of the drowning man dying is one-half if no one leaps in to save him, but that the chance that his potential rescuer will drown if he leaps in to save him is much smaller—say, one in twenty. Assume that the drowning man always drowns when his rescuer does and that he is always saved when the rescuer survives the rescue attempt. Also assume that the energy costs involved in rescuing are trivial compared to the survival probabilities. Were this an isolated event, it is clear that the rescuer should not bother to save the drowning man. But if the drowning man reciprocates at some future time, and if the survival chances are then exactly reversed, it will have been to the benefit of each participant to have risked his life for the other. Each participant will have traded a one-half chance of dying for about a one-tenth chance. If we assume that the entire population is sooner or later exposed to the same risk of drowning, then the two individuals who risk their lives to save each other will be selected over those who face drowning on their own. Note that the benefits of reciprocity depend on the unequal cost/benefit ratio of the altruistic act; that is, the benefit of the altruistic act to the recipient is greater than the cost of the act to the performer, cost and benefit being defined here as the increase or decrease in chances of the relevant alleles propagating themselves in the population. Note also that, as defined, the benefits and costs depend on the age of the altruist and recipient. (The odds assigned here may not be unrealistic if the drowning man is drowning because of a cramp or if the rescue can be executed by extending a branch from shore.)

Why should the rescued individual bother to reciprocate? Selection would seem to favor being saved from drowning without endangering oneself by reciprocating. Why not cheat? (*Cheating* is used throughout this paper solely for convenience to denote failure to reciprocate; no conscious intent or moral connotation is implied.) Selection will discriminate against the cheater if cheating has later adverse affects on his life that outweigh the benefit of not reciprocating. This may happen if the altruist responds to the cheating by curtailing all future possible altruistic gestures to this individual. Assuming that the benefits of these lost altruistic acts outweigh the costs involved in reciprocating, the cheater will be selected against relative to individuals who, because neither cheats, exchange many altruistic acts.

Human Reciprocal Altruism

Reciprocal altruism in the human species takes place in a number of contexts and in all known cultures; see, for example, Gouldner (1960).[3] Any complete list of instances of human altruism would contain the following types of altruistic behavior:

1. Helping in times of danger (such as accidents, predation, intraspecific aggression).
2. Sharing food.
3. Helping the sick, the wounded, or the very young and old.
4. Sharing implements.
5. Sharing knowledge.

All these forms of behavior often meet the criterion of small cost to the giver and great benefit to the taker.

During the Pleistocene, and probably before, a hominid species would have met the preconditions for the evolution of reciprocal altruism: long lifespan; low dispersal rate; life in small, mutually dependent, stable, social groups (Lee and DeVore 1968; Campbell 1966); and a long period of parental care. It is very likely that dominance relations were of the relaxed, less-linear form characteristic of the living chimpanzee (Van Lawick-Goodall 1968) and not of the more rigidly linear form characteristic of the baboon (Hall and DeVore 1965). Aid in intraspecific combat, particularly by kin, almost certainly reduced the stability and linearity of the dominance order in early humans. Lee (1969) has shown that in almost all Bushman fights that are initially between two individuals, others have joined in. Mortality, for example, often strikes the secondaries rather than the principals. Tool use also probably has had an equalizing effect on human dominance relations, and the Bushmen have a saying that illustrates this nicely. As a dispute reaches the stage where deadly weapons may be employed, an individual will often declare: "We are none of us big, and others small; we are all men and we can fight; I'm going to get my arrows" (Lee 1969). It is interesting that Van Lawick-Goodall (1968) has recorded an instance of strong dominance reversal in chimpanzees as a function of tool use. An individual moved from low in dominance to the top of the dominance hierarchy when he discovered the intimidating effects of throwing a metal tin around. It is likely that a diversity of talents usually exists in a band of hunter-gatherers such that the best maker of a certain type of tool is seldom the best maker of a different sort or the best user of the tool. This contributes to the symmetry of relationships, since altruistic acts can be traded with reference to the special talents of the individuals involved.

To analyze the details of the human reciprocal-altruistic system, several important distinctions are discussed here.

Kin Selection. The human species also met the preconditions for the operation of kin selection. Early hominid hunter-gatherer bands almost certainly (like today's hunter-gatherers) consisted of many close kin; and kin selection must often have operated to favor the evolution of some types of altruistic behavior (Haldane 1955; Hamilton 1964, 1969). In general, in attempting to discriminate between the effects of kin selection and what might be called reciprocal-altruistic selection, one can analyze the form of the altruistic behaviors themselves. For example, the existence of discrimination against nonreciprocal individuals cannot be explained on the basis of kin selection, in which the advantage accruing to close kin is what makes the altruistic behavior selectively advantageous, rather than its chance of being reciprocated. The strongest argument for the operation of reciprocal-altruistic selection in humans is the psychological system controlling some forms of human altruism. Details of this sytem are reviewed later.

Reciprocal Altruism among Close Kin. If both forms of selection have operated, one would expect some interesting interactions. One might expect, for example, a lowered demand for reciprocity from kin than from nonkin; and there is evidence to support this (Marshall 1961; Balikci 1964) suggests, however, that reciprocal-altruistic selection has acted even on relations between close kin. Although interactions between the two forms of selection have probably been important in human evolution, this chapter will limit itself to a preliminary description of the human reciprocally altruistic system, a system whose attributes are seen to result only from reciprocal-altruistic selection.

Age-dependent Changes. Cost and benefit were defined previously without reference to the ages, and hence the reproductive values (Fisher 1958), of the individuals involved in an altruistic exchange. Since the reproductive value of a sexually mature organism declines with age, the benefit to him or her of a typical altruistic act also decreases, as does the cost of a typical act he or she performs. If the interval separating the two acts in an altruistic exchange is short relative to the lifespans of the individuals, then the error is slight. For longer intervals, in order to be repaid precisely, the initial altruist must receive more in return than he or she gave. It would be interesting to see whether humans in fact routinely expect "interest" to be added to a long-overdue altruistic debt, interest commensurate with the intervening decline in reproductive value. In humans reproductive value declines most steeply shortly after sexual maturity is reached (Hamilton 1966), and one would predict the interest rate on altruistic debts to be highest then. Selection might also favor keeping the interval between act and reciprocation short, but this should also be favored to protect against complete nonreciprocation. W.D. Hamilton (personal communication) has suggested that a detailed analysis of age-dependent changes in kin altruism and reciprocal altruism should show interesting differences, but the anlaysis is complicated by the possibility of reciprocity to the kin of a deceased altruist (see the discussion of multiparty interactions later in this chapter).

Gross and Subtle Cheating. Two forms of cheating can be distinguished, here denoted as gross and subtle. In *gross cheating* the cheater fails to reciprocate at all, and the altruist suffers the costs of whatever altruism he has dispensed without any compensating benefits. More broadly, gross cheating may be defined as reciprocating so little, if at all, that the altruist receives less benefit from the gross cheater than the cost of the altruist's acts of altruism to the cheater. That is,

$$\sum_{i-ai} c_{ai} > \sum_{j-aj} b_{aj},$$

where c_{ai} = the cost of the ith altruistic act performed by the altruist;

b_{aj} = benefit to the altruist of the jth altruistic act performed by the gross cheater.

In this case, altruistic situations are assumed to have occurred symmetrically. Clearly, selection will strongly favor prompt discrimination against the gross cheater. *Subtle cheating*, by contrast, involves reciprocating, but always attempting to give less than one was given or, more precisely, less than the partner would give if the situation were reversed. In this situation, the altruist still benefits from the relationship, but not as much as he would if the relationship were completely equitable. The subtle cheater benefits more than he would if the relationship were equitable. In other words,

$$\sum_{i,j}(b_{qi} - c_{qj}) > \sum_{i} \ (b_{qi} - C_{ai}) \quad \sum_{i,\,j}(b_{aj} - c_{ai})$$

where the ith altruistic act performed by the altruist has a cost to him of c_{ai} and a benefit to the subtle cheater of b_{qi}, and where the jth altruistic act performed by the subtle cheater has a cost to him of c_{qi} and a benefit to the altruist of b_{aj}. Because human altruism may span huge periods of time, even a lifetime, and because thousands of exchanges may take place involving many different "goods" and with many different cost/benefit ratios, the problem of computing the relevant totals, detecting imbalances, and deciding whether they are due to chance or to small-scale cheating is an extremely difficult one. Even then, the altruist is in an awkward position, symbolized by the folk saying, "half a loaf is better than none"; for if attempts to make the relationship equitable lead to the rupture of the relationship, the altruist, assuming other things to be equal, will suffer the loss of the substandard altruism of the subtle cheater. It is the subtlety of the discrimination necessary to detect this form of cheating and the awkward situation that ensues that permit some subtle cheating to be adaptive. This sets up a dynamic tension in the system that has important repercussions, as discussed later on.

Number of Reciprocal Relationships. It has so far been assumed that it is to the advantage of each individual to form the maximum number of reciprocal relationships, and that the individual suffers a decrease in fitness upon the rupture of any relationship in which the cost to him of acts dispensed to the partner is less than the benefit of acts dispensed toward him by the partner. But it is possible that the relationships are partly exclusive, in the sense that expanding the number of reciprocal exchanges with one of the partners may necessarily decrease the number of exchanges with another. For example, if a group of organisms were to split into subgroups for much of the day (for example, breaking up into hunting pairs), then altruistic exchanges will be more likely between the members of each subgroup than between members of different subgroups. In that sense, relationships may be partly exclusive, with membership in a given subgroup necessarily decreasing exchanges with others in the group. The importance of this factor is that it further complicates the problem of dealing with the cheater and increases competition within a group to be members of a favorable subgroup. An individual in a subgroup who feels that another member is subtly cheating on their relationship has the option of attempting to restore the relationship to a completely reciprocal one or of attempting to join another subgroup, thereby decreasing to a minimum the possible exchanges between himself and the subtle cheater and replacing these with exchanges with a new partner or partners. In short, he can switch friends. There is evidence in hunter-gatherers that much movement of individuals from one band to another occurs in response to such social factors as have just been outlined (Lee and DeVore 1968).

Indirect Benefits or Reciprocal Altruism? Given mutual dependence in a group, it is possible to argue that the benefits (nonaltruistic) of this mutual dependence are a positive function of group size and that altruistic behaviors may be selected for because they permit additional individuals to survive and thereby confer additional indirect (nonaltruistic) benefits. Such an argument can be advanced seriously only for slowly reproducing species with little dispersal. Saving an individual's life in a hunter-gatherer group, for example, may permit nonaltruistic actions such as cooperative hunting to continue with more individuals. But if there is an optimum group size, one would expect adaptations to stay near that size, with individuals joining groups that are below this size and groups splitting up when they are above this size. Behavior would only be selected for to keep an individual alive when the group is below optimum size, not when it is above optimum. Although an abundant literature on hunter-gatherers (and also on nonhuman primates) suggests that adaptations exist to regulate group size near an optimum, there is no evidence that altruistic gestures are curtailed when groups are above the optimum size. Instead, the benefits of human altruism are to be seen as coming directly from reciprocity—not indirectly through nonaltruistic group benefits. This distinction is important because social scientists and philosophers have tended to deal with human altruism in terms of the benefits of living in a group, without differentiating between nonaltruistic benefits and reciprocal benefits (for example, Rousseau 1954; Baier 1958).

The Psychological System underlying Human Reciprocal Altruism

Anthropologists have recognized the importance of reciprocity in human behavior, but in ascribing functions to such behavior they have done so in terms of group benefits, that is, of reciprocity cementing group relations and encouraging group survival.[4] The individual sacrifices so that the group may benefit. Recently psychologists have studied altruistic behavior in order to show what factors induce or inhibit such behavior. No attempt has been made to show what function such behavior may serve, nor to describe and interrelate the components of the psychological system affecting altruistic behavior. The purpose of this section is to show that the preceding model for the natural selection of reciprocally altruistic behavior can readily explain the function of human altruistic behavior and the details of the psychological system underlying such behavior. The psychological data can be organized into functional categories, and it can be shown that the components of the system complement each other in regulating the expression of altruistic and cheating impulses to the selective advantage of individuals. No concept of group advantage is necessary to explain the function of human altruistic behavior.

There is at present no direct evidence regarding either the degree of reciprocal altruism practiced during human evolution or its genetic basis; but, given the universal and nearly daily practice of reciprocal altruism among humans today, it is reasonable to assume that it has been an important factor in recent human evolution and that the underlying emotional dispositions affecting altruistic behavior have important genetic components. To assume as much allows a number of predictions.

A Complex Regulating System. The human altruistic system is a sensitive unstable one. Often it will pay to cheat, namely, when the partner will not find out, when he will not discontinue his altruism even if he does find out, or when he is unlikely to survive long enough to reciprocate adequately. And the perception of subtle cheating may be very difficult. Given this unstable character of the system, where a degree of cheating is adaptive, natural selection will rapidly favor a complex psychological system in each individual regulating both his own altruistic and cheating tendencies and his responses to these tendencies in others. As selection favors subtler forms of cheating, it will favor more acute abilities to detect cheating. The system that results should simultaneously allow the individual to reap the benefits of altruistic exchanges, to protect himself from gross and subtle forms of cheating, and to practice those forms of cheating that local conditions make adaptive. Individuals will differ not in being altruists or cheaters but in the degree of altruism they show and in the conditions under which they will cheat.

The best evidence supporting these assertions can be found in Krebs's (1970) review of the relevant psychological literature. Although differently organized, much of the material supporting the assertions that follow is taken from his paper. All subsequent references to Krebs are to this review. Also, Hartshorne and May (1928-1930) have shown that children in experimental situations do not divide bimodally into altruists and "cheaters" but are distributed normally; almost all the children cheated, but they differed in how much and under what circumstances. (*Cheating* was defined in their work in a slightly different but analogous way.)

Friendship and the Emotions of Liking and Disliking. The tendency to like others who are not necessarily closely related, to form friendships, and to act altruistically toward friends and toward those one likes will be selected for as the immediate emotional rewards motivating altruistic behavior and the formation of altruistic partnerships. (Selection may also favor helping strangers or disliked individuals when they are in particularly dire circumstances). Selection will favor a system whereby these tendencies are sensitive to such parameters as the altruistic tendencies of the liked individual. In other words, selection will favor liking those who are themselves altruistic.

Sawyer (1966) has shown that all groups in all experimental situations tested showed more altruistic behavior toward friends than toward neutral individuals. Likewise, Friedrichs (1960) has shown that attractiveness as a friend was most highly correlated among undergraduates with altruistic behavior. Krebs has reviewed other studies that suggest that the relationship between altruism and liking is a two-way street: one is more altruistic toward those one likes, and one tends to like those who are most altruistic (for example, Berkowitz and Friedman 1967; Lerner and Lightman 1968).

Others (Darwin 1871; Williams 1966; and Hamilton, 1969) have recognized the role friendship might play in engendering altruistic behavior, but all have viewed friendship (and intelligence) as prerequisites for the appearance of such altruism. Williams (1966), who cites Darwin (1871) on the matter, speaks of this behavior as evolving

> in animals that live in stable social groups and have the intelligence and other mental qualities necessary to form a system of personal friendships and animosities that transcend the limits of family relationships. [p. 93]

This emphasis on friendship and intelligence as prerequisites leads Williams to limit his search for altruism to the Mammalia and to a "minority of this group." But according to the preceding model, emotions of friendship (and hatred) are not prerequisites for reciprocal altruism but may evolve after a system of mutual altruism has appeared, as important ways of regulating the system.

Moralistic Aggression. Once strong positive emotions have evolved to motivate altruistic behavior, the altruist is in a vulnerable position because cheaters will be selected to take advantage of the altruist's emotions. This in turn sets up a selection pressure for a protective mechanism. Moralistic aggression and indignation in humans was selected for in order

1. To counteract the tendency of the altruist, in the absence of any reciprocity, to continue to perform altruistic acts for his own emotional rewards.
2. To educate the unreciprocating individual by frightening him with immediate harm or with the future harm of no more aid.
3. In extreme cases, perhaps, to select directly against the unreciprocating individual by injuring, killing, or exiling him.

Much of human aggression has moral overtones. Injustice, unfairness, and lack of reciprocity often motivate human aggression and indignation. Lee (1969) has shown that verbal disputes in Bushmen usually revolve around problems of gift giving, stinginess, and laziness. DeVore (personal communication) reports that a great deal of aggression in hunter-gatherers revolves around real or imagined injustices—inequities, for example, in food sharing (see, for example, Thomas 1958; Balikci 1964; Marshall 1961). A common feature of this aggression is that if often seems out of all proportion to the offenses committed. Friends are even killed over apparently trivial disputes. But since small inequities repeated many times over a lifetime may exact a heavy toll in relative fitness, selection may favor a strong show of aggression when the cheating tendency is discovered. Recent discussions of human and animal aggression have failed to distinguish between moralistic and other forms of aggression (see, for example, Scott 1958; Lorenz 1966; Montague 1968; Tinbergen 1968; Gilula and Daniels 1969). The grounds for expecting, on functional grounds, a highly plastic developmental system affecting moralistic aggression is discussed later on.

Gratitude, Sympathy, and the Cost/Benefit Ratio of an Altruistic Act. If the cost/benefit ratio is an important parameter in determining the adaptiveness of reciprocal altruism, then humans should be selected to be sensitive to the cost and benefit of an altruistic act, both in deciding to perform one and in deciding whether, or how much, to reciprocate. I suggest that the emotion of gratitude has been selected to regulate human response to altruistic acts and that the emotion is sensitive to the cost/benefit ratio of such acts. I suggest further that the emotion of sympathy has been selected to motivate altruistic behavior as a function of the plight of the recipient of such behavior; crudely expressed, the greater the potential benefit to the recipient, the greater the sympathy and the more likely the altruistic gesture, even to strange or disliked individuals. If the recipient's gratitude is indeed a function of the cost/benefit ratio, then a sympathetic response to the plight of a disliked individual may result in considerable reciprocity.

There is good evidence supporting the psychological importance of the cost/benefit ratio of altruistic acts. Gouldner (1960) has reviewed the sociological literature suggesting that the greater the need state of the recipient of an altruistic act, the greater his tendency to reciprocate; and the scarcer the resources of the donor of the act, the greater the tendency of the recipient to reciprocate. Heider (1958) has analyzed lay attitudes on altruism and finds that gratitude is greatest when the altruistic act does good. Tesser, Gatewood, and Driver (1968) have shown that American undergraduates thought they would feel more gratitude when the altruistic act was valuable and cost the benefactor a great deal. Pruitt (1968) has provided evidence that humans reciprocate more when the original act was expensive for the benefactor. He shows that, under experimental conditions, more altruism is induced by a gift of 80 percent of $1.00 than by one of 20 percent of $4.00. Aronfreed (1968) has reviewed the considerable evidence that sympathy motivates altruistic behavior as a function of the plight of the individual arousing the sympathy.

Guilt and Reparative Altruisisms. If an organism has cheated on a reciprocal relationship and this fact has been found out or has a good chance of being found out by the partner, and if the partner responds by cutting off all future acts of aid, then the cheater will have paid dearly for his misdeed. It will be to the cheater's advantage to avoid this; and, providing that the cheater makes up for his misdeed and does not cheat in the future, it will be to his partner's benefit to avoid this, since in cutting off future acts of aid he sacrifices the benefits of future reciprocal help. The cheater should be selected to make up for his misdeed and to show convincing evidence that he does not plan to continue his cheating sometime in the future. In short, he should be selected to make a reparative gesture. It seems plausible, furthermore, that the emotion of guilt has been selected for in humans partly in order to motivate the cheater to compensate for his misdeed and to behave reciprocally in the future, thereby preventing the rupture of reciprocal relationships.

Krebs has reviewed the evidence that harming another individual publicly leads to altruistic behavior, and concludes:

> Many studies have supported the notion that public transgression whether intentional or unintentional, whether immoral or situationally unfortunate, leads to reparative altruism. [p. 267)

Wallace and Sadalla (1966), for example, showed experimentally that individuals who broke an expensive machine were more likely to volunteer for a painful experiment than those who did not, but only if their transgression had been discovered. Investigators disagree on the extent to which guilt feelings are the motivation behind reparative altrusim. Epstein and Horstein (1969) supply some evidence that guilt is involved; however, on the assumption that one feels guilt even when one behaves badly in private, Wallace and Sadalla's (1966) result contradicts the view that guilt is the only motivating factor. That private transgressions are not as likely as public ones to lead to reparative altruism is precisely what the model would predict, and it is possible that the common psychological assumption that one feels guilt even when one behaves badly in private is based on the fact that many transgressions performed in private are likely to become public knowledge. It should often be advantageous to confess sins that are likely to be discovered before they actually are, as evidence of sincerity (see the discussion that follows on detection of mimics).

Subtle Cheating: The Evolution of Mimics. Once friendship, moralistic aggression, guilt, sympathy, and gratitude have evolved to regulate the altruistic system, selection will favor mimicking these traits in order to influence the behavior of others to one's own advantage. Apparent acts of generosity and friendship may induce genuine friendship and altruism in return. Sham moralistic aggression when no real cheating has occurred may nevertheless induce reparative altruism. Sham guilt may convince a wronged friend that one has reformed one's ways even when the cheating is about to be resumed. Likewise, selection will favor the hypocrisy of pretending one is in dire circumstances in order to induce sympathy-motivated altruistic behavior. Finally, mimicking sympathy may give the appearance of helping in order to induce reciprocity; and mimicking gratitude may mislead an individual into expecting he will be reciprocated. It is worth emphasizing that a mimic need not necessarily be conscious of the deception; selection may favor feeling genuine moralistic aggression even when one has not been wronged if so doing leads another to reparative altruism.

Instances of these forms of subtle cheating are not difficult to find. For typical instances from the literature on hunter-gatherers, see Rasmussen (1931), Balikci (1964), and Lee and DeVore (1968). The importance of these forms of cheating can be inferred partly from the adaptations to detect such cheating discussed later on and from the importance and prevalence of moralistic aggression once such cheating is detected.

Detection of the Subtle Cheater: Trustworthiness, Trust, and Suspicion. Selection should favor the ability to detect and discriminate against subtle cheaters. Selection will clearly favor detecting and countering sham moralistic aggression. The argument for the other cases is more complex. Selection may favor distrusting those who perform altruistic acts without the emotional basis of generosity or guilt because the altruistic tendencies of such individuals may be less reliable in the future. One can imagine, for example, a person compensating for a misdeed without any emotional basis but with a calculating, self-serving motive. Such an individual should be distrusted because the calculating spirit that now leads this subtle cheater to compensate may, in the future, lead him to cheat when circumstances seem more advantageous (because of unlikelihood of detection, for example, or because the cheated individual is unlikely to survive). Guilty motivation seems more reliable, insofar as it evidences a more enduring commitment to altruism, either because guilt teaches or because the cheater is unlikely not to feel the same guilt in the future. A similar argument can be made about the trustworthiness of individuals who initiate altruistic acts out of a calculating rather than a generous-hearted disposition or who show either false sympathy or false gratitude. Detection on the basis of the underlying psychological dynamics is only one form of detection. In many cases, unreliability may more easily be detected through experience of the cheater's inconsistent behavior. And in some cases, third-party interactions (as discussed later) may make an individual's behavior predictable despite underlying cheating motivations.

The anthropological literature also abounds with instances of the detection of subtle cheaters (see preceding references for hunter-gatherers). Although I know of no psychological studies on the detection of sham moralistic aggression and sham guilt, there is ample evidence to support the notion that humans respond to altruistic acts according to their perception of the motives of the altruist. They tend to respond more altruistically when they perceive the other as acting "genuinely" altruistic, that is, voluntarily dispatching an altruistic act as an end in itself, without being directed toward gain (Leeds 1963; Heider 1958). Krebs (1970) has reviewed the literature on this point and notes that help is more likely to be reciprocated when it is perceived as voluntary and intentional (for example, Goranson and Berkowitz 1966; Lerner and Lightman 1968) and when the help is appropriate, that is, when the intentions of the altruist are not in doubt (for example, Brehm and Cole 1966; Schopler and Thompson 1968). Krebs concludes that, "When the legitimacy of apparent altruism is questioned, reciprocity is less likely to prevail." Lerner and Lightman (1968) have shown experimentally that those who act altruistically for ulterior benefit are rated as unattractive and are treated selfishly, whereas those who apparently are genuinely altruistic are rated as attractive and are treated altruistically. Berscheid and Walster (1967) have shown that church women tend to make reparations for harm they have committed by choosing the reparation that approximates the harm (that is, neither too slight nor too great), presumably to avoid the appearance of inappropriateness.

Rapoport and Dale (1967) have shown that when two strangers play iterated games of Prisoner's Dilemma in which the matrix determines profits from the games played, there is a significant tendency for the level of cooperation to drop at the end of the series, reflecting the fact that the partner will not be able to punish for "cheating" responses when the series is over. If a long series is broken up into subseries with a pause between subseries for totaling up gains and losses, then the partners' tendency to cheat on each other increases at the end of each subseries. These results, as well as some others reported by Rapoport and Chammah (1976), are suggestive of the instability that exists when two strangers are consciously trying to maximize gain by trading altruistic gestures, an instability that is presumably less marked when the underlying motivation involves the emotions of friendship, of liking others, and of feeling guilt over harming a friend. Deutsch (1958), for example, has shown that two individuals playing iterated games of Prisoner's Dilemma will be more cooperative if a third individual, disliked by both, is present. The perceived mutual dislike is presumed to create a bond between the two players.

It is worth mentioning that a classic problem in social science and philosophy has been whether to define altruism in terms of motives (for example, real versus "calculated" altruism) or in terms of behavior, regardless of motive (Krebs 1970). This problem reflects the fact that, wherever studied, humans seem to make distinctions about altruism partly on the basis of motive, a tendency that is consistent with the hypothesis that such discrimination is relevant to protecting oneself from cheaters.

Setting up Altruistic Partnerships. Selection will favor a mechanism for establishing reciprocal relationships. Since humans respond to acts of altruism with feelings of friendship that lead to reciprocity, one such mechanism might be the performance of altruistic acts toward strangers, or even toward enemies, in order to induce friendship. In short: do unto others as you would have them do unto you.

The mechanism hypothesized previously leads to results inconsistent with the assumption that humans always act more altruistically toward friends than toward others. Particularly toward strangers, humans may initially act more altruistically than toward friends. Wright (1942) has shown, for example, that third-grade children are more likely to give a more valuable toy to a stranger than to a friend. Later, some of these children verbally acknowledge that they were trying to make friends. Floyd (1964) has shown that, after receiving many trinkets from a friend, humans tend to decrease their gifts in return; but after receiving many trinkets from a neutral or disliked individual, they tend to increase their gifts in return, whereas receiving few trinkets from a neutral or disliked individual results in a decrease in giving. This was interpreted to mean that generous friends are taken for granted (as are stingy nonfriends). Generosity from a nonfriend is taken as an overture to friendship, and stinginess from a friend as evidence of a deteriorating relationship in need of repair. Epstein and Hornstein (1969) provide new data supporting this interpretation of Floyd (1964).

Multiparty Interactions. In the close-knit social groups in which humans usually live, selection should favor more complex interactions than the two-party interactions so far discussed. Specifically, selection may favor learning from the altruistic and cheating experiences of others, helping others coerce cheaters, forming multiparty exchange systems, and formulating rules for regulated exchanges in such multiparty systems.

Learning from Others. Selection should favor learning about the altruistic and cheating tendencies of others indirectly, both through observing interactions of others and, once linguistic abilities have evolved, by hearing about such interactions or hearing characterizations of individuals ("dirty," "hypocritical," "dishonest," "untrustworthy," "cheating louse"). One important result of this learning is that an individual may be as concerned about the attitude of onlookers in an altruistic situation as about the attitude of the individual being dealt with.

Help in Dealing with Cheaters. In dealing with cheaters, selection may favor individuals helping others, kin or nonkin, by direct coercion against the cheater or by everyone refusing him reciprocal altruism. One effect of this is that an individual, through his close kin, may be compensated for an altruistic act even after his death. If an individual dies saving a friend, for example, the friend may perform altruistic acts to the benefit of the first individual's offspring. Selection will discriminate against the cheater in this situation if kin of the martyr, or others, are willing to punish lack of reciprocity.

Generalized Altruism. Given learning from others and multiparty action against cheaters, selection may favor a multiparty altruistic system in which altruistic acts are dispensed freely among more than two individuals, an individual being perceived to cheat if in an altruistic situation he dispenses less benefit for the same cost than would the others, punishment coming not only from the other individual in that particular exchange but also from the others in the system.

Rules of Exchange. Multiparty altruistic systems increase by several times the cognitive difficulties in detecting imbalances and in deciding whether they are due to cheating or to random factors. One simplifying possibility that language facilitates is the formulation of rules of conduct, cheating being detected as infraction of such a rule. In short, selection may favor the elaboration of norms of reciprocal conduct.

There is abundant evidence for all of the multiparty interactions mentioned so far (see the preceding references on hunter-gatherers). Thomas (1958), for example, has shown that debts of reciprocity do not disappear with the death of the "creditor" but are extended to his kin. Krebs has reviewed the psychological literature on generalized altruism. Several studies (such as Darlington and Macker 1966) have shown that humans may direct their altruism toward individuals other than those who were hurt and may respond to an altruistic act that benefits themselves by acting altruistically toward a third individual uninvolved in the initial interaction. Berkowitz and Daniels (1964) have shown experimentally, for example, that help from a confederate leads the subject to direct more help toward a third individual, a highly dependent supervisor. Freedman, Wallington, and Bless (1967) have demonstrated the surprising result that, in two different experimental situations, humans engaged in reparative altruism only if it could be directed toward someone other than the individual harmed, or toward the original individual only if they did not expect to meet again. In a system of strong multiparty interactions it is possible that in some situations individuals are selected to demonstrate generalized altruistic tendencies and that their main concern when they have harmed another is to show that they are genuinely altruistic, which they best do by acting altruistic without any apparent ulterior motive, for example, in the experiments, by acting altruistic toward an uninvolved third party. Alternatively, A. Rapoport (personal communication) has suggested that the reluctance to direct reparative altruism toward the harmed individual may be due to unwillingness to show thereby a recognition of the harm done him. The redirection serves to allay guilt feelings without triggering the greater reparation to which recognition of the harm might lead.

Developmental Plasticity. The conditions under which detection of cheating is possible, the range of available altruistic trades, the cost/benefit ratios of these trades, the relative stability of social groupings, and other relevant parameters should differ from one ecological and social situation to another and should differ through time in the same small human population. Under these conditions, one would expect selection to favor developmental plasticity of those traits regulating both altruistic and cheating tendencies and responses to these tendencies in others. For example, developmental plasticity may allow the growing organism's sense of guilt to be educated, perhaps partly by kin, so as to permit those forms of cheating that local conditions make adaptive and to discourage those with more dangerous consequences. One would not expect any simple system regulating the development of altruistic behavior to exist. To be adaptive, altruistic behavior must be dispensed with regard to many characteristics of the recipient (including his degree of relationship, emotional makeup, past behavior, friendships, and kin relations); of other members of the group; of the situation in which the altruistic behavior takes place; and of many other parameters. No simple developmental system is likely to meet these requirements.

Kohlberg (1963), Bandura and Walters (1963), and Krebs have reviewed the developmental literature on human altruism. All of them conclude that none of the proposed developmental theories (all of which rely on simple mechanisms) can account for the known diverse developmental data. Whiting and Whiting (in preparation) have studied altruistic behavior directed toward kin by children in six different cultures and find consistent differences among the cultures that correlate with differences in childrearing and other facets of the cultures. They argue that the differences adapt the children to different adult roles available in the cultures. Although the behavior analyzed takes place between kin, so that Hamilton's model (1964) may apply rather than this model, the Whitings' data provide an instance of the adaptive value of developmental plasticity in altruistic behavior. No careful work has been done analyzing the influence of environmental factors on the development of altruistic behavior, but some data do exist. Krebs has reviewed the evidence that altruistic tendencies can be increased by the effects of warm, nurturant models; but little is known on how long such effects endure. Rosenhan (1967) and Rettig (1956) have shown a correlation between altruism in parents and altruism in their college-age children, but these studies do not separate genetic and environmental influences. Class differences in altruistic behavior (for example, Berkowitz 1968; Ugurel-Semin 1952; Almond and Verba 1963) may primarily reflect environmental influences. Finally, Lutzker (1960) and Deutsch (1958) have shown that one can predict the degree of altruistic behavior displayed in iterated games of Prisoner's Dilemma from personality typing based on a questionnaire. Such personality differences are probably partly environmental in origin.

It is worth emphasizing that some of the psychological traits analyzed so far have applications outside the particular reciprocal altruistic system being discussed. One may be suspicious, for example, not only of individuals likely to cheat on the altruistic system, but also of any individual likely to harm oneself; one may be suspicious of the known tendencies toward adultery of another male or even of these tendencies in one's own mate. Likewise, a guilt-motivated show of reparation may avert the revenge of someone one has harmed by cheating on the altruistic system or in some other way. And the system of reciprocal altruism may be employed to avert possible revenge. The Bushmen of the Kalahari, for example, have a saying (Marshall 1959) to the effect that if you wish to sleep with someone else's wife, you get him to sleep with yours, and then neither of you goes after the other with poisoned arrows. Likewise, there is a large literature on the use of reciprocity to cement friendships between neighboring groups that are now engaged in a common enterprise (for example, Lee and DeVore 1968).

The preceding review of the evidence has only begun to outline the complexities of the human altruistic system. The inherent instability of the

Prisoner's Dilemma, combined with its importance in human evolution, has led to the evolution of a very complex system. For example, once a moralistic aggression has been selected for to protect against cheating, selection favors sham moralistic aggression as a new form of cheating. This should lead to selection for the ability to discriminate between the two and to guard against the latter. The guarding can, in turn, be used to counter real moralistic aggression: one can, in effect, *impute* cheating motives to another person to protect one's own cheating. And so on. Given the psychological and cognitive complexity the system rapidly requires, one may wonder to what extent the importance of altruism in human evolution set up a selection pressure for psychological and cognitive powers that partly contributed to the large increase in hominid brain size during the Pleistocene.

Some Reflections on Reciprocal Altruism

My original model emphasized direct feedback from cheating by means of the discriminatory capacity of others. This must be what keeps cheating in check. I concentrated on interactions between two unrelated individuals, considering ways in which repeated interactions between them would permit a stable relationship of reciprocity to emerge. Since then I have wondered about the more general case. West-Eberhard (1975) has emphasized the artificiality of separating reciprocity from kinship and has proposed equations that naturally take both factors into account. Hamilton (1975, p. 151) has suggested that a sense of justice may require some kinship effect in addition to reciprocal interests. And it has become clear that there are complex and interesting problems of cocarrier selection in reciprocal relations, quite apart from kinship, since strongly reciprocal pairs are especially likely to have many identical genes at the loci mediating reciprocity (see Wilson 1980). In this section I consider further factors that may select against cheating.

1. Once discriminatory capacities have evolved, they will be used in new contexts. If we encounter only a limited number of genetic actors in the game of reciprocal altruism, then information learned about one particular individual may be relevant to a class of actors whose members are detected as such. Thus cheating may induce a deeper response to a *class* of genetically more similar actors in the game. It is almost automatic that learning should have this effect, since what one learns will naturally be most relevant to situations that are most similar.

2. Cheating not only alters the actions of other people, but also alters the cheater's future behavior. Cheating probably makes future cheating more likely, especially when it is initially unpunished. A *pattern* of cheating

may develop, generating responses to the pattern itself. Thus the cost of cheating may be registered outside the dyad in which it is occurring. Conversely, one act of altruism may induce in the actor a positive attitude toward a series of other opportunities, which may, in turn, richly reward the initial act.

As we go up and down in life, we are sometimes warned, on the way up, to beware of our actions lest we meet the same people on our way down. This may literally be true, as will be discussed later; but it may also be true in a figurative sense, with much the same effect. That is, we develop patterns of behavior on the way up (partly predirected on the asumption that we will not come down), and these very patterns are recognized on the way down. When we wish for the sympathy and help of others—in *our* times of need—we may discover that years of withholding these gifts from others has made us into unattractive and unlikely recipients.

3. Of particular importance to cheating is the self-deception that it automatically tends to generate. Since it is useful to maintain a facade of morality and public beneficence, cheating must be disguised—increasingly, even to the actor himself. The actor becomes less and less conscious of the true nature of his actions, and this self-deception induces a range of impaired learning that may have costs far removed from the initial acts generating the impulse toward self-deception.

4. Finally, it still seems worth emphasizing how small the world really is—that is, how often we end up interacting again with individuals we never expected to meet again. Even in large industrial societies, our patterns of behavior, our habits, and our needs continually throw us into a very narrow range of circumstances in which we are likely to come across, as if by chance, the very same people with whom we have interacted in the past. Often I have been surprised to find myself face to face with individuals I thought (and perhaps hoped) I would never see again.

Parent-Offspring Conflict

This section applies the concept of inclusive fitness to a particular relationship, the parent-offspring relationship. I will try to show that evolutionary theory not only undercuts certain assumptions that are common in psychology but also provides the basis for a biological theory of the family, in which relations between the members are understood according to certain underlying parameters, such as degree of relatedness and sex.

To subject parent-offspring relations to this kind of analysis requires that one decompose what is going on in the relationship into appropriate benefits and costs. The major thing going on, after all, is that the parent is transferring "parental investment"—caring for the offspring, feeding it, protecting it, and so on. This investment can be decomposed into a benefit for the offspring, measured as an increase in the offspring's chance of survival and hence of reproductive success, and into either a measurable cost for the parent or a decrease in the number of offspring produced. The more one gives now, the more one postpones investing in additional offspring, increases chances of one's own mortality, and so on. The advantage of this is that, from the parent's standpoint, the parent would wish with any given interaction to maximize the difference between the benefit and the cost since it is equally related to its own different offspring. The offspring, however, is related to itself by 1 but is only imperfectly related to its future sibs, namely by 1/2, assuming they are full sibs. Therefore, it wishes to maximize the difference, not between benefit and cost, but between benefit minus 1/2 the cost. "Wishes" here means, of course, that natural selection favors the individual acting as if it so wished.

As an example, weaning conflict is an obvious consequence of the difference in viewpoint between parent and offspring over maximizing each one's inclusive fitness. A picture of weaning conflict emerges if one graphs a benefit/cost ratio as a function of time beginning at, say, birth. With nursing in mammals, for instance, one starts with the assumption that benefit is high because the offspring cannot live without the milk. As time goes on, it becomes increasingly capable of living on its own; thus benefit decreases and cost probably increases for the parent. In any case, the benefit/cost ratio falls. In this imaginary species the turning point arrives when the benefit/cost ratio has fallen to 1, that is, when the benefit equals the cost. After this point, benefit is smaller than cost; if the mother continues to nurse, her eventual net reproductive success will be lower. The offspring at hand will survive better, but prolonged nursing will decrease her future reproductive success by more than the amount it increases her present reproductive success. Thus selection favors the mother withholding investment at this point. By contrast, the offspring waits, so to speak, until the benefit/cost ratio falls to 1/2—the point at which it is inflicting a cost twice as great as the benefit it is getting, which just makes up for the fact that it is only half as related to the individuals receiving the cost as it is to itself, the individual receiving the benefit. If it nurses past this point, it would in fact decrease its own inclusive fitness because it would be harming its genes located in other individuals more than it was helping its own genes.

Weaning conflict can be seen according to genetic analysis to result from an underlying conflict in the way in which parent and offspring maximize their inclusive fitness, that is, from an underlying conflict in self-interest.

The Offspring as Psychological Manipulator

How is the offspring to compete effectively with its parent?[5] An offspring can not fling its mother to the ground at will and nurse. Throughout the period of parental investment, the offspring competes at a disadvantage. The offspring is smaller and less experienced than its parent, and its parent controls the resources at issue. Given this competitive disadvantage, the offspring is expected to employ psychological rather than physical tactics. (Inside the mother the offspring is expected to employ chemical tactics, but some of the following analysis should apply to such competition.) It should attempt to induce more investment than the parent wishes to give.

Since an offspring will often have better knowledge of its real needs than will its parent, selection should favor parental attentiveness to signals from its offspring that apprise the parent of the offspring's condition. In short, the offspring cries when hungry or in danger, and the parent responds appropriately. Conversely, the offspring signals its parent (say, by smiling, or by wagging its tail) when its needs have been well met. Both parent and offspring benefit from this system of communication. But once such a system has evolved, the offspring can begin to employ it out of context. The offspring can cry not only when it is famished but also when it merely wants more food than the parent has selected to give. Likewise, it can begin to withhold its smile until it has gotten its way. Selection will then of course favor parental ability to discriminate between the two uses of the signals, but still subtler mimicry and deception by the offspring are always possible. Parental experience with preceding offspring is expected to improve the parent's ability to make the appropriate discrimination. Unless succeeding offspring can employ more confusing tactics than earlier ones, parent-offspring interactions are expected to be increasingly biased in favor of the parent as a function of parental age.

In those species in which the offspring is more helpless and vulnerable the younger it is, its parents will have been more strongly selected to respond positively to signals of need emitted by younger as opposed to older offspring. This suggests that at any stage of ontogeny in which the offspring is in conflict with its parents, one appropriate tactic may be to revert to the gestures and actions of an earlier stage of development in order to induce the investment that would then have been forthcoming. Psychologists have long recognized such a tendency in humans and have called it *regression*. A detailed functional analysis of regression could be based on the theory presented here.

The normal course of parent-offspring relations must be subject to considerable unpredictable variation in both the condition of the parent and (sometimes independently) the condition of the offspring. Both partners must be sensitive to such variation and must adjust their behavior appropriately. Low investment coming from a parent in poor condition has a different meaning than low investment coming from one in good condition. This suggests that from an early age the offspring is expected to be a psychologically sophisticated organism. The offspring should be able to evaluate the cost of a given parental act (which depends in part on the condition of the parent at that moment) and its benefit (which depends in part on the condition of the offspring). When the offspring's interests diverge from those of its parent, the offspring must be able to employ a series of psychological maneuvers, including the mimicry and regression just mentioned. Although the offspring would be expected to learn appropriate information (such as whether its psychological maneuvers were having the desired effects), one important feature of the argument presented here is that the offspring cannot rely on its parents for disinterested guidance. One expects the offspring to be preprogrammed to resist some parental teaching while being open to other forms. This is particularly true, as argued later on, for parental teaching that affects the altruistic and egoistic tendencies of the offspring.

If one event in a social relationship predicts to some degree future events in that relationship, then the organism should be selected to alter its behavior in response to an initial event, in order to change the probability that the predicted events will occur. For example, if a mother's lack of love for her offspring early in its life predicts deficient future investment, then the offspring will be selected to be sensitive to such early lack of love, whether investment at that time is deficient or not, in order to increase her future investment. The best data relevant to these possibilities come from the work of Hinde and his associates on groups of caged rhesus macaques. In a series of experiments, a mother was removed from her six-month-old infant, which remained in the home cage with other group members. After six days, the mother was returned to the home cage. Behavioral data were gathered before, during, and after the separation (see the following sections). In a parallel series of experiments, the infant was removed for six days from its mother, who was left in the home cage; and the same behavioral data were gathered, as discussed later on. The main findings can be summarized as follows.

Separation of Mother from her Offspring Affects Their Relationship upon Reunion. After reunion with its mother, the infant spends more time on the mother than it did before separation—although, had the separation not occurred, the infant would have reduced its time on the mother. This increase is caused by the infant and occurs despite an increase in the frequency of maternal rejection (Hinde and Spencer-Booth 1971). These effects can be detected at least as long as five weeks after reunion. These data are consistent with the assumption that the infant has been selected to interpret its mother's disappearance as an event whose recurrence the infant can help prevent by devoting more of its energies to staying close to its mother.

The Mother-Offspring Relationship Prior to Separation Affects the Offspring's Behavior on Reunion. Upon reunion with its mother, an infant typically shows distress, as measured by callings and immobility. The more frequently an infant was rejected prior to separation, the more distress it shows upon reunion. This correlation holds for at least four weeks after reunion. In addition, the more distressed the infant is, the greater is its role in maintaining proximity to its mother (Hinde and Spencer-Booth 1971). These data support the assumption that the infant interprets its mother's disappearance in relation to her predeparture behavior in a logical way: the offspring should assume that a rejecting mother who temporarily disappears needs more offspring surveillance and intervention than does a nonrejecting mother who temporarily disappears.

An Offspring Removed from its Mother Shows, upon Reunion, Different Effects than Does an Offspring Whose Mother Has Been Removed. Compared to an infant whose mother had been removed, an infant removed from his mother shows, upon reunion and for up to six weeks after reunion, less distress and more time off the mother. In addition, the offspring tends to play a smaller role in maintaining proximity to its mother, and it experiences less frequent maternal rejections (Hinde and Davies 1972a,b,). These data are consistent with the exception that the offspring should be sensitive to the meaning of events affecting its relationship to its mother. The offspring can differentiate between a separation from its mother caused by its own behavior or some accident (infant removed from group) and a separation that may have been caused by maternal negligence (mother removed from group). In the former kind of separation, the infant shows fewer effects when reunited because, from its point of view, such a separation does not reflect on its mother and thus no remedial action is indicated. A similar explanation can be given for differences in the mother's behavior.

Parent-Offspring Conflict over the Behavioral
Tendencies of the Offspring

Parents and offspring are expected to disagree over the behavioral tendencies of the offspring insofar as these tendencies affect related individuals.[6] Consider first interactions among siblings. An individual is only expected to perform an altruistic act toward its full-sibling whenever the benefit to the sibling is greater than twice the cost to the altruist. Likewise, it is only expected to forego selfish acts when $C > 2B$, where a selfish act is defined as one that gives the actor a benefit (B) while inflicting a cost (C) on some other individual, in this case, on a full-sibling. But parents, who are equally related to all their offspring, are expected to encourage all altruistic acts among their offspring in which $B > C$, and to discourage all selfish acts in which $C < B$. Since there ought to exist altruistic situations in which $C < B < 2C$, parents and offspring are expected to disagree over the tendency of the offspring to act altruistically toward its siblings. Likewise, whenever for any selfish act harming a full-sibling $B < C < 2B$, parents are expected to discourage such behavior, and offspring are expected to be relatively refractory to such discouragement.

This parent-offspring disagreement is expected over behavior directed toward other relatives as well. For example, the offspring is only selected to perform altruistic acts toward a cousin (related through the mother) when $B > 8C$. But the offspring's mother is related to her own nephews and nieces by $r_o = 1/4$ and to her offspring by $r_o = 1/2$, so that she would like to see any altruistic acts performed by her offspring toward their maternal cousins whenever $B > 2C$. The same argument applies to selfish acts, and both arguments can be made for more distant relatives as well. (The father is unrelated to his mate's kin and, other things being equal, should not be distressed to see his offspring treat such individuals as if they were unrelated.)

Assume, for example, that an individual gains some immediate benefit (B) by acting nastily toward some unrelated individual. Assume that the unrelated individual reciprocates in kind (Trivers 1971), but assume also that the reciprocity is directed toward both the original actor and some relative, for example, his sibling. Assuming no other effects of the initial act, the original actor will be selected to perform the nasty act as long as $B > C_1 + 1/2(C_2)$, where C_1 is the cost to the original actor of the reciprocal nastiness he receives and C_2 is the cost to his sibling of the nastiness the sibling receives. The actor's parents viewing the interaction would be expected to condone the initial act only if $B > C_1 + C_2$. Since there ought to exist situations in which $C_1 + 1/2(C_2) < B < C_1 + C_2$, one expects conflict between offspring and parents over the offspring's tendency to perform the initial nasty act in the situation described.

As it applies to human beings, the preceding argument can be summarized by saying that a fundamental conflict is expected during socialization over the altruistic and egoistic impulses of the offspring. Parents are expected to socialize their offspring to act more altruistically and less egoistically than the offspring would naturally act, and the offspring are expected to resist such socialization. If this argument is valid, then it is clearly a mistake to view socialization in humans (or in any sexually reproducing species) as only, or even primarily, a process of "enculturation" by which parents teach offspring their culture (for example, Mussen, Conger, and

Kagan 1969, p. 259). For example, one is not permitted to assume that parents who attempt to impact such virtues as responsibility, decency, honesty, trustworthiness, generosity, and self-denial are merely providing the offspring with useful information on the appropriate behavior in the local culture; for all such virtues are likely to affect the amount of altruistic and egoistic behavior impinging on the parent's kin, and parent and offspring are expected to view such behavior differently. That some teaching beneficial to the offspring transpires during human socialization can be taken for granted, and one would expect no conflict if socialization involved only teaching beneficial to the offspring. According to the theory presented here, socialization is a process by which parents attempt to mold each offspring in order to increase their own inclusive fitness, whereas each offspring is selected to resist some of the molding and to attempt to mold the behavior of its parents (and siblings) in order to increase its own inclusive fitness. Conflict during socialization need not be viewed solely as conflict between the culture of the parent and the biology of the child, it can also be viewed as a conflict between the biology of the parent and the biology of the child. Since teaching (as opposed to molding) is expected to be recognized by offspring as being in their own self-interest, parents would be expected to overemphasize their role as teachers in order to minimize resistance in their young. According to this view, then, the prevailing concept of socialization is to some extent a view that one would expect adults to entertain and disseminate.

Parent-offspring conflict may extend to behavior that on the surface is neither altruistic nor selfish but that has consequences that can be so classified. The amount of energy a child consumes during the day, and the way in which the child consumes this energy, are not matters of indifference to the parent when the parent is supplying that energy, and when the way in which the child consumes the energy affects its ability to act altruistically in the future. For example, when parent and child disagree over when the child should go to sleep, one expects in general that the parent will favor an early bedtime, in anticipation that this will decrease the offspring's demands on parental resources the following day. Likewise, one expects the parent to favor serious and useful expenditures of energy by the child (such as tending the family chickens, or studying) over frivolous and unnecessary expenditures (such as playing cards)—the former either are altruistic in themselves or prepare the offspring for future altruism. In short, we expect the offspring to perceive some behavior that the parent favors as being dull, unpleasant, moral, or some combination of these. One must at least entertain the assumption that the child would find such behavior more enjoyable if in fact the behavior maximized the offspring's inclusive fitness.

The Role of Parental Experience in
Parent-Offspring Conflict

It cannot be supposed that all parent-offspring conflict results from the conflict in the way in which the parent's and the offspring's inclusive fitnesses are maximized.[7] Some conflict also results, ironically, from an overlap in the interests of parent and young. When circumstances change, altering the benefits and costs associated with some offspring behavior, both the parent and the offspring are selected to alter the offspring's behavior appropriately. That is, the parent is selected to mold the appropriate change in the offspring's behavior; and, if parental molding is successful, it will strongly reduce the selection pressure on the offspring to change its behavior spontaneously. Since the parent is likely to discover the changing circumstances as a result of its own experience, one expects tendencies toward parental molding to appear and to spread before the parallel tendencies appear in the offspring. Once parents commonly mold the appropriate offspring behavior, selection still favors genes leading toward voluntary offspring behavior, since such a developmental avenue is presumably more efficient and more certain than that involving parental manipulation. But the selection pressure for the appropriate offspring genes should be weak; and, if circumstances change at a faster rate than this selection operates, there is the possibility of continued parent-offspring conflict resulting from the greater experience of the parent.

If the conflict just described actually occurs, then (as mentioned in an earlier section) selection will favor a tendency for parents to overemphasize their experience in all situations, and for the offspring to differentiate between those situations in which greater parental experience is real and those situations in which such experience is merely claimed in order to manipulate the offspring.

Deceit and Self-Deception

The most important thing to realize about systems of animal communication is that they are not expected to be systems for the dissemination of truth. Instead, they are expected to be systems by which individual organisms attempt to maxmize their inclusive fitnesses by communicating to others things that may be true or false. Consider a species in which males court females by offering them food (as in some scorpionflies and some birds). A female wishing to be courted by a male of this species may be selected to communicate that information. At the same time, a *male* may be selected to convey the same information—that he is a receptive female—since this may induce courtship by a male, thereby permitting him to take the food offered and put it to his own uses. That this occurs in nature is beautifully described in Thornbill (1979). The female conveys correct information, the male, incorrect; and a courting male must decide which is which.

In this example, there is some priority to the communication of correct information since deceit consists of mimicking the truth. This is probably often true of systems of animal communication, namely, that deception is a parasitism of the preexisting system of communicating correct information. In any case, this parasitism induces a coevolutionary struggle between truth and falsehood, between deceiver and deceived. In our example, a scorpion-fly male is selected to tell the difference between females and pseudo-females; and this selects for more plausible pseudofemales. If the success of pseudofemales is great enough to harm the reproductive success of true females (as when their mating is delayed by the suspiciousness of males intent on avoiding pseudofemales), then there may even be selection for females to advertise their sex more clearly.

Deceit has long been recognized in relations between members of different species. This is so, first, because it is ubiquitous and, second, because there has rarely been the presumption that members of different species naturally act so as to benefit each other. Thus predator and prey often benefit from remaining concealed to each other, and this selection has led to many remarkable instances of camouflage and mimicry (see Cott 1940; Edmunds 1974). By its nature, however, deception tends to go undetected; therefore, biologists generally underestimate the possibilities, even in interspecific relations. For example, I believe that biologists have overlooked a large category of deceptive interactions in which cryptic prey also produce a secondary image of a menacing sort, thus resembling cryptic predators. I believe the menacing image has often been selected to remain vague in order *subliminally* to frighten a searching predator from a more careful inspection while keeping it in the dark as to why it is not searching more carefully!

The great tradition of species-benefit reasoning led many biologists to assume that animals attempt to communicate the truth to members of its own species, since it is hard to see how a species benefits by having its members base their behavior on falsehoods. Thus, until recently, animal communication was analyzed entirely in terms of information and information theory (for example, Wilson 1975) without reference to misinformation and misinformation theory. Yet in social relationships there is a conflict of interest in which it may be useful to mislead one's opponent. Thus deceit is an expected feature of all relations between imperfectly related organisms. Consider four examples:

1. *Aggressive encounters.* It will often be useful to appear larger, more capable, more confident, and perhaps more moral than one actually is.

2. *Courtship.* It will be useful to appear more attractive than one is, that is, to have more to offer—in goods as in genes—than one actually possesses.
3. *Parent-offspring relations.* The fact that each partner has some concern for the interests of the other merely creates opportunities for deception based on misrepresenting cost and benefits. Indeed, a partial overlap in self-interest invites a deeper misrepresentation of self, since one may represent one's fundamental stance toward another as kindly rather than hostile, although with no overlap in self-interest, this deception, at least, must often be too implausible to attempt.
4. *Reciprocal relations.* Numerous possible deceptions have already been mentioned.

Deception is, in turn, expected to generate self-deception (see Alexander 1979, pp. 134-139). As mechanisms for spotting deception become more subtle, organisms may be selected to render some facts and motives unconscious, the better to conceal deception. In the broadest sense, the organism is selected to become unconscious of some of its deception, in order not to betray, by the signs of self-knowledge, the deception being practiced.

With the advent of language in the human lineage, the possibilities for deception and self-deception were greatly enlarged. If language permits the communication of much more detailed and extensive information—concerning, for example, events distant in space and time—then it both permits and encourages the communication of much more detailed and extensive misinformation. A portion of the brain devoted to verbal functions must become specialized for the manufacture and maintenance of falsehoods. This will require biased perceptions, biased memory, and biased logic; and these processes are ideally kept partly unconscious.

An individual's perception of its own motivation may often be biased in order to conceal the true motivation from others. Consciously, a series of reasons may unfold internally to accompany action, so that when actions are challenged a convincing alternative explanation is at once available, complete with an internal scenario ("But I wasn't thinking that at all, I was thinking . . . "). Of course it must be advantageous for the truth to be registered somewhere, so that mechanisms of self-deception must reside side by side with mechanisms for the correct apprehension of reality. The mind must be structured in a very complex fashion, repeatedly split into public and private portions, with complicated interactions between the subsections.

The essence of self-deception is the denial of deception, so that there are two very different ways to stop it: either stop deceiving others, or stop denying that you are deceiving them.

If we decide to stop deceiving others by rotting out deception as we see it, we face the awkward problem that self-deception may actually redefine some of our deceitful activities as being honest, so that we fail even to detect them. Getting rid of deception clearly depends partly on getting rid of self-deception, and vice versa.

It must, at some time, be important to specify the purpose for which our work is intended. Otherwise, our axis of self-deception, so to speak, will be unrecorded. That is, without a discussion of whose interests our work may serve, we shall be unconscious of the way our work naturally develops so as to serve those interests. Mechanisms of self-deception will naturally be activated so as to keep us in the necessary degree of darkness.

It is useless to imagine that scientists represent a class of individuals created by society to pursue truth in a disinterested fashion, thereby producing results beneficial to all. This is precisely the self-deception to which scientists are expected to gravitate (since the attendant deception enhances their apparent utility to others). Everything we know about evolution suggests that we have not been created to pursue truth in a *disinterested* fashion—quite the contrary. Thus it is our knowledge of self-deception which requires that we treat with scepticism the naive approach to social theory.

At the same time, the achievements of the weak-minded approach (to be discussed later on) should serve to remind us that any critical analysis of self-interest and social thought must begin at home, that is, with the speaker (see the Bible, Matthew 7:1-7). Otherwise, our analysis of the self-interest of others too easily becomes a screen behind which to vent our aggression on them. By raising the moral issues that the naive school fails to consider, the attackers can claim a commitment to the social good, which, in theory, should tend to decrease their self-deception. Undoubtedly this self-perception has fueled their intense moralistic aggression.

The Political Attack on Sociobiology

Wilson's (1975) review of sociobiology generated a sharp attack. The new work in biology was characterized as right wing, ultimately providing the intellectual foundation for fascism, racism, sexism, warmongering, and so forth. Although sociobiology had nothing to say about race, our work was said to be closely related to recent claims in psychology that black Americans were, on average, genetically inferior in intelligence to their white counterparts. This led to the accusation that the entire structure of sociobiology was corrupt and that hardly any part had scientific validity. Its dominant theme was said to be "biological determinism," a crude attempt to make the present distribution of power and wealth look inevitable and socially beneficent, to justify the status quo and make it appear difficult to change.

My own reaction to this attack was disappointment. Although some of the attackers were prominent biologists, the attack seemed intellectually feeble and lazy. Gross errors in logic were permitted as long as they appeared to give some tactical advantage in the political struggle. Our own work was seen as less than self-serving, since we were branded tools of the ruling elite. Because we were hirelings of the dominant interests, said these fellow hirelings of the same interests, we were their mouthpieces, employed to deepen the intellectual deceptions and self-deceptions with which the ruling elite retained their unjust advantage. Although it follows from evolutionary reasoning that individuals will tend to argue in ways that are ultimately (sometimes unconsciously) self-serving, it seemed a priori unlikely that evil should reside so completely in one set of hirelings and virtue in the other. This weak-minded approach to social theory offered to deprive its followers of the insights of evolutionary biology and to wed this deprivation to a series of intellectual errors whose purpose was to justify the deprivation.

When critics argued that sociobiology tended to *justify* existing social arrangements, they were, of course, imputing to sociobiology a pre-Darwinian, species-advantage perspective, which they embraced but which the objects of their criticism had repudiated. Arguments in terms of natural selection only appear to justify that which has evolved when one imagines—incorrectly—that traits evolve for the benefit of the species. Likewise, in coining the term *biological determinism*, critics were describing their view of genetics as if it were the view of those they attacked. Sociobiology emphasizes facultative traits, based on genes, which permit individuals to adjust themselves adaptively to a great array of environmental (including social) contingencies. Every individual human alive today possesses numerous genes selected in the past because they aided the individual as a parent, offspring, female, male, nonreproductive, reproductive dominant, subordinate, altruist, cheater, deceiver, deceived, and so on. The fact that we are highly evolved social actors means that each of us has the genes with which to play almost all the roles. Although many of these genes are held in common, there is naturally some real variation. But admitting to this is no more than admitting to the *fact* of ongoing biological evolution, one of the surest facts in all of biology. It is no cause for alarm.

The charge that sociobiology provided intellectual support for American racism was almost entirely false, and one can only speculate on the motives for spreading a story with such hostile effect for black Americans: on the one hand, giving an unfriendly section of the populace the impression that racist ideas had new and unexpected scientific support; on the other hand, discouraging black Americans from learning the new discipline. Such are the achievements of human hypocrisy.

While I was doing my own work, it never occurred to me that the work was actually serving deeply regressive political aims. On the contrary, reciprocal altruism, for example, seemed to enlarge the possibilities for socially beneficial action beyond the sometimes narrow limits of kinship. Systems of reciprocal altruism tend to generate a sense of justice in the participants; and a sense of justice with genetic components seemed reassuring, since it thereby had a deeper and more secure foundation than if it were entirely the product of cultural influences acting on an indifferent, or even hostile, genotype. The fact that a sense of justice would not evolve unless it increased the inclusive fitness of those with the sense of justice hardly seemed a drawback. Instead, it suggested that the trait was more personally valuable than was commonly admitted.

Under the alternative view, a person with a commitment to justice must recognize that this is individually harmful and is embraced in spite of all natural organic strivings. It therefore puzzled me that those who claimed a commitment to social justice should have found an evolutionary approach to the subject so unattractive. Perhaps this was partly because they imagined that if justice were made self-interested it would somehow become selfish.

A second puzzling case was that of parent-offspring conflict. As mentioned earlier, the repudiation of the group-selection, species-advantage heritage had the beneficial effect of drawing attention to the self-interest of *all* actors in a social scene, especially submerged actors. For example, in parent-offspring relations, the offspring could no longer be viewed simply as the agent of its parents' self-interest, created and molded to do what was good for the parent. It had an independent self-interest, different from that of the parents but equally legitimate. The fact that conflict was—in the new view—a natural and expected feature of parent-offspring relations (as well as of all other relations between imperfectly related individuals) did not frighten us. After all, such conflict is widespread in nature, quite independently of our ability to explain it. Explanations in the species-advantage tradition merely mislead us regarding the cause, and do so in a politically biased fashion, in this case, by obscuring the offspring's self-interest.

Certainly sociobiologists have sometimes contributed to the impression that their work gives support to narrow and selfish orientation to life. Consider the phrase, "the selfish gene" (Dawkins 1976). Leaving aside the fact that genes themselves are not selfish, the proper phrase is "the self-promoting gene" or "the self-benefiting gene." Selfishness refers to only one limited aspect of self-benefit, namely, self-benefit coupled with harm to others. We do not say of an individual who works hard for his children, helps his relatives, loves his friends, treats strangers with respect, and avoids spite toward enemies, "What a selfish wretch he is!" Philosophers have long told us that the meaning of a word is, in Wittgenstein's phrase, "its use in the language game," and the word *selfish* is not used in this way in our language game. It is more nearly used to denote someone who is content to inflict costs on others as long as there appears to be some slight gain to self, where gain is measured as some increment in personal satisfaction.

There is a theme here that is worth underscoring. Natural selection seems to insist, so to speak, that traits prove themselves at a very local level if they are to become part of life. Typically, they must either sustain the life of the individual bearing them or increase its level of reproduction. Failing this, they must aid closely related individuals; the less related the recipient, the larger must be the net benefit. In addition, there are some traits that do not immediately benefit the organism or its relatives but that do so only by somehow inducing a return benefit. The less certain the return, the greater must be its net benefit. Thus evolution is conservative, tending to build up life-sustaining systems via their local effects, and insisting that the more locally a trait is harmful, the more beneficial must be its net effect, if it is to become part of life.

In our desire to see some unity and harmony in life, we sometimes wish that this were not so. How nice it would be, we think, if evolution favored traits that were good for the species, the biosphere, or the universe. Perhaps wisdom lies in trying to see virtues in the way in which life actually evolves. If traits that are locally useful are favored, life is provided a secure foundation for improvement. Traits negative to themselves are rapidly eliminated. We can see what kind of nonsense develops when creatures unable to benefit those closest to themselves claim to aid the species itself.

In summary, as biologists we have some confidence that our work is tending to clear away mistakes that have had biased political effects. Our destruction of group-selection thinking has removed the chief prop from the comfortable belief that the dominant interests naturally rule in everybody's self-interest. And we have uncovered a series of submerged actors in the social world, for example, females and offspring, whose separate self-interest and evolutionary adaptation we emphasize. By concentrating on explaining the natural selection of altruistic behavior, we have given a deeper and more reassuring image to the concept of self-benefit. Finally, we have been deriving a scientific theory of self-deception, which can be turned on ourselves.

Notes

1. Trivers, "Evolution of Reciprocal Altruism," p. 35.
2. Ibid., pp. 35, 36.
3. Ibid., pp. 45-47.
4. Ibid., pp. 47-54.
5. Trivers, "Parent-Offspring Conflict," pp. 257-259.
6. Ibid., pp. 259-260.
7. Ibid., p. 262.

References

Alexander, R. 1979. *Darwinism and Human Affairs*. Seattle: University of Washington.

Almond, G.A., and Verba, S. 1963. *The Civic Culture*. Princeton, N.J.: Princeton University Press.

Aronfreed, J. 1968. *Conduct and Conscience*. New York: Academic Press.

Baier, K. 1958. *The Moral Point of View*. Ithaca, N.Y.: Cornell University Press.

Balikci, A. 1964. "Development of Basic Socioeconomic Units in Two Eskimo Communities." National Museum of Canada Bulletin no. 202, Ottawa.

Bandura, A., and Walters, R.H. 1963. *Social Learning and Personality Development*. New York: Holt, Rinehart and Winston.

Berkowitz, L. 1968. "Responsibility, Reciprocity and Social Distance in Help-Giving: An Experimental Investigation of English Social Class Differences." *Journal of Experimental Social Psychology* 4:664-669.

Berkowitz, L., and Daniels, L. 1964. "Affecting the Salience of the Social Responsibility Norm: Effects of Past Help on the Response to Dependency Relationships." *Journal of Abnormal Social Psychology* 68:275-281.

Berkowitz, L., and Friedman, P. 1967. "Some Social Class Differences in Helping Behavior." *Journal of Personality and Social Psychology* 5:217-225.

Berscheid, E., and Walster, E. 1967. "When Does a Harm-Doer Compensate a Victim?" *Journal of Personality and Social Psychology* 6:435-441.

Brehm, J.W., and Cole, A.H. 1966. "Effect of a Favor Which Reduces Freedom." *Journal of Personality and Social Psychology* 3:420-426.

Campbell, B. 1966. *Human Evolution*. Chicago: Aldine.

Cott, H.B. 1940. *Adaptive Coloration in Animals*. London: Methuen.

Darlington, R.B., and Macker, C.E. 1966. "Displacement of Guilt-Produced Altruistic Behavior." *Journal of Personality and Social Psychology* 4:442-443.

Darwin, C. 1871. *The Descent of Man and Selection in Relation to Sex*. New York: Random House.

Deutsch, M. 1958. "Trust and Suspicion." *Journal of Conflict Resolution* 2:267-279.

Edmunds, M. 1974. *Defense in Animals*. Essex: Longman.

Epstein, Y.M., and Horstein, H.A. 1969. "Penalty and Interpersonal Attraction as Factors Influencing the Decision to Help Another Person." *Journal of Experimental and Social Psychology* 5:272-282.

Fisher, R.A. 1958. *The Genetical Theory of Natural Selection*. New York: Dover.

Floyd, J. 1964. "Effects of Amount of Award and Friendship status of the Other on the Frequency of Sharing in Children." Ph.D. dissertation,

University of Minnesota. (Reviewed in D. Krebs, "Altruism—An Examination of the Concept and a Review of the Literature," *Psychological Bulletin* 73:258-302.)

Freedman, J.L.; Wallington, S.A.; and Bless, E. 1967. "Compliance without Pressure: The Effect of Guilt." *Journal of Personality and Social Psychology* 7:118-124.

Friedrichs, R.W. 1960. "Alter Versus Ego: An Exploratory Assessment of Altruism." *American Sociological Review* 25:496-508.

Gilula, M.F., and Daniels, D.N. 1969. "Violence and Man's Struggle to Adapt." *Science* 164:395-405.

Goranson, R., and Berkowitz, L. 1966. "Reciprocity and Responsibility Reactions to Prior Help." *Journal of Personality and Social Psychology* 3:227-232.

Gouldner, A. 1960. "The Norm of Reciprocity: A Preliminary Statement." *American Sociological Review* 47:73-80.

Haldane, J.B.S. 1955. "Population Genetics." *New Biology* 18:34-51.

Hall, K.R.L., and I. DeVore, 1965. "Baboon Social Behavior." In *Primate Behavior: Field Studies of Monkeys and Apes*, ed. I. DeVore, pp. 53-110. New York: Holt, Rinehart and Winston.

Hamilton, W.D. 1964. "The Genetical Evolution of Social Behavior." *Journal of Theoretical Biology* 7:1-52.

_____ . 1966. "The Moulding of Senescence by Natural Selection." *Journal of Theoretical Biology* 12:12-45.

_____ . 1969. "Selection of Selfish and Altruistic Behavior in Some Extreme Models." Paper presented at Man and Beast Symposium. Washington, D.C.: Smithsonian Institution, forthcoming.

_____ . 1975. "Innate Social Aptitudes in Man: An Approach from Evolutionary Genetics." In *Biosocial Anthropology*, edited by R. Fos, pp. 133-155. New York: Wiley.

Hartshorne, H., and May, M.A. 1928. *Studies in Deceit*. Studies in the Nature of Character, vol. 1. New York: Macmillan.

_____ . 1929. *Studies in Self-Control*. Studies in the Nature of Character, vol. 2. New York: Macmillan.

_____ . 1930. *Studies in the Organization of Character*. Studies in the Nature of Character, vol. 3. New York: Macmillan.

Heider, F. 1958. *The Psychology of Interpersonal Relations*. New York: Wiley.

Hinde, R.A., and Davies, L.M. 1972a. "Changes in Mother-Infant Relationship after Separation in Rhesus Monkeys." *Nature* 239:41-42.

_____ . 1972b. "Removing Infant Rhesus from Mother for 13 Days Compared with Removing Mother from Infant." *Journal of Child Psychology and Psychiatry* 13:227-237.

Hinde, R.A., and Spencer-Booth, Y. 1971. "Effects of Brief Separation from Mother on Rhesus Monkeys." *Science* 173:111-118.

Hrdy, S. 1978. *The Langurs of Mt. Abu*. Cambridge, Mass.: Harvard University Press.

———. 1979. "Infanticide among Animals: A Review, Classification, and Examination of the Implications for the Reproductive Strategies of Females." *Ethology and Sociobiology* 1:13-40.

Kohlberg, L. 1963. "Moral Development and Identification." In *Yearbook of the National Society for the Study of Education*, part 1: "Child Psychology," edited by H.W. Stevenson, pp. 277-332. Chicago: University of Chicago Press.

Krebs, D. 1970. "Altruism—An Examination of the Concept and a Review of the Literature." Psychological Bulletin 73:258-302.

Lee, R. 1969. "!Kung Bushman violence." Paper presented at meeting of American Anthropological Association, November 1969.

Lee, R., and De Vore, I. 1968. *Man the Hunter*. Chicago: Aldine.

Leeds, R. 1963. "Altruism and the Norm of Giving." *Merrill-Palmer Quarterly* 9:229-240.

Lerner, M.J, and Lightman, R.R. 1968. "Effects of Perceived Norms on Attitudes and Altruistic Behavior Toward a Dependent Other." *Journal of Personality and Social Psychology* 9:226-232.

Lorenz, K. 1966. *On Aggression*. New York: Harcourt, Brace and World.

Lutzker, D. 1960. "Internationalism as a Predictor of Cooperative Game Behavior." *Journal of Conflict Resolution* 4:426-435.

Marshall, I.K. 1959. "Marriage among !Kung Bushmen." *Africa* 29:335-365.

———. 1961. "Sharing, Talking and Giving: Relief of Social Tension among !Kung Bushmen." *Africa* 31:231-249.

Montague, F.M.A. 1968. *Man and Aggression*. New York: Oxford University Press.

Mussen, P.H.; Conger, J.J.; and Kagan, J. 1969. *Child Development and Personality*. 3rd ed. New York: Harper and Row.

Pruitt, D.G. 1968. "Reciprocity and Credit Building in a Laboratory Dyad." *Journal of Personality and Social Psychology* 8:143-147.

Rapoport, A., and Chammah, A. 1965. *Prisoner's Dilemma*. Ann Arbor: University of Michigan Press.

Rapoport, A., and Dale, P. 1967. The "End" and "Start" Effects in Iterated Prisoner's Dilemma." *Journal of Conflict Resolution* 10:363-366.

Rasmussen, K. 1931. "The Netsilik Eskimos: Social Life and Spiritual Culture." Report of the Fifth Thule Expedition, 1921-1924, vol. 8(1.2). Copenhagen: Gyldendalske Boghandel.

Rettig, S. 1956. "An Exploratory Study of Altruism." *Dissertation Abstracts* 16:2220-2230.

Rosenhan, D. 1967. *The Origins of Altruistic Social Autonomy*. Princeton, N.J.: Educational Testing Service.

Rousseau, J.. 1954. *The Social Contract*. Chicago: Henry Regnery Company.

Sawyer, J. 1966. "The Altruism Scale: A Measure of Cooperative, Individualistic, and Competitive Interpersonal Orientation." *American Journal of Sociology* 7:407-416.

Schopler, J., and Thompson, V.T. 1968. "The Role of Attribution Process in Mediating Amount of Reciprocity for a Favor." *Journal of Personality and Social Psychology* 10:243-250.

Scott, J.P. 1958. *Aggression*. Chicago: University of Chicago Press.

Tesser, A.; Gatewood, R.; and Driver, M. 1968. "Some Determinants of Gratitude." *Journal of Personality and Social Psychology* 9:232-236.

Thomas, E.M. 1958. *The Harmless People*. New York: Random House.

Thornhill, R. 1979. "Adaptive Female—Mimicking Behavior in a Scorpionfly." *Science* 205:412-414.

Tinbergen, N. 1968. "On War and Peace in Animals and Man." *Science* 160:1411-1418.

Trivers, R.L. 1971. "The Evolution of Reciprocal Altruism." *Quarterly Review of Biology* 46:35-57.

———. 1972. "Parental Investment and Sexual Selection." In B. Campbell, ed. *Sexual Selection and the Descent of Man, 1871-1971*, edited by B. Campbell, pp. 136-179. Chicago: Aldine-Atherton.

———. 1974. "Parent-Offspring Conflict." *American Zoologist* 14:249-264.

Ugurel-Semin, R. 1952. Moral behavior and moral judgment of children. *Journal of Abnormal Social Psychology* 47:463-474.

Van Lawick-Goodall, J. 1968. "A Preliminary Report on Expressive Movements and Communication in the Gombe Stream Chimpanzees." *Primates*, edited by P. Jay, pp. 313-374. New York: Holt, Rinehart and Winston.

Wallace, J., and Sadalla, E. 1966. "Behavioral Consequences of Transgression: The Effects of Social Recognition." *Journal of Experimental Research in Personality* 1:187-194.

West-Eberhard, M.J. 1975. "The Evolution of Social Behavior by Kin Selection." *Quarterly Review of Biology* 50:1-33.

Williams, G.C. 1966. *Adaptation and Natural Selection*. Princeton, N.J.: Princeton University Press.

Wilson, D.S. 1980. *The Natural Selection of Populations and Communities*. Menlo Park, Calif.: Benjamin-Cummings.

Wilson, E.O. 1975. *Sociobiology: The New Synthesis*. Cambridge, Mass.: Harvard University Press, Belknap Press.

Wright, B. 1942. "Altruism in Children and the Perceived Conduct of Others." *Journal of Abnormal Psychology* 37:218-233.

Wynne-Edwards, V.C. 1962. *Animal Dispersion in Relation to Social Behaviour*. Edinburgh: Boyd.

2

A Biological Critique of Sociobiological Theory

William Etkin

Synopsis

The Genetic Basis of Evolutionary Change

There is a tendency in sociobiological discussion to accept oversimplified concepts of the working of the genetic mechanisms in relation to evolutionary change. Whereas current concepts do give a reasonably clear account of the way in which even mild selection can shift the genome balance in a population by changing the proportion of well-established genes, certain fundamental processes are still obscure. The short-term advantage of sexuality is one of these. A related difficulty is that of understanding how new mutations become established in the genome. Current interpretations emphasize the role of stochastic processes operating on a highly variable demographic and ecological base. These concepts fit better the scenario for evolution developed by Sewall Wright than the simplified mathematical models based on deterministic statistics that are presented in most general discussions. Some geneticists even question the basic concept of the individual gene as the unit of selection. These considerations lead us to question the tendency in sociobiological thinking to assume that any new mutation that is thought to offer an appreciable selective advantage to individuals under a given set of conditions would necessarily be able to establish itself in the genome. Natural selection of individual genes is too often viewed as an omnipotent solution to any problem of adaptation, without consideration of the complexity of countervening factors.

Genes, Learning, and Culture

Perhaps a more fundamental difficulty in sociobiological theory of behavior is the lack of consideration of the significance of the role of learning and its interaction with the genetic mechanism. From the ecological viewpoint, learning may be viewed as an uncoupling of a stimulus from its response as these are fixed in genetically determined behavior. Learning capacity, once built into an animal's genome, allows adaptation for varied circumstances without further genetic change. Such variability in response

45

is especially important in longer-lived and more active animals, particularly in mammals, where it effectively takes the place of detailed tracking of environmental conditions by the genome. Learning as a mode of adaptation reaches its maximum expression in humans and is the basis of cultural evolution by intergenerational transmission of learned behavior. Behavioral evolution by cultural change is vastly more rapid and effective than change through the genetic mechanism. Once established in human evolution, it must have largely displaced genetic change as the mode of adaptation. Thus behavioral charcteristics that are similar in animals and humans may be based on entirely different mechanisms, and the analogy between them may be deceptive. As we proceed to examine specific behavioral problems, we should keep these two general limitations of sociobiological thinking in mind.

The Paradox of Altruism

Some degree of altruistic behavior on the part of individual members of social groups appears to be necessary and is often evident. Basic evolutionary theory has been dogged by the difficulty of explaining how such altruism could be reconciled with natural selection. The resort to group-selection concepts formerly frequently adopted (from Darwin to Wynne-Edwards) is generally denigrated today in favor of selection operative at the individual and gene level. Hamilton's theory of inclusive fitness and kin selection offers a mechanism consistent with this newer emphasis and provides a clear mechanism to account for many examples of apparent altruism. This theory is examined in relation to Hamilton's original paradigm of hymenopteran social organization and also in the light of modern studies of alarm calling, an apparently altruistic activity, in rodent colonies. I conclude that within limits this theory makes a highly significant contribution in these two cases.

The Role of the Male in Social Organization
in Vertebrates

The male/female sex ratio in vertebrates is generally maintained at near 1:1 by a simple selective mechanism first explicated by R.A. Fisher. Since a male may inseminate many females, there is an effective surplus of males and, especially in polygynous species, intense competition among them for opportunities for mating. As a consequence such males show highly developed competitive features, which are deleterious to both their own and, often, the species survival (the expendable-male phenomenon). Infanticide by males is a striking example of this paradoxical effect. Under the conditions of Langur-monkey life, such male infanticidal tendencies would be expected to occur, as postulated by Trivers and confirmed in Hrdy's detailed observational studies. Although I find Hrdy's argument for genetic determination of the behavior to be strong, I think that learning probably also plays an important role in this phenomenon and helps account for its variation in different areas.

Parent-Offspring Conflict

Trivers has pointed out that a degree of parent-offspring conflict with respect to whose genes are to be favored might be expected from gene-selection theory. We confine our attention here to the problem of weaning conflict between mother and offspring as the example of most interest to social scientists. Although there appears to be some evidence of genuine conflict in some larger mammals, I believe its occurrence and significance is exaggerated by Trivers. Much of what appears to be dysgenic conflict may be better interpreted as a mechanism that allows flexibility by learning to operate in determining the progress of the weaning process and to adapt it to local circumstances. The supposed conflict may actually favor the survival of the genes of both mother and offspring.

Reciprocal Altruism

Trivers proposed reciprocal altruism as a mechanism to supplement Hamilton's kin-selection theory as an explanation of the development of altruistic behavior. He proposes that reciprocity by an animal for altruistic acts by another would convey selective advantage to both and, therefore, would tend to be incorporated into the genetic system. He illustrates this by the "cleaning" behavior in coral-reef fish and goes on to extend it to primates, including humans. He proposes the development of genetically fixed "cheating" and "countercheating" behaviors in these animals as extensions of reciprocity. I find this discussion unconvincing, particularly as it presumes unacceptable mental capacities in lower animals and a greater efficiency in the capacity of the genetic system to fix new genes than is reasonable under the circumstances considered. The cleaning behavior in fish can, I think, be readily explained on a straight Darwinian basis if plausible intermediate stages are envisaged. Descriptively, Trivers's discussion of the phenomenon in humans is realistic enough and is our common experience in human social relations. But such human behavior depends on a capacity for foresight and planning and can hardly be applied to animals.

Such human ablity must have had a much broader-base in evolution than Trivers suggests in his one-gene one-character approach. Trivers's discussion suffers from a basic confusion arising from a fallacious analogy between cultural and genetic determination.

Introduction

In this chapter I attempt to evaluate from a biological perspective the contributions and limitations of some current sociobiological thinking, with particular attention to the stimulating studies of Robert L. Trivers. The topics for consideration were selected for their interest to students of the social sciences. The preceding synopsis was given to provide an overview of the interrelations of the parts of the argument.

Personal Orientation

My interest in social behavior goes back to the 1930s, when I was a research associate in the behavior laboratory that was established by G.K. Noble at the American Museum of Natural History for the study of the newly emerging science of ethology, and was carried on after his death by Frank Beach. Although my own research was primarily in neuroendocrinology and animal development, I was intrigued by the behavior research around me and developed a course in ethology at the City College of New York, where I was then teaching. In 1964 I edited an introductory text in ethology for the Committee on Social Behavior of the American Society of Zoology (Etkin 1964). I accepted the invitation to write this critique as a challenge—an opportunity to see how the new developments have changed the field. I was particularly intrigued by the synthesis of population genetics with ethology introduced in E.O. Wilson's magnificent *Sociobiology* (1975) and the several brilliant theoretic papers by R.L. Trivers (1971, 1972, 1974; Trivers and Hare 1976) applying these concepts to specific evolutionary problems. My approach to the subject here, however, must be essentially negative for two reasons. First, these authors, as well as Dawkins (1976) and Barash (1977), have already presented the new outlook with the characteristic enthusiasm of pioneers. Second, my own background in experimental physiology makes me skeptical of the theoretic and speculative presentation characteristic of much of this writing, although I recognize that, given the present status of biology, this approach is both necessary and useful. I hope here by a critical examination to afford social scientists, to whom this book is addressed, a different perspective that may be useful in balancing their evaluation of the potential of the field for their own exploitation.

Some General Considerations: Science as
Mechanistic Explanation

I do not propose to analyze the philosophical problem of reductionism in the explanation of behavior, but it may be advisable for me to indicate my personal viewpoint in order to eliminate confusing interpretations.

In dealing with natural events (outside of human behavior), science has been successful only insofar as it has been mechanistic in its thinking. The term *mechanism* I understand to refer to cause-and-effect relations in which causes are understood as events that must necessarily antecede the effects they influence. In contrast, *teleological* explanation uses the concept of final causes toward which, in time, events are directed. In human affairs, these are referred to as goals, purposes, motives, and so forth. These are future events, which exert their influence through the human capacity for imaginative foresight, a capacity not generally demonstrable in animals. In its study of animal behavior, biology excludes teleology on the purely pragmatic grounds that it has not contributed to "successful" science, that is, to science that permits falsifiable, testable prediction and allows the synthesis of coherent systems for the extension and rationalization of experience. A biologist may, indeed, see reasons to believe that animals have consciousness (Griffin 1976); but until objective methods of examining such suggestions as factors in behavior are developed, the use of teleological explanations must remain a "cardinal sin" in animal biology. Should convincing evidence of foresight be demonstrated in any animal, biologists should be as ready to "sin" as anyone else.

I see no a priori guarantee that this mechanistic approach will work as well with human affairs as with natural events, nor do I see the need to deny purposefulness as a factor in human behavior since it is the most immediate of my own experiences and indispensible in my interaction with others. To reject our own experience of purposefulness in favor of an a priori mechanistic dogmatism would indeed be a cardinal sin (without quotes) in science. Something more of my own perspective will emerge later in this essay. For the present we must cling to both horns of the dilemma—mechanism versus teleology, animal versus human—trying to understand human behavior in mechanistic terms where we see an opportunity and in teleological terms where that seems more fruitful. The role of biology is to exploit the mechanistic approach as far as it will go and to note its limits. That, in the area of social behavior and organization, is what I wish to concentrate on here.

Evolution as a Pseudoteleological Science

Difficult as it is to hold on to both horns of a lively thrashing dilemma such as the study of behavior in animals and humans presents today, the task is made more difficult by the fact that natural selection, the basic mechanism in evolutionary theory, is itself pseudoteleological. It appears superficially to offer explanation in terms of an end to be accomplished—adaptation to the "demands" of survival. Thus we say that birds are adapted *for* flight, that horses' legs are adapted *for* running. The teleology implied in this language is a false one, however, because selection is a mechanistic process that operates on hereditary characteristics not in terms of whether they lead to an adaptive goal for the species but rather of whether they have immediate competitive advantage over alternatives. The terminological confusion arises from the fact that the long-term effect on the species—that is, the evolutionary outcome—is most easily described in the teleological thinking (anthropomorphisms). Biologists—journeyman scientists, in Frank Beach's phrase (Beach 1978)—are, of course, acutely aware of the possibility for confusion produced by using anthropomorphisms in writing for a general audience. Characteristically, they explain the reason for the use of anthropomorphisms and, having made their apologies, often feel free to indulge in such expressions as animals "deceiving," "trying," "investing," "being confident," and so forth. A minor difficulty is that the license provided for anthropomorphisms sometimes genuinely obscures the scientific interpretation, confusing the author's analytical thought with the animals' motivation. What can we think when an author writes: "Adult male harassers are probably attempting to prevent a male competitor from inseminating a troop female?" Attempting to prevent insemination? Particularly troublesome, to me at least, is the reference commonly made to gene selection as an "ultimate" cause of behavior and to physiological factors (experience, hormones, neural elements) as proximate causes, as though two independent systems of causation were involved. Such terminology oversimplifies to the point of distortion. Natural selection operates on the phenotype, not directly on genes. The phenotype is a product of a complex interaction of many genes, developmental processes, environmental influences, learning, and other feedback processes. It is our task to consider these as specifically and realistically as possible in our analysis. As a general orientation I prefer Mayr's (1977) distinction between open and closed behavioral programs. Although both have a genetic basis to be explained in terms of the evolution of the genome, open systems are more subject to environmental and experiential influences.

Genetic Interpretation of Behavioral Evolution

Historical Comments

It would be well to take a brief historical look at the relation of evolutionary and genetic theory so that we can better appreciate the dominant current viewpoint in terms of its likely stability. Darwin had no clear concept of the mechanism of heredity to guide him and saw no reason to deny a place to the notion of the inheritance of acquired characters along with natural selection in producing evolutionary change. He did, indeed, formulate a theory of inheritance—pangenesis—based on the idea that the germ cells receive components from all the organs of the body. This would allow for the possibility of acquired characteristics being transmitted to offspring. But this theory died aborning as cytological studies in the latter part of the nineteenth century displayed the manner of origin of the gametes and the central role of the cell nucleus in inheritance.

The prevailing concept of sexual inheritance in the nineteenth century was that of a mixing and blending of fluids (blood relationships). Not only was this too vague to be useful in clarifying the mechanism of evolution, but it even presented a formidable barrier to the understanding of this mechanism. It implied that favorable variations in one parent would be diluted by half in each successive generation and thus reduced to insignificance. Darwin had no effective answer to the problem of the genetic mechanism by which evolution proceeds.

Things did not improve immediately with the development of Mendelism in the early twentieth century; it too seemed to present insuperable barriers to an understanding of how natural selection could operate effectively. The early work of the Morgan school depicted mutations as minor variations, almost always recessive, and physiologically deleterious. The situation at that time was made worse by the quirkness of human events. The mathematical biologists then interested in inheritance (Galton's biometrical school) strongly opposed Mendelism; it was left to Bateson and other naturalists who were, in R.A. Fisher's charitable phrase, "unfortunately unprepared to recognize the mathematical aspects of biology," to carry on for Mendelism. Even well into the 1920s, one of my professors at the University of Chicago "had his doubts" about the reconcilability of Mendelism with evolution and opted for evolution. But the late 1920s and early 1930s brought a revolution in biology on this point. The experimentalists by then had built up a more complete picture of gene effects and interactions. The basic concept of the gene as a highly stable particulate unit subject to predictable rates of mutation opened the field to detailed mathematical treatment. Such units could be handled as numbers with all the apparatus of modern mathematics. The establishment of the Hardy-Weinberg law (1908) laid the basis for the mathematical modeling of genome change under the influence of natural selection. In the hands of S.S. Chetverikov in the USSR, R.A. Fisher and J.B.S. Haldane in England, and Sewall Wright in the United States, this produced the discipline of population genetics and its derivative, the synthetic theory of evolution, which is standard teaching today. This is commonly assumed to provide a satisfactory basis for understanding the workings of natural selection in evolution (Ravin 1965; Carlson 1966; Provine 1971; Mayr 1977; Berry 1977; Jameson 1977).

In recent years the ethological study of social behavior—also developed largely in the 1930s under the leadership of Konrad Lorenz and Niko Tinbergen—has been integrated with population genetics to produce the hybrid discipline of sociobiology. Although this movement has many sources, it was crystallized by E.O. Wilson's presentation in *Sociobiology* (1975).

Current Genetic Concepts and Their Limitations

Population-genetic analysis generally proceeds on the basis of the statistical analysis of models of populations in which the various parameters of the equations are assigned values that, although arbitrary, are presumed to be relevant to natural cases. The calculated consequences in terms of evolutionary change over successive generations are, of course, limited by the assumptions, implied or expressed, that are included in the model and in the statistical theory used. Where possible, the inferences derived from theory may be tested by laboratory experiments or in known instances of evolutionary changes in nature. Far more frequently, however, such data are not available and the researcher must resort to comparative studies of variation between species or populations in order to seek examples testing the predictions of the analysis (Davies and Krebs 1978). In actual practice, however, the procedure is usually reversed, with the examples from nature as the starting point and the models offered as explanations. With respect to the problems of social behavior, this is where population genetics links up with field ethology to create sociobiology.

It is commonly accepted that population-genetic analysis has shown the effectiveness of selection in producing moderate shifts in gene frequency in a reasonably small number of generations under the influence of appropriate selection pressures. This is supported by experimental and comparative types of evidence. It is this theory that is commonly explicated in general discussions of evolutionary theory (see, for example, E.O. Wilson 1975, chaps. 4, 5, 15). However, detailed analysis in the literature of population genetics also reveals many basic difficulties with the theory and the assumptions in the models. Some consideration of these is necessary for proper perspective in evaluating the applicability of current theory to understanding the evolution of social behavior in animals and humans.

A general limitation of population-genetic analysis is inherent in the nature of mathematical models as applied in evolutionary problems. In such models the parameters of the equations should represent real and measurable quantities and, of course, must take cognizance of all the operative factors. Astronomy and physics are often taken as the paradigms of exact science (Ziman 1979). In predicting the movements of the planets, astronomers deal essentially with only one type of interaction, gravitation acting on inertial masses in movement. The mathematical analysis is eminently satisfactory, although even here it is theoretically incomplete as applied to more than two bodies. Population genetics appears to mimic this mathematical method, for the concept of average selective advantage applied to genes seems to offer the same simplicity as gravitational pull in relation to mass. Unfortunately, selective advantage is not a readily measurable quantity, especially under natural conditions. It is not stable and is subject to the interplay of innumerable ecological and genetic variables. A partial list of these would include variations of climate and seasons, of food supply, of predators, of parasites, of population size and rates of change, of age distribution in a population, of inbreeding and outbreeding, of migration, of genetic isolation of groups and subsequent cross-breeding, of reproductive patterns, and so on (Hartl and Cook 1977). These could not all be spelled out in any manageable way even if the investigator were to accept arbitrary values for any he wished to consider. As Crow and Kimura (1970) expressed it in the introduction of their text in population genetics:

> A mathematical theory that could take into account all the relevant phenomena of even the simplest population would be impossibly complex. Therefore, it is absolutely necessary to make simplifying assumptions. To a large extent the success or failure of a theory is determined by the choice of assumptions—by the extent to which the model accounts for important facts, ignores trivia and suggests new basic concepts.

For particularly instructive examples of the difficulties of mathematical modeling in ecology, see D.S. Wilson (1975) and E.O. Wilson (1973). In using a mathematical model, it is easy to overlook even the assumptions made explicitly. For example, Trivers (1972) assumes that differential survival between the sexes after they become independent of their parents would not influence the cost of investment involved in their production. He justifies this assumption on the basis of a mathematical model proposed by Leigh (1970). Yet this model assumes that males mate only once and hence is of very limited applicability in natural populations of the types under discussion.

The interface between population genetic theory and ecology that explores the parameter of species survival is one of the principal areas of current biological research, and the application of the results of such research is a basic component of any understanding of evolutionary change. See summarizing works by Crook (1970), as well as works by Eisenberg and Dillon (1971); Baerends, Beer, and Manning (1975); Bateson and Hinde

(1976); Karlin and Mevo (1976); Berry (1977); Stonehouse and Perrins (1977); Krebs and Davies (1978); and Brussard (1978). Unfortunately, the task is barely begun; and, in view of the vastness of the field, it is not surprising that the critical information is seldom available. We are, therefore, often reduced to offering plausible but unsubstantiated hypotheses of selective advantage. It is well to bear in mind that for every selective pressure that may be suggested, counterpressures can be envisaged resulting from variations in ecological, demographic, or other factors. In the absence of ecological evaluations, all conclusions must thus be suspect. The frequent practice of citing examples from nature may be useful by way of illustration, but it cannot carry conviction since nature offers such a tremendous wealth of variation that examples can be found to fit almost any hypothesis. Even the careful evaluation of all available comparative data as practiced in critical studies often produces no clear-cut solution (see the discussion later on of the value of sex). As we consider individual cases later in the section on the role of the male in social organization, I think we shall find this a primary weakness of population-genetic interpretations of behavioral problems.

As with other sciences, introductory or general discussions stress the successes and understandings that have been achieved. The more technical literature deals with the still unsolved aspects, which, of course, are of greatest interest to workers in the field. Although familiar with this phenomenon in my own specialty of neuroendocrinology, I must confess that I was somewhat taken aback to discover how deep and fundamental are many of the problems that obscure the foundations of population-genetic theory. For example, the significance of sexual reproduction has recently been subjected to a searching reinterpretation (Williams 1977; Maynard Smith 1978). A critical difficulty is the genetic cost or penalty of meiosis (the process whereby the chromosome number is halved in the formation of gametes).

In contrast to asexual modes of reproduction (for example, by spores or parthenogenetic eggs), in which two (diploid) sets of genes are passed on by the parent to each offspring, sexual reproduction involves the transmission of only a single (haploid) set of its genes by each parent. Thus the parent may be said to suffer a 50-percent loss of its genes in reproducing sexually rather than asexually. In the modern view that selection operates to favor particular genes (see the discussion of group-selection versus selfish-gene theory), we would expect that sexual reproduction would in general be displaced by asexual methods. Yet in higher animals sexual reproduction characterizes all but a few species. In vertebrates only some forty species are known to reproduce parthenogenetically (Schultz 1977).

The standard explanation that every textbook (including three of my own) emphasizes is that sexual reproduction allows for new combinations of characters, especially in bringing together mutations that arise in different individuals. This provides a broader use for the evolution of new adaptations. Although this concept is logical enough, it provides only a long-term advantage for sexual reproduction. But since genes presumably are not teleologically guided by future consequences, the explanation does not tell us how sexual reproduction is brought about or maintained at the immediate expense of the individuals concerned, each of which suffers a 50-percent loss in gene transmission. One would expect, therefore, that in species that have achieved sexual reproduction, by whatever means, mutations that permit eggs to develop parthenogenetically would take over rapidly and eliminate the necessity of fertilization. Of course, the asexual species would be less flexible in the face of changing conditions and therefore subject to extinction. But this long-term effect on the species does not seem adequate to compensate for the 50-percent cost of meiosis to the individuals on which selection operates. In any case, the long-term advantage of sexual reproduction must depend on the often denigrated process of group selection rather than on the survival of individual genes. Indeed, even R.A. Fisher in 1930 accepted group selection as the explanation of the prevalence of sexual reproduction; and both Williams and Maynard Smith basically concur. Williams wrote:

> I am sure many readers have already concluded that I really do not understand the role of sex in either organic or biotic evolution. At least I can claim on the basis of the conflicting views in the recent literature, the consolation of abundant company. [1977, p. 169]

Maynard Smith wrote:

> Indeed on the most fundamental question—the nature of the forces responsible for the maintenance of sexual reproduction and genetic recombination—my mind is not made up. On sex, the relative importance of group and individual selection is not easy to decide. [1978, preface]

The clarity and candor of these authors brings out most clearly the limitation of deductive reasoning when applied to the complexities of animal life. Without wishing to compound the uncertainties, I may point out further that sexual reproduction may have physiological as well as genetic consequences. There is some evidence to indicate that synapsis of chromosomes (part of the meiotic process) may serve in the repair of disturbed DNA (Bernstein 1977; Bernstein 1979). This may be an important advantage in sexual reproduction and a basic factor in its evolution.

Beyond the problem of sexual versus asexual reproduction, the cost of meiosis seems to me to raise a fundamental problem with respect to the survival of new mutations such as are frequently evoked in sociobiological explanations. The sexually reproducing individual that carries such a mutation passes it on to only half of its offspring. Since in a species with a stable population size each individual leaves on the average only one descendant, the mutation has a considerable chance of being lost with each new generation. Because of the complications of diploidy and variance in the number of offspring, the calculation of the chance of extinction of a new gene is complex. Fisher (1930, p. 83) published a table estimating this chance after fifteen generations at approximately 11 in 100. Interestingly, if the gene conveys a 1-percent advantage, the chance of its survival is improved by only a fraction of 1 percent. As Fisher states, "a mutation, even if favorable, will have only a very small chance of establishing itself in the species if it occurs once only." He suggests that fifty occurrences would provide reasonable assurance of survival. With a gene with a mutation rate of $1:10^6$, this would require a population of 50 million; a rare gene ($1:10^7$), 500 million. If an adaptive change depends on several genes acting in combination, the required demographic base for its successful transmission approaches astronomical figures. Such population sizes may be available in some small organisms such as insects, but are questionable possibilities among larger vertebrates living in partially isolated groups. Such considerations also illustrate the difficulties of mathematical genetic analysis, as emphasized by Crow and Kimura throughout their textbook. It thus appears that the first step in introducing a mutation into a species is a complex matter not adequately envisaged in the simplistic concept that if a selective advantage is given by a particular characteristic, then the selection of the gene or genes responsible must inevitably lead to their incorporation into the species. Williams (1977) expresses this sentiment in his preface, and Maynard Smith (1978) agrees in his: "I share with him a distaste for the Panglossian belief that if some characteristic can be seen as benefiting the species, then all is explained."

Current theory in population genetics appears to be in a state of considerable ferment as a result of new insights provided by modern biochemical methods for detecting protein variability. When applied intensely to the analysis of the phenotypes of previously well-studied organisms, these methods have revealed vastly more variability than had previously been suspected (Dobzhansky et al. 1977, chap. 9). Since protein structure reflects the DNA composition of the genes, this seems to indicate much more variablity in gene structure than can be accommodated by present theory. Haldane (1957) first proposes the concept that selection within a species can be effective on only a limited number of genetic loci at any one time. The reason for this is that selection proceeds by eliminating individuals carrying the less-effective genes, in other words, by causing "genetic deaths." The number of such deaths cannot add up indefinitely without decimating the species, hence the limitation on the amount of variability a species can carry under selective pressure.

One escape from the paradox presented by the high level of protein polymorphism that is favored by some investigators is the assumption that much of this variability is selectively neutral. Under this concept, most of the variations do not affect the functioning of the proteins and therefore do not count in selection. Only the relatively few codon changes that affect phenotypic characteristics enter into the selective process. The rest must be considered as background "noise" of no evolutionary significance (King and Jukes 1969; Kimura and Ohta 1971; Kimura 1979). Other investigators favor a more radical explanation. In connection with other evidence they question whether the individual gene is the basis of selection and suggest that some larger assemblage of coordinated genes furnishes the basic unit on which natural selection operates (Lewontin 1974; Dobzhansky et al. 1977; Selander 1976). Until genetic research clarifies these concepts, we cannot incorporate them into our considerations. But it is well for us to recognize here that the fundamental bases of population-genetic analysis are not definitively established and therefore may undergo basic changes in the near future. In my opinion, the confidence with which current theory is often applied in sociobiological discussions and projected into the future development of science is far from deserved.

Group-Selection versus Selfish-Gene Theory

We have referred previously to natural selection acting at the level of the gene as the modern view, the logical inference from the Mendelian understanding of genetics. In this view only those genes are selected that operate to favor their own survival regardless of the effect on the species as a whole. We shall refer to this concept by Dawkins' felicitous term: the "selfish-gene" theory. Although this view was thoroughly appreciated by the pioneers of population genetics in the 1930s, the fuller exploitation of the concept took many years to develop. Earlier writers frequently found it necessary to fall back on the notion that competition between groups within a species will ensure that the better-adapted group will win out in the end. This would account for the occurrence of many cooperative activities of social animals that benefit the species. This concept of group selection reached a high point of support with the publication of Wynne-Edwards (1962) book on animal dispersion. In this he argued effectively that many group phenomena contribute to species survival in spite of any disadvantage they may have for the individuals of the species. For example, he considered that colonial nesting, common in marine birds, was advantageous for the species despite its evident disadvantages for the individual breeding pairs in forcing on them greater exposure to interference, predation, and competition for space. In his view, colonial nesting enabled them to regulate their reproductive activities to the species' advantage. This, he explained, comes about by sensory feedback from the colony size made apparent in colonial nesting and thus enables them to restrain or stimulate individual reproductive effort. Almost all who speculated on evolutionary mechanisms tended until recently to fall back on this type of argument from the good-of-the-species point of view, since we are impressed on every side with the wonder of the adaptation of each species to the details of its ecological requirements (Maynard Smith 1964; Etkin 1979). It is of interest to social scientists to note that Wynne-Edwards (1962) points out that the sociologist Carr-Saunders had already developed a similar interpretation of the role of much conventional behavior in human societies. He ascribed the mechanism of origin of cultural conventions to group selection, quoting Carr-Saunders as follows: "those groups practicing the most advantageous customs will have an advantage in the constant struggle between adjacent groups."

Particularly strong support for group-selection concepts comes from the difficulty in understanding altruistic behavior in animals on the basis of individual gene selection. As we shall see in the section on altruism, this sticking point for selfish-gene theory was cleared away by Hamilton's (1964) concept of kin selection. With that roadblock gone, the selfish-gene concept came into its own and has fueled the new burst of creative thinking in sociobiology.

Dawkins (1976, p. 147) has expressed this view uncompromisingly (even if anthropomorphically): "There is really only one entity whose point of view matters in evolution, and that entity is the selfish gene." Much of Trivers' highly original interpretations have been likewise based on the relentless insistence on the gene-selection viewpoint. He expressed this in an early paper by saying of the group-selection concept that it is "not consistent with the known workings of natural selection" (Trivers 1971, p. 44).

Despite the new enthusiasm for selfish-gene theory on the part of some sociobiologists, most population geneticists and Wilson himself (1975; see the section on interdemic selection, p. 107) continue to maintain an open mind on the question, at least with respect to the short-term advantage of sexuality. Consequently, we will examine this point a bit further here.

As we have seen, the basic explanation of the action of selection in Mendelian inheritance is quite complex and presents some unresolved ambiguities. Two different approaches, developed by R.A. Fisher and Sewall Wright, respectively, continue to contend for acceptance. This is well described by Crow and Kimura in their textbook on population genetics, as follows:

> The views of Fisher and Wright contrast strongly on the evolutionary significance of random changes in the population. Whereas, to Fisher

random change is essentially noise in the system that renders the deterministic processes somewhat less efficient than they would otherwise be,
Wright thinks of such random fluctuations as one aspect whereby evolutionary novelty can come about by permitting novel gene combinations.
[1970, p. 222]

Fisher emphasized the statistical effectiveness of selection based on deterministic mathematical models, which assume large populations with free
interbreeding and consistent selective coefficients. Wright stressed the difficulties presented by this concept. In its place he proposes that evolutionary change is greatly favored when a species is subdivided into a
multitude of small, partially isolated populations, each subject to
somewhat different selective forces in different habitats. Small population
size, acting by itself, leads to strong differences in genome composition as
a result of purely random fluctuations in the distribution of genes from
generation to generation. An analogy with coin tossing may be helpful
here. If one tosses a million coins one may expect a fairly close approx-
imation to a 50:50 ratio of heads to tails. However, if we toss 100,000
groups of 10 coins each, we would expect many of these groups of show
ratios of 10:0, 9:1, and so on. In natural selection, a small group of
animals that by random distribution acquired an unusual assemblage of
genes might progressively extend this in a process of random drift. Variations of conditions in different situations of the groups would further
compound the variability between groups. A change in conditions that
then brings these groups into close contact would permit those with more
favorable overall adaptive genomes to displace the others before interbreeding becomes extensive. In essence, this concept of Wright's over-
comes the difficulties inherent in models based on deterministic statistics
of large population and allows for a kind of intergroup selection (Wright
1932; Crow and Kimura 1970; Maynard Smith 1964; Berry 1977).

Obviously, without a great deal of information on the demography and
ecology of a species during its evolution, we cannot evaluate the relative
roles of Fisher's and Wright's models in any particular case (compare West-
Eberhard 1975, p. 3). In any case, in the face of the complexity of real-life
situations, the theoretic distinction between individual and group selection
fades out. For example, Brown (1974) explains the social evolution of New
World jays very realistically by invoking different types of selection
operating in different phases of the species evolution. Later we shall consider some studies of rodent population relevant to this point, but I think it
fair to say now that many ecological studies emphasize variability among
subgroups. To quote Crow and Kimura again: "Whether random gene frequency drift is a way of creating new favorable epistatic combinations or is
more like background noise, there is increasing evidence that it is
prevalent" (1970, p. 322).

Where there is so much diversity of judgment among experts, we cannot pretend to make a judgment. But we can draw two relevant conclusions at present.

1. The concept of competition and selection between groups is a theoretically permissible option. This is particularly important for the larger mammals and humans, among which population size is restricted and partial isolation of social groups often exists (Gajdusk 1960).
2. Selfish-gene theory and individual selection has an advantage as an explanation wherever it can be successfully applied, since it makes fewer assumptions of unknown variables and thus permits mathematical analysis.

This last point is, I believe, a real strength of the sociobiological approach. In my mind, it justifies my enthusiasm (kept under severe restraint in this "critical" chapter) for the new insights into social behavior in animals that selfish-gene theory is now providing and, it is hoped, will continue to provide. We will consider specific examples of this in the section on the role of the male.

Genetics, Learning, and Culture

The fundamental potential contribution of sociobiology to the analysis of social behavior lies in the application to that analysis of our understanding of the genetic basis of evolution. The emphasis in sociobiological writing on genetic change is, therefore, understandable. Nevertheless, it is to be regretted that the subject of learning and its interaction with the genetic system receives so little attention from sociobiologists. Wilson devotes a few pages to it in *Sociobiology* (and gives it more proportionate space in a 1977 essay) but Dawkins and Trivers do little more than mention the topic. Yet I think the basic change that learning introduces into the genetic system is crucial for understanding animal social evolution and, of course, indispensable for interpreting the emergence of culture. Although this is too large a topic to be treated in any detail here, I should like to outline why, from a strictly biological view, I regard learning as introducing a fundamental reconstruction into the genetic system regulating behavior, and why culture is a phenomenon that is largely independent of the operation of natural selection on genetic alleles (although it is dependent on the human genome, paradoxical as that may seem).

Biologists assume that animal behavior is a product of evolution and is, therefore, the result of natural selection of genes. Of course, the genes work through intermediate mechanisms, the various physiological and developmental processes of the organism. This path of action of genes in expressing their influence on the animal's soma is indeed a complex one of which, regrettably, little is presently understood. However, the details of that process need not concern us as long as we can assume a one-to-one correspondence between gene and phenotype in normal development. The fundamental assumption implicit in much popular sociobiological reasoning is that as long as the outcome is within the capacities of the physiological mechanisms, allelic substitutions of genes can direct evolution to any result that serves to increase fitness. Stated more colloquially, if it pays to do it in terms of fitness, then the genes can get it done automatically and mechanistically by natural selection of random variations among genes.

What I attempted to show in the previous section is that even from the genetic point of view this concept is, in Maynard Smith's phrase, Panglossian. The stochastic processes involved are really of limited effectiveness and cannot be taken for granted as providing a "universal solvent" for all problems of genetic fitness. Too much depends on the variability of demographic and environmental factors in making gene substitutions possible.

We may now consider another difficulty in accepting the implied omnipotence of genic substitution in evolution—the limit to the burden of information that can be borne by the genome. When conditions are changing, adaptation implies that the change itself must be monitored. Thus Trivers and Willard (1973) suggest that it is advantageous for females to produce a higher ratio of male offspring when they are in especially good health, and Wilson (1975, p. 317) concurs. But if the genome were to regulate the sex ratio in terms of the mother's health, it would have to provide mechanisms not only to control the ratio but also to monitor the state of health of the females and to link the two. We will consider sex-ratio theory in more detail later on. Here I merely wish to point out the enormity of the information load with which the genome must deal if it is to regulate every detail of organismic reactions in a changing environment. As we bear in mind Haldane's conclusion, discussed previously, that selection can operate effectively on only a limited number of genes at any one time, we must stop to ask, "Isn't there a better way?" And indeed there is. Feedback mechanisms can be developed for each change. This brings us to the subject of learning, which is perhaps the most pervasive, although not the only, such feedback mechanism developed in evolution. Many physiological and developmental feedback mechanisms are known. These enable the genome to operate effectively under varied conditions without the burden of innumerable specific genes for each contingency. An illustration of a physiological feedback mechanism relevant to our later discussion is the control of lactation by stimulation of the nipples in nursing. Continued nursing sends nerve messages to the hypothalamic centers of the brain, which control the hormones necessary for maintenance of milk production. When stimulation of the nipples ceases, the endocrine system shifts away from support of milk production. Thus variables in the time of weaning are coordinated with milk production.

Learning capacity in animals similarly makes a flexible link between environmental changes and adaptive responses. It substitutes for a one-to-one linkage between stimulus and response one dependent on the past experience of the animal. Where the animal's ecological niche presents little variability, the genome need not be burdened with learning capacity, and we find little. But where variability characterizes the ecological situation, we find animals endowed with the requisite learning capacity. This is true almost independently of the size or complexity of their nervous system. Thus digger wasps learn and preserve an exact memory of the spot where they have prepared a nest hole days before, despite the smallness of their brains. Nestling birds are prime examples of rigid instinctual linkage between food-giving parents and the food-getting gaping response, whereas with much the same brain structure chicks and pigeons, which have to scrounge for themselves for food, are excellent subjects for learning experiments involving food discrimination. Similarly, rats, whose survival depends primarily on hiding to escape predators, have a persistent drive to learn the details of their environment. They make excellent subjects for maze-learning experiments and will explore and become familiar with the structure of a maze independently of any material reward (latent learning). Their sexual behavior, however, requires no learning and is only with difficulty modified experimentally. This princple, long stressed by ethologists (see Hediger 1955; Etkin 1964; Tinberger 1972; Barash 1977), has only in recent years gained much recognition among experimental psychologists, although animal trainers have long appreciated it. Hediger, for example, asserted that it is hardly necessary to train sea lions to balance balls on their snouts. These manipulative capacities, which they use in fish catching, they also employ spontaneously in play with floating objects. The trainer has only to condition this natural activity to some reward in order to make a circus act. The fundamental principle is clear throughout the animal kingdom. Learning capacity is closely correlated in specific detail with the animal's ecological requirements. Animals are genetically programmed to learn readily with respect to those characteristics whose variability is important for their survival in nature. Learning is not a generalized capacity in animals but, as Tinbergen has expressed it, "each animal is programmed for learning in its own, and adapted way" (1972, p. 398). The failure of many experimentalists to appreciate the ecological restriction of learning capacity may have vitiated much laboratory work on conditioning (Cronhelm 1970; Moore and Stuttard 1979).

A striking example of the intimate interaction of genetic and experiential factors in the regulation of animal social behavior is provided in Barash's

(1974) summary of his classical analysis of social organization in several species of marmots. In this he correlated their behavioral characteristics with the requirements of their ecological situations—their *socioecology*, to use his apt term. He found that Olympic marmots, which are subject to great variation in overwintering survival and therefore of population growth, have a (presumed) genetically programmed behavior for maintaining friendly relations among colony members. They do this by the extensive practice of a greeting ceremony between members of the colony. He found that this interaction favors the dispersal of the two-year-old animals from the colony. Since this ceremony is performed much more frequently in the more successful and growing colonies, the dispersal rate from these is stepped up, thereby coordinating dispersal with population growth. In this way the behavioral system is adjusted to colony size by the conditioning effect of the animal's experience of greetings. Barash, in the spirit of sociobiological thinking, emphasizes the genetic aspect in the greeting ceremony rather than the involvement of the animal's learning experience in this adaptation.

The specificity shown in learning capacities in animals demonstrates clearly that such capacities, like their other characteristics, are based on their genome composition. From the sociobiological viewpoint, learning capacities are merely another of the techniques by which selfish genes "achieve" survivability. The tendency seen in sociobiological writing to emphasize a one-to-one relation between gene and behavioral phenotype without consideration of learning is, I think, in good part due to the greater simplicity of argument that such an assumption permits. Unfortunately, it incorrectly implies that behavioral evolution by genetic change and by learning are mutually exclusive. In my view, the relationship appropriate to sociobiological thinking is better expressed by saying that, in animals generally, the impact of experiential factors on behavior is circumscribed by limitations imposed by the animal's genetic system. They must be viewed together in the ecological framework of the animal's life in order to be understood. Genetic change serves to alter the locus of learning capacities that are inherent in all complex nervous systems, rather than to step up a generalized learning capacity. The introduction of learning at any point into a behavioral system requires genetic change making for sensitivity to experiential factors intervening between stimulus and response. Once this occurs, behavioral adaptation of the animal under different conditions can be achieved by learning and does not require new specific genes.

Although we cannot here go into the phylogenetic aspects of the relationship between genes and learning, it would be helpful before taking up this program in relation to humans to point out that the greatest flexibility between genes and learning in behavior would be expected to evolve in mammals, for several reasons. They are generally long lived; they have, of necessity, intergenerational contact, at least between mother and young; being homothermal, they can adapt to wide-ranging environments and seasons; and they have complex large nervous systems affording a wide basis for learning. Unlike birds, which share some of these characteristics, they lack the capacity for efficient flight, which makes complex learning capacities often irrelevant in birds (Heinroth and Heinroth 1958). (An often quoted epigram of Heinroth's is that birds are so stupid because they can fly.) The larger social primates, on the other hand, appear to have advanced considerably in freeing their learning capacities from close restriction to specific environmental conditions. Social interactions appear to be more important in their lives than do their problems with other ecological factors, and social learning is a conspicuous factor in their behavior. Can these be steps by which humans achieved a generalized type of learning ability and a culture-dependent survival pattern? We shall not attempt to inquire into the difficult problem of the manner of origin of human cultural capacities here but will try to identify their basic components as a mode of adaptation.

As plausible as I find this view of the relation of genes to learning in animals in general, it breaks down when applied to humans. It is in this breakdown that I believe the sociobiological view, with its emphasis on specific gene changes, further loses relevance when applied to human social behavior, making the facile application of sociobiological thinking to human social behavior unfortunate. This is, of course, a complex matter going far beyond the limits of this biological critique. Nevertheless, I think it necessary and appropriate here to outline my concept of the special character of the behavior system in humans.

Since the concept of uniqueness in humans often is greeted with skepticism, let me begin by pointing out that uniqueness is by no means unique to humans. In a real sense every valid species is unique, that is, separated from all other species by some characteristics. But in a more important way the major animal groups (phyla, classes, and so on) are almost entirely isolated from each other. Projected back in evolutionary time, of course, they have common ancestors; but the contemporary forms are generally well separated from each other by the absence of intermediates. The reason for this, as Darwin well recognized, is that each major evolutionary achievement, although arising out of a common background with others, has, by perfecting its own special mechanisms, preempted the available evolutionary opportunities and caused the extinction of the less well-adapted intermediaries. Thus birds and their feathers are unquestionably derived from reptilian ancestry, but no intermediates remain alive today. In evolutionary theory we expect connecting links to be missing, as in general they are. Of course, fossil evidence exists connecting birds and reptiles. Unfortunately, however, behavior is not fossilized; only the scantiest of indirect evidence of past behaviors, such as nests or other artifacts, are left to attest to them.

From that point of view we need not be surprised that humankind with its cultural mode of social organization is unique and that no array of intermediate forms is found today.

We then face the question of what the basic change is that has been perfected in human evolution and has made man alone the cultural animal. This has, of course, long intrigued the philosophically inclined evolutionists. With the emergence of the ethological interpretation of social behavior, the subject has produced a large literature of its own, beginning in the 1950s (Bartholomew and Birdsell 1953; Etkin 1954; Spuhler 1959) and continuing into the contemporary concern in ethology and sociobiology (DeVore 1971). We will not consider the problem of the evolutionary transition involved but will concentrate on the question of the outcome of that transition. What are the charcteristics of the human mind that make cultural organization possible for humans and not for animals generally?

The behavioral distinctiveness of humans lies in cultural organization. By this I mean that the predominant characteristics of human social behavior are determined by intergenerational social learning. Such patterns of behavior differ among human groups as a result of differences in experiences that are transmitted by intergenerational learning (see chapter 9 by E. White).

As we have seen, animals are sensitive to opportunities for learning only in situation-specific ways. On the contrary, the basic learning characteristic that makes the human cultural pattern possible is sensitivity in all respects to social learning. Human behavior is governed not so much by conditioning based on individual experience with the general environment as it is by imitation of social companions. Thus we learn on what and how to feed, how to pattern and express dominance and submission, how to recognize and respond to friends and enemies, how and with whom to form mating relations, how to care for offspring, how to regard territory, and so forth. We learn these not by individual experiences but by adapting the patterns of the group in which we are raised. Such social learning is, of course, present in other social animals, even birds (Cronhelm 1970; Curio, Ernst, and Vieth, 1978) but is particularly well developed in primates (Jolly 1968; Crook 1970). This is, however, at a much lower level. Social learning in humans makes for a more generalized learning, less restricted to specific relations than is the predominant characteristic in animals. The capacity for intergenerational learning in primates and wolves (Schaller 1973; Peters 1978)—*protoculture*, as it has been called—is not to be seen as a series of intermediate steps toward man. Rather like flight in pterodactyls, bats, and airplanes in relation to that of birds, it is a separate, self-limited development in each case.

The predominance of generalized social learning frees the process of evolutionary adaptation to a considerable extent from dependency on gene substitutions as a mechanism of evolutionary change. It substitutes the vastly more rapid and effective process of accumulating learned adaptations from generation to generation, thereby "short-circuiting" the generation-consuming stochastic processes of natural selection. The consequent diversification of human behavior permits human adaptation to numerous different ecological niches without the development of basic genetic differentiation. Humans have become adapted to different habitats not by forming separate species, genetically differentiated and isolated from each other, as animals do, but by forming different cultural units. By being the first to arrive at this evolutionary achievement, humans have preempted this evolutionary mode and have prevented competing groups of primates from continuing their lines of development in this regard, thus making the gap between cultural humans and noncultural apes broad and permanent.

Much has been made out of the existence of social learning in monkeys and apes (Etkin 1964, p. 292; Wilson 1975, p. 170). However, if one takes a broad view, what is striking is how small a role social learning and intergenerational transmission (that is, tradition) plays in their lives. A striking example that comes to mind is Jane Goodall's observation of the chimp that learned to terrorize and dominate its companions by making noise with a large tin. Apparently others failed to take up this technique despite its evident availability to them, nor did a new custom become established in the group.

The elaboration of social learning was presumably furthered during the transitional period in the emergence of cultural man by genetic changes (gene selection) that made for more effective communication by the development of language. I regard language as being based on a much more profound change than an elaboration of signal systems as seen in animal communication (Etkin 1963a). It provides communication between one stream of consciousness (mind) and another. Doubtless, as previously noted, some sort of consciousness exists in animals; but we have almost no means of communicating with this aspect of the animal. [However, see the work on cognitive maps in wolves by Peters (1978) and on animal dreaming by Allison and Twyver (1970) and Mogenson (1977) for possible new approaches.] On the other hand, I accept as evident that humans do each have a stream of consciousness and that individuals communicate by language with each other's conscious minds, as I am trying to do now with the reader's mind. I do not pretend to understand consciousness in physiological terms any more than I understand how gravitational attraction operates through empty space. But to deny its existence because of some arbitrary theory of scientific methodology would be fatuous.

I do not propose to attempt to characterize the human language faculty here beyond saying that it is generally built into humans and into humans alone and is central to the supremacy of social learning in him (DeVore

1971). Recent work on the teaching of language to apes supports this interpretation (Peng 1978; Terrace 1979). This work seems to me (if not to most
students) to demonstrate merely a great aptitude on the part of the animals
for learning complex signal system as means of access to material rewards.
But the ape, unlike the human being, is uninterested in communication for its
own sake as a means of socialization between minds (Menzel 1971). Only the
most meager evidences of play with or enjoyment of "language" communication have been offered in ape studies despite intensive and extensive
training. In contrast the child's motivation to talk is almost irrepressible, and
attempts to condition it to material rewards are often counterproductive
(Moskowitz 1978; Chevalier-Skolnikoff 1979). It is the motivation of one
mind to socialize with another irrespective of other rewards that distinguishes
human communication from that of other animals (Bateson 1972). As I expressed the role of language in socialization previously, "Adult monkeys
groom. Adult humans make do with small talk, committee meetings and
other nonfunctional exchanges of social stimulation" (1967, p. 73).

In our consciousness we transcend the limitations of time and space in a
way we do not regard as possible for animals. We react to what our imagination presents to us as the contents of past and future situations and of
happenings that are beyond our present range of sensory contact.
Philosophers have spoken of this aspect of the human mind as time and
space binding (Montagu 1953). It is this time- and space-binding content of
the human stream of consciousness that language enables us to communicate to each other and that I think is lacking in animals. [However, see
Menzel (1971) and Sharp and Sharp (1978) for a different viewpoint.]

One consequence of time-binding capacity is that our behavioral system
receives input from an anticipated future. As a consequence human
behavior is not a completely mechanistic system but is, in part, determined
by what is interpreted as part of the future. Our behavior is thus to some extent goal directed, capable of changing direction to keep in line toward
something that does not yet exist. In short, we are teleologically directed (as
defined previously) insofar as our anticipated goals, existing only as images
in our consciousness, guide our present behavior. In this view, a completely
mechanistic interpretation of human behavior is impossible because feedback from the anticipated future modifies the present nexus of causes and
changes them. This changed state is still not determinate since it is itself
negated by feedback from the new anticipation, and so on in an infinite
regression. I do not propose to discuss the metaphysical paradoxes and implications of this breakdown of mechanisms in human behavior. I introduced it here because I think it is central to the problem of the applicability
of sociobiological thinking to the social sciences. Without exploring this
problem further, I believe we can legitimately draw the following inferences
as relevant to our present concerns.

1. Adaptation to ecological requirements by culturally transmitted variations in behavior is so much more rapid and effective that further evolution by genetic mechanisms must have largely ceased once humans had achieved an effective cultural level of behavior. Just as automobiles largely displaced horses in transportation in our society, so culture must have displaced gene substitution as the primary method of evolutionary adaptation in human evolution. Humankind, of course, originally came into the cultural mode with genes for specific learning capabilities; but the attainment of culture necessarily tended to dispel these. Once the capacity for culture was built into the human genome, it largely, albeit perhaps not completely, displaced gene substitution as the means of further human evolution.

2. The development of imaginative consciousness giving the human mind a time- and space-binding capacity and the ability to balance alternative modes of response further outmoded genetic mechanisms for attaining adaptation. I regard this imaginative capacity as the basis of human thinking or reasoning. Even in its most elementary form, such anticipatory reason further outpaced genetic change. It would therefore be expected to produce a counterselection suppressing genetic limitations to cultural control. An illustration of the substitution of cultural for genetic determination is seen with respect to the differential social role of the sexes, which appears to be genetically determined even in higher primates. In humans, however, a remarkable plasticity appears to exist, permitting genetic males to be raised quite successfully as social females although some physical characteristics of play (tomboyism) appear to resist complete cultural determination (Money and Ehrhardt 1972; Barlow and Silverberg 1978).

In previous essays on the emergence of humans as cultural creatures (Etkin 1954, 1963b, 1967), I concluded that ethological insights give us only vague hints of how the initial steps in that process could have been brought about as humans shifted from the vegetation-gathering ecology characteristic of primates to a dependence of hunting. Today, despite the extensive speculative literature and many paleontological findings that had added glittering lights and some new insights, I still find the biology of the origin of the human mind a mystery wrapped, as the saying goes, in an enigma. It may be enjoyed even if unresolved (Humphrey 1976; Etkin 1979), provided we do not confuse the analogy between culture and genetic adaptation with homology between them. Let us now examine that last point.

The carryover of the concept of homology from morphology to behavior can be the source of much confusion (Ravin 1979). In tracing phylogenetic patterns, biologists depend greatly on the concept that structures, despite profound functional changes during evolution, maintain morphological relations that betray their evolutionary sources. A classic example is found in the bones of the middle ear. In mammals these transmit vibrations from the eardrum to the inner ear. In reptiles they constitute the joint by which the lower jaw is articulated to the upper skull. This became clear in the nineteenth century because, although minute in the mammal, these bones maintain the same relations to other bones, including those containing the inner ear as in reptiles. In the embryonic development of mammals, they start out as the suspension of the lower jaw, as is their present condition in reptiles. As the mammalian embryo develops, they change their position and function to the adult condition. Subsequent fossil discoveries have confirmed this path of their evolution through intermediate conditions in which they serve both functions simultaneously.

This concept that the fundamental anatomical relations of parts in animals (homologies) reveal their evolutionary pathways is often carried over uncritically to the behavioral field, and behavioral characteristics are thought to persist nonadaptively from one evolutionary level to another. For example, it is often implied that male aggressivity, territorial behavior, and so forth in humans are genetic holdovers from a primate ancestry. I regard such thinking as essentially false. It is true that Konrad Lorenz and later ethologists have demonstrated homologous behavioral elements in the courtship patterns of various animals. But what these studies show are modifications of specific action patterns (neuromuscular coordinations) transferred from one functional context to another in closely related animals.

I certainly do not wish to denigrate the value of homology in such details of action patterns, based as they are on built-in patterns of nervous structures. What I wish to stress is that many of an animal's general behavior patterns, like its skin, are intimately correlated with ecological requirements and are therefore extremely flexible in adaptation. Closely related animals differ greatly in skin adaptations (color, hair, glands, and so forth) in relation to different environments. Similarly, general behavioral characteristics are not tied to morphological constants but are readily modified in closely related animals to suit different ecological niches. As functional requirements change, behavioral patterns are readily modified. Phylogeny and homology are not significant determinants of such behavioral characteristics. For example, closely related species such as lions and tigers, redwing and tricolor blackbirds, woodchucks and Olympic marmots have different territorial and mating systems as suits their different ecological adaptations (Schaller 1967; Tinbergen 1972; Barash 1974). These behavioral characteristics are functional activities, which, unlike morphological components, are readily modified in adaptive evolution. Analogies may be useful in suggesting functional interpretations but not in indicating genetic relations (Scharrer 1956; Washburn and Lancaster 1968).

A comparison with architecture might be helpful here. Basic techniques of construction such as stone, wood or steel framing, types of arches, and so forth can be traced historically because their similarities are homologies. Yet each can be put to a variety of different uses such as dwelling, factories, or churches. Similarities of use, unlike similarities of structural patterns, tell us little about the historical connection between buildings of different periods. Similarly, social-behavioral characteristics such as polygamy, hierarchy, role differentiation between sexes, and learned or instinctual patterns are functional adaptations available to all morphological types. These vary primarily with ecology, not with phylogeny. The popular inference of important carryover of such behavioral patterns from ancestral species, as is prominently inferred in popular literature, is unjustified. More significant for our consideration here is that the emphasis on genetic determinants of behavior as implied by homology tends to a confusion of analogy with homology. If modern man does indeed have genetically limited behavioral flexibility in social characteristics (which I by no means deny), it must be because these traits were of selective value in the ecological adaptations of primitive humans, not because they were carried over from prehuman primates with different ecological adaptations. This will be one of the principles to be kept in mind in the later sections of this chapter, where we will consider specific problems in social behavior.

The Problem of Altruism

As explained previously, the existence of altruistic behavior on the part of individuals poses a frustrating puzzle for evolutionists. Darwinism seems to imply that, except in the case of parental care, only selfish behavior has selective value. Some zoologists, anxious to avoid the "raw in tooth and claw" interpretation of Darwinism, stressed group selection as a possible mode of origin of self-sacrificing behavior; but with the clarification of the genetic basis for evolution after 1930, this option seemed less acceptable than ever. In 1964 Hamilton introduced his concept of inclusive fitness as an explanation of altruism. This avoided the concept of group selection and made apparent altruism comprehensible on a strictly "selfish"-gene basis. It has thus become a foundation principle of contemporary sociobiological theory. Hamilton applied his concept initially to one of the most striking cases of altruism, that of the caste system of social hymenopteran insects: wasps, bees, and ants. In the most advanced species, sterile castes of workers, soldiers, and so on do the work of the colony and defend it with their lives, but do not reproduce. Therefore, we begin our analysis of this concept with Hamilton's explanation of hymenopteran social organization.

By *fitness* of a gene we mean the potential for success in transmission to succeeding generations. By *altruism* (better called apparent altruism) we refer to behavior that increases fitness of others at the expense of the fitness of the actor. It is to be noted that Hamilton explicitly restricted his discussion to genetically determined behavior, saying that it applied "in the world of our model organism, whose behaviour is determined strictly by genotype" (1964, p. 16). This is a point often ignored in general discussions of his concept. Starting with the familiar concept that in normal sexual species a child receives half its genes from each parent, Hamilton points out that a gene could increase its own survival potential (fitness) by aiding the survival of relatives that bear the identical gene (that is, DNA replicas). The likelihood of a relative bearing the same gene can be calculated according to the degree of relatedness between them, as estimated on Mendelian principles. Thus siblings have half their genes in common, on average, since each gets one of the two alleles possessed by each parent and therefore has a 50-percent chance of sharing any particular gene it possesses with a sib. First cousins are related at the one-eighth level and have one chance in eight of sharing a particular gene from a common ancestor. Thus a gene that determines altruistic behavior would be selected for (that is, increase its fitness) if the sum of its contributions to fitness in relatives added up to more than the loss of fitness of the altruist due to the action. In more dramatic terms, a gene that led a soldier to sacrifice his life for three brothers or nine cousins would thereby increase its own fitness and be favored by natural selection. This calculation is referred to as *inclusive fitness*, and selection based on this process is called *kin selection*. Note that the altruism referred to is not genuine altruism as understood in human discourse but only apparent altruism, more allied to what in human terms could be called nepotism. This is a remarkably fertile concept, adumbrated earlier by Haldane but not systematically developed until Hamilton took it up.

Hamilton applied his concept in detail to explain the long-standing puzzle of why the hymenopterans show so many species with highly developed social organization in which altruistic behavior by sterile castes is conspicuous. Here, if anywhere, self-sacrifice is to be seen in what is clearly genetically determined behavior. He pointed out the peculiar reproductive system in this group whereby males are all haploid, being developed from unfertilized eggs, and the females are diploid, coming from normally fertilized eggs. As a consequence, the female workers are related to each other at the 3/4 level instead of the ordinary 1/2 level. This is beause they each bear an identical set of genes derived from their haploid fathers and share one of the two sets of genes from the diploid queen. Therefore, genetic females would be expected to favor investment of effort in raising their sisters rather than offspring of their own to whom they would be related only at the 1/2 level. This produces a selection for females to be strongly altruistic to sisters but much less concerned with brothers, with whom they have only one chance in four of sharing any particular gene.

Thus the concept of inclusive fitness provides a neat explanation of the strong tendency evident throughout the hymenopterans to evolve social colonies in which workers sacrifice individual fitness for the sake of sisters. In some wasps overwintering females found colonies caring for the first brood themselves, but these then remain in the colony and help in raising subsequent sister broods while the original founder concentrates on egg laying. Other species form colonies on a more permanent basis. Among ants and bees, some reach extreme specialization of sterile castes. Since the application of the concept of fitness to the hymenopterons is the paradigm of the concept of inclusive fitness, it would be well to examine this case in more detail in order to see its limitations as well as its strengths.

First, we are forewarned that the matter is more complex than appears initially since the termites that do not have the haploidiploid condition nevertheless achieve complexities of social organization entirely comparable to that of ants. Their sterile castes consist of both male and female individuals, all arising from fertile eggs and therefore all related to each other at the conventional 1/2 level. This, of course, does not contradict the effectiveness of haploidiploidy for the promotion of social organizations in hymenopterans; but it does show that haploidiploidy is not a necessary condition for altruistic social organization. Biologists had offered other interpretations of the origin of highly developed social structure prior to Hamilton's 1964 suggestion. These draw on complex interactions of selective forces (Williams and Williams 1957). We will not attempt to consider these since we are concerned here only with the validity of the concept of inclusive fitness and the support given to it by its explanation of hymenopteran evolution.

Another fact of natural history that raises doubts about the effectiveness of the inclusive-fitness theory here is that in many unrelated species of insects, none of which show particular development of social organization, haploidiploidy also occurs. In some of these (coccids) haploidiploidy appears to function by enabling the females to regulate the number of males being produced at a given time. For example, in the spring, rapid reproduction without males (parthenogenesis) builds up a large population. At the end of the season, males in appropriate numbers are produced to give rise to fertilized eggs that winter over (Berry 1977). This ability to regulate the number of males by withholding sperm from some eggs may have constituted the original usefulness of haploidiploidy in hymenopteran evolution and, aided by other factors, may have produced the strong trend to highly social species. Certainly such a view is consistent with the fact that many contemporary wasps and bees are solitary species and that others show various degrees of suppression of breeding by workers. Of course, these considerations indicate only that haploidiploidy is neither a necessary nor a sufficient condition for the evolution of complex societies (eusociality) in insects. There is no reason to doubt that it is a strong factor in promoting it and in accounting for the prevalence of eusociality among hymenopterans.

Other aspects of the problem may be brought out by imaginatively reconstructing intermediate steps in the evolution of eusociality in hymenopterans. Upon emergence from hibernation, a female mates, builds a nest, and provisions some cells for the eggs to be laid therein. The daughters advance their genes best by remaining together with their mother, helping her raise their sisters rather than going off to start a new nest. The success of the original nest is thus greatly helped in terms of the number of wasps produced and their ability to defend the nest against predators or usurping rivals (Gamboa 1978). But the success of this strategy depends on ecological circumstances such as available food and nesting places, population density, and so forth (West-Eberhard 1975). Thus selective pressures vary, and various grades of organization would be expected to evolve in different species. But counterpressures also would tend to build up.

When ecological conditions make for success in establishing new colonies, the advantages of dispersion and multiple colony formation may outweigh those of a single cooperative colony. Different strategies fit different situations, and variations in the extent of social organization are to be expected as different degrees of elaboration of colony formation require different cost-effectiveness ratios.

The calculations of inclusive fitness discussed here apply only to rare genes. Once a gene for altruistic behavior accumulates in the population, the difference between the effects of the altruistic act on relatives versus its effect on nonrelatives tends to decrease. Thus once the gene has reached the 50-percent level in an interbreeding population, the extent to which an altruistic act toward a random member of the population furthers survival of the gene approaches that when done to a sibling. (It would still be somewhat less, however, because the probability of a sibling sharing the same gene would also increase.) The general principle is clear, however. The effectiveness of the principle of inclusive fitness is greatest in promoting propagation of genes in the initial stages of gene spread and loses effectiveness as the gene progresses toward fixation. Since the spread of new (rare) genes through a population is very slow, as we have seen, this consideration emphasizes the importance of inclusive fitness at early stages in the evolution of an altruistic trait. It would, therefore, be crucial to the establishment of new altruistic genes but less effective in later stages of colony evolution.

With respect to the evolution of insect sociality, a factor operating against the continued progress of colony differentiation is that workers must be expected to "resist" their exclusion from reproduction. Since workers are females, they are potentially capable of laying unfertilized eggs, which would develop into males. This is an economic way for a worker to propagate its own genes. The laying of male-producing eggs is well known in hymenopteran colonies of various degrees of differentiation and even appears to occur to some extent in advanced ants (Alexander and Sherman 1977). But in fully developed eusocial ants, egg laying by workers is largely suppressed (Oster and Wilson 1978). The sterile condition of the workers is the basis of the population analogy of ant colonies to individual multicellular organisms, with the workers being comparable to somatic cells and the queen to an ovary (Emerson 1937). Of course, unlike somatic cells, each sterile worker has its own unique genome; but if workers play no part in reproduction, then this would appear to be of no evolutionary consequence. It does not seem to me possible to account for the complete suppression of egg laying in workers except by selection operating on colony queens. Although workers share half their genes with queens, their interests with respect to worker egg laying are antagonistic, rather than concordant as they are with respect to altruistic acts. Therefore, the calculations of inclusive fitness as done with respect to altruism are irrelevant; only genes making for greater fitness of the queens can prevail. This requires suppression of egg laying by workers. Hamilton's principle of inclusive fitness thus cannot account for the suppression of egg laying by workers. [For a contrary interpretation, that workers interests can prevail, see Trivers and Hare (1976) and a critique of their position by Alexander and Sherman (1977); also see Noonan (1978); Macnair (1978); Charnov (1978).]

Apparent Altruism in Vertebrate Societies

As we have seen, the appearance of altruism in social insects is explained away in kin-selection theory. That is to say, it is not really altruism at all, but only the selfish gene operating under the constraints of inclusive fitness in the haplodiploid reproductive pattern. Perhaps the highest levels of eusocial evolution must be viewed on the basis of selection operating between colony reproductives in traditional Darwinian manner. In such species the distinction between kin and group selection is obscured by the assumption by the colony of characteristics of an individual with separate reproductive and somatic organs (superindividual). No such source of confusion exists among vertebrates, where every "individual" reproduces for itself. Yet among vertebrates, too, apparent altruism is commonplace. We will confine our attention here to one of the best-studied examples, alarm calling. This is the sounding of an alarm call by individual members of a group on detecting the appearance of predators. Such signals have the effect of alerting others to take cover or escape. Many birds and small mammals vocalize with specific, generally loud notes before taking to cover themselves, thus apparently drawing attention to themselves and delaying

delaying their own escape. The problem may be generalized to other forms of signaling, such as stotting by African antelopes and release of chemical signals by fish. Of course, there is no presumption that the variety of such phenomena have a common social function or an evolutionary explanation. Even the response to such signals may vary, as some small birds respond to alarm signals by "mobbing," that is, joining in common aggressive actions against an offending owl.

Alarm calling offers many possibilities for interpretation (Charnov and Krebs 1975). Since the alarm caller is not necessarily the closest to the predator, it may not be exposing itself to increased predation at all (Barash 1975). In addition, depending on circumstances, it may be indirectly protecting itself by stirring up confusion. In birds and ungulates the alarm leads to the formation of a tight flock that a predator would be unable to attack without danger of injury to itself. If the animal simply disappeared without issuing the alarm, the predator's success would encourage its return at another time, thus exposing the silent animal to later attack. Theoretical speculation of this kind suggests endless variants in the interaction of ecological factors. Only detailed analysis of concrete situations can untangle the numerous possibilities.

We will confine our attention to two splendid studies on rodents: Barash's (1974) seven-year study on marmots and Sherman's (1977) three-year study on Belding's ground squirrel. Sherman's study is particularly detailed, as he followed his animals by marking animals individually so that their genetic relationships as well as their responses could be analyzed. The most significant conclusion of these studies for us is that the data fit in well with kin-selection theory. For example, when a predatory mammal appeared near a colony of ground squirrels, old resident females were most likely to call first, as kin-selection theory predicts. Also as expected, males were commonly among noncallers. This correlates with kinship relations since females generally stay near each other as they grow up, whereas males tend to leave the neighborhood. The most frequent callers are old females, who have lost most of their reproductive potential and therefore sacrifice least by calling. Less clear were indications that the callers really do expose themselvles to greater danger; some 13 percent of callers were seen to be attacked, as opposed to only 5 percent of noncallers. Other possible functions of calling, such as diversion of predators, were strongly contraindicated. Other possibilities, such as helping the group irrespective of kinship or warning only reciprocating callers, although not ruled out, were not supported by Sherman's data.

Barash's observations on three species of marmots also support kinship theory. Males of the Olympic marmot maintain harems in their neighborhood and thus live among relatives. They also are callers, as kinship theory predicts. Such detailed and difficult long-term studies are stimulated by population-genetic theory and serve to give us confidence in the results of theoretic analyses generally and of kinship explanation of altruistic behavior in particular.

Role of the Male in Social Organization

One of the aspects of social behavior to which sociobiological analysis brings fresh insights is that of the behavioral differences between male and female. Older views took for granted that mating and reproduction was an enterprise in which female and male functioned cooperatively and efficiently in propagating the species (good-of-the-species orientation) (Etkin 1979). But the modern emphasis on selection at the gene level implies that each sexual partner operates to maximize the survival of its own genes. Consequently, there is the possibility of competition and conflict between the sexes with dysgenic consequences for the species. That the characteristic differences between the sexes present perplexing anomalies was long apparent to naturalists and was considered in some detail by Darwin in *The Descent of Man*. Darwin's puzzlement is well expressed at the conclusion of his discussion of the general equality in the numbers of the two sexes: "I formerly thought that when a tendency to produce the two sexes in equal numbers was advantageous to the species it would follow from natural selection, but I now see the whole problem is so intricate that it is safer to leave its solution for the future" (2d ed., 1860, p. 298).

Darwin developed his concept of sexual selection to explain and reconcile natural selection with some of the anomalies seen in the biology of sex. Trivers (1972) has reviewed the somewhat checkered history of the concept of sexual selection and has interpreted many aspects in modern sociobiological terms, providing numerous fresh insights that have been incorporated into the literature of sociobiology.

We will not try to analyze this wide-ranging subject here but will instead concentrate on male aggressivity as it relates to the conflict between mates for the propagation of their genes. The problem arises from the fact that in many species of mammals, especially polygynous ones, the males are larger and more aggressive than females and are provided with weapons such as enlarged canine teeth, horns, antlers, and so forth that equip them for destructive fighting (aggressive potential) (Etkin 1964). In many species of cats, pinnipeds, ungulates, and primates, males not only do not contribute to raising the young but often actively interfere with that process.

The sociobiological explanation of this high development of aggressivity goes back to the concept developed by Fisher (1930) that the ratio of males to females is kept approximately equal (ratio = 1) despite the fact that a single male is physiologically capable of inseminating many females.

From the species point of view fewer males than females would be expected. The reason for the equality is that any mutations making for an increase in proportion of males would create a counterselection premium for females, which would then be in short supply. The competition among males for females in polygynous mating systems leads to selection pressure on males for exaggerated development of aggressive potential. One effect of this is to lower the level of physiological efficiency in males, since they must invest undue resources in components with aggressive-potential components. Males are thus expected to be less hardy and to have shorter life spans than females. I have called this phenomenon the expendability of the male (Etkin 1964, 1979). The lower viability of the male requires a slightly higher initial production of males in order to maintain the equality of numbers called for in Fisher's theory, and this is what is commonly found. Furthermore, under unfavorable conditions more male fetuses die, further distorting the ratio. The ratio in the American population, for example, is currently estimated to be at least 120:100 at conception and 104:100 at birth (McMillen 1979). I regard the preceding explanation of the deviation from the 1:1 ratio as sufficient to account for these ratios and their deviations with the health of mothers (Etkin 1979). However, Trivers and Willard (1973) developed an ingenious concept relating a selection pressure for the production of excess males to the health of the mother. This is accepted by Wilson (1975, pp. 317-138) and presented in syllogistic form. I regard this concept as flawed by the faith it requires in the perfection of the process of natural selection, which is here called on to track temporary variations in environmental conditions affecting maternal health. The reader is invited to compare the brief presentations of the two points of view and to judge for him- or herself. The outcome, however, is the same. The life of the male in many mammals is short, brutish, and nasty; and some of this spills over to the females and their young. No better illustration of this is seen than in the life of the Indian langur monkeys so elegantly studied and graphically recounted by Hrdy (1977).

In her studies Hrdy has described infanticide by males and has given a sociobiological interpretation in terms of the competition between mates for the propagation of their respective genes. Trivers (1972, p. 159), on the basis of earlier and less complete observation of Sugiyama (1967) on the same species, had first offered this theoretic interpretation and had stressed the pervasiveness of competition between the sexes in animals and humans. We may concentrate on this case in some detail as a paradigm of the genetic interpretation of behavior so much emphasized in sociological thinking.

Hrdy's study extended with interruptions over three years and covered a number of troops of langurs living near the town of Abu in central India. She described several instances in which she observed behavior at the time of a takeover of a troop by a new overlord. In the course of a few weeks after each takeover, she noted that the nursing young all disappeared. In several cases the male was seen to attack the mother that was carrying the infant, severely injuring or killing the young. Other direct confirmations of such killings were provided by native informers. Combining her observations with those of others on which she had data, she found fifteen takeovers of which eleven showed male attacks on nursing young with the destruction of some thirty-nine infants of up to one year in age. All females vigorously defended their young, often with the help of other females; but they were no match for the males. Infants born some months after the male takeover apparently were not molested. (Because of the seasonal nature of the langur reproduction and the interruptions of the observation periods, the data on this point are not as complete as could be wished.) In several instances the recently deprived mother was seen subsequently to show apparent estrous behavior (as judged by behavior signs) and to be mounted by the male. One of the females whose nursling had been killed a few days before was seen to show estrous solicitation of the male and was mounted by him. She gave birth after an appropriate (circa six-month) gestation period. In another instance a female who appeared to be in early pregnancy was seen to display estrus and to mate and to give birth in about four months. In this instance estrous behavior was interpreted as dissembling by the female to appease the male.

Trivers's original interpretation was that the male destroyed the young fathered by the previous overlord and thereby freed the mothers to start estrous cycles again and to breed with him. Thus the takeover male appeared to hasten the propagation of a set of his genes at the expense of a set of those of the female and, of course, to the disadvantage of the species. The display of estrous behavior by the recently deprived females fits into that explanation and corresponds to the endocrinological findings that lactation generally inhibits breeding in primates. Although Dr. Hrdy planned her study of langurs with special attention to the problem of infanticide, she nevertheless was surprised to find so extensive a confirmation of Trivers's suggested explanation.

It has repeatedly been suggested that the killing of infants in langurs, like that in many other mammals, is an incidental result of the battles between males. Such infanticide, for example, is seen in elephant seals (Le Boeuf 1974) where the male appears to ignore the young (which they may or may not have fathered during the previous year) and sometimes crushes them in battles with rivals. The completeness with which infanticide occurs at Abu might be due to special stress of crowding or of contact with humans. Since the classic study of Zuckerman (1932), it has often been noted that few infants survive in monkey colonies that are under stress (Vandenberg 1967). Some writers see a population-control mechanism in infanticide along the lines of Wynne-Edwards's ideas of group selection. In agreement with Hrdy, I do not think these suggestions stand up to the evidence. It appears evident that the new overlord specifically attacks the infants, snatching them away from the mother and only incidentally injuring her, if at all. The behavior of the females in defending the young likewise supports the concept that the males' behavior is specifically directed at the destruction of the infants. The evidence on female solicitation of the male after loss of a nursling is also supportive of the Trivers-Hrdy concept. Unfortunately, the evidence here is not as clear as could be desired. Langur females do not show the swelling of the sexual skin that makes estrus anatomically evident in many other primates. Sexual presentation is a common appeasement gesture in primates. Thus solicitation, which was seen at Abu within a few days after loss of an infant (Hrdy 1977, p. 280), even when accompanied by estrous type of head shaking, does not necessarily indicate physiological estrus, which would require a complete readjustment of the endocrine system and time for the maturation of an ovarian follicle. Nevertheless, I see no reason to question the basic conclusion that the male langur at Abu does advance the propagation of his genes by the practice of infanticide.

However, I find it difficult to conceive the mechanism involved to be a purely genetic, one-to-one linkage of specific genes to the specific act. It seems to me that conditioning by experience probably plays a considerable role here. Hrdy considers learning in only a single sentence, saying, "To what extent infanticide is learned behavior is unknown; it seems unlikely to me, however, that adequate opportunity for such learning is present" (1977, p. 281). I cannot agree with this.

The chief difficulty I find in the concept of a purely genetic control of this behavior is its variability in different areas of India, as discussed by Hrdy. The genetic interpretation makes it necessary to suppose that specific genetic modulation would be able to keep up with the instability of the demographic and ecological factors in different regions in order to adjust the intensity of the male's aggression to local conditions. Hrdy, for example, discusses the conditions under which infanticide would be profitable for the male. These include the average length of tenure of the overlord; if too short, he would risk the loss of all offspring to the next overlord; but too long a tenure would bring on other penalties, such as the loss of future breeding females among the slaughtered young. To suppose that natural selection could adjust the genome to the vagaries of the environmental factors governing population density and male competiton seems to me unrealistic (Panglossian), as previously explained, especially as the different populations are not isolated from each other. A genetically determined sensitivity to environmental conditioning (learning) in the species, as discussed in the section on learning and culture, appears more realistic as an interpretation. The local differences in behavior would thus be environmentally and not genetically determined.

It is well known from laboratory and field studies that monkeys and other primates are capable of excellent learning by observation of social companions. Every male langur would appear to have many opportunities to observe at close range the incessant battling of the males and subsequent behavior in the troop. They may well be capable of learning the lesson that the female bearing a young is not available for sexual activity but becomes so after the loss of the infant. We must disassociate our anthropomorphic conception of the nursling as a potential future member of the troop from the animal's perception of it, presumably as a squirming appendage attached to the female and associated with her unavailability for copulation. The destruction of such an impediment, which would be incidental to the common fighting activities and which would lead to subsequent sexual availability of the female, would be no more difficult for a monkey to learn than the association of a particular type of tree with edible fruits. Further, should a more vigorous and perceptive male develop a conditioned behavior of "deliberate" infanticide, the copying of such behavior and the establishment of a strong infanticide tradition in the troop would be expected, much as the well known "potato washing" tradition was established in some monkey colonies (Etkin 1964, p. 292). Different levels of infanticide in different groups may thus have a protocultural learned basis. There is much evidence of such subtle social learning in monkey colonies. For example, young males become adept at using displays of care giving to infants as a method of inhibiting the aggression of dominants (Crook 1977). Whether or not this hypothetical scenario would "play well in Abu," I think my contention that sociobiological thinking needs to pay more attention to learning as a factor in behavioral adaptation is well illustrated in Hrdy's study.

Learning as a factor is also implicit in the fact that the overlord does not kill the infants born after his initial takeover period. Hrdy quotes specific instances of offspring born about six months after an observed mating, which were not attacked by the male. She raises the question of the possibility of males being able, in some manner, to recognize their own offspring; but she offers no evidence to substantiate such a concept. The resolution of this problem may lie more with the phenomenon of familiarization (Zajonc 1971). This is a well-recognized factor in decreasing aggression, fear, and other negative responses in animals. For example, in many birds—gulls, song sparrows, and so forth—the coming together of mates in courtship necessitates a reduction of aggression between male and female. This occurs as the animals become accustomed to each other. Rats, like many other animals, avoid new objects until they have had time to familiarize themselves with them. I think this general characteristic of animal (and human) learning is sufficient to account for the reduction of tension and aggression between established overlords and the troop females. In any case, the newly born are kept close and are inconspicuous at first, only gradually becoming distinct visual components associated with the female. Of course, only future observational and experimental data can establish the value of such speculations. But as long as the attention of sociobiologists is given only to genetic factors, such data will not become available and sociobiology will repeat the unfortunate history of the early ethologists (Lehrman 1953), and of the social Darwinists before them, in turning some good biology into simplistic sociology of higher animals and humans.

Parent-Offspring Conflict

Trivers (1974) has raised the question of parent-offspring conflict as an inference from the concept of selection at the gene level. Clearly it is possible that behavior that favors the fitness of the offspring should run counter to that of a parent since, although they share one-half of their genes, they differ with respect to the other half. Trivers has adduced several examples to illustrate this possibility and has drawn the inference that such conflict provides a genetic basis for intergenerational conflict in animals and in humans. Let us examine this problem as it manifests itself in the prime example in mammals, the weaning period.

It is clear that at weaning the female in many species acts to break the tie with the young. Not only does her milk production decrease; but she may also, by withdrawing or failing to assume appropriate positions, prevent nursing. She also tends to neglect the young, allowing them to leave her in favor of exploring the environment and associating with other members of the social group. Such behavior varies considerably in different species. Rats, for example, which run an estrous cycle shortly after parturition and are therefore commonly pregnant during nursing, taper off their nursing and attention to the young while the young increasingly leave the nest to feed and fend for themselves. Consequently, before the next litter is born they have lost contact with the mother and are on their own. There is little evidence of active rejection between mother and young (Rosenblatt and Lehrman 1963). In ungulates (sheep, goats, deer, moose, and elk) (Linsdale and Tomich 1953; Hersher, Richmond, and Moore 1963; Altmann 1963) the young start foraging for themselves as they develop and associate with peers. They too gradually lose their close attachment to the mother with only occasional active rebuff by her, particularly if they try to nurse when her next birth is due. However, they may be permitted to return to nursing subsequently along with the younger sibling. In cats, studied in detail under laboratory conditions by Schneirla, Rosenblatt, and Tobach (1963) weaning likewise proceeds in a highly adaptive manner. They write: "The mother evidently contributes to weaning not only by incidentally emphasizing sources of solid food behaviorally, but in particular by making the infantile mode of feeding more and more difficult at a time when the young are more and more capable of getting their food independently'' (p. 154). In monkeys the arboreal langur's young are given protection and assistance as their nursing period is ending, not only by the mother but also by other females and even males in the troop (Jay 1963). In ground-living baboons, which are more exposed to predation, much more aggressivity is seen in all social interactions, including the weaning process. Initially the young feed with the mother, learning from her on what and how to feed. As they mature, the mother is less and less tolerant and sharing and treats the offspring more and more like any other competing members of the troop. Left more to themselves, the young associate more and more with others, including males who are quite protective. In this way they establish their position in the social group through play with peers and experiences with adults (DeVore 1963; Jay 1963). Of the chimpanzees Lawick-Goodall remarks that "in the wild chimpanzee mothers do not appear to play an active part in weaning behavior" (1967, p. 302).

Thus described, the relationship between mother and young in mammals would appear to be essentially a harmonious one in which the mother supports the young in all ways, including nursing, but also encourages the emerging independence of the young as they mature and learn to feed and fend for themselves. The conventional interpretation of the weaning process is, therefore, that the "interests" of mother and young are both well served in that the mother is freed again for breeding as the child is led and directed toward its independent life. Such rejection of the young by the mother as appears in different species is not to be regarded as necessarily or seriously detrimental to the young but rather as helpful in the acquisition of the skills required for independent adult life. The period of "conflict" may work to give a measure of flexibility to the separation so that when circumstances are favorable the young may accept the separation sooner, whereas when its needs are greater an offspring will persist longer in its demands on the mother (Hinde 1966).

Trivers, taking the "selfish-gene" point of view, rejects this conventional interpretation, as follows:

> Weaning conflict is usually assumed to occur either because transitions in nature are assumed always to be imperfect or because such conflict is assumed to serve the interests of both parent and offspring by informing each of the needs of the other. In either case, the marked inefficiency of weaning conflict seems the clearest argument in favor of the view that such conflict results from an underlying conflict in the way in which the inclusive fitness of mother and offspring are maximized. Weaning conflict in baboons, for example, may last for weeks or months, involving daily competitive interactions and loud cries from the infant in a species otherwise strongly selected for silence (DeVore 1963). Interactions that are inefficient

within a multicellular organism would be cause for some surprise, since, unlike mother and offspring, the somatic cells within an organism are identically related. [1974, p. 251]

This viewpoint presumes that any extension of care beyond the physiological minimum is favorable to the young at the expense of the mother's capacity to reproduce and that variability in weaning behavior is "inefficient." There are many good reasons to doubt this. In social mammals, particularly larger species, experience in group living and peer relations are essential to the animal's growing up. In temperate climates the independent capabilities of the young for surviving the trials of winter are crucial. Their life cycles are adaptively ordered, with birth occurring in early spring followed by a period of extremely rapid growth and maturation of the young during the most favorable season. But nature's variability makes this only a rough adjustment, which is improved by a measure of flexiblity (that is, "conflict") in the separation. In many species nursing does not interfere with sexual cycling and breeding of the nursing females in the fall. Such rejection as occurs comes in the spring before the new birthing time. The yearling may later be admitted to nurse again with the new infant, as in moose (Altmann 1963). In unfavorable seasons the female may miss a breeding season, allowing longer continued nursing for the young. Variability is characteristic of larger mammals, and flexibility based on experiential factors and learning plays a conspicuous role. As explained earlier, the endocrinological system maintaining nursing (principally prolactin production) is keyed to the stimulation of the nipples during nursing. This permits some interaction between the success of the young in feeding for itself and the continuance of milk flow in the mother. In large mammals of temperate climates, the spacing of successive births is largely regulated by the limited annual breeding period; nurslings at this time do not interfere with mating. In other mammals, such as the tropical primates, the cessation of nursing comes into play as one of many factors regulating the resumption of sexual cycling, as seen in the previous discussion of infanticide. The interplay of factors is complex, however. The validity of Trivers's concept that a significant conflict necessarily exists between maternal care and reproduction can be judged only by detailed experimental and observation studies, such as are reported in H. Rheingold's symposium volume (1963). I find little support for Trivers's interpretation in this literature.

Following the selfish-gene approach to a logical extreme, Trivers suggests that the offspring might be selected for deception of the mother in order to extract additional sacrifice from her and that she in turn might evolve capacities for detection and negation of such deception. The possibilities need not stop here but could go on to an indefinitely extended

feedback of strategy and counterstrategy on the part of mother and offspring considered as opponents. Trivers writes:

> But once such a system has evolved, the offspring can begin to employ it
> out of context. The offspring can cry not only when it is famished but also
> when it merely wants more food than the parent is selected to give.
> Likewise, it can begin to withhold its smile until it has gotten its way. Selec-
> tion will then, of course, favor parental ability to discriminate the two uses
> of the signals but still subtler mimicry and deception by the offspring are
> always possible. Parental experience with preceding offspring is expected to
> improve the parent's ability to make the appropriate discrimination. Unless
> succeeding offspring can employ more confusing tactics than earlier ones,
> parent-offspring interactions are expected to be increasingly biased in favor
> of the parent as a function of parental age. (1974, p. 245]

Here again we face the speculation of an infinite regression of strategies
based on the presumed unlimited effectiveness of natural selection to refine
genetic adaptation to each separate circumstance. Since I have already
discussed the objections to such a Panglossian concept of genetic selection
and have also previously indicated why I believe learning capacities make
such genetic adaptation unnecessary, I will not further belabor the point
here.

The concept of adaptation by genetic selection, which is the basic orientation in Trivers's analysis, is, like other speculative approaches, a two-
edged sword. For any single imagined pressure, a counterpressure of equal
plausibility can generally be suggested. For example, it is possible that a
mother might be selected to give *more* aid to a weanling than is beneficial
for it, as in the following argument. An offspring reaching weaning age is
worth, in terms of maternal fitness, far more than a young to be produced
in the future, since in nature a considerable proportion of neonates die
before reaching weaning age. The mother's own prospect of survival and
success in having another offspring is also at risk. One might speculate,
therefore, that a mother should be selected to invest more in a weanling
than is good for it in terms of its need to achieve ultimate independence and
social position in its group. For a mother to invest the minimum in order to
get on to the next young would be to risk the loss of a well-established set of
her genes in favor of a dubious future offspring. One could thus conjure up
a gene for maternal overindulgence, a "spoil-the-child" gene (with the
fascinating possibilities such a gene provides for making analogies to
human behavior.) Needless to say, I would put little stock in such narrowly
genetic arguments. Rather, I consider the significance of the highly
developed learning capacity shown as a genetic trait by mammals to lie in its
provision of an efficient system for producing behavioral responses adaptive to the variability in the ecological and social conditions of their lives, as
discussed earlier. Conflict between mother and offspring at weaning in

mammals, insofar as it is real, would seem to be better interpreted, as by several authors in the Rheingold volume (1963), in terms of the complex interactions of the learning experiences of the interactants with each other. These must be seen in the context of the environmental and social variables they encounter rather than in terms of the direct molding of the genome by a multitude of hypothetical selective forces.

Evolution of Reciprocal Altruism

As we have seen, the appearance of altruism may be explained genetically in animal social behavior in terms of Hamilton's concept of inclusive fitness and kin selection. Trivers (1971), in a paper that stirred a great deal of interest among social scientists, has added another concept that he suggested as a factor in promoting cooperative behavior in animal and human societies, namely reciprocal altruism. His thesis, briefly stated, is that an animal by reciprocating altruistically toward another that had performed an altruistic act for its benefit may, on balance, promote its own genes by establishing such reciprocity between them. His introductory model example is that of a man making a sacrifice of time, effort, and risk in order to rescue another who is drowning. He may be promoting his own genes if the rescued person has genes for comparable altruistic behavior that would pay back more than the cost to the first actor of his altruism. Although this mechanism may not be widely applicable, the potential for it, Trivers avers, exists in larger, longer-lived animals living in small social groups where opportunities for altruistic interactions may be frequent—in short, the conditions envisaged for primitive humans. Hence, the inference is that human altruism may be genetically based through selection for reciprocal altruism.

Before considering the application to humans, Trivers develops his thesis in two instances from lower animals. The first is the "cleaning" action of a small fish (a wrasse) on the body of a large grouper, a phenomenon seen commonly in certain coral reefs. The wrasse picks and eats ectoparasites off the grouper, which holds still and otherwise cooperates in the action. Although the grouper normally feeds on such small fish, it refrains from eating the wrasse. Since the cooperating animals belong to different species, Hamilton's concept of kin selection cannot be applied here for explanation.

Trivers recognizes that in part this behavior is explicable in terms of classical Darwinian natural selection. The cleaner clearly profits from the convenient source of food and might be expected to have evolved the requisite abilities in avoiding capture. The grouper also profits by getting rid of its parasites. But the behavior appears to go far beyond this exploitation of mutual profit. For example, the grouper comes regularly to a particular spot for cleaning, stays quiet—even permitting the cleaner to explore its mouth cavity—and finally signals its intention to depart with special movements. It also chases away predators of the wrasse. Trivers feels that such acts of altruism can be explained only on the basis that reciprocal helpfulness between the species yields sufficient genetic gain for each of them to lead to the selection of genes in both species to further the behavioral coordination.

Darwin and the post-Darwinian writers faced many such problems raised by naturalists critical of evolution theory. An obvious approach to solving them lies in adducing possible intermediate steps in the development of what appears as an excessively perfect adaptation. A classic example of this type of problem is that of the evolution of the electric organs of some fish, which use their ability to produce high-voltage shocks to stun their prey. Although this electric weapon was clearly developed from the minute electric potentials formed in all muscle contraction, the intermediate stages could not be understood by Darwin. The initial stages in the buildup of a discharge by evolving electric organs would seem to be disadvantageous in driving the prey away rather than immobilizing it. Darwin confessed himself stumped by this problem. But modern physiological research has shown that an intermediate stage of great utility exists in many predaceous fish. These produce electric fields of low potential, which are disturbed by other organisms swimming into them. In muddy tropical waters where vision is obscured, these electric fields serve as the sensory basis for the food hunting of several species of fish (Bennett 1971). The progressive development of electric organs from low to high potential thus becomes comprehensible.

Returning to the grouper-wrasse problem, it is not difficult to suggest possible intermediate steps leading to the perfection of their cooperative relation. For example, many small coral-reef fish develop poison glands and conspicuous markings that protect them from predators, which, by either genetically determined or learned behavior, avoid them. Such a protected fish might find the cleaning technique particularly profitable and evolve in the direction of the grouper-wrasse partnership. It appears to me that some such indirect evolutionary pathway is much more plausible than the concept of reciprocal altruism, which implies mental capacities far beyond those apparent in any animals other than perhaps higher primates. Evidence of the limitation of grouper psychological capacities is seen in the fact that another small fish, a blenny, has evolved a behavioral pattern that fools the grouper. It looks and swims much like the wrasse and thus manages to come in close to the grouper. But instead of helpfully removing parasites, it nips a bit of the bigger animal's flesh and escapes. The grouper has not succeeded in evolving the capacity for distinguishing it from the wrasse, and in the presence of many blennies the smooth functioning of the cleaning operation breaks down (Anderson 1978).

The second example that Trivers considers as requiring reciprocal altruism for explanation is the use of warning cries by birds. A warning cry that helps conspecific members, as we have seen previously, can be understood on the basis of kin selection. However, in many birds these warnings operate across species lines, serving to alert members of other species. Kinship selection is thus excluded as a basis for this aspect of their evolution.

Nonetheless, the effectiveness of warning cries in alerting members of other species is not difficult to explain on simple natural-selection principles. In the first place, warning cries, like other loud or unusual noises, evoke attention; in view of the fact that warning cries do indeed alert the animals to danger, it is not surprising that all animals should be selected to respond to them genetically or by learning, just as they respond to the sight or sound made by a predator. Furthermore, field observers have often noted the similarity of the warning cries of different species; sound-spectrum analysis confirms this finding. The explanation of this similarity is that the sounds used in warning cries (high pitch, and so on) are such as to minimize the possibilities of localizing their source, thus protecting the criers to some extent from the predators. The similarity between warning cries by different species, therefore, is a result of convergence in their functional effectiveness (Marler 1955, Collias 1960). There is thus no need to invoke selection for reciprocal altruism to account for their effectiveness between species.

The application of his concept that Trivers makes to human social life is in many ways the most intriguing and pertinent to the general problem of the sociobiological interpretation of human behavioral adaptation. The human being, as Trivers points out, is the species that satisfies best his criteria for the effectiveness of reciprocal altruism in behavior (long life, permanent association in small groups, advanced mental capacity). Although he considers that much human altruism is to be accounted for by kin-selection theory, he concentrates here on phenomena not involving kin interactions. Admitting that no direct evidence of the degree of reciprocal altruism practiced during human evolution is available, he nevertheless says that "it is reasonable to assume that it has been an important factor in recent human evolution and that the underlying emotional dispositions affecting altruistic behavior have important genetic components" (1971, p. 48). He then proceeds to detail the human interactions that indicate advantages to each partner of participation in reciprocal altruisms or, in less technical terms, of mutual helpfulness. Going beyond these, he interprets cheating and countercheating strategies, drawing on the evidence from the literature of psychological investigations to spell out supporting details of human mentality. For example, speaking of the formation of friendship and the emotion of liking and disliking, he draws the inference that "selection will favor a system whereby these tendencies are sensitive to such parameters as the altruistic tendencies of the liked individual" (1971, p. 48). In other words, genes will be selected that favor liking those who are themselves altruistic.

In the subsequent pages of Trivers's discussion I find some ten instances (the exact number differing with the interpretation of phraseology) in which the human genome is described as bearing determinants for specific behaviors of reciprocal altruism. Some examples are: a gene for altruism, a gene for the detection of subtle forms of cheating by apparent altruists, a gene for moralistic aggression and indignation on being cheated, a gene for the emotion of gratitude for altruistic acts, a gene for sympathy, a gene for guilt, a gene for establishing reciprocal relationships, a gene for learning about establishing reciprocal relationships, a gene for learning about altruistic and cheating tendencies in others (1971, pp. 48-52). Considering the heterozygosity prevalent in the human genome, we humans presumably differ among ourselves in the distribution of these genes. If you, the reader, for example, are so unfortunate as to lack the gene for detecting cheating on the part of apparent altruists, then nothing can be done for you. Like the grouper, you are destined always to be victimized by the blennies of this world. It is all foretold in the genes.

The difficulty with this approach, with its infinite regression from motive to countermotive to counter-countermotive, becomes apparent in Trivers's subsequent discussion. In the concluding paragraphs of his paper, he says "under these conditions one would expect selection to favor developmental plasticity of those traits regulating altruistic and cheating tendencies and responses to these tendencies in others" (1971, p. 53). The term "developmental plasticity" I take as a euphemism for learning. He concludes as follows:

> Given the psychological and cognitive complexity the system rapidly acquires, one may wonder to what extent the importance of altruism in human evolution sets up a selection pressure for psychological and cognitive powers which partly contribute to the large increase in hominid brain size during the Pleistocene. [p. 54]

I presume the "powers" referred to here are those of intelligence, imagination, foresight, empathy, ethical sensitivity, and so forth. We have here an abandonment of the basic position of sociobiology in its application to humans, since the powers referred to are not specific products of the selective agents but, rather, general capacities operative throughout human behavior and therefore selected on a much broader base than the individual items Trivers enumerated. As with langur infanticide, as discussed earlier, the specific items may be viewed as expressions of a general trait as it is expressed under particular circumstances, rather than as genetically fixed. The interaction of genes and environment in behavior is far more complex than is often considered in sociobiological speculations.

In animals such as insects, and to some extent in lower vertebrates with stereotyped behaviors, natural selection may operate on behavior as on other characteristics by selecting those genetic factors that promote their own propagation on the basis of phenotype, since under usual conditions there is a one-to-one correspondence between genotype and phenotype. In mammals, particularly primates, the modification of response by learning takes over some of the burden of adjusting to specific variants in ecological and social conditions; and selection of specific genes for each adjustment is no longer effective. In humans, learning capacities have become so generalized, and cultural transmission of learned adjustments thus so far outpaces specific gene selection, that further human evolution has little input from genetic selection. In his concluding paragraphs Trivers returns us to the thesis defended by numerous authors and supported earlier in this chapter that humans have evolved a capacity for imagination, intelligence, foresight, empathy, and so forth that is so far superior to that of other animals as a means of behavioral adaptation as to make the human cultural system unique. The basis for this change, as indicated in the section on learning and culture, is related to the complexities of social interdependence. Trivers's discussion has very well illuminated the subtlety of social interactions required of humans as members of society. I agree with the inference that this probably helped in generating the evolution of human mentality (Etkin 1954). However, Trivers's predilection for hypothesizing separate genes for adaptation to each element of selection pressure, a one-gene one-character approach, however useful in understanding the evolution of behavior at the instinct level, is simplistic in ignoring learning in higher vertebrates and completely misleading as applied to humans, where cultural change has supplanted gene selection in behavioral evolution. The mystery of the many evolutionary forces that have cooperated to produce man's special mentality remains to challenge us (Etkin 1954; Humphrey 1976). Fundamentally, the social sciences dealing with humans face a unique problem and will have to find their own unique solution, without depending on extrapolation from the successes of sociobiology in dealing with instinctual behavior in lower animals.

Summary

After some introductory remarks at the beginning of this chapter, the next section examined the application of population-genetic theory to determine social-behavioral traits. This reveals a number of theoretic weaknesses centering around the complexity of the interplay of ecological factors in animal life. It is emphasized that natural behavior cannot be adequately treated in the simplified mathematical models characteristic of socio-biological reasoning. Even the basic Mendelian unit on which natural selection acts is not satisfactorily established at present. The implications drawn in many sociobiological scenarios of the directive role of natural selection at the level of the gene must be viewed as simplistic and suggestive rather than firmly based, even for behaviors whose determination is accepted as genetically controlled.

The next section considers the interaction of learning (or the experiential factor) and genetic determination. Genetic determination (selection of a gene for a particular behavioral trait) establishes a one-to-one relation between the gene and its phenotypic expression. Learning capacity introduces flexibility into this relationship, permitting the individual animal in its lifetime to adapt behaviorally to short-term variations in the environment. The capacity for learning in animals is itself under genetic control. However, in animals it is limited in range to situations where variability in response is adaptive to the animals's particular ecological niche. This genetically limited learning capacity sensitizes the animal to its previous experiences as a factor intervening between the gene and its phenotypic expression and breaks down the one-to-one relation between gene and behavior characteristic of instinctual systems.

In the final sections of the chapter these principles are applied to the analysis of specific sociobiological interpretations, particularly those of R.L. Trivers. The section dealing with the theory of altruism and inclusive fitness is followed by one that deals with selfish-gene theory in male-female relations, one on parent-offspring conflict, and, finally, a section dealing with Triver's concept of reciprocal altruism, with a special focus on human behavior.

The human behavioral system displays a generalized capacity for learning from social companions. There is also the intercession of a time- and space-binding consciousness that gives rise to goal-directed behavior and to communication by language. The origin in evolution of these aspects of the human behavioral system is obscure and not discussed here. However, their presence is accepted as the basis for the unique human capacity for evolution by cultural change. This system is vastly more effective in adaptation to new environments than is genetic change, and it is thought to have largely replaced genetic change in subsequent human behavioral evolution, possibly even repressing aspects of previously existing genetic determination.

References

Alexander, R., and Sherman, P. 1977. "Local Mate Competition and Parental Investment in Social Insects." *Science* 196:494-500.

Allison, T., and Twyver, H. 1970. "The Evolution of Sellp." *Natural History* 79:56-65.

Altmann, M. 1963. "Naturalistic Studies of Maternal Care in Moose and Elk." In *Maternal Care in Mammals,* edited by H. Rheingold, chap. 7. New York: Wiley.

Anderson, A. 1978. *The Blue Reef.* New York: A. Knopf.

Baerends, G.; Beer, C.; and Manning, A. 1975. *Function and Evolution in Behavior.* Oxford: Clarendon Press.

Barash, D. 1974. "The Evolution of Marmot Societies: A General Theory." *Science* 185:415-420.

_____. 1975. "Marmot Alarm Calling and the Question of Altruistic Behavior." *American Midland Naturalist* 94:468-470.

_____. 1977. *Sociobiology and Behavior.* New York: Elsevier.

Barlow, G., and Silverberg, J. 1978. *Sociobiology: Beyond Nature/Nurture?* American Association for the Advancement of Science (AAS) Symposium. Boulder, Colo.: Westview Press.

Bartholomew, G., and Birdsell, S. 1953. "Ecology and the Proto-hominids." *American Anthropologist* 55:481-498.

Bateson, G. 1972. *Steps in an Ecology of Mind.* New York: Ballantine.

Bateson, P., and Hinde, R. 1976. *Growing Points in Ethology.* New York: Cambridge University Press.

Beach, F. 1978. "Sociobiology and Interspecific Comparisons of Behavior." In *Sociobiology and Human Nature*, edited by M. Gregory, A. Silvers, and D. Sutch, chap. 6. San Francisco: Jossey-Bass.

Bennett, M. 1971, "Evolution of Electric Organs." In *Fish Physiology,* edited by W.S. Hoar and D. Randall, vol. 5, pp. 561-564.

Bernstein, C. 1979. "Why Are Babies Young? Meiosis May Prevent Aging of the Germ Line." *Perspectives in Biology and Medicine* 22:539-545.

Bernstein, H.Y. "Germ Line Recombination May Be Primarily a Manifestation of DNA Repair Processes." *Theoretical Biology* 69:371-380.

Berry, R. 1977. *Inheritance and Natural History.* London: Collins.

Brown, J. 1974. "Alternative Routes in Sociality in Jays." *American Zoologist* 14:63-81.

Brussard, P. 1978. *Ecological Genetics:* New York. Springer-Verlag.

Carlson, E. 1966. *The Gene: A Critical History.* Philadelphia: W.B. Saunders.

Charnov, E. 1978. "Evolution of Eusocial Behavior: Offspring Choice or Parental Parasitism. *Journal of Theoretical Biology* 75:451-465.

Charnov, E., and Krebs, J. 1975. "The Evolution of Alarm Calls: Altruism or Manipulation? *American Naturalist* 109:107-112.

Chevalier-Skolnikoff, S. 1979. "Kids." *Animal Kingdom* (New York Zoological Society 82, no. 3:11-18.

Collias, N. 1960. "An Ecological and Functional Classification of Animal Sounds." In *Animal Sounds and Communications,* edited by

W. Lanyon and W. Tavolga, pp. 368-391. Washington, D.C.: American Institute of Biological Science.

Crook, J.H. 1970. "The Socio-ecology of Primates." In *Social Behavior in Birds and Mammals,* edited by J. Crook. New York: Academic Press.

_____ . 1977. "On the Integration of Gender Strategies in Mammalian Social Systems." In *Reproductive Behavior and Evolution*, edited by J. Rosenblatt and B. Komisural, pp. 18-38. New York: Plenum Press.

Cronhelm, E. 1970. "Perceptual Factors in Observational Learning in the Behavioral Development of Young Chicks." In *Social Behavior in Birds and Mammals,* edited by J. Crook, pp. 393-441. New York: Academic Press.

Crow, J., and Kimura, M. 1970. *An Introduction to Population Genetics Theory.* New York: Harper and Row.

Curio, E.; Ernst U.; and Vieth, W. 1978. "Cultural Transmission of Enemy Recognition: One Function of Mobbing." *Science* 202:899-901.

Davies, N., and Krebs, J. 1978. "Ecology, Natural Selection and Social Behavior." In *Behavioral Ecology,* edited by J. Krebs and N. Davies. Sunderland, Mass.: Sinauer Associates.

Dawkins, R. 1976. *The Selfish Gene.* New York: Oxford University Press.

DeVore, I. 1963. "Mother-Infant Relations in Free Ranging Baboons." In *Maternal Behavior in Mammals*, edited by H. Rheingold, chap. 10. New York: Wiley.

_____ . 1971. "The Evolution of Human Society." In *Man and Beast,* edited by J. Eisenberg and W. Dillon, chap. 9. Washington, D.C.: Smithsonian Institution.

Dobzhansky, T.; Ayala, F; Stebbins, G.; and Valentine, J. 1977. *Evolution.* San Francisco: W.H. Freeman.

Eisenberg, J., and Dillon, W. 1971. *Man and Beast.* Washington, D.C.: Smithsonian Institution.

Emerson, A. 1937. "The Termite Problem." *Natural History* 39:249-254.

Etkin, W. 1954. "Social Behavior and the Evolution of Man's Mental Faculties." *American Naturalist* 88:129-142.

_____ . 1963a. Communication among animals. In *The Psychology of Communication,* edited by J. Eisenson, J. Auer, and J. Irwin, chap. 10. New York: Appleton-Century-Crofts.

_____ . 1963b. "Social Behavioral Factors in the Emergence of Man." *Human Biology* 35:299-310.

_____ . 1964. *Social Behavior and Organization among Vertebrates.* Chicago: University of Chicago Press. (Paperback ed., 1967.)

_____ . 1967. "Behavioral Factors Stabilizing Social Organization in Animals." In *Comparative Psychopathology,* edited by J. Zubin and H. Hunt, pp. 63-75. New York: Grune and Stratton.

_____ . 1979. "The Expendable Male Animal, with a Sociobiological Interpretation." *Perspectives* in *Biological Medicine* 22:559-564.

Fisher, R. 1930. *The Genetical Theory of Natural Selection*. Oxford: Clarendon Press.

Gajdusk, D. 1960. "Factors Governing the Genetics of Primitive Human Populations." *Cold Spring Harbor Symposium* 29:121-135.

Gamboa, G. 1978. "Intraspecific Defense: Advantage of Social Cooperation among Pacer Wasp Foundresses." *Science* 199:1463-1465.

Griffin, D. 1976. *The Question of Animal Awareness*. New York: Rockefeller University Press.

Haldane, J. 1957. "The Cost of Natural Selection." *Journal of Genetics* 55:511.

Hall, R., and Sharp, H. 1977. *Wolf and Man*. New York: Academic Press.

Hamilton, W. 1964. "The Genetical Evolution of Social Behavior." *Journal of Theoretical Biology* 7:1-52.

Hartl, D., and Cook, R. 1977. "Stochastic Selection and the Maintenance of Genetic Variation." In *Population Genetics and Ecology*, edited by S. Karlin and E. Nevo, pp. 593-616. New York: Academic Press.

Hediger, H. 1955. *Psychology of Animals in Zoos and Circuses*. New York: Criterion Books.

Heinroth, O., and Heinroth, K. 1958. *The Birds*. Ann Arbor: University of Michigan Press.

Hersher, L.; Richmond, J.; and Moore, A. 1963. "Maternal Behavior in Sheep and Goats." In *Maternal Behavior in Mammals*, edited by H. Rheingold. New York: Wiley.

Hinde, R. 1966. *Animal Behavior*. New York: McGraw-Hill.

Hrdy, S. 1977. *The Langurs of Abu*. Cambridge, Mass.: Harvard University Press.

Humphrey, N. 1976. "The Social Function of Intellect." In *Growing Points in Ethology*, edited by P. Bateson and R. Hinde, pp. 303-318. New York: Cambridge University Press.

Hutchinson, J. 1978. *Biological Determinants of Sexual Behavior*. New York: Wiley-Interscience.

Jameson, D. 1977. *Evolutionary Genetics*. Stroudsberg, Pa.: Dowden, Hutchinson and Ross.

Jay, P. 1963. "Mother-Infant Relations in Langurs." In *Maternal Behavior in Mammals*, edited by H. Rheingold. New York: Wiley.

Jolly, A. 1968. "Lemur Social Behavior and Primate Intelligence." *Science* 153:501-506.

Karlin, S., and Nevo, E. 1976. *Population Genetics and Ecology*. New York: Academic Press.

Kimura, M. 1979. "The Neutral Theory of Molecular Evolution." *Scientific American* 241 no. 5:98-129.

Kimura, M., and Ohta, T. 1971. "Protein Polymorphism as a Phase of Molecular Evolution." *Nature* 229:467-469.

King, J., and Jukes, T. 1969. "Non-Darwinian Evolution." *Science* 164:788-798.

Klopfer, P. 1962. *Behavioral aspects of Ecology.* Englewood Cliffs, N.J.: Prentice-Hall.

Krebs, J., and Davies, N. 1978. *Behavioral Ecology.* Sunderland, Mass.: Sinauer Associates.

Lawick-Goodall, 1967. "Mother-Offspring Relationships in Free-Ranging Chimpanzees." In *Primate Ethology*, edited by D. Morris, chap. 9. Chicago: Aldine.

LeBoeuf, B. 1974. "Male-Male Competition and Reproduction Success in Elephant Seals." *American Zoologist* 14:163-176.

Lehrman, D. 1953. "A Critique of Konrad Lorenz's Theory of Instinctive Behavior." *Quarterly Review of Biology* 28:337-363.

——— . 1958. "Introduction of Broodiness by Participation in Courtship and Nest-Building in the Ring Dove (*Streptopelia resoria*)." *Journal of Comparative Physiology and Psychology* 51:32-36.

Leigh, E. 1970. "Sex Ratio and Differential Mortality Between Sexes." *American Naturalist* 104:205-210.

Lewontin, R. 1974. *The Genetic Basis of Evolutionary Change.* New York: Columbia University Press.

Linsdale, J., and Tomich, P. 1953. *A Herd of Mule Deer.* Berkeley: University of California Press.

MacArthur, R., and Connel, J. 1966. *The Biology of Populations.* New York: Wiley.

Macnair, M. 1978. "An ESS for the Sex Ratio in Animals, with Particular Reference to the Social Hymenoptera." *Journal of Theoretical Biology* 70:449-459.

Marler, P. 1955. "The Characteristics of Some Animal Calls." *Nature* 176:6-8.

Maynard Smith, J. 1964. "Group Selection and Kin Selection." *Nature* 201:1145-1147.

——— . 1978. *The Evolution of Sex.* Cambridge: Cambridge University Press.

Mayr, E. 1977. "Concepts in the Study of Animal Behavior." In *Reproductive Behavior and Evolution*, edited by J. Rosenblatt and B. Komisaruk, pp. 1-16. New York: Plenum Press.

McMillen, M. 1979. "Differential Mortality by Sex in Fetal and Neonatal Deaths." *Science* 204:89-91.

Menzel, E. 1971. "Communication about the Environment in a Group of Young Chimpanzees." *Folia Primatologia* 15:220-232.

Mogenson, G. 1977. *The Neurobiology of Behavior.* New York: Wiley.

Money, J., and Ehrhardt, C. 1972. *Man and Woman, Boy and Girl.* Baltimore, Md.: Johns Hopkins University Press.

Montagu, M. 1953. "Time Binding and the Concept of Culture." *Scientific Monthly* 77:148-153.

Moore, B., and Stuttard, S. 1979. "Dr. Guthrie and *Felis domesticus*, or Tripping over the cat." *Science* 205:1031-1033.

Moskowitz, B. 1978. "The Acquisition of Language." *Scientific American* 239 no. 11:92-108.

Noonan, K. 1978. "Sex Ratio of Parental Investment in Colonies of the Social Wasp *Polistes fuscatus*." *Science* 199:1354-1356.

Oster, G., and Wilson, E. 1978. *Caste and Ecology in the Social Insects*. Princeton, N.J.: Princeton University Press.

Peng, F. 1978. *Sign Language and Language Acquisition in Man and Ape*. AAAS symposium. Boulder, Colo.: Westview Press.

Peters, R. 1978. "Communication, Cognitive Mapping and Strategy in Wolves and Hominids." In *Wolves and Man*, edited by R. Hall and H. Sharp, pp. 95-107. New York: Academic Press.

Provine, W.B. 1971. *The Origins of Theoretical Population Genetics*. Chicago: University of Chicago Press.

Ravin, A. 1965. *The Evolution of Genetics*. New York: Academic Press.

_____ . 1979. "The Amorality of the Gene." *Medicine on the Midway*. 33:11-15.

Rheingold, H. 1963. *Maternal Behavior in Mammals*. New York: Wiley.

Rosenblatt, J., and Komisaruk, B. 1977. *Reproductive Behavior and Evolution*. New York: Plenum.

Rosenblatt, J., and Lehrman, D. 1963. "Maternal Behavior of the Laboratory Rat. In *Maternal Behavior in Mammals*, edited by H. Rheingold. New York: Wiley.

Schaller, G. 1967. *The Deer and the Tiger*. Chicago: University of Chicago Press.

_____ . 1973. *Golden Shadows, Flying Hooves*. New York: Alfred A. Knopf.

Scharrer, E. 1956. "The Concept of Analogy." *Pub. Staz. Zool. Napoli* 28:204-213.

Schneirla, T.; Rosenblatt, J.; and Tobach, E. 1963. "Maternal Behavior in the Cat." In *Maternal Behavior in Mammals*, edited by H. Rheingold. New York: Wiley.

Schultz, R. 1977. "Evolution and Ecology of Unisexual Fishes." *Evolutionary Biology* 10:277-331.

Selander, R. 1976. "Genetic Variation in Natural Populations." In *Molecular Evolution*, edited by P.J. Ayala, pp. 21-45. Sunderland, Mass.: Sinauer Associates.

Sharp, H., and Sharp, S. 1978. "Wolf Studies." In *Wolf and Man*, edited by R. Hall and H. Sharp, pp. 81-93. New York: Academic Press.

Sherman, P. 1977. "Nepotism and the Evolution of Alarm Calls." *Science* 197:1246-1253.

———. 1979. Insect Chromosome Numbers and Eusociality." *American Naturalist* 113:925-935.

Spuhler, J. 1959. *The Evolution of Man's Capacity for Culture.* Detroit, Mich.: Wayne University Press.

Stonehouse, B., and Perrins, C. 1977. *Evolutionary Ecology.* London: Macmillan.

Sugiyama, Y. 1967. "Social Organization of Hanuman Langurs." In *Social Communication among Primates,* edited by M. Altmann, pp. 221-236. Chicago: University of Chicago Press.

Terrace, H. 1979. *Nime.* New York: Alfred A. Knopf.

Tinbergen, N. 1972. "Functional Ethology and the Human Sciences." *Proceedings of the Royal Society* (London) 182:385-410.

Trivers, R. 1971. "The Evolution of Reciprocal Altruism." *Quarterly Review of Biology* 46:35-57.

———. 1972. "Parental Investment and Sexual Selection." In *Sexual Selection and the Descent of Man,* edited by B. Campbell, pp. 126-130. Chicago: Aldine Press.

———. 1974. "Parent-Offspring Conflict." *American Zoologist* 14:249-264.

Trivers, R., and Hare, H. 1976. "Haplodiploidy and the Evolution of the Social Insects." *Science* 191:243-263.

Trivers, R., and Willard, D. 1973. "Natural Selection of Parental Ability to Vary the Sex Ratio of Offspring." *Science* 179:90-92.

Vandenberg, J. 1967. "The Development of Social Structure in Free Ranging Rhesus Monkeys." *Behaviour* 29:179-194.

Washburn, S.; Jay, P.; and Lancaster, J. 1965. "Field Studies of Old World Monkeys and Apes." *Science* 150:1541-1547.

Washburn, S., and Lancaster, C. 1968. "The Evolution of Hunting." In *Man the Hunter,* edited by R. Lee and I. DeVore, pp. 293-303. Chicago: Aldine Press.

West-Eberhard, M. 1975. "The Evolution of Social Behavior by Kin Selection." *Quarterly Review of Biology* 50:1-33.

Williams, G. 1977. *Sex and Evolution.* Princeton, N.J.: Princeton University Press.

Williams, G., and Williams, D. 1957. "Natural Selection of Individually Harmful Social Adaptations among Sibs with Special Reference to Social Insects."*Evolution* 11:32-39.

Wilson, D.S. 1975. "A Model of Group Selection." *Science* 189:870-871.

Wilson, E.O. 1973. "Group Selection Audits Significance for Etiology." *Bioscience* 23:631-638.

———. 1975. *Sociobiology*. Cambridge, Mass.: Harvard University Press.

Wright, S. 1932. "The Roles of Mutation, Inbreeding, Cross-breeding and Selection in Evolution." Proc. VI Int. Cong. Genet., *1*, 356-366. Reprinted in D. Jameson. 1977. *Evolutionary Genetics*. Stroudsberg, Pa.: Dowden, Hutchinson and Ross.

Wynne-Edwards, V. 1962. *Animal Dispersion in Relation to Social Behavior*. New York: Hafner Publishing.

Zajonc, R. 1971. "Attraction, Affiliation and Attachment." In *Man and Beast*, edited by J. Eisenberg and W. Dillon. Washington, D.C.: Smithsonian Institution Press.

Ziman, J. 1979. *Reliable Knowledge*. New York: Cambridge University Press.

Zuckerman, S. 1932. *The Social Life of Monkeys and Apes*. New York: Harcourt, Brace.

3

Domesticating Nature: Thoughts on the Ethology of Modern Politics

Hiram Caton

If you mentioned nature to a social scientist two decades ago, he thought you were talking about the out-of-doors. "Nature" was not in the social-scientific lexicon, having long since been replaced by "experience." As for biology, it was known to have some bearing on the sociological bypath of gerontology, but otherwise was thought to be of no interest.

This happy neglect of hard questions was shaken by the ecology alarm, which suggested that nature, and the biological sciences, might have something to say about the way we live and the political goals we may hope to reach. Since then biologists have been grabbing headlines with dramatic and sometimes disturbing announcements of new discoveries and biological manipulations. Neurologists have probed minds surgically and teased them pharmacologically. Organs have been transplanted. Geneticists have hinted at the possibility of creating new forms of life. As if this were not enough for the ordinary person, already perplexed about the ethics of abortion and euthanasia, ethology popularizers have contributed stirring tales of "naked apery" in African forests.

Political scientists have been no better prepared than others to digest or evaluate the suddenly conspicuous biological sciences. There is, as always, the arduous labor of boning up on alien disciplines. Burdened already by self-tutoring in half a dozen of the latest fashions, the unfortunate political scientist who dipped into ecology or ethology found not one science but, rather, platoons of disciplines loosely deployed across appallingly wide fronts. He might be excused if he washed his hands, invoked the division-of-labor principle, and left the field to newcomers.

So it happened that ecology was entered in the research ledgers as another item on the political landscape, like urban renewal or state-federal relations, to be investigated by specialists and reported as part of the general fund of knowledge. Certainly there is no evidence that American political science (not to mention sociology) has adjusted its basic thinking to encompass the problem horizon disclosed by ecology.

I am grateful to S.A. Barnett, professor of zoology at the Australian National University, for detailed comments on this chapter. He and Professor John Gibson of the Research School of Biological Sciences, A.N.U., have patiently explained to me many of the idioms and assumptions of ethology and genetics. Needless to say, they are blameless for my errors.

It remains to be seen whether ethology will get the same treatment. That brave new word, *biopolitics*, signifies a resolve not to let that happen. Its exponents claim that the incorporation of biological thinking into political science implies reorientation of the discipline and detailed changes in research programs to take account of variables hitherto ignored.[1] Ethology differs from ecology in that, whereas the latter is pertinent to political science primarily as a policy option, ethology potentially informs *all* research on behavior. Its advocates envisage not only biopolitics, but also biosociology, bioanthropology, and so forth, right across the behavioral spectrum. Such changes are thinkable, we are told, because the prevailing concept of behavior, based on conditioning theory, will be replaced by a concept of behavior in which human biology plays a deep and variegated role. Professor Triver's work on inclusive fitness and reciprocal altruism, rooted in Darwinian theory and population genetics, exemplifies one—albeit only one—type of biological approach to the study of humankind.

But the primary object of this chapter is not to speculate on the future of the disciplines, but, rather, to speculate ethologically on the past and future of modern politics. The reader will know that ethologists study animal behavior, especially adaptations over time, against the background of environment affecting the animal's ecological niche. Human groups have their ecological niches as well; a fascinating study could be written on the development of parasitism wherever a few crumbs drop regularly from the table.[2] But the larger fact about human beings is that they do not so much occupy a niche as create one called "culture." Until about 1900, our created niche harmonized tolerably well with local environments, despite some ecological depredations. But nowadays our niches smack hard against local environments and global biochemical cycles as well: ours could be the niche to end niches. We behave this way not only as individuals but also as politically organized beings whose institutions and public policy aim us in that direction. I suggest that institutions and policy aim as they do partly because of the mechanical notions of nature and human nature that they assume. Mechanical thinking is tailor made for a politics of domesticating nature; indeed, historically the two conceptions arose together. The antipathy to organic thinking of this politics is epitomized by the conception of animals as machines. Lacking any concept of life as an ordered, interacting whole, it did not suspect and certainly did not predict the collision of mechanical civilization with its environment. Similarly, the notion of humans as passive, unstructured machines responding to stimuli effectively blocks any concept of human nature and thus prevents us from entertaining the thought that modern politics might also bring humans into conflict with one another. I suggest that ecology and ethology are conceptually linked in a new concept of nature that is at variance with the mechanism assumed by contemporary practice. My ethological perspective—rather more metaphorical than literal—is given by my focus on the fits and misfits between the behavior of modern political systems and their biosocial "organs." This chapter is a speculation on natural fitness, including Trivers's model of the evolution of sociability. I call it a speculation because it moves rapidly over brambled terrain by flying three feet off the ground. Empiricists are invited to read it as a recreation from hard science.

Ecology and Modern Politics

In 1900, and again in 1955, it was not far fetched to believe that the productivity problem had been solved. At the turn of the century, industrial nations had for some time enjoyed dramatic increases in productivity, sparked largely by technological innovation so novel and persistent that even the least imaginative were dazzled. Edward Byrn, surveying a half century of invention in the *Scientific American* in 1896, wrote:

> It has been a gigantic tidal wave of human ingenuity and resource, so stupendous in its magnitude, so complex in its diversity, so profound in its thought, so fruitful in its wealth, so beneficent in its results, that the mind is strained and embarrassed in its effort to expand a full appreciation of it.

As one knows, the resourceful ingenuity was twice turned to destructive purposes. Yet by the mid-1950s economists graphed the recovery miracles in Germany and Japan and spoke confidently of "fine tuning" the economy to changing labor and market conditions.

Solving the productivity problem meant that the dismal science of political economy and its Mathusian base were refuted, since there appeared to be no impediment to producing enough to supply a modest bounty for large, growing populations. Partly for this reason, political scientists supposed that the main political question reduced to the problem of allocating resources; in other words, politics was about the rules of the game for dividing up the largesse of the industrial cornucopia. The same idea, expressed less academically by politicians, was that revolutionary movements were withered stumps at home and that the recovery of Germany and Japan under imposed democracy gave good hope that the system could be transplanted. It was thought that, whatever the external threats might be, high productivity plus social mobility eliminated fundamental, divisive issues. And that was the end of ideology.

This phase of liberalism (and we are still in it) supposes that very broad individual liberties may be combined with mild political institutions, provided that the ethos of acquisitive innovation, and the rising expectations it spawns, can be satisfied by increasing productivity. The ecological crisis directly menaces these political assumptions. For ecologists are saying that the abundance-through-productivity political settlement induces two new sets of disorders that *undermine the settlement*. One set stands at the output end (pollution and related ecological maladies), the other at the input end (resources). At both ends the politics of abundance discovers nature delivering an oracle: "No, not *that* way." Although interpretations of the oracle differ, that it was delivered at all confounds the assumption that nature is a linear, nonreactive, noninteractive, inexhaustible resource for exploitation. We learn instead that the consequences of the politics of abundance must receive negative feedback from an array of ecological disequilibria that menace production, public health, and even the very atmosphere.

This is the new problem horizon. No politics of abundance, whether capitalist or socialist, can achieve its objectives exclusively within the domain of human action; nature too must be a willing sponsor.

But how willing? Opinion varies between the extremes of those who believe that nature sets an absolute limit to abundance, and those who deny that the ecology crisis represents a novel situation that cannot be handled by the time-honored methods of technological innovation and control. The first group includes geophysicist M.K. Hubbert, who sketched this austere portrait of the future:

> [I]t is clear that the episode of exponential industrial growth can only be a transitory epoch of about three centuries duration in the totality of human history. It represents but a brief transitional phase between two very much longer periods, each with rates of change so slow that it may be regarded as essentially a period of nongrowth. This circumstance can hardly fail to force a profound revision of those aspects of our current social and economic thinking which stem from the assumption that the growth rates which have characterized this temporary period can somehow be sustained indefinitely. [1971]

Exponential industrial growth must stop, Hubbert thinks, because it drives population growth, environmental contamination, and resource use beyond tolerable levels. Left to itself, the system would collapse under its own weight, like a great dinosaur.

Informed opinion, it seems, does not deny this calamitous trend; to that extent, opinion has shifted significantly. Nevertheless, most expect or prophesy that new energy technologies, coupled with population control, will enable global expansion to continue indefinitely.

Let us hope that they are right. Yet the horizon of our hope is not the new heaven and earth that Henry Adams saw with wonder and vague apprehension at the 1900 Paris Exposition. Today we hope that unpredicable science will discover the right technologies in sufficient time, and that political skill will bring numerous contingencies under control in a coordinated manner. And somehow the burgeoning new industrial nations, as well as the many more about to modernize, must be persuaded to accept ecological compromises before even tasting the sweetmeats of abundance.

The Dynamo of Progress

These preliminaries suggest that the ecology problem is too narrowly conceived if we call it merely the balking of the ecological horse at the industrial harness. Rather, it is an unforeseen collision of the major tendencies of modern politics with nature. Both the tendencies and the unforeseen collision are in part the outcome of the mechanistic conception of nature and man's relation to it; but they may also be due in part to certain genetic and demographic dynamics that we are only now beginning to discern. In this section I want to probe both tendencies in order to determine more exactly the character of the collision with nature. These remarks will also describe the proximate political context of the entry of the biological sciences into the social sciences.

As we saw, Hubbert regards history up to the industrial revolution as a steady state, relative to the exponential growth it unleashed. But if we consider that period in itself, we notice that it was not entirely steady. *Homo sapiens* remained a hunter-gatherer for about 200,000 years after his emergence, until he settled in villages and began to cultivate the soil about 10,000 years ago. That was a turning point; agriculture was quickly followed by growth in population, productivity, and technology (Darlington 1969; Washburn 1961; Lee and DeVore 1968). We must suppose, too, a change in social organization from tribal organization with loose hierarchies to a class structure stable enough to command the material resources and political aptitude to build cities and establish kingdoms. We may estimate the astonishing acceleration of change between 10,000 B.P. and 5000 B.P. by comparing the achievements of ancient civilizations in the Fertile Crescent with rustic Neolithic cultures. In that period, the grand style in architecture and politics was invented and carried to heights not often surpassed. We do not know what dreams of glory may have tempted or tormented the hunter-gatherer. We do know, from monuments and inscriptions, that a few lords were able to command the labor and compliance of millions and that the intoxication of this power was heady. Thus we read of a mythic Sumerian king: "This too was the work of Gilgamesh, the king, who knew the countries of the world. He was wise; he saw mysteries and knew secret things." It seems natural that the Gilgameshes should have practiced war and invented slavery.

It is significant that technical and political development were more or less continuous despite the low social status of artisans and tradesmen, and despite the absence of religious or secular cosmologies that endorsed expansion. Cosmologies, indeed, tended to portray the world in a steady state; or in a cycle of birth, growth, and decline; or as a decline from an original golden age. Even the rationalists of antiquity, who displaced the earth from the center of the visible cosmos, consigned gods to the void between atoms, affirmed the evolution of human beings from animals, and lived in an age of rapid expansion, did not discern the developmental dynamic clearly visible historically, despite epicycles of decline. This is a very curious fact. How could the notion of progress—of a future for humanity that would not resemble the past—have eluded thinkers who believed that humanity itself had evolved from the slime of the earth? If culture had evolved in the past, as they believed, why should it not evolve further in the future?

We may answer this question indirectly by considering what was thought to be the essential ingredient of a developmental dynamic when the notion of progess first appeared in the seventeenth century. According to Bacon, Descartes, and their successors, this absolutely new idea involved a new attitude toward nature—the conquest of nature for the relief of man's estate—coupled with a mathematical, manipulative natural science able to tap nature's vast powers by the invention of an "infinitude of arts" that could orchestrate them to improve the human condition (Rossi 1968; Caton 1973). Needless to say, I cannot map here the highways and byways that lead from this idea through the Royal Society and Newton's science of machines to eighteenth-century liberalism and the industrial revolution (Purver 1967; Webster 1975). A few comments must suffice.

The conquest of nature was a notion of such amplitude that, as its originators predicted, decades were needed for its assimilation and centuries for its fruition. The notion challenges an assumption so evident until then that it was seldom expressed and never, to my knowledge, critically discussed. The assumption was that observed natural scarcity represents a firm if labile natural limit on the increase of wealth and relief from natural adversities, such as disease and age. It was thought that agriculture can increase yields and medicine sometimes cure disease, but only by cultivating what nature directly provides. the conquest notion denies this seemingly evident fact, asserting instead that there is no natural limit to growth, to expansion, to new things. The initial evidence for the conquest idea was the observation that the powers of nature are great, and that the mechanical arts, which until Galileo were based mainly on empirical rules of thumb, had succeeded in tapping those powers. Might they not be tapped systematically by a mechanistic natural science able to calculate natural powers with mathematical precision? The discoveries of seventeenth-century scientists settled that question. By 1750 the developmental dynamic inherent in the idea of conquering nature had been fleshed out into a jubilant politics of progress advocated by most European thinkers and even by many medioc-

rities (d'Alembert 1963; Hume 1953). I want to discuss two aspects of the
new politics that highlight the dynamism it unleashed, and in such a way as
to move us toward the concerns of Professor Trivers's paper.

A theory of human nature lay at the base of the new politics. Humans
were thought to be self-interested creatures, mainly because they inhabit
bodies that nature, in a thousand ways, suggests and sometimes impels them
to put first. Although they quietly suspected that human cruelty was innate,
eighteenth-century liberal thinkers rejected Hobbes's *Homo lupus*. War was
thought to stem mainly from civic or tribal pride due to political arrangements or arbitrary customs that need not endure and that would not
endure under the new progressive dispensation. The interests of the mass of
people were seen as political and material security and acquisition. Security
was to be provided by political liberty and a conception of property that
derived all value from labor. Acquisitiveness was to be satisfied by a system
of political economy that sustained incentive by rewarding "industrious-
ness." In addition, a principle of sociability, called "sympathy," was
discovered. By sympathy was meant the capacity of human beings to share
the feelings of a conspecific, or even in those of animals. Its operation was
not unlike what Konrad Lorenz called "mood convention," since it is able
to efface preoccupation with self or kin and to transpose individuals into a
sympathetic relation with persons of any quality or origin. It was therefore
posited as the basis of the cosmopolitan virtue of "benevolence" (Caton
1980). Trivers's notion of man as a selfish individual bears a marked
resemblance to the eighteenth-century liberal notion, except that nothing in
his theory corresponds to sympathy.

A second aspect of the politics of progress, the equality doctrine, was
intended to give maximum scope to self-interested action. A program that
posits labor as the source of value is obviously not favorable to patricians
who happen to be about. The equality doctrine was meant to underwrite the
derivation of value from labor, while at the same time providing a principle
of justice and legitimacy that opposed patrimonial institutions. For if all are
equal by nature and enjoy "natural rights," then inherited status and
privilege cannot be right. The equality doctrine was a critique of the class
society of the eighteenth century, and its significance is hardly limited to its
implications for the patriciate. The equality doctrine complemented sympathy as a *cosmopolitan* principle of sociability, for it was not intended to
deny natural differences so much as to affirm clearly what people have in
common. Patrimonial relations, which have a vertical structure, were to be
replaced by contract, into which all free men can enter. Transition to con-
tractual relations facilitated mobility, both social and geographic, by
diminishing the importance of ties to family, village, religion, and other
forms of association.

But mobility increases outbreeding, and it is a theorem of population genetics that outbreeding increases genotypic and phenotypic diversity. Here we find a suggestive thought that is unfortunately difficult to test. We know that class societies tend to inbreed within classes. Inbreeding tends toward greater homogeneity in the gene pool of the breeding population, and therefore toward greater similarity among the individuals of that population. Some authorities believe (as inclusive fitness would seem to predict) that greater cohesiveness of the inbred group (relative to other populations) is a behavioral consequence of inbreeding. Conversely, increased outbreeding creates increased phenotypic diversity, whose behavioral consequence might be increased "individualism" (Haldane 1949; Darlington 1969; Hamilton 1971).

Whether these inferences from genetic theory to behavior are probable for the period under discussion is for others to say. The conjecture deserves mention because liberal theory and practice behaved as if maximization of individualism through outbreeding were an aim of the program. Liberal institutions were contrived to accommodate great diversity of individual talent and purpose, so that each would have an equal opportunity to compete for success, esteem, and power. Open competition, it was believed, would select the "natural aristocracy" (Jefferson) of talent to conduct affairs of business and government. It was essential to the program, especially as implemented in the United States, that performance alone should judge a man's quality; for openness—a chance at all the prizes—was to be a major cause of the dynamic of progress. One sees, then, that the equality doctrine was understood in a way compatible with contemporary genetic theory (Dobzhansky 1973; White 1975). The doctrine was a device for replacing institutions of inherited inequality by a natural inequality that would sort itself out in every generation through institutions that assured open competition. It was social Darwinism a century before Darwin, with the important qualification that the struggle was not for existence, but for a greater portion of wealth and power.

The program would scarcely have been feasible without the Baconian-Cartesian answer to the limits of natural scarcity. It would be folly to conjure a politics meant to excite acquisitiveness if nature itself sets limits to the growth of wealth. But Bacon's promise, which by 1750 was a settled conviction and by 1850 a material fact, made the program seem practicable while simultaneously creating the avenue for achieving the virtually utopian future he had sketched.

Today the question arises whether, once this program reaches escape velocity, it can be diverted into a safe orbit, and if so, under what conditions. The main alternative discussed until now has been the "steady-state economy," whose defining assumption is that present levels of goods and services will be maintained, or perhaps marginally increase, as new technologies become available. As yet there seems to be no mathematical model of a steady-state politics. Consideration of the parameters that may reasonably be ascribed to a steady-state politics exposes some of the political change that transition to a steady state might entail, and in that way helps us to evaluate the future of the politics of progress. Let us consider the model.

Assuming a policy goal of zero population growth, and current levels of longevity, there would be a demographic shift toward much greater average age relative to the averages that have prevailed in industrial nations for some time. Greater average age would tend to decrease social mobility, if it is true that older persons tend to be more settled. This effect would be reinforced by zero or nearly zero economic growth assumed by a steady-state economy. The existence of more of the old, and fewer of the young, would tip the political scales to the advantage of the former, who would frame morality in terms of loyalty, experience, steadiness, prudence, and respect for elders. This moral suasion would be used in a struggle sharpened by decreased mobility and expansion. For in the absence of expansion, competition for advantageous positions, especially among the young, would tend to increase, generating in turn a strong interest in the protection of status once acquired. The old could be expected to consolidate their positions further by strengthening family ties and obligations, since in the family (as Professor Trivers would readily agree), parents enjoy natural superiority to offspring. All these factors would provide favorable conditions for the return to apprentice systems and to inherited status of some sort, possibly including inherited classes (Ophuls 1977).

These changes are so wildly at variance with current expectations that the mere thought of them would mortify an elected official. Circumstances might conceivably compel a modern nation to adopt, unawares, a steady-state politics; but one does not easily imagine the public opting for such a course even to avert a threatening disaster. The dynamics of opinion and institutions are wholly against it. And perhaps not only opinion is against it. It might be that centuries of outbreeding have so hybridized the populations of advanced nations that their individual diversity is not compatible with the static social conditions that a steady-state politics appears to imply. Should that be true, a natural dynamic operating at the demographic level adds momentum to a trajectory that collides with nature at the ecological level. As we have learned from Darwin, analogous collisions are not uncommon in the plant and animal kingdoms.

Ethology and Social Man

At first glance, the problem horizon disclosed by ethology seems to be an academic debate rather than a set of describable predicaments. Ethologists and others maintain that human behavior is in many ways influenced, and in some ways determined, by biological endowments, or by biological parameters such as health and disease. Social scientists generally claim, to the contrary, that nearly all significant social behavior is caused by society, culture, or some form of convention—the old nature-nurture debate.

On closer inspection of the political context of the controversy, however, we find parallels to the ecology problem. Over the past seventy-five years, the social sciences have abandoned the liberal concept of human nature previously sketched and have replaced it by the notion of social man. Human behavior is thought to be a product of society rather than the expression of a fixed human nature. Human biology may contribute a few constraints or drives, such as hunger, sex, and senescence; and somatic pathology may disturb behavior. But biology does not shape behavior and cannot explain typical behavior.

The principle support for this outlook has been conditioning theory of behavioral psychology, which holds that all human behavior is learned by reinforcement of contingent responses to environmental stimuli. The range and variety of possible responses is held to be virtually infinite, and there is no intrinsic order among them: anything goes. In particular, behaviorists deny that the biological (or psychological) properties of organisms imposes any order on their behavior: the organism is a "black box," whose contents are irrelevant to the prediction of behavior. As a result, social-science research assumes that behavior is almost infinitely malleable and is shaped in one way or another by contingencies of social milieu, which provide the stimuli to which individuals respond.

This model of social man came into vogue at the turn of the century when laissez-faire liberalism had run into difficulties over what was called the social question. It had turned out that the free and open competition prompted by liberal institutions resulted in great inequalities of wealth and power, which produced a dilemma for liberal thought and practice. Heavily committed to individualism in laws regulating liberty, property, and contract, it needed a rationale for moderating its commitments. The rationale was provided by the concept of social man and that of social justice, understood as a necessary complement to political and legal justice. The result of this modification was phase-two liberalism, which prevails today in non-Marxist advanced nations. Typical of its policies are welfare legislation funded by a progressive income tax, as well as the extension of liberties to classes of persons who formerly did not enjoy them (women) or who, owing to their condition, could not exercise them (the poor). The idea that economy operated under natural laws that were beneficient when left alone was replaced by the notion that creative intervention and planning were necessary to ensure a just distribution and equal opportunity for all, and indeed to prevent the system of free competition and market economy from destroying itself through an imbalance between rich and poor. Cooperation was to be favored more than competition, primarily by creating a large sector of public-service employees whose jobs were protected against market fluctuations and lackluster performance.

Under the auspices of the idea of social man, the concept of equality underwent considerable change. If humans are highly malleable creatures, then phase-one liberalism must have ascribed to natural inequality of talents what was really due to favorable or unfavorable environmental conditions. One of the chief institutional means for correcting socially induced inequalities was the state school system, to which enormous efficacy was ascribed, particularly by social scientists. Although today the enthusiasm for the school system has waned (Jencks et al. 1972), the demand for equality of opportunity has nonetheless escalated to a demand for equality of result, which one who holds the social-man theory should expect. These attitudes stem from a new manifestation of the old "social question." Despite all attempts to control inequality (on the assumption that it is unjust), it still asserts itself in what geneticists have called the paradox of democracy. The paradox is that it is precisely the society that provides everyone an equal opportunity, and that assigns social position according to achievement rather than status, that will tend to maximize the effects of natural (genetic) inequality and thereby generate a "meritocracy."[3]

The social-man theory has performed other policy and rationalizing functions as well, recently in the form of John Rawls' *A Theory of Justice*. Its stress on the dependency of the individual on others has justified togetherness at a time when masses of people were bunching in huge governmental, commercial, and industrial organizations. It has provided assurance that human beings can adjust to rapid social and environmental change, such as widespread social mobility and densely packed cities. The social man is accordingly not only a theoretical construct; a good deal of the daily practice as well as the expectations of policy take this idea for granted to some extent (Miller 1980). It follows that the ethological and, generally, biological critique of this concept constitutes or implies a critique of a range of current practices. In broad terms, the critique seems to be this. Just as the ecological crisis resulted from neglect or misunderstanding of nature, so at least some of today's social ills perhaps arise from an attempt to mold and adjust human beings to conditions for which they are not naturally suited, and which they cannot endure without distress or neurosis. It is claimed that there is a species-specific repertoire of behaviors that can be successfully combined only in certain ways; and that to plan or hope in ignorance of them, or directly contrary to what they appear to allow, must lead to frustration in individuals and confusion in society.

Nature and Nurture

Since social scientists tend to ascribe nearly all behavior to nurture, attempts to sort out this complex relationship have gone by default to biologists and ethologists, although recently some anthropologists and political scientists have begun to contribute as well. There is some agreement that the relation between nature, nurture, and environment may be broadly characterized as "interactionist," meaning that the causes, function, and development of behavior is to be understood as the product of the interaction between the organism, its behavior, and its environment (Masters 1979).

The interactionist approach has replaced the old "learned/instinctive" classification of behavior with complex new approaches that divide the monoliths "organism" and "environment" into fine-grained causal and functional parts. In general, all learning occurs on a physiological background, within the context of other behaviors and many kinds of developmental influences that may engender larger or smaller deviations from anticipated behavior. A critic of the learned/instinctive dichotomy, S.A. Barnett, illustrates the subtle distinctions drawn in current research by reference to the sucking of infants:

> Very early, it has a standard rhythm, readily recorded during sleep. But the rhythm and the precise character of the movements of sucking are quickly adjusted in accord with what produces the best yield of milk. . . . Hence, within the seemingly single act of sucking, we find components of varying developmental ability. [1972; also, Hinde 1966]

The infant's capacity to modify its sucking differentiates this behavior from "fixed action patterns," where the information feedback from the consequence of the behavior to its modification does not exist.

Perhaps no human behavior occurs according to a pattern fixed by the neurophysiology of our bodies. Instead we are endowed with behavioral propensities, some parallel to types observed in lower animals, others unique to humans. To illustrate this conception, let us look at the notion of sensitive learning times, which humans have in common with animals.

The development of an infant's behavioral repertoire, like his or her physical growth, is correlated with age; both are believed to be genetically regulated. In the first days after a normal pregnancy, the infant can be provoked to display about seventeen behaviors that mark human phylogenetic origins (Eibl-Eibesfeldt 1975). Placed in water, he will try to swim. If he is thrown into the air, his arms will spread wide, like those of primate neonates. He will clutch so tightly with his fists that he can be suspended even on the first day after birth, again like his primate cousins. Most of these behaviors disappear in days or weeks. Meanwhile, he begins to acquire his human repertoire of behavior. He begins to learn to see. Gregory and his associates have shown that neonates are initially more responsive to bright objects than to moving objects, but that at about eight weeks of age it is the other way around (Gregory 1966). At that age, learning to see begins to require coordinating body motions with objects, by handling them, for example. Since developmental times are observed as the neonate learns to move and control his limbs, to babble and speak, to interact with his mother.[4] None of these behaviors develops normally if the neonate is deprived of the requisite sensory environment and nurturant care. The widely publicized studies of Harlow and Harlow (1966) on behavioral disturbances in rhesus monkeys deprived of normal nurturant care illustrate the importance of interaction.

The numerous parallels between animal and human behavior, not merely with respect to type (for example, courtship and sexual display), but also with respect to function and often highly comparable physiology (sexual dimorphism based on genetic and hormonal differences) suggests that humans too might have a species-specific behavioral repertoire. That the enumeration of such a repertoire must at the present time remain conjectural is not a good reason for ignoring the evidence suggesting that one or another behavior perhaps belongs on the list. The evidence, in any case, varies in kind and quality.

There are experimental grounds for believing that language, emotions, need for association, exogamy, handedness, intelligence, sensitive learning times, and sleep and dreams are biologically founded propensities or states. Investigation of states whose biological base has never been doubted, such as sickness and senescence, is beginning to reveal significant correlations between state and attitude (see especially the bibliography in Somit 1976). Physiology and ethology suggest that family, dominance and status, sexrole differentiation, courtship ceremonies and adornment, sexual competition, male rivalry, social spacing, territoriality, group association and collaboration, and perhaps some nonverbal signals are species specific (Bolby 1958; Eibl-Eibesfeldt 1975; Reynolds 1966; Sommer 1969; Bateson and Hinde 1976; Leakey and Lewin 1977).

The ethnographic literature suggests that marriage rules, the incest taboo, customs of avoidance and methods of settling disputes, possession and gift, initiation ceremonies, obligation and right, male association, myth, legend, dance and song, gambling, tool and weapon making, punishment, alpha males and wise men, deceit and betrayal, honor and propriety, the outcast, a distinction between "them" and "us," art, subtle observational skills, adultery and homosexuality, homicide, suicide, schizophrenia, and neurosis naturally develop in every society (Count 1973; Tiger 1969; Fox 1971; Lee and DeVore 1968; Gellner 1963).

Whereas these behaviors may be observed as cultural constants, their integration into a new outlook requires the premise that humans by nature make culture because cultural selection made man the cultural animal. Until recently that proposition would have been received as a paradox, for it was imagined that the capacity for culture was an all-or-nothing proposition. It now appears that 2 million years ago there were hominids with a brain capacity of 435-600 cc and bipedal locomotion who hunted, built shelters, and made tools (Leakey and Lewin 1977). This previously unsuspected combination of traits yields a picture of rudimentary culture within which it is thinkable that man could evolve. The rudimentary culture would have been a proximate environment on which natural selection operated to induce behavioral adaptations for culture. Subsequent hominids would evolve as *products of antecedent stages of culture;* that is, cultural adaptations would have become genetically fixed. Anthropologist Robin Fox (1971) put the matter graphically when he wrote that "man's anatomy, physiology, and behavior therefore are in large part the result of culture . . . we are not simply *producers* of institutions such as family; we are a *product* of them."

Until recently this interpretation would have lacked requisite foundation, since it smacks of Lamarckian inheritance of acquired characters. But C.H. Waddington has achieved some satisfactory results with his model of "genetic assimilation," which explains how the effect of Lamarckian theory can be obtained from orthodox theory (Waddington 1959; Wallace 1968). Further work on genetic assimilation shows that a behavioral adaptation might become fixed in a breeding population in ten generations (300 years), assuming no more than moderate selection pressure. The demonstration of such rapid assimilation rates has suggested the possibility of the "genetic tracking" of culture, meaning that the operation of natural selection through culture may fix in a breeding population an array of behavioral traits peculiar to a culture (Wilson 1971).

These experimental and theoretical developments throw new light on the evaluation of cultural diversity and cultural constants. Social scientists usually believe, mistakenly, that biology explains only traits that are uniform and frozen; hence from the diversity of behaviors they deduce the absence of biological influence. Biological sciences explain uniformity *and* diversity of traits, relative fixity *and* plasticity of behaviors. The biology of individuality illustrates this point. Each individual is a unique genotype, who differs somatically and behaviorally from his conspecifics; yet his somatic constitution and behavior clearly belong to classes that are species specific. One may therefore not infer that observed differences in individual behavior are due exclusively to socialization; this will be true in many instances, but false in others.[5] Analogous reasoning holds for the evaluation of cultural differences. No one doubts that certain physical adaptations, such as skin pigmentation and above-normal lung capacity of mountain dwellers, result from natural selection operating in particular environments.

The adaptations amount to genetic tracking, in certain populations, of the environment. Given the immense capacity of human DNA for variation (there may be as many as 1 million genes and 5.3 billion base pairs in human DNA), genetic theory provides ample basis for the hypothesis of genetic tracking of culture. That until recent times cultural groupings usually correspond to breeding groups, and that even today viable states are based on nationality, itself suggests a relation between social cohesion and breeding groups—a relation that inclusive fitness attempts to explicate.

These suggestions are not dogmas meant to be swallowed, but researchable hypotheses. Some geneticists awaken the contrary impression. They play a game of genesmanship, which assumes a gene for any given behavior and computes the conditions for its spread. One hears of a selfish gene, an altruistic gene, a homosexual gene, a whisker-flicking gene—the list is endless. This procedure, which has a specific use in population genetics, leads to problems when used to explain human (or animal) behavior directly. There is an element of genesmanship in Hamilton's theory of inclusive fitness, and we shall see that it affects our evaluation of Trivers's theory of the evaluation of reciprocal altruism.

Inclusive Fitness and Reciprocal Altruism

Professor Trivers's model is an ingenious attempt to explain sociability by linking sociobiology with anthropology and psychology to construct a hypothesis concerning the evolution of significant social behavior and attitudes. The model arrives at the familiar, although not trivial, conclusion that human beings behave so as to "maximize their own interests regardless of what they say they are trying to do." (Trivers 1977) I shall examine three aspects of what they say they are trying to do." I shall examine three aspects of the model: its presuppositions, its proof strategies, and its psychology, in that order, although these aspects cannot always be neatly separated.

Trivers begins with a "back to Darwin" statement that affirms two postulates, the first being that natural selection operates on individuals, not on groups or species. This postulate establishes the basic interpreative rule that the function of any somatic or behavioral adaptation is for the benefit of the individual. The second postulate states the purposiveness of individuals, which is that organisms "are assumed to be attempting to maximize their own reproductive success. . . ." Trivers stresses the importance of these postulates, since the selfish origin of altruism is contained in the first, and the mechanism of its evolution in the second. The postulates need emphasis because, as Krebs and May put it, reviewing Trivers's work in *Nature* (1976): "It is an astonishing fact that many professional biologists still do not understand the essence of Darwinian natural selection. Many people still think and write, that adaptations evolve by natural selection because they are 'good for the species as a whole' . . . natural selection is a matter of differential survival and reproduction of individuals (or to be precise, of genes), not of species." [Krebs and May 1976]

It is indeed curious that professional biologists disagree about Darwin's meaning. We catch a glimpse of the difficulty of interpreting Darwin in the small discrepancy between Krebs and May's phrase "differential survival *and* reproduction" and Trivers's identification of survival *with* reproduction. It makes a great difference to the interpretation of purposiveness whether survival and reproduction are distinguished or identified. Trivers identifies them, agreeing in that with his eminent colleague Ernst Mayr, who wrote: "Let it be clearly understood that what really counts in evolution is not survival but the contribution made by a genotype to the gene pool of the next and subsequent generation" (1963).

Darwin, however, did not think this way, but distinguished survival, or struggle for existence, from differential reproduction, which he called "sexual selection."[6] The struggle for existence includes competition for food, flight or deception of predators, immunity to disease, and so on. It is a distinct, observable purposiveness regularly presupposed in the study of animal behavior. True, Darwin was prepared to include sexual selection as *part* of the struggle for existence when that term was taken in the "large, metaphorical sense." Yet because the behaviors related to survival and to reproduction are distinct, he distinguished differential *mortality* from differential *reproduction*. The distinctions were closely related to the way he conceived evolution to occur. He supposed "the most severe struggle between individuals" so that "any variation, however slight . . . if it be in any degree profitable to an individual of any species . . . will tend to the preservation of that individual, and will generally be inherited by its offspring." But the idea that only differential reproduction matters seems to be compatible with the complete absence of a struggle for existence. It does, at any rate, abstract from it. The abstraction alters Darwin's conception of how evolution occurs, which is as follows. The struggle for existence, which begins at birth, is a prereproductive test of fitness. Individuals bearing slight favorable variations tend to survive (differential mortality), succeed in the intense sexual competition, and pass on their traits to offspring (differential reproduction). The inheritance of favorable variations eventually leads to the evolution of new behaviors, organs, and species.

The assimilation of survival to differential reproduction expresses the specific bias or point of view of population genetics, which is interested in gene frequencies; the bias involves, in other words, a tendency to disregard phenotypes. It seems to lead to several paradoxes.

1. If we postulate with Trivers that the purposiveness of organisms is to maximize their reproductive success, as measured by surviving offspring,

then they would be well advised to steer clear of sexual reproduction. Sexual reproduction means that the individual must share its genetic contribution with another individual, thereby halving its contribution to a common legacy, whereas asexual reproducers (and hermaphrodites) have it all their way. Why, then, is all reproduction not asexual? The standard answer is that sexual reproduction increases heterozygosity of the species, which in turn increases the survival chances, not of a particular individual, but of the breeding population (Mayr 1963). One must recognize, it seems, a purposiveness beyond individual benefit. Biologists, as Trivers reminds us, tend to shy away from group selection and group benefit, although, as he surely knows, it is acknowledged by Hamilton, and E.O. Wilson devoted a chapter to the subject in his *Sociobiology*. According to Mayr, that crucial moment in natural selection, speciation, occurs by the isolation of a breeding population.[7] If I understand Mayr correctly, it follows that evolutionary selection operates *only* on groups.

2. If the purposiveness of organisms were only reproductive success, it follows that life beyond the age of fertility is superfluous. We might—must —expect organisms to expire, since *ex hypothesi* they evolved only to reproduce. Nature has in fact arranged this cruel but efficient system in some arthropod species and among the small marsupial, *Antechinus,* where the male expires immediately after his first copulation. This problem in a related form persists in Trivers's application of reciprocal altruism to human beings, since the calculation of return benefit must be tied to the period of fertility of the altruist. On that basis, infertile individuals cannot benefit from altruistic behavior toward unrelated individuals, nor, for that matter, from selfish behavior. We should expect reciprocal altruism to be a trait expressed by prefertile and fertile individuals only. I hope it is not impertinent to suggest that this seems not to be the case with *Homo sapiens* or even with some primate species. The aged receive care and consideration, even though they cannot return a benefit that enhances someone's reproductive success, or even when their existence becomes a burden. Conversely, sterile or infertile individuals bestow benefits, even among primates, although they can receive none.[8]

I have tried to devise escape routes from these difficulties. One is that altruistic traits that were evolved to maximize fertility continue to exercise their influence despite their irrelevance. But this seems an ad hoc conclusion in view of what natural selection has done to poor *Antechinus* and might do to others. More to the point, it ignores the fact that individuals strive to live, as well as to reproduce.

3. I have suggested that kinship theory and reciprocal altruism express the bias of population genetics, where calculi of gene frequencies are paramount. There is a built-in tendency to gloss over behavior and the diversity of phenotypic traits in one's hurry to the gene pool. The bias is expressed by

E.O. Wilson's remark, "Samuel Butler's famous aphorism, that the chicken is only an egg's way of making another egg, has been modernized: the organism is only DNA's way of making more DNA" (1975). With the reader's indulgence, I call this bias "the phenotypization of the genotype," since it attributes phenotypic traits to genes, as in the locutions "altruistic gene," "selfish gene," and so forth. Genes, of course, have no such traits. The locutions are shorthand for the complex way in which genes are supposed to cause traits. The bias and the shorthand are usually harmless in population genetics, but they do produce an equivocation or ambiguity that ceases to be harmless when it is applied directly to the explanation of behavior. It appears from Trivers's model that "kinship" has become a systematically misleading expression. My examination will, I hope, clarify ambiguities likely to pop up in applications of population genetics.

Hamilton worked out his theory from Sewall Wright's idea that fitness should be measured not only by an individual's reproductive success, but also by that of his genetic kin, since siblings and cousins carry a fraction of the genes of their kinfolk. Hamilton proposed a formal theory of inclusive fitness, consisting of an individual's fitness plus the sum of all the effects he or she has on the related parts of the fitness of his or her relatives. Kinship is therefore defined as the fraction of genes shared by an individual with his relatives. Let this be called *genetic kinship* (kinshipG). Now the genetic bias goes to work. Inclusive-fitness theory posits kinshipG as the sole meaning of kinship, so that phenotypic kinship (kinshipP) is covertly identified with the former. In other words, the phenotype is geneticized (if the reader will tolerate another atrocious phrase), and the ambiguity of a systematically misleading expression is produced.

The ambiguity may be specified by considering kinshipG and kinshipP as they affect mother and offspring of rats. Usually there is a clean fit between the two kinships. The female gives birth, then marks her litter with pheromones so that she recognizes them. But if a neonate from another litter is placed in the nest soon after parturition, it will be marked and accepted as an offspring, whereas if one of her genetic offspring is removed before marking and later returned, it will be rejected or attacked (Barnett 1975). These facts show that kinship among rats is not established by the mere fact of kinshipG, but rather is based on characteristics of maternal and neonate behavior (kinshipP). As far as the rat is concerned, only kinshipP exists, since a marked neonate *is* phenotypically the mother's "child," although not her offspring. And the same is true for many other species, including *Homo*. The male langur that Trivers discusses with evident satisfaction appears to be one of the very few animals that seems to behave as if it insisted on kinshipG. Supposing this interpretation to be correct, this unusual case serves by its rarity to emphasize that actual animal behavior toward kin is based on kinshipP.[9]

From all this one might conclude that the geneticist who says that organisms strive to maximize the spread of their genes is reporting the reflection of selection equations in the gene pool, rather than actual behavior. It is not a description of behavior to say that organisms try to maximize their inclusive fitness; it is a description of a particular calculus based on special assumptions, one being that individual A can propagate his genes by benefiting a kinsman in whom there are some replica genes of A. Using the hypothesis that each organism strives to maximize the diffusion of his genes, we infer that A, if the cost does not outweigh the benefit, will act altruistically toward B. That is all very well. Consider, however, that *any* conspecific will have replica genes of A, since they are all genetically related. The fact that for any two "unrelated" conspecifics one cannot a priori assign a relatedness coefficient is a problem for the geneticist, but not for animals, who are familiar only with kinshipP and who perhaps behave accordingly. Trivers may object that this begs the question. Such an objection may be returned: in order to prove his case, it would be necessary to note carefully the differences between the two types of kinship. While I cannot judge Trivers's field studies of *Hymenoptera,* to which his theory of altruism implicitly appeals, it seems appropriate to remark that his observations have been criticized (Alexander and Sherman 1977).

The choice of number of shared genes as a measure of kinshipG—and in general, the use of gene frequencies as a measure in population genetics—is a mathematical simplification. This is not in itself a criticism, since all sciences simplify. But let us examine the actual situation. Genes produce not traits, but gene products, such as enzymes and other proteins, which built the phenotype that expresses traits. The one gene—one trait assumption simplifies the more complex fact that most, perhaps all, genes are pleiotropic, whereas most traits are polygenic—that is, a single gene's product affects several traits, whereas most traits result from the products of many genes. Trivers maintains that the one gene—one trait assumption is harmless, and doubtless it is for many applications. But according to Dobzhansky (1973), the actual picture is this:

> The concept of a pleiotropic action of genes . . . is very important for understanding the action of selection. This concept leads us to the idea of the genotypic milieu which acts from the inside on the manifestation of every gene in its character. An individual is indivisible not only in its soma but *also in the manifestation of every gene it has.*

If I understand correctly, pleitropy (and polygeny) cut the ground from under the interpretation of reproductive purposiveness as *fractional* propagation of genes, since the dynamics of inheritance depends not merely on the number of genes but also on the way all genes function in the genome (Alexander and Sherman 1977). It is thus not convincing to attribute to the individual organism a selfish interest in propagating a fraction of its genes. What makes it a "self," its genome, is just what is *not* heritable, whereas its genes, considered abstractly as a divisible aggregate, belong to the species. Biologically speaking, individuals can have a selfish interest only in their unique genome, whereas a selfish interest in genes is impossible, since here there can be only a species interest. Nor does the problem end here. The attempt to explain how an altruistic gene can maintain itself is a misbegotten exercise if the genetic expression of altruism is pleiotropically inseparable from a variety of other traits, such as immediate responsiveness to a conspecific. I do not know whether that is true, and I gather from one of his passing remarks that Professor Trivers does not know either.

Possibly the belief that fractional gene representation in another individual adequately interprets phenotypic reproduction and kinship draws on the ancient belief that one's offspring is "another self," and that "one's own" are "blood kin." Perhaps the geneticist substitutes "genes" for "blood" and supposes that his theory captures the truth of an ancient mysterious prejudice. but "blood" is a metaphor for the manifold phenotypic social bondings that accompany conception, birth, upbringing, shared life. Certainly, my offspring are my own partly because there is something of me in them; they are "of my seed." But "seed" too is phenotypic. It expresses the awe and mystery before life—from this mystery there comes another, whom I recognize as another self because the child resembles me. This is part of the ancient belief in blood. Other aspects are the many ways in which human beings bond together. The *Phenotypic* origin of the bond explains why individuals form associations. Trivers's abstraction from phenotypic bonds leads him into reasoning about weaning conflicts that proves nothing because the very same conflicts are found among adopted children.

This discussion shows, I think, that inclusive-fitness theory is at best a partial account of the reproductive behavior even of insects, and certainly could not be generalized to explain the basis of human behavior. Inclusive fitness incorporates the intrinsic bias of population genetics—abstraction from phenotype and from genome, which is imposed by the limitations of probability equations. Not observation, but requirements of mathematical simplicity suggest that the purposiveness of organisms is reducible to one type. Rather than questioning, as one might, Trivers's right to purposive psychological terms, I have attempted to show how his equivocal use of them links genes with traits in what seems to be something like a causal proof of the genetic origin of traits and behavior. Let us consider now what his proofs actually are.

Proof Strategies

Professor Trivers developed the theory of reciprocal altruism as a hypothesis to explain how unrelated animals and human beings act altruistically. Altruism toward kin does not require reciprocity, since the behavior itself promotes the fitness of the altruist. Altruism toward unrelated individuals, however, can be explained only if there is a return benefit that compensates for the genetic cost of the original altruistic act. ("To explain," we may remind ourselves, means to explain how a self-sacrificing gene can be maintained in the gene pool.) As Trivers points out, there is an asymmetry between inclusive fitness and reciprocal altruism behavior in that there is, or should be, *less* reciprocity among kin than among unrelated individuals, since offspring have no inclusive-fitness reason to benefit their parents. According to Trivers, in other words kinfolk are *less* altruistic among themselves than among strangers.

Trivers presents his argument as a reconstruction of the evolution of a range of attitudes and behavior from an initial Pleistocene protoaltruistic position. We are meant to see how the postulates of the initial position induce a natural-selection dynamic that evolves altruistic behavior exclusively from selfishness. I say this is the manner of presentation, for it is not the proof strategy. We know little about the psyche of the Pleistocene hominid. We know even less about how hominid psychodynamics changed over time as adaptation evolved for subtle cheating, moralistic aggression, and so forth. We do not know for a fact whether guilt evolved after the ability to detect subtle cheating, as it must have according to Trivers's model; or whether hominids were initially guileless creatures who were corrupted by property, as Rousseau believed; or whether, as the behavior of some primates suggests, the emotions Trivers discusses were all initially present together and became sharply differentiated as intelligence evolved. The evidence does not, I repeat, enable us to decide between these and other alternatives, although Trivers's model is compatible with only one alternative. Moreover, although his model refers to Pleistocene man, his evidence does not, since it is drawn exclusively from present-day humans in surviving Neolithic cultures and among undergraduates in American universities. Trivers arranges these data into evidence for certain psychological traits, posits a supposed order of genesis, and explains the genesis by applying the initial hypothesis (selfishness plus material dependency on others) to a behavioral situation (the initial altruistic act).[10]

This proof strategy closely resembles a method of textual interpretation familiar in the humanities. Just as the humanist interprets the meaning of a book systematically by explicating each unit in terms of a few initial hypotheses, so Trivers attempts a systematic interpretation of human cooperative behavior by explicating each psychological-behavioral trait in terms of selfishness and selection dynamics. A text that initially appears to contain selfishness and cooperation, generosity and self-seeking, is reduced by systematic explication to selfishness only. The proof strategy is of course circular: the initial hypotheses generate systematic, coherent meaning; and, conversely, the coherence certifies the hypotheses. Circular arguments are logically impeccable: they are tautologies. Yet they are open to tests of various sorts. Are all the relevant phenomena explicated? Has each been convincingly explicated? Have the phenomena been divided in the right way? With these questions in mind, we turn to Trivers's psychology.

Psychology

No one will be startled by the argument that human motives, virtues, and social behavior are convoluted expressions of calculation of return benefit, that is, self-interest. It is the cardinal doctrine of phase-one liberalism, expressed in Pope's couplet.

> That REASON, PASSION, answer one great aim
> That here SELF-LOVE and SOCIAL are the same.

It is the working assumption of interest politics. It is implicit in the very jargon of sociology. All this testimony creates a presumption that the theory cannot be entirely mistaken.

Despite the theory's familiarity, one reads Trivers's version with admiration for its ingenuity, so often reminiscent of Darwin's incomparable skill at elucidating the evolutionary adaptiveness of traits. One notices with surprise, however, that Trivers makes no use of Darwin's *Expression of Emotion in Men and Animals*, nor of the ethological literature that stems in part from this book. In particular, the literature on attachment and affiliation, which seems so pertinent to his subject, is ignored. Trivers pushes to the limit his hypothesis that natural selection of the genetic basis of behavior is the sole cause of behavioral adaptation. He does not countenance a group process, even though human and animal association seems for all the world like a group process (Crook 1971). But having chosen the neo-Darwinian approach, he does not specify whether he assumes random or assortive mating—this because, curiously enough for a geneticist, his model abstracts from gene flow. Yet relevance of gene flow is clear. When altruists pair with selfish individuals, they are at a disadvantage, whereas when they pair assortively, the reverse is true (Hamilton 1971). Trivers will perhaps say that he assumes that all individuals are equally selfish. But what might this mean empirically, in view of the factual social differentiation among humans and animals? In Trivers's model, not even sexual differentiation is relevant to the evaluation of cooperative behavior.

Pertinent as discussion of this and other omitted material would be, I will conclude on a more political note. Reciprocal altruism resembles what liberals called "enlightened self-interest," a sociable selfishness motivated by awareness that we must after all rely on others. There have been many attempts to set up a calculus of return benefits. Utilitarians based theirs on a calculus of pleasure and pain. More recently, decision theory and rational-choice models have attracted much attention and have enjoyed limited success in stable decision environments. But as Trivers points out in regard to his own calculus, it is difficult to assign reliable probabilities to reciprocation at some future time because there is an element of the incalculable in human beings (and in animals). Still, if individual and group behavior were not roughly calculable, life would be totally unpredictable—a madhouse.

Part of our calculating about others amounts to discerning and guessing at motives. The anthropological material Trivers cites bears out his contention that one motive humans count on is the self-interest of others. Subtle psychological probing by authors as diverse as St. Augustine, La Rochefoucauld, and Nietzsche bears this out as well. There probably are few behaviors absolutely impervious to selfish motives at some level. Does a mother sacrifice all for a child? But it is her own. Does a man act generously toward his enemies? He may hope to win them over. And so on with the *arrière pensée*. But how shall we evaluate these facts? Do they mean that moral distinctions—for example, between pettiness and generosity—are illusory insofar as they imply that the generous act is not selfish? It is not quite clear what Trivers thinks about that. Speaking of trust and suspicion, he writes in chapter 1 of this book that

> . . . human beings respond to altruistic acts according to their perception of the motives of the altruist. They tend to respond more altruistically when they perceive the other as acting "genuinely" altruistic, that is, voluntarily dispatching an altruistic act as an *end in itself*. . . .

And a little later he writes:

> Lerner and Lightman (1968) have shown experimentally that those who act altruistically for ulterior benefit are rated as unattractive and treated selfishly, whereas those who apparently are genuinely altruistic are rated as attractive and are treated altruistically.

But Trivers does not believe in genuine, unselfish altruism, for in summary he subscribes to the "cynical view of human behavior" that everyone acts on "his own lowly selfish impulses." Genuine altruism is an illusion; moral distinctions are unreal. Yet our constant experience, as well as the evidence Trivers cites, indicates that the illusion effectively motivates behavior, because human beings treat the calculating and uncalculating altruist differently: one cannot count on the calculating altruist. It follows that those who advocate Trivers's view make themselves suspect and forfeit the benefit of being regarded as honest.

This dilemma has been faced before, once by the Sophists of antiquity, and later by liberalism. The solution in antiquity was this. Since whoever says that human beings strive exclusively for their own aggrandizement is suspect, he should, out of self-interest, preach the opposite of what he believes. He should declare his warm esteem for the social virtues and affect devotion to the common good, while acting on the opposite opinion. He should, in short, preach justice and practice injustice, or, in Trivers's terms, cheat and deceive and practice sham moralistic aggression to the hilt (Masters 1977).

The evident difficulty with this code is that it works only for tough, cold-blooded types who can take care of themselves. The general run of people are too moral or too timid to practice that rough code; and if they did, fang and claw would prevail. But liberalism came up with a generally applicable solution. If people's selfish motives were publicly acknowledged to be normal, then these motives would be blameless, calculable, and susceptible to political institutionalization. The idea was to enlighten people about their true nature, and the enlightenment was thought to confer a benefit so great that it would alter the character of human association. For if individual self-interest is the true foundation of sociability, then the tribe, city, or state can have no other rational purpose than to serve the interests of its members. Such a determination of the "public interest" bids fair to eliminate from politics the effects of moralistic aggression—sectarian strife over good and evil, which depends on the illusory belief that leaders genuinely espouse a genuine common good. This solution to the political question depended, of course, on the aggregate of self-interests being compatible. This was thought to be the case. The self-interests of the great majority are directed toward a small range of immediate goals that they can be satisfied by a politics based upon acquisitiveness.

Trivers does not address the questions raised here. He provides no analysis of the interests people typically seek to satisfy nor of the self who bears those interests. He implicitly assumes the self as defined in liberal theory as an apolitical, private person. We are therefore not surprised to find that a spectrum of commonplace experiences are omitted from his analysis: love, loyalty, dignity, generosity, and sacrifice; also malice, envy, cruelty, jealousy, arrogance, and revenge. Nor is there attention to the possibility that the meaning of "self" may change significantly as one moves from the middle range of the average person to the top and bottom ends of the scale. We see no grand passion; no glimmer of self-transcedence and hard demands on oneself; no inkling of the springs of art, religion, or politics. Nor do we see in his *Homo* the possibility of implacable hatred, cruelty as a credo and way of life, or viciousness as pleasure and stimulus. Trivers's man is at bottom a reproductive utiltarian. Like other utilitarians, Trivers reduces the enormous range of human behavior and feeling to the homogeneity of selfishness. Accordingly, his theory needs an addendum that explains the observed heterogeneity of selfishness: small-minded, petty selfishness; agreeable selfishness; modest selfishness; voracious, ambitious selfishness; self-destructive selfishness; magnanimous selfishness; and so on.[11]

This diversity is well documented. A pertinent documentation, from the point of view of his theory, is Solzhenitsyn's depiction of the extreme social Darwinism of the Gulag Archipelago. For the *zeks*, life is reduced to struggle for existence, which, daily and hourly in jeopardy, vanishes with the least misstep. The jailers have been selected for "firmness," that is, pitilessness and cruelty. They may commit any outrage against prisoners with impunity. Camp regimen is not moderated by requirements of productive efficiency or occasional visits by an inspector general. The bosses expect most of the prisoners to perish. What are the ethics of these forlorn human beings, thrown together by despotic caprice to hew frozen Arctic forests?

The Law of the Taiga is the prisoner's code for survival, and its first commandment is to trust no one. Any unselfish act is suspect, since kindness is likely to be a ruse to snatch the "second skin"—those paltry but precious possessions (the bread ration, the battered rump of dignity) that hold death at bay. The second commandment completes the first by counseling new arrivals to suppress all fellow feeling and to be pitiless toward everyone, according to the maxim, "Even if you are croaking right next to me, it's none of my affair." This rule, which experienced prisoners break selectively, seems in the Gulag to be a defense against natural sociability rather than the frank expression of its "real" selfish basis. For withholding attachments is the means of maintaining psychological equilibrium in a milieu where jailers deliberately break any attachments that may be formed; where every day one would helplessly see his friends abused, diseased, and dying; where energy is so reduced that there is not enough even for self-pity, for prisoners must learn to be indifferent to *their own grief* (Solzhenitzyn 1972-1976, vol. 2, p. 501; vol. 1, p. 563).

Pitilessness is not the same as malice or exploitation, which exists among a special category of prisoners, the "thieves" or nonpolitical prisoners. Thieves are encouraged by the jailers, since they add yet another torment to the life of the *zeks*. Whereas the *zek*'s law forbids theft and counsels indifference to the man dying in the next bunk, the thief enjoys pushing him into death, adding a final humiliation if he can. The *zek's* law forbids him to squeal to jailers, but the thieves cooperate with them.

Brutalized though it is, the Law of the Taiga expresses rules of survival with as much decency and dignity as the condition of continuous predation will allow. The wonder is that any decency remains at all. Indeed, reading these dismal archives, one wonders why men and women who survived punishment, starvation, disease and cold did not die of despair. Solzhenitsyn explains it this way:

> But probably the most interesting psychological twist here is the fact that the zeks perceive their own stable state of equanimity in these primitive and wretched circumstances as a victory for *love of life*. It is quite enough for the sequence of misfortunes to slow down a little, for the blows of fate to slacken just a little, for the zek to express his *satisfaction with life* and take pride in his own conduct in it. [vol. 2, p. 502]

In those moments he is apt to say, "The climate is cold, but the company is good."

This brief glimpse into the Gulag shows the persistence of moral distinctions in extreme conditions of depravity and injustice. The Law of the Taiga commands the preservation of one's own existence as the first law of life; yet, as we have seen, the lives of the *zeks* are morally different from those of the jailers and thieves. Since he has been stripped of the capacity to help or harm others very much, the most substantial moral act remaining to the *zek* is to endure; for to endure is to defy the persecution, to express mutely but eloquently *"the secret thirst for justice"* (vol. 2, p. 504). A consistent interpretation of morality as interest would declare that the zek's longing for justice is only a morally aggressive way of expressing his thirst for revenge, or for improving his condition—in either case at the cost of the selfish interests of the jailers. This outcome shows that the interest interpretation cannot evaluate moral difference of persons or actions, since that approach is based on a decision to eliminate moral difference by reducing it to individual interest, assumed to be equal or to have the "same value" for each. Such plausibility as this approach can muster fades, I believe, when we put the interests of jailers and their victims on the same footing. The mind balks, not merely because we feel sympathy for the victims, or cannot "identify" with the jailers—the existence of jailers shows that to be a contingent psychological limitation. It is because the Gulag and its likes systematically assault nearly every human quality that we reasonably treasure, while encouraging those that we reasonably condemn.

In liberal nations, the interest interpretation of morality was for a long time muted by religious convictions. But as conscience eroded under the steady flow of secularism, people began to see themselves "as they really are." By 1835 Tocqueville was to write of his countrymen: "Men are no longer bound together by spirit, but by interests; and it would seem that human opinions are reduced to a sort of intellectual dust, unable to collect, unable to cohere.'' Since then things have gone much farther. The selfish person's contempt for his own smallness combines with doubt or cynicism about moral restraint (moral grandeur is not even in the vocabulary), stirring social mobility into a whirling confusion. The demiexecutive protagonist of Heller's *Something Happened* expressed this conscience when he said, ''Deep down inside, I might really be great. Deep down inside, I think not. I hope I never live to see the real me come out. He might say and do things that would embarrass me and plunge him into serious trouble, and I hope I am dead and buried by the time he does.'' Such despair searches fitfully, often pathetically, for something to believe in, some conquering idea, some hero of integrity to redeem the mediocrity and narrowness of lowly self-interest that grinds people into interchangeable parts of well-managed organizations.

Surveying these ashen landscapes of distempered souls, one may doubt that the enlightened settlement of the great political questions is an unqualified success. Certainly it has succeeded in propagating rationalism through institutions and in the *mentalité* of modern publics. But science as a *mentalité* is cosmopolitan, heedless of localism—a vivisectionist, as Nietzsche called it, of all living belief. This is very well for the vivisectionists. Yet by impressing, however incompletely, its form on institutions, it has generated a society whose dynamics cut away all localisms and roots in the interest of cosmopolitan homogeneity. Never before have humans lived in such conditions; and the danger of this has been noted recently by the biologist Jacques Monod, who wrote:

> Modern societies have been robbed, by science itself, of any firm, coherent, acceptable ''belief'' upon which to base their value systems. This, probably, is the greatest revolution that ever occurred in human culture. I mean the utter destruction by systematic pursuit of objective knowledge, of all belief systems . . . which had, for thousands of years, served the essential function of justifying the moral code and social structure. [1971]

Modern people have not only lost faith. They have also lost the sense of continuity of generations, certainty of status, the network of kinfolk and allies, the naturalness of diurnal time and bounded spaces, limited contingencies, and the commitments for life for which one risks life. All these changes and more were perceived as losses decades ago by artists and writers. The losses have been masked by excitement with new things—numerous gadgets and trinkets, urbanization, entertainment, the euphoria of release from the old restraints.

But evidence accumulates that the keel of human sociability was laid down long ago in tribal association. Whether and how humanity can abide

the unprecendented rupture with natural sociability is an urgent question.
Our hope now must be that intensive investigation of this question will not
be impeded by complacency or militant dogmatisms. I suspect that in the
coming decades we must shoulder the burden of Tinbergen's (1972) dis-
quieting thought: "The functional ethologist, who is continuously faced
with the precariousness of survival in animals, is in a position to see at least
some aspects of Man's unique position—and he is extremely alarmed by
what he sees."

Notes

1. The Paris Conference on Biology and Politics (1975) is a useful index of the anticipated importance of biology to politics, as conceived by
political scientists who have been the first to develop the field. The conference proceedings were published by Somit (1976) in a book that contains
a bibliography. But anthropologists were the first social scientists to adopt
biological findings and approaches to their subject; that is, a few anthropologists did so, against a disciplined orthodoxy. See Gellner (1963),
Freeman (1966), Fox (1971), Lee and DeVore (1971), and Count (1973).

2. Alexander Solzhenitsyn describes the thieves of the Gulag Archipelago, themselves prisoners, who strip other prisoners of their last
possessions if they can. The thieves are organized and are tolerated by the
camp commanders, who for their part plunder rations meant for prisoners.
This is a particularly graphic example of niche filling, but comparable ones
are described in James Clavell's *King Rat*, MacKinley Kantor's *Anderson-
ville*, and Bettelheim's *The Informed Heart*.

3. This argument, which originated with Fisher, has been repeated by
Dahlberg, Dobzhansky, Herrnstein, and Mayr, although Wilson (1975)
doubts its validity. Apart from political influences that might act against a
tendency toward meritocracy, two genetic countervailing forces might be
mentioned. One is that outbreeding (random mating) among persons of
very different genotypes (that is, who stem from previously isolated
breeding populations) can produce inharmonious gene combinations affecting somatic and behavioral traits. It is not known to what extent this
may be occurring in nations with heterogeneous populations, but it is
something that geneticists flirting with eugenics invariably mention.
Curiously, H.J. Muller and J.B.S. Haldane, who were once Communists,
stress this point, which agrees so well with ancient prejudice against the
"impurity" of outbreeding. More recently it has been discussed by
Medawar. The other consideration is the so-called dysgenic effects of urbanization and advanced culture. Muller was especially concerned about the
accumulation of lethal genes, echoing from the perspective of genetics Darwin's naked-eye observation:

> There is reason to believe that vaccination has preserved thousands, who from weak constitution, would formerly have succumbed to smallpox . . . no one who has attended to the breeding of domestic animals will doubt that this must be highly injurious to the race of man.

Other authors, such as Dobzhansky, dismiss this concern, since lethals would introduce a disturbing factor only if requisite medicines were no longer available. But Dobzhansky and many others are alarmed by genetic predictions of decreasing intelligence. Huxley wrote that

> . . . man's genetic nature has degenerated and is still doing so. . . . There is also the fact that modern industrial civilization favors the differential decrease of genes concerned with intelligence. It seems now to be established that . . . people with higher intelligence have, on the average, a lower reproductive rate than the less intelligent. . . . If this process were to continue, the results would be extremely grave. [1953]

In this vein, Mayr (1963) protests against "innumerable administrative rules and law of the government that discriminate inadvertently against the most gifted members of the community. Changing these laws so as to place a premium on performance (the 'opportunity' of true democracy, rather than identicism) is entirely different from distributing privileges. . . ." The process in train is that the progressive increase of ever higher demands for professional skills required in modern society is accompanied by a relative decrease in the number able to perform them. This could lead to an "intelligence crash," or, more likely, to a political struggle between the gifted and the average.

4. The fact that language acquisition is subject to sensitive learning times, and in quite specific neurophysiological ways, is one of the more severe blows to the notion that all human behavior is learned, in the Skinnerian sense. There is reason to believe that speech competence is neurologically and ultimately genetically programmed, in much the same way as is vision or locomotion; that is, we naturally walk, talk, and see by virtue of our biological constitution. Yet all three of these behaviors are nurtured to some degree. If it is true that speech does not develop in persons deprived of a speech environment, then that distinctively human trait is just the one in which the nuture of nature reaches its maximum. The rudimentary speech that has been taught to chimpanzees is by contrast a circus trick, like a bear riding a bicycle: it does not come naturally, and it fades rapidly.

5. Hirsch (1963) has given an especially lucid exposition of the behavioral geneticist's approach to uniformity and diversity of behavior traits. He argues that facts of genetics overthrow "the common behaviorist assumption that individuals are uniform at birth and become differentiated only by environmental differences." He also opposes the reductionist assumption that would explain behavior by reference to only one biological system, such as the neurological. Whereas a disease or pathology is usually traceable to a fault in one system, normally behavior is "the integration of

most of these systems rather than the expression of any one of them." The capacity of biology to explain both uniformity and diversity rests ultimately on the properties of DNA, which is capable of both enormous variation and great stability. That one and the same substance can produce *opposite effects*, that it is a union of contraries, makes DNA a rich subject of reflection and the deepest puzzle for geneticists. See the discussion by Thoday (1962).

6. Chapter 3 of *The Origin of Species* is entitled, "The Struggle for Existence," and chapter 4 is called "Natural Selection." Sexual selection is introduced only in chapter 4, where Darwin says:

> And this leads me to say a few words on what I call Sexual Selection. This depends, not on a struggle for existence, but on a struggle between the males for possession of the females; the result is not death to the unsuccessful competitor, but few or no offspring. Sexual selection is, therefore, less rigorous than natural selection.

I draw particular attention to this distinction because it is often ignored by biologists, including Michael Ghiselin, author of *The Triumph of the Darwinian Method*, who writes that "Natural selection explains evolutionary change as due to reproductive competiton between members of the same species" (1971). Like Krebs and May, Mayr, and others, Ghiselin emphasizes the difficulty of Darwin's evolutionary mechanism: "Even within biology, few understand it." Waddington, who puzzled over the mechanism during a lifetime of prolific study, eventually concluded that the matter was obscure because "the origin of species is just the facet of evolution on which Darwin's theories throw the feeblest illumination" (1960). He also declared Darwin's formulation of natural selection to be a tautology, and said of the supposed evolution of characters through random mutation: "This explanation is a very powerful one. It could, in fact, explain anything . . . I should not dream of denying it—as far as it goes—but I wish to argue that it does not go far enough" (Waddington 1959, 1975). Waddington developed his theory of genetic assimilation as an explicitly Lamarckian attempt to explain anagenesis, which Darwin himself believed had to be explained by Lamarckian theory.

7. See Mayr (1963, pp. 489, 518, 588). Like Waddington, Mayr claims that Darwin did not understand the origin of species: "Even now we are only beginning to understand the speciation process and, at that, in only a few groups of animals" (1963, p. 426). Since genetics does not endorse Darwin's conjectures about the properties of the inheritance material, it retains with difficulty his concept of evolutionary mechanisms. The differences between Darwin and neo-Darwinism are briefly these:

1. "Fitness" for Darwin meant above all phenotypic survival fitness (rejected by Trivers and others).

2. Darwin imagined that the "least advantage" an organism acquired by mutation or variation of its soma or behavior would be passed on to offspring, and that through successive generations the advantage would accumulate, resulting in the evolution of an organ or behavior, or some modification of such. But genetics recognizes evolution through "random drift" of variations. It also recognizes that normalizing selection tends to return variations to a phenotypic mean, and concludes therefore to "the survival of the ordinary" (Mayr 1963, p. 280).

3. Genetics declares that if most mutations are not adaptively neutral, then organisms could not survive the selection pressure of deleterious mutation; whereas if they are mainly neutral, the most important source for genetic innovation is drastically curtailed. How evolution occurs thus becomes an ever darkening mystery.

It would be salutary if biologists admitted more openly that speciation, which has never been observed (Mayr, 1963, p. 488; Dobzhansky 1972, p. 277), is not understood.

8. Although it is pertinent to his analysis, Trivers fails to mention the field work on "aunt behavior" among primates. Aunts are usually grooming companions of a mother who take interest in the infant and help with its care. They may or may not be near kin of the mother, and they may be either socially dominant or subordinate to her; aunting does not change the relative social status of mother and aunt. The behavior is initially resented by the mother (how human!), then accepted. Aunts have been reported to adopt a child on the death of the mother. "Uncling" has also been reported among primates. For a review, see Crook (1971).

9. Infanticide among male langurs is a striking apparent confirming instance of inclusive fitness. Yet is would be rash to infer from one instance to a general statement. Further investigation is required to determine whether *all* polygamous male animals behave as the langur does. If this is not the case—and it seems not to be (Eibl-Eibesfeldt 1975)—then we require an explanation of why inclusive fitness produces infanticide among langurs but not among other species. Conversely, on Trivers's premises as I understand them, all infanticide should be related to inclusive-fitness theory, yet it occurs in circumstances that have no apparent connection with inclusive fitness, for example, under stress.

Furthermore, there is a difficulty about polygamy that Trivers does not explain. If each individual strives to maximize his progeny, by what mechanisms has evolution produced redundant males? This is the problem of sex ratios, or, alternately, the problem of the evolution of a group behavior inharmonious with individual biology. If one focuses on genetics and behavior simultaneously, the following problem emerges. Polygamy insures that all langur offspring are offspring of a dominant male. Continuous assortive mating of this kind ought to increase dominance among the harem. Yet this behaivor is somehow inhibited, which suggests a group benefit of some kind. On the genetics of polygamy, see Hamilton (1971).

10. Trivers's account of the origin of altruism is no less ambiguous than that offered by liberal theorists. In Hobbes's state of nature, all are at loggerheads. Locke softened this by assuming altruism within the family, whereas Hume claimed that sympathy is a genuine principle of sociability equal in weight to selfishness. For Hobbes the initial reciprocal altruistic act is self-interested submission to a common power that secures life; for Locke it is probably parent-offspring mutualism. Trivers can use neither of these origins. It is curious that in his account, the *initial* altruistic act is unproblematic; he assumes a being who computes the probabilities of a return benefit for saving a drowning man. According to him, the problem arises only at the second stage, when we require an explanation of why the benefited individual should reciprocate. But if B has reasons for cheating, then A must know it (since they are identically selfish); why then, if reciprocity were not ensured, for example, by some pre-existing custom, should A perform the initial altruistic act? An infinite regress arises here that either postpones the initial altruistic act indefinitely, or presupposes sociability, which then must be explained. This suggests that the notion of an initial altruistic act by beings supposed to be completely selfish is not very coherent. Everything we know about primates and hominids suggests that humans never passed through a Hobbesian state of nature, since they evolved from a gregarious species.

It is noteworthy that Trivers's account of the origin of sociability refers to moral aggression, but never to physical force. It is worth remarking in this connection that sociability need not imply mutuality. Various insect parasites have broken the social code of their hosts so that they and their offspring are protected and fed by the hosts, even though the parasites devour larvae in the hosts' nests (Wilson 1975).

11. On this problem, see Masters (1978).

References

Alexander, R.D., and Sherman, P.W. 1977. "Local Mate Competition and Parental Investment in Social Insects." *Science* 196:494-500.
Barnett, S.A. 1972. "The Ontogeny of Behaviour and the Concept of Instinct." In *Brain and Human Behaviour*, edited by A.G. Karczman and J.C. Eccles. Berlin: Springer.
_____. 1975. *The Rat: A Study in Behavior*. Chicago: University of Chicago Press.
Bateson, P.P.G., and Hinde, R.A., eds. 1976. *Growing Points in Ethology*. Cambridge: Cambridge University Press.

Bolby, J. 1958. "The Nature of the Child's Tie to His Mother." *International Journal of Psychoanalysis* 41:89-113.

Caton, H. 1973. *The Origin of Subjectivity: An Essay on Descartes*. New Haven: Yale University Press.

———. 1980. "Toward a Diagnosis of Progress." Paper presented at the Symposium on Modernity, Washington, D.C. To appear in *Independent Journal of Philosophy*.

Count, E.W. 1973. *Being and Becoming: Essays on the Biogram*. New York: Van Nostrand.

Crook, J.C. 1971. "Sources of Co-operation in Men and Animals." In *Man and Beast: Comparative Social Behaviour*, edited by J.F. Eisenberg and W.S. Dillon. Washington, D.C.: Smithsonian Institution Press.

d'Alembert, Jean Le Rond. 1963. *Preliminary Discourse to the Encyclopedia of Diderot*. New York: Library of Liberal Arts.

Darlington, C.D. 1969. *The Evolution of Man and Society*. London: Allen and Unwin.

Dobzhansky, T. 1972. "Natural Selection in Mankind." In *The Structure of Populations*, edited by G.A. Harrison and A.J. Boyce. Oxford: Oxford University Press.

———. 1973. *Genetic Diversity and Human Equality*. New York: Basic Books.

Ebl-Eibesfeldt, I. 1972. *Love and Hate: The Natural History of Behaviour Patterns*. New York: Holt, Rinehart and Winston.

———. 1975. *Ethology*. 2nd ed. New York: Holt, Rinehart and Winston.

Fox, R. 1971. "The Cultural Animal." In *Man and Beast: Comparative Social Behaviour*, edited by J.F. Eisenberg and W.S. Dillon. Washington, D.C.: Smithsonian Institution Press.

Freeman, D. 1966. "Social Anthropology and the Scientific Study of Human Behavior." *Man* 1:330-341.

Gellner, E. 1963. "Nature and Society in Social Anthropology." *Philosophy of Science* 30:236-251.

Ghiselin, M.T. 1971-1972. "The Individual in the Darwinian Revolution." *New Literary History*, 3:113-134.

Gregory, R.L. 1966. *Eye and Brain*. New York: McGraw-Hill.

Haldane, J.B.S. 1949. "Human Evolution: Past and Present." In *Genetics, Paleontology, and Evolution*, edited by J.L. Despen, E. Mays, and G.G. Simpson. Princeon, N.J.: Princeton University Press.

Hamilton, W.D. 1971. "Selection of Selfish and Altruistic Behavior in some Extreme Models." In *Man and Beast: Comparative Social Behavior*, edited by J.F. Eisenberg and W.D. Dillon. Washington, D.C.: Smithsonian Institution Press.

Harlow, H., and Harlow, M. 1966. "Learning to Love." *American Scientist* 54:244-272.

Hinde, R.A. 1966. *Animal Behavior*. 2nd ed. New York: McGraw-Hill.

Hirsch, J. 1963. "Behavior Genetics and Individuality Understood." *Science* 142:1436-1442.

Hubbert, M.K. 1971. "Energy Resources." In *Environment, Pollution and Society*, edited by W.M. Murdoch. Stamford, Conn.: Sinauer, Associates.

Hume, D. 1953. *The Political Essays of David Hume*, edited by Charles W. Hendel. New York: Library of Liberal Arts.

Huxley, J.S. 1953. *Evolution in Action*. New York: Harper and Row.

Jencks, Christopher; Smith, M.; Ackland, H.; Bane, M.J.; Cohen, D.; Gintis, H.; Heyns, B.; and Michelson, S. 1972. *Inequality: A Reassessment of Family and Schooling*. New York: Basic Books.

Krebs, J., and May, R.M. 1976. "Social Insects and the Evolution of Altruism." *Nature* 260:9-10.

Leakey, R., and Lewin, R. 1977. *Origins*. New York: Dutton.

Lee, E.B., and DeVore, I., eds. 1968. *Man the Hunter*. Chicago: Aldine.

Masters, R.D. 1975. "Politics as a Biological Phenomenon." *Social Science Research* 26:7-63.

_____. 1977. "Human Nature, Nature, and Political Thought." In *Human Nature in Politics*, edited by J.R. Pennock and J.W. Chapman. New York: New York University Press.

_____. 1978. "Classic Political Philosophy and Contemporary Biology." Paper presented at Conferences for the Study of Political Thought, Loyala University.

_____. 1979. "Beyond Reductionism: Five Basic Concepts in Human Ethology." In *Human Ethology*, edited by W. Lepenics and M. von Cranach. Canbridge: Cambridge University Press.

Mayr, Ernst. 1963. *Animal Species and Evolution*. Cambridge, Mass.: Harvard University Press.

Miller, H.L. 1980. "Hard Realities and Soft Social Science." *The Public Interest*, no. 59, pp. 67-82.

Monod, J. 1971. "On the Logical Relationship between Knowledge and Values." In *The Social Impact of Modern Biology*, edited by W. Fuller. London: Routledge and Kegan Paul.

Ophuls, W. 1977. *Ecology and the Politics of Scarcity*. San Francisco: Freeman.

Purver, M. 1967. *The Royal Society: Concept and Creation*. London: Routledge and Kegan Paul.

Reynolds, V. 1966. "Open Groups in Hominid Evolution." *Man* 1:444-452.

Rossi, P. 1968. *Francis Bacon: From Magic to Science*. Chicago: University of Chicago Press.

Solzhenitsyn, A. 1972-1976. *Gulag Archipelago*. 3 vols. New York: Harper and Row.

Somit, A., ed. 1976. *Biology and Politics*. The Hague: Mouton.

Sommer, R. 1969. *Personal Space*. Englewood Cliffs, N.J.: Prentice Hall.

Thoday, J.M. 1962. "Natural Selection and Biological Progress." In *A Century of Darwin*, edited by S.A. Barnett. London: Mercury.

Tiger, L. 1969. *Men in Groups*. New York: Random House.

Tinbergen, N. 1972. "Functional Ethology and the Human Sciences." *Proceedings of the Royal Society* (London) 182:385-410.

Trivers, R. 1977. Transcript of "Symposium on Sociobiology and Politics." Temple University, Philadelphia, Pa., p. 51.

Waddington, C.H. 1959. "Evolutionary Adaptation." *Perspectives in Biology and Medicine* 2:379-401.

_____. 1960. *The Ethical Animal*. London: G. Allen.

_____. 1975. *Evolution of an Evolutionist*. Ithaca, N.Y.: Cornell University Press.

Wallace, B. 1968. *Topics in Population Genetics*. London: Duckworth.

Washburn, S.L. 1961. *Social Life of Early Man*. New York: Wenner-Gren.

Webster, C. 1975. *The Great Instauration*. London: Duckworth.

White, E. 1975. "Genetic Diversity and Democratic Theory." Paper Presented at the annual meeting of the American Political Science Association, San Francisco.

Wilson, E.O. 1971. "Competitive and Aggressive Behavior." In *Man and Beast: Comparative Social Behavior*, edited by J.F. Eisenberg and W.S. Dillon. Washington, D.C.: Smithsonian Institution Press.

_____. .1975. *Sociobiology*. Cambridge, Mass.: Harvard University Press.

4 The Value—and Limits—of Sociobiology: Toward a Revival of Natural Right

Roger D. Masters

Sociobiology has sparked increasing attention—and polemic—in the last few years. For some, this approach promises a revolution in our understanding of human social behavior that will cast new light on old problems while integrating the natural and social sciences. For others, however, it is a reductionist if not reactionary exercise, doomed to futility and marred by ideological presuppositions. Given the political implications of this debate, it is essential that the issues be confronted dispassionately and knowledgeably.

Unfortunately, many discussions of sociobiology have been based on superficial impressions or on popularized, journalistic accounts. To be fair, judgment must be based on the work of reputable scientists, such as Edward O. Wilson (1975); William Hamilton (1964); Richard Alexander (1974, 1975, 1976, 1977, 1978); David Barash (1976); and Richard Dawkins (1976). To avoid the risk of constructing a "straw man" out of disparate citations, I will focus on the influential work of Robert Trivers (1971, 1972, 1974).[1] Although divergences in the field will be noted, for most purposes Trivers is an excellent representative of contemporary sociobiology.

It should not be assumed, of course, that *all* evolutionary biologists—much less ethologists, geneticists, and other specialists—are in agreement. But it is probably not too early to suggest both the great importance of recent work in sociobiology and its limitations when extended to human behavior. Social scientists have much to learn from this approach, although it should neither be accepted uncritically nor applied indiscriminately.

My procedure will be as follows. In the first section sociobiology will be related to the Western tradition of political thought and shown to be a valid approach to social analysis. The next section will survey limitations of sociobiological theories, distinguishing superficial criticisms from serious objections. In the final sections, I will suggest how a balanced assessment of sociobiology points to the revival of a conception of "natural right" derived from classical political philosophy.

The Value of Sociobiology

Darwin's concept of natural selection is now generally accepted as the basis of evolutionary theory, albeit with numerous technical modifications (Mayr 1978). One important change is that biologists no longer speak of the "survival of the fittest." Survival is now measured by the genes carried by those who leave behind the most offspring. Natural selection thus refers to the fate of genes in populations, not to that of individual organisms.

The contemporary concept of natural selection is called *inclusive fitness* because it *includes* relatives when calculating the evolutionary effects of an individual's traits and behavior. As Trivers puts it:

> If in calculating the selective value of a gene one not only computes its effect on the reproductive success of the individual bearing it, but adds to this its effects on the reproductive success of related individuals, appropriately devalued by the relevant degrees of relatedness, then one has computed what Hamilton (1964) calls *inclusive fitness*. [1974, p. 250]

The popular notion of Darwinian selection has thus been modified in two important ways. First, *fitness* now means success in reproduction, not idealized excellence in all respects. And second, an individual's reproductive success refers not merely to the number of direct offspring but also to the number of other organisms sharing the same genetic heritage.

From this point of view, inclusive fitness not only serves as an updating of Darwin's theory of natural selection, but also suggests a different mode of analysis. As Trivers notes, one can use

> the language of strategy and decision, as if each individual contemplated in strategic terms the decisions it ought to make at each instant in order to maximize its reproductive success. This language is chosen purely for convenience to explore the adaptations one might expect natural selection to favor. [1972, p. 146]

Hence *social* behavior can be treated as resulting from a calculus of *individual* costs and benefits.

No attempt will be made here to restate in detail Trivers's explanation of altruistic behavior in terms of inclusive fitness, measured by "the benefit/cost ratio of the act, times the chance that the recipient has the gene" (1974, p. 250). Trivers provides a good introduction to this subject (1971, 1977, 1978), although interested political scientists have a responsibility to consult the somewhat different formulations of Wilson, Hamilton, Alexander, Barash, Dawkins, and others.[2] Rather than repeat what biologists clearly have done, it will be more useful to situate this new approach in terms of traditional political philosophy and contemporary social science.

Inclusive Fitness and Social-Contract Theories

At first sight, theories of inclusive fitness may strike the social scientist as a radical departure from accustomed models of reasoning. For many non-scientists, biology is a field devoted to the intricacies of cell structure, DNA, and ecological system; when animal behavior is at issue, most of us think of the biologist as studying "instincts" coded in the genes. In contrast, game theory and calculations of self-interest are familiar to the economist or student of international politices—and seem a world away from the behavior of "lower" creatures.

Contemporary sociobiologists like Trivers cut across this traditional division of mental habits, adopting a style of thought developed by social scientists. For example, the prisoner's dilemma in game theory can be used to analyze "symmetrical reciprocal situations" between any two animals (Trivers 1971, p. 38). As Tullock (1978), Hirshleifer (1978), and Chase (in press) have shown, Trivers's sociobiological theory of reciprocal altruism is formally identical to economic theories of collective or public goods.

Little matter that the calculation of advantage need not be fully rational: game theorists, economists, and nuclear strategists have noted the utility of a cost-benefit approach even—indeed, especially—in situations where participants do not perform the same rational calculus as the observer. Nor is it critical that sociobiologists define benefits in terms of the number of "surviving offspring" (relative genetic contribution to succeeding generations) rather than of the organism's pleasure; the similarity in approach concerns the cost-benefit mode of anlaysis, not the way of measuring a benefit.

Whatever the superficial differences between the cost-benefit calculus of sociobiologists and that of game theorists, economists, or students of collective choice, the underlying kinship of approach should be evident. In both cases, a social pattern is derived from the balancing of advantages and disadvantages as measured by the individual. To be sure, some sociobiologists speak of the calculation from the perspective of a "selfish gene" (Dawkins 1976), whereas others consider the entire genome as the relevant unit of selection (Alexander and Sherman 1977). But for Trivers and many other sociobiologists, social systems do not have an autonomous status, since natural selection is said to operate at the level of "individual reproductive success" and *only* at this individual level (Trivers 1977, p. 5; 1978, p. 3).

This mode of analysis is not new in the West. On the contrary, it can be traced to the beginning of Western political philosophy and recurs wherever social-contract theories have been formulated to account for human politics. Like the pre-Socratics, not to mention the tradition of Hobbes, Locke, and Spinoza, recent sociobiologists account for cooperative behavior—and especially for altruism—in terms of the long-range or rational advantage of individual participants. And like such social-contract theories, the concept of inclusive fitness leads one to treat selfishness as a natural given, transcended only when circumstances make it profitable to do so.

I hope that it is unnecessary to belabor this point. Elsewhere, I have cited Antiphon the Sophist and other pre-Socratics, as well as the speeches of Thrasymachus in Plato's *Republic,* to show the striking parallels between what can be called the classical theory of "individualistic hedonism" and contemporary analysis of inclusive fitness (Masters 1978a).[3] To be sure, the ancients speak of "advantage" of the individual *organism,* whereas today's biologists stress the advantage of the individual's *genes.* But this would seem to be a redefinition of the notion of self-interest (or at least of enlightened self-interest) rather than a fundamental departure.

Viewed from this perspective, the natural-law teachings of Hobbes and Locke appear to be the forerunners of Trivers's notion of reciprocal altruism. In both cases, a rational calculus of long-range interest indicates the mixture of cooperation and hedonistic or selfish behavior that produces the optimum situation for all. Hence the relative unfamiliarity of many specific terms and the focus on animal examples should not obscure the extent to which sociobiological approaches represent a perfectly legitimate approach to political life.[4]

In short, current theories of inclusive fitness can claim to provide the scientific rationale for a long-standing tradition in Western political thought (Masters 1978b,c), not to mention the many contemporary economic, sociological, and political models based on a cost-benefit calculus by individual actors. But insofar as such approaches appear to have widespread applicability in all the social sciences, the implication is exciting indeed. In a generation that has bemoaned scientific specialization and the gaps betwen disciplines, sociobiology seems to show how Darwinian natural selection provides a theory integrating an impressive range of social phenomena.

Sociobiology as a Unifying Discipline

Robert Ardrey (1966) has suggested that humans exhibit a "territorial imperative"; but most scientists are embarrassed to appear to defend their own field against outsiders, regardless of logic or evidence. Still, one cannot avoid the impression that many of the objections to sociobiological reasoning are of this order. Although it is worrisome to see theorists from another discipline cast imperialistic glances on one's "own" subject matter, particularly if the outsiders seem to make trivial errors in so doing, Trivers's approach need not be viewed in this way.

To be sure, some biologists have spoken paternalistically of the social sciences as "branches" of biology to be absorbed or reduced to biological explanations (Wilson 1975, chap. 1; Simpson 1969, pp. vii, 39). But this exuberant reaction to the promise of sociobiological theory is understandable; for over a century, the Durkheimian view that human societies are somehow *sui generis* has contrasted sharply with the nominal acceptance of Darwinian theories of evolution.

It can hardly be denied that until the last few years social scientists generally ignored the heritage of Darwin. Since this gulf between biology and human behavior occurred during a generation in which biological science made astonishing advances, it was especially paradoxical. Having unraveled the genetic code, discovered what long appeared to be missing links in our primate ancestry, and explained an awesome variety of biological processes, biologists can hardly be blamed for their annoyance that social scientists failed to pay attention.

The most frequent objections to sociobiological reasoning, such as that of Sahlins (1977), only confirm the impression that social scientists may be guilty of bad faith. Again and again we are told that the incursion of biology into the social sciences is untenable *because* it is reductionist. The theory of inclusive fitness is dismissed as genetic determinism. And the autonomy of the social sciences is proclaimed on the basis of the ubiquity of human learning and cultural variability.

The reasons for dismissing these objections can only be outlined briefly here. Theories of inclusive fitness concern the calculus of natural selection. But natural selection explains how the *effects* of a trait can lead to its spread or disappearance. Hence biologists generally describe theories of natural selection as functional explanations, to be carefully distinguished from causal analysis (Masters 1976b). Genetic determinism is a *cause,* invoked as a plausible hypothesis in many biological phenomena. Natural selection is an *effect,* which can be mediated by individually "learned" behaviors as well as by narrowly programmed or "instinctive" ones. It follows, as George Gaylord Simpson put it, that total reductionism in biology is "scientifically absurd" (1969, p. 21). As Alexander points out, inclusive fitness theory presumes nothing "more complex or deterministic than learning through ordinary positive and negative reinforcement schedules" (1976, p. 13).

Those social scientists or humanists who insist that human learning is somehow unique must still account for the origin of this ability to learn. As biologists cannot fail to observe, any exemption of *Homo sapiens* from the laws of evolution is, since Darwin, hardly scientific. Assuming that human learning and cultural variability are different from anything else in the animal world, it is necessary to explain how such traits as speech and extensive individual learning arose in our species. Sociobiology provides such an explanation, based on the evolving tradeoffs between costs and benefits among competing genotypes. Hence Trivers uses inclusive-fitness theory to account for the emergence of "developmental plasticity" in humans (Trivers 1971, pp. 53-54).

Sociobiology thus appears as a bridge between the natural and social (or human) sciences, placing social life in a Darwinian theoretical context without reducing humans to unthinking beasts. Lest this appear forced, consider the relationship between Trivers's approach to inclusive fitness and some well-known political theories in the social-contract tradition. Rousseau's "general will," Kant's "categorical imperative," and Rawls's "veil of ignorance," to mention only three representative formulations, all seem to share formal attributes with Trivers's "reciprocal altruism."

Like today's sociobiologists, Rousseau, Kant, and writers in the Rawlsian perspective try to show how social cooperation, ethical restraint, and self-sacrifice can follow from a rational analysis of long range self-interest. To be sure, Rousseau limits the "general will" to a single community, on the grounds that the extension of an altruistic calculus to the entire human species is irrational (*Geneva Manuscript* I, ii [ed. Masters 1978, pp. 157-63]). In contrast, Kant's "categorical imperative" extends the range of reciprocity to the entire species of rational beings (*Fundamental Principles of the Metaphysics of Ethics* [ed. Manthey-Zorn, 1938, pp. 36-58]). In any case, Trivers's explanation of altruistic behavior can be seen as a scientific ground for political and ethical theories that have played a vital role in the Western intellectual tradition. Little wonder that biologists are excited by the promise that neo-Darwinian theory can transcend long-standing divisions between academic disciplines (Alexander 1975).

Evidence in Favor of Inclusive-Fitness Theory

One indication of a fruitful scientific theory lies in the formulation of counterintuitive hypotheses subject to empirical verification. If an approach gives rise to apparently paradoxical or unexpected predictions that are nonetheless confirmed by the evidence, then we must take its claims seriously. And if the same perspective simultaneously explains many things that have been emphasized by traditional theories, it becomes even more attractive. Recent sociobiology makes precisely these claims.

Most social scientists have stressed the variability of human behavior. As Trivers points out, the idea of inclusive fitness leads to a straight forward Darwinian explanation of the "plasticity" of our species. Philosophers and anthropologists alike have related this obvious fact to the likelihood that some individuals will behave "badly" toward others. In

Trivers's terms, "the human altruistic system is a sensitive unstable one"—especially since "often it will pay to cheat" (Trivers 1971, p. 48). Political theorists since Thrasymachus have said much the same thing, albeit without basing their observation on neo-Darwinian biology.

In his writings, Trivers has indicated how inclusive fitness helps to integrate a wide range of findings in such diverse social sciences as anthropology, economics, game theory, and psychology. But although sociobiology confirms many obvious insights of traditional approaches, it also suggests some unexpected hypotheses. As an example, consider how Trivers describes "the parent-offspring relationship" and suggests that "evolutionary theory tends to undercut certain assumptions that are common in at least psychology" (Trivers 1977, p. 19; 1978, p. 37).

We tend to approach the relationship of parents and offspring in terms of "maternal instinct," infant dependency, and familial love. But analyzing parent-offspring relations from the perspective of inclusive fitness "means you have to decompose what is going on in the relationship into appropriate benefits and costs" (Trivers, 1978). As a result, Trivers shows how the behavior of parents and their offspring can reflect a "conflict" between their genetic "interests."

"Weaning conflict is usually assumed to occur either because transitions in nature are assumed to be imperfect or because such conflict is assumed to serve the interests of both parent and offspring by informing each of the needs of the other" (Trivers 1974, p. 251). In contrast, sociobiology reveals "an underlying conflict in the way in which parent and offspring maximize their inclusive fitness" (Trivers 1977, pp. 21-22; 1978, p. 39). Similarly, the manipulation of parents by their offspring, sibling rivalry, socialization of the young—and youthful resistance to parental norms of altruism—can all be explained by inclusive-fitness theory (Trivers 1974, pp. 257-262).

These applications of inclusive-fitness theory are not merely unverifiable hypotheses: in many cases they can be tested empirically. For example, Hinde and others have shown that primate infants display precisely those responses one might predict from Trivers's conception of mother-offspring conflict (White 1974, pp. 29-68). Human learning ability, long treated primarily in terms of cognitive problems, now appears to be especially adapted to monitoring social interactions and gauging others' *intentions* (Humphrey 1976). Although predictable from inclusive-fitness theory, it is not generally expected that either new-born human infants or the young of other species are capable of intentional or purposive analysis of adult behavior (Von Cranach et al. 1979). And when applied to adults, social interaction (Alexander 1977), economic activity (Hirshleifer 1977a), and politics (Willhoite 1978) can be seen in a new light.

The Limits of Sociobiology

The foregoing discussion suggests that sociobiology is a legitimate and promising approach to the study of human behavior, ultimately relevant to politics. But to promise something does not guarantee delivery, and exaggerated claims are bound to breed future disappointment. Little wonder, therefore, that many social scientists have been—and remain—skeptical. Since there is more than a germ of truth in the reservations that have been expressed about Trivers's reasoning, let us turn to the *limits* of inclusive-fitness theories.

Exaggerated Claims

It is hardly surprising that the proponents of a new point of view will exaggerate its benefits; it is often tempting to advertise an innovation in unduly favorable terms. Indeed, inclusive-fitness theories lead to the prediction of such behavior whenever access to desirable resources depends on convincing others to accept something novel. In the development of science, however, a theory should not be sold like a refrigerator; and overblown claims must be subjected to independent verification.

On three different levels, proponents of sociobiology have occasionally made extreme claims for their approach. It has been implied that the idea of inclusive fitness will permit the discovery of genetic causes for all manner of human behavior, that sociobiology points to a deterministic or causal theory of politics, or that this mode of analysis is the only way of approaching the subject. Critics have a point when they reject each of these three claims.

Reductionism. In order to present the theory of inclusive fitness in a clear and generally understandable way, sociobiologists have spoken of a "gene for altruism." As Trivers puts it, there would be no difference in the logic of his analysis if altruism "required 100 genes at 100 different loci in an individual"; hence, "the tendency to imagine a single gene and ask whether it is in a relative or not is just a didactic device" (Trivers 1977, p. 32; 1978, p. 52). Like many didactic devices, this one has its dangers.

The notion of a single "gene" that programs highly complex and variable behavior exemplifies the reductionist project of showing simple, particulate causes for widely observed phenomena. Critics of sociobiology have often leaped at this implication, asserting that Trivers's approach necessarily implies reductionism, and that such a reductionist analysis is bound to fail. One can agree with the critics' conclusion without accepting their premise: sociobiology need not be reductionist, but claims that it could resolve complex patterns of human behavior into simple genetic components are untenable.

The crucial arguments on this score, however, are not those typically made by critics. The issue is not metaphysics or epistemology. Rather, the main point is that such reductionist claims are inconsistent with contemporary biology (Alexander 1976)—not to mention physics (Anderson 1972; Capra 1975). Simpson's remark that genetic reductionism is "scientifically absurd" is confirmed by such general developments as "hierarchy theory" (Pattee 1973), as well as by the empirical data studied by ethologists.

A thoroughly reductionist approach to altruism becomes questionable, for example, as soon as one describes more concretely the specific behaviors involved. In most primates, as well as in humans, the traits defined as "altruistic" are typically combined with capabilities or behaviors that are conventionally called "selfish" or "hedonistic." If the dominant male *both* copulates with females more frequently than do subordinates *and* has a greater tendency to defend the group against intruders, is this complex of behavioral traits altruistic? Or is it selfish? On inclusive-fitness grounds, it is obvious that the answer is "both" (Masters 1978a).

Trivers's claim that there would be no difference in his argument if it referred to 100 genes ignores the multifunctionality of many genetic loci. That is, Trivers does not take into consideration the fact that a particular gene can influence more than one trait. Nor does he emphasize the multiple functions or consequences of a particular bodily trait or behavior pattern. For example, differences in the average sizes of males and those of females may have a major effect on the breeding structure of the group; but they also can influence patterns of social cooperation, defense against predators, childrearing, and food supply. Although the simple genetic models of inclusive fitness may be useful for didactic illustration, they can be theoretically misleading.

There is much irony in this conclusion. Many of the critics of sociobiology share Marvin Harris's view that the sociobiological frame of reference can be dismissed once it is agreed that "the most important factor in determining human social life is culture rather than genes" (Harris and Wilson 1978). To the contrary, the information coded in the genes and that transmitted by a culture seem to be causally distinct mechanisms for satisfying analogous functions (Masters 1970). The functional patterns underlying natural selection can thus operate in the historical changes in human cultures; although it is genes that are selected in other species, similar processes occur in the evolution of ideas or cultural symbols (Masters 1975). Oddly enough, for example, Harris—one of the leading critics of sociobiology—uses sociobiological variables to explain many differences between human cultures (Harris 1977).

In other words, Trivers's approach is a functional analysis of the way consequences of behavior influence future social development, and need not be viewed as genetically reductionist theory. There is no reason to treat genetic mechanisms as the sole agents of the evolutionary adaptations described by Trivers. Hence there is plenty of room for nonreductionist factors and explanations, consistent with, albeit sometimes modifying, the inclusive-fitness model discussed previously (for example, Hartung 1976). Conversely, the attempt to convert sociobiology into a rigorously reductionist interpretation of complex systems will continue to attract deserved criticism, for reductionism of this sort is biologically improbable (Barkow 1978; Masters 1979).

Determinism. A related claim often made by overly optimistic sociobiologists, and typically rejected by critics, concerns the search for a deterministic model of social systems. It could be argued that even if one includes individually learned as well as genetic causes of behavior, the theory of inclusive fitness leads to a deterministic solution of the mixtures of traits in a population. If this were so, sociobiology would lead to an unambiguous, predictive theory, perhaps even making possible the improved design of a human culture.

It is not hard to see why such an implication generates considerable hostility. One thinks immediately of Huxley's *Brave New World* or Orwell's *1984*. Combined with the fears generated by new biomedical technologies like cloning, recombinant DNA, and the fabrication of interspecies chimeras, the pretension to achieve a perfect society through total genetic and behavioral control no longer appears merely fictional. Insofar as sociobiology lends credence to this danger, it too seems untenable.

As a matter of fact as well as of theory, biological analysis of social systems is not necessarily—nor even typically—determinist. In the first place, the image of the natural sciences as determinist is a curious relic of nineteenth-century optimism; in physics as in biology, recent research has led to the general abandonment of deterministic theories in favor of probabilistic ones (Capra 1975). Second, a probabilistic approach is particularly necessary in the study of animal populations, especially if they reproduce sexually; as population genetics has shown, the presence of genes in a population is hardly an all-or-nothing factor, since selection operates on the entire gene pool as well as on component organisms (Mayr 1978; Wright 1978).

I will return to this last point. But since many biologists reject Trivers's view of population genetics, for the moment it will suffice to say that rigorously deterministic models appear only to describe large systems or long time series. This is, of course, the characteristic of most probabilistic phenomena: reliable predictions can be made only for aggregates over time, not for single events. But when social scientists think of a deterministic or causal model, they have in mind a physical system that is *not* probabilistic in this way. Hence the attribution of determinist prediction to sociobiology is as misleading as the claim of genetic reductionism.

Paradoxically enough, rigorous determinism is unlikely in biological phenomena precisely because evolutionary trends so often lead to *"over*determination." This concept was used by Freud, of course, to describe how a given set of symptoms could simultaneously result from more than one "cause," even though each causal configuration might be capable of producing the symptoms independently. Much the same redundancy can be found in the genetic code, leading Waddington (1953) to speak of "buffering" or "channelized selection." Yet whenever more than one causal mechanism emerges to guarantee the performance of a given behavior (particularly if it is truly essential), these mechanisms can be subject to independent evolution (Masters 1975).[5] Hence it is particularly difficult to arrive at simple deterministic models in evolution.

The same conclusion could arise from the study of population genetics. In this field, the parameters and variables influencing the evolution of a population are quantified. Although some of the resulting systems of equations have unambiguous solutions, others are intrinsically unstable—oscillating over long time periods, for example, or exhibiting unexpected responses to small changes in a key variable. Nothing in population genetics guarantees, *in principle,* a deterministic outcome for an entire ecological system. Sociobiology cannot emancipate itself from these characteristics of population genetics, for the concept of inclusive fitness concerns one element in the system of equations describing the evolution of species.

Note that here, again, the limitation arises from exaggerated claims for sociobiological theory, not from the theory itself. As Trivers's discussion of "human reciprocal altruism" (1971, pp. 45-54) and "sexual plasticity" (1972, p. 146) illustrates, a biological approach to human behavior can be presented in a probabilistic and nondeterministic form. Just as biologists are generally aware of the unpredictability of future evolutionary trends, inclusive-fitness theories can hardly lead to an ambiguous specification of the next stages of human history. Indeed, one of the most extraordinary achievements of modern biology is that it shows how chance events and necessary causes combine, in complex systems, to produce living populations whose behavior is at least comprehensible.

Theoretical Exclusivity. A third exaggeration in the claims made for sociobiology arises from the implication that all contrary theories are replaced or contradicted by the calculus of inclusive fitness. Trivers implies such a claim when insisting that "Darwinian reasoning properly applied centers on the individual, or . . . on genes within individuals" (1977, p. 1; 1978, p.8). In attacking the notion that natural selection concerns the extent to which an attribute "is good for the species or some unit larger than the individual" (1977, p. 11; 1978, p.8), Trivers apparently treats his theoretical model as generally applicable, to the exclusion of others.

Once again, this is a strategy that one might expect in terms of inclusive-fitness theory itself. If ideas—or, as Dawkins (1976) calls them, "memes"—evolve in ways analogous to the evolution of genes, then the propagation of an idea would only be enhanced by the impression that it makes alternative ideas irrelevant. An idea that simply replaces a wide variety of other ideas is more advantageous to those who choose to adopt it; hence individuals seeking to influence the development of scientific theory often tend to exaggerate the claims of their own perspective.

However great the explanatory power of inclusive-fitness theory, it need not follow that other approaches are thereby rendered obsolete or redundant. On the contrary, there is a good deal of evidence that other evolutionary processes operate simultaneously, so that the selective advantage of individual genes is not the only factor involved in biological adaptation. For example, Trivers emphasizes "reciprocal altruism" and "kin selection" as possible models that might explain cooperative behaviors, thereby rejecting "group selection" (that is, natural selection as it applies directly to an entire population). Yet evidence in favor of inclusive fitness as the explanation of altruism need not exclude selection at the level of groups or populations, at least in some specialized contexts (see Alexander 1974, pp. 376-377).

Critics sometimes express this difficulty by saying that inclusive-fitness theories are tautological. That is, sociobiologists seem to begin by describing a behavior and devising a calculus of cost and benefit that might justify the behavior as a means of increasing an individual's "inclusive fitness." Then these reasons are stated as causes or sources of the behavior, even though the actual process of reasoning was just the reverse.

This criticism is to some extent unfair, since empirical test of inclusive-fitness theories are not subject to the charge of tautological reasoning. Nonetheless, the critics have a point. All too often one finds that inclusive-fitness theories are couched in terms like "may," "might," "would," or "could." Frequently a behavior pattern is treated as though it could be isolated from other elements in an ongoing social structure, although in practice this is not feasible. Above all, inclusive-fitness theorists typically stress the genetic *differences* between organisms, rather than the genetic traits that members of a species *share*.[6]

To see the precise bearing of this point, it will be necessary to turn to two technical issues that constitute the major substantive limitations to Trivers's approach. Claims that inclusive fitness makes possible a reductionist, determinist, or exclusive explanation of complex behavior can be attributed to exaggeration. But the sociobiological approach in question also has several shortcomings, even when it is formulated in more cautious and responsible terms.

The Population and the Species as Units of Evolution

Trivers's analysis assumes that the individual is the essential, if not the only, unit on which natural selection operates. Or, to be more precise, Trivers treats the selective process solely in terms of its differential effect on individual genes. At most, he views a constellation of genes influencing a single trait as the element that determines whether an individual is or is not at a selective "advantage."

There is no question, of course, that Darwinian natural selection operates in this way. The issue is whether it operates *only* in this way, and here the answer is in the negative. As Ernst Mayr has pointed out, evolutionary processes exist at the level of entire species:

> Uniquely different individuals are organized into interbreeding populations and into species. All the members are "parts" of the species, since they are derived from and contribute to a single gene pool. The population or species as a whole is itself the "individual" that undergoes evolution; it is not a class with members. [Mayr 1978, p. 52]

To show the implications of Mayr's remarks, it is useful to consider several evolutionary concepts that Trivers tends to underemphasize: environmental variability, the gene pool as a coordinated system, and extinction. When the relevance of each of these concepts is assessed, it will become apparent that Trivers's approach has a more limited applicability than he himself has admitted.

Environmental Variability. Being a good biologist, Trivers is of course aware that species evolve in environments, and that these environments are subject to change. He does not, however, stress the extent to which environmental variability can operate as a means of selection on entire populations, *without reference to differences between individuals in the group.* Assuming that members of a local population share most of their genes and that different local populations face different microenvironments, there is no reason that divergences should not occur between local populations (provided that their breeding structure results in their relative isolation from each other).

There are, of course, many situations in which these conditions do not arise. In such situations, "group selection" is not expected. But population geneticists have carefully worked out the equations describing situations in which group selection *can* occur as a response to environmental variation (Wilson 1975, chap. 5). In such circumstances, natural selection cannot be simply "reduced" to calculations of individual inclusive fitness, for the relevant selection forces operate on *all* members of a population simultaneously. To take an extreme but important example, the late Mesozoic "was a time of worldwide faunal extinctions" associated with a major climatic change (McLean 1978). Sociobiologists like Trivers tend to ignore this level of evolution, on which entire populations and species compete for scarce ecological resources.

This point is far from trivial, even though environmental variability only results in "interdemic" or "group selection" under rare conditions. Some evolutionary theorists believe that it is precisely these unusual conditions that give rise to new species and genera. As Gould (1977) has persuasively argued, the evidence does not confirm the assumption that the differentiation of species is always due to incremental structural mutation. On the contrary, the fossil record is often more consistent with a picture of apparently sudden or discontinuous changes, especially in response to environmental variability.

But even if the evolution of a single species or genus, through time, could be entirely deduced from inclusive-fitness theory, there would remain a higher level of analysis that could not be so explained. "The coevolution of species within ecosystems gives rise to interesting patterns in the total number of species found in a given area, in their relative abundances and in the overall structure of the local food web" (May 1978, p. 161). At this level, "trends in numbers of species are correlated with geographic variation in climactic measures"; for example, "species densities of vertebrates in North America increase toward lower latitudes; those of Australian vertebrates generally do not" (Schall and Pianka 1978, p. 685). In comparing the evolution of ecosystems, the species is—as Mayr put it (1978, p. 52)—an "individual."

A comprehensive theory of population genetics must therefore be complex, including processes that operate on the various levels of individuals, of local populations, of entire species, and of ecosystems. In concluding his monumental four-volume treatise, *Evolution and the Genetics of Populations,* Sewall Wright put it this way:

Finally, natural selection occurs not only among genes (against mutability), among individuals, and among local populations, but also among species of different higher categories that compete for the same ecological niche. This does not affect the course of transformation among the species themselves but has had an enormous effect on the course of the living world as a whole. The successful species have tended to give rise to multiple daughter species, sometimes involving extensive adaptive radiation and occasionally the origin of new higher categories, while the unsuccessful ones and often the higher categories to which they belong, become extinct or nearly so. It was noted that about 98% of the current families of vertebrates (some 40,000 species) probably trace to only eight of the many thousands of species that presumably lived at the beginning of the Mesozoic, and that only about two dozen of the latter have left any descendents at all.

It may be well to note again that all of the diverse results of natural selection are ultimately consequences of ecological opportunities. [Wright 1978, pp. 524-525]

In the short run, of course, one can often assume that major environmental parameters are constant; hence evolutionary processes may appear to operate primarily on individuals. But a general theory must also include other levels of natural selection.

Insofar as relatively sudden shifts in species character cannot be fully explained by selection operating solely on individuals, inclusive-fitness theory needs to be complemented by a consideration of entire species as the relevant breeding unit. In no case would this be more important than for *Homo sapiens,* for the latest work in hominid evolution challenges the assumption of a gradual evolution in a single phyletic line (Kurtèn 1972, Pilbeam 1978). Human beings may therefore be an excellent illustration of the inability to provide a totally adequate account of a species based entirely on a gradualist theory of natural selection on individuals.

The Gene Pool as a System. Trivers's approach to inclusive-fitness theory assumes that one can equate a selective process at a single locus with the selective process at 100 different loci. This argument has been criticized with reference to the biological properties of the individual genome, and it is also questionable at the level of the species as a whole. At least from the theoretical point of view, evolutionary processes exhibit some mathematical properties at the level of the entire gene pool that cannot be simplistically reduced to individual members (Moorhead and Kaplan 1967).

Formal demonstration of this point is beyond my competence and in any event is of little interest to most social scientists. But the practical consequences are extremely important to any theory of human nature. Trivers's approach to inclusive fitness assumes that the individual organism adopts a strategy to maximize the proportion of its genes in succeeding generations (Trivers 1972, p. 146). But many evolutionists have pointed out that one can also speak of an entire species as having a "strategy" of adaptation (Slobodkin 1964; Wilson 1975, pp. 99-100).

Sociobiologists like Trivers might well object that such terminology is mystical. A concrete example might help. In a family vegetable garden, some crops are grown from large seeds (beans, corn, and so on) and others from small ones (lettuce, leeks, carrots, and so on). This difference means that the latter normally require extensive thinning, whereas the former do not. If people stop thinning their vegetables, the long-range consequences of an environmental change may therefore be greater for lettuce than for beans. Even apart from differences in varieties of beans, corn, or lettuce, these characteristics mean that environmental differences can have a distinct kind of impact in various species and genera.

Nowhere is this factor more important than in hominid evolution. Since the breeding structure of a population establishes the probability that any two genotypes will be recombined in sexual reproduction, Trivers's theory of inclusive fitness can hardly take as given the parameters within which individuals mate. For example, the way of life of early hominids—including the size of the social units as well as the prevailing mode of livelihood—necessarily had a significant effect on *how* individuals could maximize inclusive fitness.

Perhaps a concrete example will clarify this point. It has long been thought that the transition to the hominid way of life was, in part, a response to climatic change in Africa; the conventional view holds that, as the forest home of our distant primate ancestors receded, some early hominids ventured out onto the savannah, where small bands adapted to a mixture of hunting, scavenging, and gathering. Bipedal stature, year-round sexual receptivity, and prolonged infant dependency are often related to this transition (Fox 1967).

The most recent findings have added much specificity to this picture. For example, the work of Richard Leakey, Glynn Isaac, and others indicates that early hominids carried tools, or the materials for making them, over considerable distances; combined with data on the distribution of artifacts and fossil remains, this has suggested the importance of food sharing and a probable division of labor at least 2 million years ago (Coppens et al. 1976; Leakey and Lewin 1977; Isaac 1978). The feedback effects of differences in individual traits could well be very strongly influenced by this adaptive "strategy" of the early hominids, since a single male could no longer maximize his inclusive fitness with the behaviors characteristic of the langurs discussed by Trivers (1972, p. 159; 1977, pp. 6-10; 1978, pp. 4-7).[7]

In other words, consideration of the gene pool as an integrated system places Trivers's theory in a different perspective. Inclusive fitness explains the marginal advantage of one individual behavior compared to another; in some contexts, such a marginal advantage can indeed explain an observed trait. But in other situations this logic may be incomplete or misleading. To show this concretely, the example of year-round sexual receptivity in the human female is both convincing and substantively important.

The human female—unlike other primate females—is sexually receptive throughout the year. Although Trivers does not discuss this problem when reviewing the sexual availability of females over time (1972, pp. 159-160), this fact might be explained from the perspective of inclusive-fitness theory: year-round sexual activity would seem to increase the reproductive potential of females, particularly by establishing the possibility of prolonged male interest in the mother-infant dyad. The difficulty, of course, is that if this rationale explains the year-round receptivity of the human female, why does it not function in an analogous way for other primate species? Why is the human reproductive system so different on this point from those of our nearest relatives?

One plausible answer has been suggested by J.N. Spuhler (1976). Reflecting on the continuities and differences between *Homo sapiens* and other primates, Spuhler noted the critical importance of our species' "persistent bipedalism." This trait can be viewed as the result of natural selection in favor of a "greater capacity for endurance running" as a means of taking prey (1976, pp. 3-4).[8] One physiological consequence, however, is that human "men and women have greatly larger thyroid glands, and significantly larger adrenal glands and consequently greater hormone output than in rhesus monkeys and chimpanzees" (1976, p. 7). As a result, the human female has proportionately higher levels of androgens than do other primate females.

Differences in the sexual receptivity of human and primate females seem directly related to the extent to which androgens are "libido hormones." It follows that year-round sexual receptivity could be a secondary result of natural selection in favor of the capacities needed for bipedal hunting in savannah environments:

> Hominids responded to the selective challenge of endurance walking and running in order to take large game animals by developing hypertrophied thyroid and relatively larger adrenal glands. A side effect was the higher degree of continual sexual receptivity in hominid females. [Spuhler 1976, p. 12]

If the capacity to run until one's prey drops from exhaustion is highly adaptive, and if there is no strong countervailing selection against high androgen levels in both sexes, then year-round sexual receptivity could occur without primary reference to sexuality at all.

As this example suggests, the difficulty with Trivers's approach is not that he is completely wrong, but that he focuses on a single variable in dealing with events that are more complex. Inclusive fitness may indeed be an important facet of evolutionary processes in humans as in other species. But other characteristics of populations in their natural environments also must be taken into consideration in the development of a general theory. In particular, one cannot deny that the selective pressures *against* a given trait require as much emphasis as the pressures *for* it.[9] And when we consider the risks of extinction as well as the benefits of adaptation, the theory of inclusive fitness becomes somewhat easier to combine with other components in evolutionary theory.

Extinction: r Selection versus K Selection. If the foregoing argument is valid, Trivers's point of view places insufficient emphasis on changes in the ecological setting that influence entire populations or species. In particular, because Trivers does not treat the gene pool as a system, he fails to see how some populations become extinct and others change very rapidly in response to adaptive "opportunities" (such as a vacant ecological niche). When placed in broader perspective, therefore, Trivers's version of inclusive fitness has to be complemented by other biological processes if we are to have a full picture of neo-Darwinian theory.

This criticism can be stated in terms of contemporary population genetics. In this field, a distinction is made between two variables: r (representing reproductive potential) and K (representing the carrying capacity of the environment). Different species have quite diverse strategies: some maximize r, for example by broadcasting large numbers of young—most of which die before reaching maturity. Others maximize K, for example by limiting the number of viable offspring—each of which receives a high degree of parental "investment."

As Wilson points out, this difference can be analyzed in terms of the degree and kind of environmental threat to the species as a whole. He describes this in terms of a distinction between "r extinction" and "K extinction":

> When populations are more subject to r extinction, altruist traits favored by group selection are likely to be of the "pioneer" variety. They will lead to clustering of the little population, mutual defense against enemies, and cooperative foraging and nest building. The ruling principle will be the maximum *average* survival and fertility of the group as a whole; in other words, the maximization of r. In K selection the opposite is true. The premium is now on "urban qualities" that keep population size below dangerous level. . . . Mutual aid is minimized, and personal restraint in the forms of underutilization of the habitat and birth control comes to the fore. [Wilson 1975, pp. 108-109]

In these terms, Trivers has stressed attributes of species subject to K selection, and underemphasized the properties selected to counter "r extinction."

It may well be that *Homo sapiens* is, in general, a species characterized by greater vulnerability to K extinction than to r extinction (Gould, 1977, pp. 399-404). Simply put, the main problem for most humans has probably been insufficient resource supply for the entire population, rather than a sudden environmental shift providing a new microenvironment open to human habitation. But this general tendency is not a rigid law, and human technology sometimes produces conditions favorable to an "r selection" strategy of higher birth rates and higher individual risk. Colonization is not an unknown phenomenon among humans, and the constraints on other colonizing species (Wilson 1975, pp. 94-95) presumably apply in human history as well.

Trivers's approach, although valid within limits, cannot therefore be taken as a general theory to the exclusion of all other approaches. On the contrary, the strength of inclusive-fitness explanations is increased if they are not treated as universal keys to the explanation of everything. Scientific prudence should lead us to assume that nature is complicated, and that selective processes that operate on entire populations may contradict as well as reinforce adaptations improving individual "inclusive fitness." Far from a resort to mysticism, such a balanced view seems to be the broad thrust of contemporary biology.

Empirical Inadequacies of Inclusive-Fitness Explanations

A final indication of the problem posed by Trivers's approach may be useful. When inclusive-fitness theories have been used to explain social behavior in humans, some of the conclusions are at first striking. But on closer examination, the arguments are not always as conclusive or as narrowly derived from the theory as they first appear. As an example of this difficulty, consider John Hartung's provocative interpretation of the inheritance of wealth in human populations (1976).

Using inclusive-fitness theory, and stressing differences in male and female reproductivity, Hartung concludes that there is a tendency for natural selection to favor inheritance of wealth in the *male* line.[10] Without going into the details of this argument, we can see that Hartung's conclusion has obvious political implications. If patrilineal inheritance is "naturally" favored in our species, then the conception of sexual equality currently endorsed by many would appear to be a mistake.

Hartung's analysis is not marred by some of the criticisms raised in previous sections of this discussion. He makes no claim that the system of inheriting wealth depends directly on genetic causes, suggesting instead that natural selection will tend to operate on cultural variation as well as on genes (with the sole difference that "culturally transmitted behavior is, fortunately, more subject to rapid adaptive change than is genetically transmitted behavior"). Hartung's reasoning is thus neither reductionist nor determinist; on the contrary, he insists specifically that "natural selection, whether operating on culturally or on genetically transmitted behavior, is necessarily and in all cases a quantitative process."

The fundamental issue is rather different. As evidence of his hypothesis, Hartung surveyed the data in Murdock's *Ethnographic Atlas.* He found that:

Of 165 cultures in which it has been determined that rules for inheritance of real property favor either the male or female line, 144 favor the male line and 21 the female. Similarly, for the inheritance of movable property, 176 out of 211 favor the male line and 35 the female. [Hartung 1976, P. 612]

Although he admits the importance of the "deviant" cases, Hartung emphasizes that they depend to a great extent on the existence of three factors: first, a "long" tradition of monogamy "without too much promiscuity or too high a divorce rate"; second, insufficient "heritable wealth to affect reproductive success"; and third, "sexual habits which are not conducive to a high probability of paternity" (that is, habits that make it difficult to identify the father with a high degree of certainty).

It is obvious why the first and third of these conditions are inconsistent with male inheritance. For both parents to improve their "inclusive fitness" by leaving property or wealth to male descendants rather than to females, it is necessary in principle that the male line be identifiable. If there is a high degree of promiscuity and male parents cannot be identified, then the presumed selective advantages do not follow. Conversely, if all adults form monogamous couples, and there is no reproduction outside of marriage, there is little or no selective advantage in patrilinial transmission of wealth. In other words, Hartung's reasoning applies most fully to a society in which a male is likely to inseminate more than one female—but can be identified as the parent of his offspring.

If one turns to the primate literature, which Hartung himself does not do, there is a striking confirmation of his reasoning. In a number of primates, such as rhesus monkeys, it has been found that high social status is to some extent heritable. But the transmission of status is through the *female* (for a review of the literature, see Willhoite 1975). One reason for this seems to be that sexual behavior is relatively promiscuous, with short consortships between males and females—and hence uncertain paternity. It follows that the primates seem to conform to the principle behind Hartung's reasoning, precisely because they do *not* exhibit patrilineal transmission of differential advantages in status and wealth.

A closer look, however, reveals Hartung's reasoning to be incomplete. Consider first the rhesus monkeys who transmit high social status through the female line. In these species, groups are formed in which females and their young remain at the center of the band, along with highly dominant males; subordinate males move to the periphery of the group and often remain there as adults. Both males and females form dominance hierarchies. As a result, the offspring of the high-status female is able to secure his mother's protection, and is far more likely to remain at the center of the band than are the male young of subordinate females.

This structure seems to fit into inclusive-fitness theory, because adult males and females maximize their reproductive potential by favoring the offspring of a high-status female (allowed to remain longer in the core of the band, and thus more likely to become dominant on reaching adulthood). But note that in this social system, there is no "heritable wealth" in the human sense; if mere social status can induce a selective advantage for unilineal descent preferences in rhesus monkeys, then why would the absence of heritable wealth be an independent factor in humans?

Without reference to ecology, moreover, inclusive-fitness theory cannot fully explain why some primates form bands like those of rhesus monkeys, whereas others have very different social structures, ranging from the largely independent behavior of orangutans to the one-male groups of Patas monkeys, Hamadryas baboons, and langurs. Even within individual species, there are often considerable variations in breeding structure as a response to environmental factors. And since the breeding structure determines the "probability of paternity"—that is, the likelihood that the identity of the father is knowable—this variation from group to group cannot be ignored by the theory.

In other words, Hartung's approach does not solve the problem of the supposed tendency of human societies to transmit property and wealth in the male line because, for such a tendency to manifest itself, a number of other factors have to come into play. Inclusive-fitness theories lead us to see how, in some primates, status can be transmitted in the female line; some human societies are, in this respect, probably similar to the rhesus case. Hence Hartung is able to identify one factor that may indeed operate in the inheritance of wealth. But unless one has specified the full range of variables that lead to the evolution of social systems, inclusive fitness is incomplete. And if one has specified all of these variables, the logic of inclusive fitness has no longer explained, *by itself,* all the variation observed.

A number of other criticisms of Hartung's analysis and of similar exercises in inclusive-fitness theory have been raised. But the point should be clear by now. This approach touches on one factor that seems to be relevant to the social systems of evolving species, including our own. But such calculations cannot be taken, in the abstract, as a universal formula that is supposed to explain all the differences between one society and another.

In Hartung's case, for example, it is crucial to know the causes of various kinship systems. Since breeding patterns lead to a difference in the probability that males and females will reproduce—and to different probabilities that the paternal line will be identifiable—no theory of the heritability of wealth can take kinship systems as given. On the contrary, one might as well argue that the causes of human kinship patterns are decisive variables—and that Hartung's complex rationale concerning inclusive fitness is merely a secondary factor.

Even sociobiologists who reject this argument would have to agree that the same theory cannot account for transmission of status in the female line (among rhesus monkeys) and in the male line (in many human societies) without also accounting for the differences between the social structures of rhesus and humans. And since these differences arise in part from the basic "biogrammar" of the species concerned, and in part from the way populations adapt to their environmental setting, it simply will not do to erect inclusive fitness into a universal "law" from which empirical behavior can supposedly be deduced. Sociobiology thus points to the multiplicity of factors needing to be integrated in a general theory of social behavior.

Toward a Return to Natural Right

The foregoing discussion may appear much too technical for most social scientists. This doubtless results from the tendency to academic specialization, a tendency that improves the individual's chances for success at the cost of narrowing scientific breadth and interdisciplinary communication. If we reconsider the Western intellectual tradition, it becomes apparent that such radical specialization of the individual was not always the case. Thinkers as diverse as Aristotle and Rousseau were simultaneously at home in the ethics and biology of their own day (Masters 1978b,c). Consistent with this tradition, what are the human implications of the claims and limits of Trivers's theory of inclusive fitness?

On the other hand, it would seem that the potential for competitive rivalry between individuals or kin groups is very much a natural characteristic of our species. The intellectual tradition of the pre-Socratics, as well as the social-contract theories of Hobbes, Locke, and Rousseau, thus rest on an aspect of human nature that cannot be ignored. Human selfishness, which the moderns emphasize under the name of the "right to self-preservation," is not merely a cultural artifact, since it has a grounding in the basic processes of natural selection in our species.

On the other hand, however, cooperative behavior is equally fundamental to the species—not only because it increases an individual's reproductive potential ("reciprocal altruism"), but because our species' strategy for survival has apparently stressed social cooperation for several million years (Isaac 1978). In this sense, the tradition of Plato and Aristotle among the ancients, or of Hegel and Marx among the moderns, has an equally solid claim to biological soundness.

Ultimately, therefore, human nature must be seen in terms of balances between contradictory pressures (Chase, in press). We are *not* simple animals, easily described as either "naturally good" or "naturally wicked." Rather, our species has evolved what Trivers aptly calls "a complex psychological system" (1971, p.48) that combines different behavior patterns that are subject to variation within and between groups. In different environments, one can expect to find very different social behaviors. Yet despite this variability there are certain general tendencies or trends that permit one to speak of "human nature."

This way of thinking is hardly new. It suggests the need to combine the two modes of analysis that have dominated Western social science. As Brian Barry (1970) has thoughtfully argued, contemporary theories tend to follow one of two basic approaches: some, inspired by economics, start from a calculus of individual costs and benefits; others, following sociological tradition, insist that society must be treated as a whole. Within sociology itself, C. Wright Mills (1959) made a similar distinction between methods that start from the individual and those that begin from the social aggregate. This same duality can be traced throughout the Western tradition of political thought (Masters 1977).

Trivers's theory of inclusive fitness represents the more individualistic or "economic" pole of thought; his critics often take a more "sociological" group approach. But from the perspective of current biology, neither can be entirely reduced to the other. Hence we would do well to focus on theories that treat human nature in a complex, nonreductionist fashion. Although it is consistent with Trivers's account of human psychology (1971, pp. 47-54), this approach can also be illuminated by the research of critics of sociobiology like Harris (1977).

In the tradition of Western political thought, this means a willingness to take seriously the individualism of the pre-Socratics and Hobbes as well as the group orientation of Plato and Hegel. On another occasion, I have argued that Aristotle is the model of a political thinker who transcended the dichotomy between individualistic and group-oriented social analysis (Masters 1978b). As a careful reading of the *Politics* confirms, Aristotle's approach to human life is strikingly consistent with modern biology. Even those who do not agree must admit that one implication of contemporary sociobiology is inescapable: whereas the fact-value dichotomy has proved relatively sterile, biology is impelling us toward a reconsideration of the ways of life that are "according to nature."

This conclusion will seem doubly paradoxical. On the one hand, it appears that political philosophy—long treated as a humanistic escape from the scientific approach of our age—is consistent with the natural sciences. Indeed, the philosophical tradition is *more* scientific than an apparently empirical approach that totally ignores the biological dimensions of human nature (Wahlke 1979). But on the other hand, philosophers cannot claim that their disciplines are entirely grounded on "humanistic" intuition, without reference to the natural sciences. On the contrary, not only have past political thinkers clearly understood human life in terms of the scientific evidence available to them, but their thought can best be assessed in the light of contemporary science (Masters 1978c).

Many social scientists will respond that the foregoing discussion is more a promise than a demonstration of the compatibility of sociobiology and political theory. But the premature demand for definitive conclusions is unfair. Serious attempts to relate biological and social science, renewing the traditional concern for human nature in the light of contemporary science, have begun only in the last few years.

It may well be, for example, that sociobiology can never show a human behavior to be natural. Rather, this approach seems most useful as a means of defining situations that are *unnatural* to our species. This notion is worth stressing because biological reasoning was for so long erroneously viewed as determinist and reductionist.

The argument here has stressed the probabilistic and nonreductionist character of biology; inclusive fitness concerns the functional analysis of *effects,* not the demonstration of *causes.* But this means that sociobiological theory cannot prove that one and only one pattern of social behavior is "natural" to the human species. On the contrary, for even among primates there are often a variety of social patterns exhibited by a single species.

Sociobiology is thus not likely to be able to prove that there is a single form of human society that is "naturally" preferable in all situations. But theories of inclusive fitness and natural selection can indicate the costs and benefits of alternatives. In particular, such approaches suggest tensions or contradictions that necessarily arise in our species. To cite an example, an ethological study of *Homo sapiens* can readily show that although it is possible for humans to live in large, high-density populations, the consequences will typically include additional strains in a species that lived in relatively small groups for over 3 million years.

The discovery of agriculture made large-scale civilization possible; cities of more than a million human inhabitants obviously *can* exist because they *do* exist. But such social institutions as the highly impersonalized crowd create tensions for our species, because—as Trivers's theory of reciprocal altruism shows—much of our ethical life depends on the ability to identify personally the other actors with whom we come into contact. In this respect, analysis of contemporary life in terms of inclusive fitness can lead to quite radical conclusions.

If human altruism requires the capacity to identify others—and to punish "cheaters" at least some of the time—then impersonal social systems are intrinsically dangerous. The attempt to replace altruistic behavior with bureaucratic control will, from this point of view, necessarily increase the frequency of selfishness. One could find evidence for such a conclusion in the chronic failures of Soviet agriculture or the irrational economic consequences of Hitler's totalitarianism, not to mention the decline of all early forms of high civilization.

It should be emphasized that such applications of sociobiology are not trivial merely because they focus on what is *"un*natural." A better understanding of those social patterns that are *not* consistent with human nature—or that engender extraordinary costs—can provide a salutary guide for public policy and individual happiness. Yet this approach fully recognizes the plasticity of our species, the role of individual or group learning, and the possibility of social change. Indeed, naturalistic standards of judgment could well have salutary consequences precisely because they arise from a nonreductionist and nondeterministic science of social behavior.[11]

Sociobiology thus points toward the revival of a concern for those social and cultural practices that are consistent with human nature. Although this involves reviving a tradition that can be traced to classical philosophers like Aristotle, such applications of recent sociobiology remain to be worked out. But it is already clear that inclusive-fitness theory can be of incalculable importance in improving our understanding of human behavior—provided, of course, that its acceptance rests on a balanced understanding of other evolutionary factors. For the present, therefore, suffice it to say that social scientists have every reason to consider biology with the same seriousness with which past philosophers, from Heraclitus to Rousseau, insisted that one study both "nature" and "human nature."

Notes

1. In addition to these well-known articles, Trivers restated his ideas in a presentation to the Symposium on Sociobiology and Politics organized by the Department of Political Science, Temple University, Philadelphia, Penna. (April 11, 1977). All references to this paper will cite both the verbatim transcript of the lecture (Trivers 1977) and an edited version including selections from Trivers's published papers (Trivers 1978). For an example of Trivers's influence on other sociobiologists, see Dawkins (1978).

2. Wilson's *Sociobiology* (1975) is perhaps the best-known work in this area, although its massive size and forbidding detail may deter the unspecialized reader. Hamilton's paper (1964) is generally recognized as a milestone in the historical development of sociobiology. Barash's solid introduction (1976) can be supplemented by an excellent and brief restatement for a broader audience (1978). Dawkins's work (1976) is somewhat popularized and has been subject to particular criticism (Stent 1977). For a recent summary, see Smith (1978). Alexander's papers (1974, 1975, 1976, 1977, 1978) are exceptionally subtle and thoughtful.

3. For the relation of the pre-Socratics' "individual hedonism" to later forms of political thought, and especially to the modern versions of individual hedonism represented by Hobbes, see Masters (1977).

4. It is often objected that a biological approach to human behavior is

intrinsically reductionist, leading to genetic determinism or worse. Although reasons for rejecting this criticism are suggested later on in this chapter, the grounds for legitimate comparisons between species have been set forth elsewhere in detail (Von Cranach 1976).

5. "Evolutionary increments (or decrements) in the hereditary material occur largely by means of duplications (or deletions) of DNA segments: the duplicated segments can then evolve toward new functions while the preexisting segments retain the original function" (Ayala 1978, p. 59). In addition, it is possible to speak of the "twofold redundancy" of DNA at the level of information coding (Hershey 1968); curiously enough, a similar "redundancy of 50%" has been found in the "distinctive features" of human languages (Gerard, Kluckhohn, and Rapoport 1956).

6. The measure of "relatedness" between organisms used by sociobiologists like Trivers tends to exaggerate genetic differences: "For example, in a diploid species (in the absence of inbreeding) an individual's [relatedness] to his or her full-siblings is 1/2; to half-siblings, 1/4; to children, 1/2; to cousins, 1/8" (Trivers 1974, p. 250). This typical mode of calculation could mislead the unwary reader into presuming that full-siblings have the same genes at 50 percent of their genetic loci, and different alleles at the remaining 50 percent (for example, Barash 1977, p. 86; Wilson 1975, figure 5-9). Such a conclusion is incorrect, as can be seen from Wilson's precise definition: "Designated by r, the coefficient of relationship is the fraction of genes in two individuals *that are identical by descent,* averaged over all loci" (Wilson 1975, p. 74). Genes shared by unrelated members of a population are thus not counted in this statistic. In other words, the coefficient of relatedness is a direct measure not of gene frequences, but of common genetic inheritance—for example, it measures *chromosomes* held in common rather than the actual number of identical *genes.* The "coefficient of relationship" thus minimizes the proportion of genes shared by members of a single species—not to mention those shared by related species. Yet it has been estimated that humans and chimpanzees share more than 99 percent of their genetic material (King and Wilson 1975). Although two unrelated humans are less alike genetically than siblings, they are more alike than a human and a monkey. And as Plato showed long ago, the intellectual quest begins with the realization that the attributes of greater and less can be predicated of the same object (*Republic,* VII.523b-525c).

7. On the langur populations discussed by Trivers, in which peripheral males chase off the previously dominant male and kill the young, see Sugiyama (1967). In another population of langurs, however, this behavior was not observed (Jay 1963). Note, moreover, that langurs are noted for the variability of their social structures (Napier and Napier, 1967, pp. 281-282).

8. In one study of olive baboons, who live in a savannah environment

often compared to that of early hominids, surprisingly frequent predation was observed, "including several instances when males in relays ran down prey" (Strum 1975, p. 687). From the perspective of inclusive-fitness theory, cooperation between male baboons is *not* expected (Smith 1978, p. 184).

9. One example of this point that is of awesome importance for our own species is the evolutionary increase in the size of the human brain. Most discussions of this phenomenon have assumed that larger brain size was an unqualified benefit, without considering the *cost* of this mutation in more difficult childbirth and hence more frequent mortality to mother and/or infant (see Masters 1978a, appendix).

10. Hartung's argument is summarized as follows:

> Greater reproductive variance among males than among females has been presented as a component of natural selection's influence in determining preferential treatment of males in the inheritance of wealth. In conjunction, the transmission of sex chromosomes and the attendant probabilities that ancestor and descendant will have genes identical by descent have been traced for several generations in order to illustrate a male bias in a species whose male sex is heterogametic (XY) while the female sex is homogametic (XX). The effect (direct and additive) of this bias on coefficients of relationship leads to the hypothesis that transmission of wealth along the male line is more efficient, in terms of maximizing ancestral fitness, than transmission along the female line, [Hartung 1976, p. 613].

11. It is not possible to explore this point further in the present context. But one apparently trivial example may indicate how biological analysis can lead to a nonreductionist, "negative" definition of natural rights in terms of what is *un*natural to our species. Excretion is a necessary function in *Homo sapiens*. Yet no one dares assert that, merely because the human child must be toilet trained, urination or defecation are entirely cultural. In some societies these acts are public (for example, ancient Rome); in others they are private. Given the variation in learned taboos, there is clearly not one and only one "normal" way to perform excretion. But it is clearly *un*natural to prevent another human from urinating or defecating. Indeed, this is a particularly vicious form of torture. One can thus say that all humans have a natural right to perform the culturally accepted behaviors associated with excretion, and that any denial of this right is prima facie unethical. Note that it is the cultural variable that is a biological universal, and that such universals can generate negatively defined natural rights constituting the limits of a decent culture.

References

Alexander, R.B. 1974. "The Evolution of Social Behavior," *Annual Review of Ecology and Systematics* 5:325-383.

_____ . 1975. "The Search for a General Theory of Behavior."*Behavioral Science* 20:77-100.

_____ . 1976. "Evolution, Human Behavior, and Determinism." *PSA 1976*. 2:3-21.

_____ . 1977. "Natural Selection and the Analysis of Human Sociality." In *The Changing Scenes in Natural Sciences, 1776-1976*, pp. 283-337. Philadelphia: Academy of Natural Sciences.

_____ . 1978. "Natural Selection and Societal Laws." In *Morals, Science, and Society* edited by T. Engelhardt and D. Callahan, Vol. 3, chap. 7. Hastings-on-Hudson, N.Y.: The Hastings Center.

Alexander, R.D., and Sherman, P.W. 1977. "Local Mate Competition and Parental Investment in Social Insects." *Science* 196:494-500.

Anderson, P.W. 1972. "More Is Different." *Science* 177:393-396.

Ardrey, 1966. *The Territorial Imperative*. New York: Atheneum.

Ayala, F.J. 1978. "The Mechanisms of Evolution." *Scientific American* 239:56-69.

Barash, D. 1977. *Sociobiology and Behavior*. New York: Elsevier.

_____ . 1978. "The New Synthesis." *Wilson Quarterly*, Summer, pp. 82-94.

Barkow, J.H. 1978. "Culture and Sociobiology." *American Anthropologist* 80:5-20.

Barry, B. 1970. *Sociologists, Economists and Democracy*. London: Collier-Macmillan.

Capra, F. 1975. *The Tao of Psysics*. Berkeley, Calif.: Shambala.

Chase, I.D. In press. "Cooperative and Non-cooperative Behavior in Animals." *American Naturalist*.

Coppens, Y.; Howell, F.C.; Isaac, G.L.; and Leakey; R.E.F. 1976. *Earliest Man in the Lake Rudolf Basin*. Chicago: University of Chicago Press.

Dawkins, R. 1976. *The Selfish Gene*. New York: Oxford University Press.

_____ . 1978. Letter: "Are Genes 'Selfish'?" *Hastings Center Report* 8(August):4.

Fox, R. 1967. "In the Beginning: Aspects of Hominid Behavioral Evolution." *Man* September:415-433.

Gerard, R.; Kluckholn, C.; and Rapoport, A. 1956. "Biological and Cultural Evolution: Some Analogies and Explorations." *Behavioral Science* 1:6-34.

Gould, S.J. 1977. *Ontogeny and Phylogeny*. Cambridge, Mass.: Harvard University Press.

Hamilton, W.D. 1964. "The Genetical Theory of Social Behavior," I and II. *Journal of Theoretical Biology* 7:1-52.

Harris, M. 1977. *Cannibals and Kings*. New York: Random House.

Harris, M., and Wilson, E.O. 1978. New York Times, February 26, E-18.

Hartung, J. 1976. "Natural Selection and the Inheritance of Wealth." *Current Anthropology* 17:607-622.

Hirshleifer, J. 1977a. "Economics from a Biological Viewpoint." *Journal of Law and Economics* 20(April):1-52.

_____ . 1977b. "Shakespeare *vs.* Becker on Altruism: The Importance of Having the Last Word." *Journal of Economic Literature* 15:500-502.

_____ . 1978. "Competition, Cooperation, and Conflict in Economics and Biology." *American Economic Review* 68:238-243.

Hershey, A. 1968. "The T4-   Universe." *Carnegie Institution of Washington Year Book.* 67:562-568.

Humphrey, N.K. 1976. "The Function of Intellect." In *Growing Points in Ethology*, edited by P.P.G. Bateson and R.A. Hinde. Cambridge: Cambridge University Press.

Isaac, G.L. 1978. "The Food-sharing Behavior of Protohuman Hominids." *Scientific American* 238(April):90-108.

Jay, P. 1963. "The Indian Langur Monkey (Presbytus entellus)," In *Primate Social Behavior*, edited by C. Southwick, pp. 114-123. Princeton, N.J.: Van Nostrand.

Kant, I. 1938. *The Fundamental Principles of the Metaphysics of Ethics*, translated by O. Manthey-Zorn. New York: Appleton-Century-Crofts.

King, M.C., and Wilson, A.C. 1975. "Evolution at Two Levels in Humans and Chimpanzees." *Science* 188:107-116.

Kurten, B. 1972. *Not from the Apes*. New York: Vintage.

Leakey, R.E., and Lewin, R. 1977. *Origins*. New York: Dutton.

Masters, R.D. 1970. "Genes, Language, and Evolution." *Semiotica* 2:295-320.

_____ . 1975. "Politics as a Biological Phenomenon." *Social Science Information* 14:7-63.

_____ . 1976a. "The Impact of Ethology on Political Science." In *Biology and Politics*, edited by A. Somit, pp. 197-233. The Hague: Mouton.

_____ . 1976b. "Functional Approaches to Analogical Comparisons between Species." In *Methods of Inference from Animal to Human Behavior*, edited by M. Von Cranach, pp. 73-102. The Hague: Mouton.

_____ . 1976c. "Exit, Voice, and Loyalty in Animal and Human Behavior." *Social Science Information* 15:955-978.

_____ . 1977. "Human Nature, Nature, and Political Thought." In *Human Nature in Politics*, edited by R. Pennock and J. Chapman, chap. 3. New York: New York University Press.

_____ . 1978a. "Of Marmots & Men: Human Altruism and Animal Behaviors." In *Altruism, Sympathy, and Helping*, edited by L. Wispe, chap. 3. New York: Academic Press.

_____ . 1978b. "Jean Jacques in Alive and Well: Rousseau and Contemporary Sociobiology." *Daedalus* (Summer), pp. 93-105.

_____ . 1978c. "Classical Political Philosophy and Contemporary Biology." Paper presented at Conference for the Study of Political Thought, Loyola University of Chicago, April 7-9.

_____ . 1979. "Beyond Reductionism: Five Basic Concepts in the Field of Human Ethology." In *Human Ethology: Claims and Limits of a New Discipline*, edited by M. von Cranach. Cambridge: Cambridge University Press.

May, R.M. 1978. "The Evolution of Ecological Systems." *Scientific American* 239(September):161-175.

Mayr, E. 1978. "Evolution." *Scientific American* 239(September):47-55.

McLean, D.M. 1978. "A Terminal Mesozoic 'Greenhouse': Lessons from the Past." *Science* 201:401-406.

Moorhead, P., and Kaplan, M.M., eds. 1967. *Mathematical Challenges to the Neo-Darwinian Interpretation of Evolution*. Philadelphia: Wistar Institute.

Mills, C.W. 1959. *The Sociological Imagination*. New York: Oxford University Press.

Napier, J.R., and Napier, P.H. 1967. *A Handbook of Living Primates*. London: Academic Press.

Pattee, H., ed. 1973. *Hierarchy Theory*. New York: George Barziller.

Pilbeam, D. 1978. "Rearranging Our Family Tree." *Human Nature* 1(June):38-45.

Rousseau, J.J. 1978. *On the Social Contract*, edited by R.D. Masters. New York: St. Martin's Press.

Sahlins, M. 1977. *The Use and Abuse of Sociobiology*. Ann Arbor: University of Michigan Press.

Schall, J.J., and Pianka, E.R. 1978. "Geographical Trends in Numbers of Species." *Science* 201(25 August):679-686.

Simpson, G.G. 1969. *Biology and Man*. New York: Harcourt, Brace, Jovanovich.

Slobodkin, L. 1964. "The Strategy of Evolution." *American Scientist* 52:342-357.

Smith, J.M. 1978. "The Evolution of Behavior." *Scientific American* 239 (September):176-192.

Spuhler, J.N. 1976. "Continuities and Discontinuities in Anthropoid-Hominid Behavioral Evolution: Bipedal Locomotion and Sexual Receptivity." Paper presented at 75th Annual Meeting, American Anthropological Association, November 20.

Stent, G.S. 1977. "You Can Take the Altruism But You Can't Take the Altruism Out of Ethics." *Hastings Center Report* 7(December):33-36.

Strum, S.C. 1975. "Life with the Pumphouse Gang." *National Geographic Magazine* 147(May):687.

Sugiyama, Y. 1967. "Social Organization of Hanuman Langurs." In *Social Communication among Primates*, edited by S. Altmann, pp. 221-236. Chicago: University of Chicago Press.

Trivers, R. 1971. "The Evolution of Reciprocal Altruism." *Quarterly Review of Biology*, 46:35-57.

——— . 1972. "Parental Investment and Sexual Selection," in *Sexual Selection and the Descent of Man*, edited by B. Campbell, pp. 136-179. Chicago, Aldine.

——— . 1974. "Parent-Offspring Conflict." *American Zoologist* 14:249-264.

——— . 1977. "Sociobiology and Politics," verbatum transciption of lecture at Symposium on Sociobiology and Politics (Department of Political Science, Temple University, Philadelphia, Pa.), April 11.

——— . 1978. "Sociobiology and Politics," edited text with excerpts from published papers (Department of Political Science, Temple University, Philadelphia, Pa.)

Tullock, G. 1978. "Altruism, Malice, and Public Goods." *Journal of Biological and Social Structures* 1:1-9.

von Cranach, M., ed. 1976. *Methods of Inference from Animal to Human Behavior*. The Hague: Mouton.

von Cranach, M.; Foppa, K.; Lepenies, W.; and Loog, P., eds. 1979. *Human Ethology: Claims and Limits of a New Discipline*. Cambridge: Cambridge University Press.

Waddington, D.H. 1953. "The Evolution of Adaptations." *Endeavor* 12(July):134-139.

Wahlke, J. 1979. "Pre-Behavioralism in Political Science." *American Political Science Review* 73:9-32.

White, N., ed., 1974. *Ethology and Psychiatry*. Toronto: University of Toronto Press.

Willhoite, F. 1975. "Equal Opportunity and Primate Particularism." *Journal of Politics* 37:270-276.

——— . 1978. "Rank and Reciprocity: Notes Toward a Sociobiological Political Theory." Paper presented at Conference for the Study of Political Thought, Political Theory and the Question of Human Nature. Chicago, April 7-9.

Wilson, E.O. 1975. *Sociobiology*. Cambridge, Mass.: Harvard University Press.

Wright, S. 1978. *Evolution and the Genetics of Populations*, vol. 4: *Variability Within and Among Natural Populations*. Chicago: University of Chicago Press.

5 Human Nature as the Central Issue in Political Philosophy

Albert Somit

Human Nature: The Convergence of Sociobiology, Ethology, and Political Philosophy

The basic objective of ethology and sociobiology, as we all know, is to explain the "nature of human nature"—what is, how and why it got that way, and the degree to which we can realistically hope to control or change it. What is sometimes not so readily grasped, even by political scientists, is that these same questions, slightly restated, have constituted the central core of political speculation from Plato to the present.

In this chapter I will attempt to show how different conceptions of the nature of "political man" almost invariably provide the point of departure for competing political philosophies and profoundly varying interpretations of political phenomena. The nature of human nature, as manifested in political behavior, is thus a matter of critical importance to political science in general and political philosophy in particular.

The study of politics is the study of political man. At the micropolitical level, party policies are made by a relative handful of leaders rather than by the collective membership; executive, legislative, and judicial decisions reflect the choices of individual executives, legislators, and judges; elections turn on the preferences of individual voters; and bureaucracies, the suspicions of their clients notwithstanding, are run by people, not by automatons. At the macropolitical level, people, not "states," make and execute foreign policy. As the careers of Roosevelt, Churchill, Stalin, De Gaulle, and Hitler demonstrated, a nation's destiny can be profoundly influenced by the beliefs and character, not to mention the eccentricities, of those who occupy high office.

The human factor, to be sure, is not the only one involved. Social and political institutions affect, subtly or otherwise, the behavior of their members. The structure of the political system may make some decisions, however unwise, relatively easy and attractive while rendering others, however sound, difficult and hazardous. Past events may seriously limit present options. Consequently, political phenomena cannot and should not be reduced to a matter of individual or collective psychology. They are much better understood as the outcome of a complex interplay of psychological forces, ideological commitments, institutional and systemic factors, history, immediate circumstances—and sheer chance.

Still, in the final analysis, political behavior is *human* behavior. Only human beings are political actors. Other forces and factors enter into the political process only as they are perceived by, or act on, people. Human nature thus constitutes the grist for the political mill. What emerges from the mill as political behavior is substantially a function of the quality and limitations of this human material. It is not surprising, then, that "the nature of political man" has long been a major bone of contention among those concerned with political phenomena.

The issue, indeed, cuts across several aspects of political science. First, our conception of human nature has a direct bearing on the way in which we perceive and account for political actions, a nexus that finds classical expression in Machiavelli. Those who wish to understand politics, wrote the great Florentine in his *Discourses on the First Ten Books of Titus Levius*, must start with the realization that

> . . . all men are bad and ever ready to display their vicious nature. . . . If their evil disposition remains concealed for a time, it must be attributed to some unknown reason; and we must assume that it lacked occasion to show itself; but time . . . does not fail to bring it to light.

Just as did Machiavelli, so do contemporary political scientists build a number of assumptions about human nature into their models. Too often, however, these assumptions are implicit rather than explicit; their implications for other aspects of the conceptualization have not been fully considered; and they take little cognizance of recent work in psychology and biology. As John Wahlke (1979, p. 24) has argued in his American Political Science Association presidential address, the discipline is unlikely to develop a very powerful body of explanatory theory until it handles the question of political man in a more satisfactory fashion.

Second, competing views of human nature, translated into ideological positions, generate much of the phenomena with which political science is concerned. The differences between, or among, the various ideologies for which endless political battles have been fought, and on behalf of which countless millions have died within the past two centuries alone, in large part spring from divergent conceptions of human nature. To the degree, then, that ideologies motivate human behavior, these rival views of *homo politicus* literally make history. To explain how and why this happens is, of course, one of our major objectives.

Third, in almost every field of political science there are consistently recurring patterns of behavior for which the nature of the human animal is proferred as a plausible, if not necessarily correct, explanation. Warfare, undoubtedly the most serious threat to our continued survival as a species, affords the most obvious case in point—but by no means the only one. Students of urban affairs, alarmed by increasing manifestations of violence and aggressive behavior, speculate that these may spring in part from the growing difficulties encountered in adjusting to the pressures of urban existence by members of a species ". . . programmed for survival in a group of nomadic hunter-gatherers living on the African savannas . . ." (Reynolds 1976, p. 157). As specialists in parties and organizational behavior are aware, the regular emergence of self-serving factions and cliques within a bureaucracy or a party seems to conform almost to an iron law of human behavior for which a genetic basis has often been suggested. There is no need to belabor the point: wherever we turn in political science, there is almost an irresistible tendency to account for "undesirable" behavior (that is, behavior that is seen as essentially counterproductive for the general system) by recourse to some theory of innate tendency.

Fourth, and most important from the vantage point of this chapter, is the centrality of human nature for political philosophy. The history of Western political thought could readily be written in terms of the various stands taken on this question. A philosopher's approach to the nature of political man has a direct bearing on his treatment of almost every major issue, ranging from the origin of the state to his conception of the "ideal" political society. The concept of human nature is so pivotal, moreover, that the manner in which a political philosopher handles any one of these questions is often a reliable clue to his stance on the others. In this chapter I will attempt to illustrate this twofold relationship.

Since the broader concerns of ethology and sociobiology overlap those of political philosophy, research in these fields may well have, or can be apprehended to have, far-reaching political implications—especially during a period of great ideological sensitivity. The violent reactions elicited by the attempt to study the possible genetic bases of human behavior, let alone to any findings resulting from that study, spring as much from ideological as from scientific opposition to the undertaking. For this reason, I have drawn my illustrations, wherever possible, from the "great" political philosophers rahter than from the more contemporary, and likely more controversial, political ideologies. But the "fit" is the same in both cases. Ideology, no less than political philosophy (and the line is by no means easy to draw), rests on an underlying, if not always articulated, conception of human nature. Marxists, to take an obvious example, might find it quite difficult to accommodate their doctrine to unambiguous biological evidence that human genetic programming makes human beings unlikely prospects for life in a "classless" society.

The Nature of Political Man: A Historical Overview

"Man," said Aristotle," is by nature a political animal," a concept which, restated by Aquinas, became an integral aspect of Catholic political thought. On the other hand, a distinguished contemporary political scientist (Dahl 1965, p. 81) maintains that, "if we must have an axiom, then it would probably be healthier to assume that man is not by nature a political animal." The quarrel, like so many others in political science, may be more apparent than real. Aristotle certainly did not believe that a person emerged from the womb fully prepared for citizenship and, if we may presume to speak for him, would probably have found nothing exceptional in Dahl's thesis that a lengthy period of "political socialization" is needed in order for *Homo sapiens* to become *Homo politicus*.[1]

Still, to agree that man is (potentially) a political animal advances our knowledge very little unless we have some consensus as to what that term connotes. Here, political science lags far behind economics. At least for analytic purposes, most economists have agreed to agree on the impelling motives and psychological attributes of that otherwise mythic entity, *economic man*. From these traits—a single-minded pursuit of gain, dedicated self-interest, and decisions made fundamentally in terms of material gain and loss, to mention the more endearing—they have developed the most sophisticated and rigorous body of theory in the social sciences. Political scientists, on the other hand, have yet to arrive at a common understanding of *political man*. Much of political philosophy has been, and continues to be, devoted to arguing such basic questions as: "Are men good or evil?" "Are men basically selfish or essentially altruistic?" "Are men fundamentally equal or unequal in their capacity to govern themselves?" and, of course: "To what degree can we modify existing patterns of political behavior by changing the social and political environment?"

These have been key issues in Western political speculation for almost twenty-five centuries; in fact, the major schools of thought can be discerned by the close of Roman times and had pretty much crystallized by the end of the seventeenth century. Subsequent contributions have served primarily to elaborate on or refine previously established positions. The controversies remained unresolved for a very simple reason: advocates of almost any given viewpoint could find historical support for almost any conception of political man—good, bad, or indifferent. Even where the bulk of the evidence seemed to point in a contrary direction, it was easy enough to insist that the particular kind of human nature postulated *did* exist but that it had simply been corrupted or repressed by society. Post-sixteenth-century efforts to draw inferences about "natural" political man from studies of newly discovered American, African, or Pacific peoples also proved fruitless,

since most of these societies had a history that equalled, or in many instances actually antedated, that of their European brethren. The political
structure of primitive societies, Western students reluctantly realized, was
anything but "natural."

Not until well into the twentieth century were social scientists able to advance beyond a priori argument and finally bring to bear something akin to
scientific data. These contributions came first from psychology and more
recently from biology, ethology, and sociobiology. To be sure, the old
issues have by no means been resolved. Nonetheless, the frontiers of
ethological and sociobiological knowledge have advanced sufficiently to
warrant the hope that, if this is not the beginning of the end, then we are at
least approaching the end of the beginning. The irony is that the mere
possibility of being able to do more than debate these questions has vastly
perturbed many of those who previously had been enthusiastic parties to the
debate itself.

This brief overview accomplished, we can proceed to review some of the
key issues traditionally discussed by political philosophy under this general
heading. As previously mentioned, the answers have implications far
beyond the particular point being controverted.

Political Man: Good or Evil, Self-Centered
or Altruistic?

Simplistic and naive though these dichotomies appear, they state what is
perhaps the single most important issue in political thought. The position
we take colors no less than it reflects our understanding of the way political
man has acted in the past and is likely to act in the future. It also tends to
preclude other responses to a variety of questions ranging from the origin of
the state to the rights of the individual.

Nowhere are these interconnections more strikingly manifest than in the
writings of the two great English seventeenth-century "contract" theorists,
Thomas Hobbes and John Locke.[2] Both used as a springboard the idea of a
"state of nature"—that is, that time in human history before political society (the state) came into being. Both set themselves the same fourfold task:
to describe the quality of life in the state of nature; to explain why this was
so; to account for man's decision to enter into formal political society; and
to draw from this pseudohistorical reconstruction conclusions conceivably
relevant to the political issues of their own day. That they arrived at
philosophical and political antipodes stems largely from their fundamental
disagreement on the morality—or amorality—of political man.

Hobbes gave classic expression to a conception of human nature that
can be traced through Machiavelli all the way back to the Greek Sophists.

For Hobbes, in the *Leviathan* (chap. 11), the basic human motivation was a "perpetual and restless desire of power after power that ceaseth only in death."[3] Starting from this premise, he drew a remarkably unappetizing picture of existence in the state of nature. Men being what they were, he declared, in an extraordinarily pungent phrase, life could only have been "nasty, brutish, and short." But if they were brutish and power hungry, they were also cunning—cunning enough to realize that the only way to ensure the security of their own lives and property was to create some entity capable of maintaining law and order. To protect themselves against themselves, then, they joined together in a "covenant" whereby they voluntarily left the state of nature and entered into political society. So originated the state.

Having derived political society from the selfish—to put it charitably—traits of human beings, Hobbes pushed his argument to its logical conclusion. Those who drafted the original contract (covenant) were aware that, given human nature, there would be chaos in any sphere of human affairs that was left unregulated. They therefore turned the task of governance over to a state of such sweeping and awesome power that it well merited Hobbe's descriptive term, Leviathan. Of necessity endowed with almost unlimited authority, the state literally cannot exceed its proper bounds. And if Leviathan cannot overstep its powers, then there could hardly be any lawful right of revolution. Faced with what he saw as a choice between absolutism and anarchy, Hobbes endorsed the former.

We see the consequences of starting with a more benign view of human nature when we turn to Locke's version of events. He, too, postulates a prepolitical state of nature, but one that has little resemblance to that described by Hobbes. It was, rather, "a state of peace, good-will, mutual assistance, and preservation . . ." (*Second Treatise*, par. 9; see Ashcroft 1968, pp. 898-915). Why would people ever choose to leave so idyllic a condition? Locke has a ready answer. Although life in the state of nature was ordinarily peaceful and secure, there were occasional disagreements, usually about the ownership of property. Aware that only an impartial adjudicator could equitably resolve these disputes, men contracted together to create such an entity, the state. Given the sterling qualities of human nature, relatively little in the way of political control was needed and the contract accordingly limited the state to the task of securing "life, liberty, and property." Should these limited powers be exceeded, then the contract was breached, and revolution was morally and legally justified. The choice, Locke insisted, was between freedom and depotism, not absolutism and anarchy.

The difference between Hobbes and Locke mirrors a deep-seated division that runs through both formal political philosophy and the ideologies that derive their doctrinal substance from those philosophies. Democratic thought, drawing heavily on Locke, his predecessors, and his successors, presupposes an essentially "good" political man—or one capable of becoming good. In contrast, authoritarian ideologies postulate, as did Hobbes and those who came before and after him, an essentially "evil" human nature—or one that would quickly become so if freed of political restraint. To be sure, these are not absolutely necessary assumptions: it is logically possible, by a somewhat convoluted and ideologically unappealing line of reasoning, to defend democracy without arguing that people are essentially good, and to justify authoritarianism without insisting that they are basically bad. The fact remains, nonetheless, that democratic theory usually proceeds from the former premise, authoritarian doctrine from the latter.

Political Man: Equal or Unequal?

Here some terminological underbrush must first be cleared away. The concept of equality has at least three meanings, and acceptance of one carries no necessary commitment with regard to the others. First, there is the kind of equality that Jefferson had in mind when he wrote that "all men . . . are endowed by their Creator with certain inalienable rights; that among these are life, liberty, and the pursuit of happiness." With few exceptions (German National Socialism immediately comes to mind), Western political philosophers agree that all men are equal before what the Stoics called "eternal law," what Deists call God, and what Jefferson called the "laws of nature and of Nature's God." They also agree that, both historically and in our own day, we have yet to solve the problem of translating this moral and legal equality into satisfactorily tangible reality.

A second usage looks to the distribution of ability, wisdom, and knowledge among people. In the abstract, at least, less disagreement might be expected. If few theorists accept Aristotle's dictum that "some men are by nature free, and others slaves, and that for these latter slavery is both expedient and right," equally few share Cicero's conviction that "no single thing is so like another, so exactly its counterpart, as all of us are to one another." Most disagreements on this point tend to center less on the fact of unequal intellectual ability, and other such factors than on the causes of such differences and the extent to which they might be minimized, if not eliminated entirely, by a better educational system or a more equitable social system.

Once *some* degree of "operational" human inequality is conceded, and even the most staunchly egalitarian make this concession, the critical question arises: are people so disparate in political talent that the more able minority has a rightful (moral) claim to rule over the majority? Or, to restate the question: do the many have sufficient political acumen, individually or collectively, to justify granting them a determining voice, direct or indirect, in the formulation of public policy? On this point, democratic and anti-democratic ideologies part company.

Antiegalitarian theory has the longer and, it must be conceded, philosophically more distinguished history. The prototypic case for rule by the few is stated in Plato's *Republic*. Men (and women), he argues, can be classified into three categories (philosopher-kings, warriors, and workers) on the basis of their innate psychological makeup and intellectual powers. Only a tiny minority, the philosopher-kings, are capable of mastering true wisdom; only the truly wise should rule; ergo, all power should be vested in the philosopher-kings. Other writers have since rung changes on the theme, but the basic contention remains the same. Perhaps the only significant addition has been the complementary thesis, advanced by Machiavelli, Burke, Carlyle, and Neitzsche, among others, that the masses actually do not want political responsibility and are happier when they can unthinkingly obey their betters.

Democratic theory, on the other hand, is of relatively recent origin. In fact, one is hard pressed to identify a single truly satisfactory exposition of the idea that the great majority of people are capable of wisely governing themselves. Pericles' *Funeral Oration*, often cited, was more a eulogy of Athenian political genius than a reasoned defense of democracy. Aristotle, critical of Plato's elitism, conceded that "the cook is not always the best judge of the feast" but himself preferred to limit political participation to the propertied classes. Cicero, arguing the quality of men, fell back on the fatal qualifying phrase ". . . if bad habits and false beliefs did not twist the weaker minds. . . ." Centuries later, the struggles among and between the popes, emperors, kings, nobles, and higher clergy produced staunch defenses of *representative* government; but all these espoused the claims of particular minorities, rather than of the masses. Even Calvin and Luther, radical as they might have been on religious issues, rejected any notion of vox populi, vox dei—although generally extending to all, regardless of class, the right to religious martyrdom.

Something akin to a notion of popular democracy was voiced by the seventeenth-century Levellers, although in their literature the demand for political equality is simply enunciated rather than justified. As for the contract theorists, Locke's *Second Treatise* hardly looked to universal suffrage, whereas Rousseau was careful to distinguish between the "general will" and the will of the majority. In the New World, the compacts and other civic testaments of the founders almost invariably made political rights contingent on property; and Jefferson, believing in a "natural aristocracy of wealth and talent," was hardly an advocate of one man, one vote.[4] Surprising though it may be, the first carefully reasoned justification of democracy is found in J.S. Mill's *Representative Government*—and Mill, with characteristic honesty, supports it as the system most conducive to the development of human character, not because of its wisdom or efficiency.

Needless to say, the nineteenth-century demand for a vastly expanded suffrage did not wait on the formulation of an intellectually coherent defense of popular government. Nor did it need to; as suggested previously, a suitable substitute was already at hand. Starting with the ideas of Marsiglio of Padua and Nicolas of Cusa, the basic tenets of a theory of representative government had already been fashioned during earlier efforts, in church and state alike, to secure for the well born, the wise, and the wealthy a greater share of the political authority exercised by monarchs and in previous centuries claimed, with varying degrees of success, by the papacy as well. The ideologues and politicians of the French Revolution, of British Chartism, and of Jacksonian democracy simply carried this idea to its logical conclusion by broadening the right of representation from class to mass. If the argument left something to be desired by purely philosophical standards, it was nonetheless remarkably efficacious as an instrument of popular propaganda.

A third conception of equality is concerned less with intelligence than with the capacity to make rational political decisions. In this sense, "rational" means decisions that are informed and carefully reasoned and that, above all, look to the long-term well-being of the body politic as a whole, rather than only to short-run consequences and/or the special interest(s) of some group(s) within the society. Democratically inclined doctrine, starting with the Roman Stoics and running through Aquinas, Sidney, Rousseau, the Mills, evolutionary socialism, and twentieth-century liberalism, holds that political man is by nature (aided, it is often stipulated, by some process of education yet to be devised) capable of consistently acting in such a fashion. The authoritarian tradition, from Plato, the Epicureans, Machiavelli, Filmer, Hume, Bossuet, Burke, Coleridge, fascism, and—operationally—Stalinist Marxism, insists that only a small minority are capable of manifesting any meaningful degree of political rationality, as defined here. It holds, consequently, that whatever the outward trappings of popular participation, real political power should be wielded by the relative few truly qualified to do so.

Human Nature: Malleable or Fixed?

Neither the practical nor the philosophical implications of this issue require lengthy explication. It is, however, perhaps the question to which the others eventually return. One can concede all types of shortcomings to political man *if* these can be attributed to an imperfect environment and/or education, rather than to any genetically influenced or otherwise innate aspect of human nature. Alternatively, one may comfortably confess to defects in the existing social order if these can be attributed to humankind's inherent and ineluctable behavioral tendencies.

The beliefs that human nature is essentially constant over the ages, and that political, social, and economic institutions reflect rather than shape the basic characteristics of human nature, usually go hand in hand. If these two propositions are accepted, it follows that at any given time the status quo pretty well marks the limits of what is politically, socially, and economically practicable. Consequently, any effort to change society radically flies in the face of human nature and is utopian, in the pejorative sense. Quite different conclusions follow when one insists that human nature is not really fixed and that, in the final analysis, it is determined by, rather than determinant of, culture and society. Should this be the case, the present order and its institutions have neither any necessary permanency nor any necessary inherent value. They can be regarded, in fact, as perverting rather than reflecting human nature. Radical change is thus possible, in principle; by transforming existing institutions we can profoundly alter human nature, presumably for the better. Utopia, in the best sense of the term, is attainable.

It is evident that we have here the age-old riddle: are people fundamentally the product of their heredity or of their environment? Those who hold liberal, democratic, utopian, socialist, and even quasi-anarchistic views incline to the latter notion; conservative, antidemocratic, and facist opinion favors the former. Very few in either camp, we should note, take an all-or-none position—that is, that people are absolutely unchangeable or, alternatively, infinitely plastic. Most align themselves somewhere between the two polar positions, although, it should be noted, closer to one than to the other.

The conviction that human nature can be changed greatly, if not actually perfected, occurs in the Stoics and was dear to the heart of St. Augustus and most of the Church Fathers, embraced by Thomas More, ardently argued by Rousseau, more charily accepted by Bentham; it can be found in the literally hundreds of utopian blueprints for a better world. It received classic formulation by Robert Owen in the early nineteenth century.[5] Drawing on his experience at New Lanark, the great British industrialist and philanthropist insisted that "human nature, save the minute differences which are ever found in all the compounds of the creation, is one and the same in all; it is without exception universally plastic." Anticipating behavioral psychology by a century and a half, Owen was convinced that "any general character, from the best to the worst, from the most ignorant to the most enlightened, may be given to any community, even to the world at large—a notion to which he devoted his life and his fortune, albeit with little tangible success. (Owen, 1963) A similar belief in human malleability, not always stated so baldly, runs through the socialist and Marxist literature of the past century; in attenuated form, it is often implicit in democratic thought.

The wisdom or practicality of efforts to change basic social instructions is a matter of practical as well as theoretical concern. Proposals aimed at drastically modifying or abolishing private property, for example, invariably trigger a furious debate. The conventional wisdom holds that there is almost a human "instinct" that impels people to the acquisition of property, in whatever form it may take within a given society. From Aristotle to Adam Smith to Herbert Spencer, philosophers have regarded the desire for material possessions as natural to human beings, the ensurance of property rights as basic to political order and social stability, and the protection of these rights as a—if not *the*—major responsibility of the state.

Nonetheless, there have been dissenters. Plato considered that the desire for property was inborn but, believing the pursuit of individual gain to be a prime source of social disorder, recommended that the philosopher-kings be denied personal wealth. There are a few who go much further, insisting that people are not naturally acquisitive and that they seem always to seek personal gain only because they have been taught to do so by society. In a world organized along other lines, they argue, people would as "naturally" scorn such behavior as they now honor it. Variants of this belief can be found among the Cynics and the early Stoics; similar notions were voiced during the peasants' rebellions of the fourteenth century, by the Anabaptists a bit later, and by the English Diggers during the Cromwellian era. The tenet that the desire for private property is fundamentally social rather than genetic in orgin characterizes much of socialist and utopian writing from Babeuf to Bellamy to Huxley. Just where the present day Soviet Marxists stand on this issue is somewhat puzzling. The ultimate goal of the USSR, presumably, is the abolition of private property and of economic inequality; actual practice suggests a more conservative view of human malleability.

Human Nature and War

This discussion would be manifestly incomplete without some mention of the relationship between theories of human nature and that most pervasive of all political phenomena, war. With few exceptions (Proudhon, Treitschke, and certain of the nineteenth century social Darwinists), political philosophers have sought the abolition of war. From Dante, Kant, and Lenin, up to the present day, the literature abounds with plans for the attainment of perpetual peace. On this issue, ethology and sociobiology may have contributed more to the conceptualization of the problem than they have, as yet, to its solution.

Historically there have been as many explanations for the cause of war as there have been authors attempting to deal with the subject. Among the theories advanced have been the will of God (or the gods), the economic rivalry of nations, nationalistic feelings, the personal ambitions of political leaders, the exploitative tendencies of propertied classes, the struggle for survival and dominance among "races," and—more recently—the redirection of aggression resulting from personal and societal frustrations. In most, although not all, of these theories, aggression and war are seen as the consequences of a faulty social order; the solutions proposed, therefore, have called for sweeping transformations of society and even of our system of national states.

Some of the most widely read ethologists, such as Lorenz, have argued, however, that the basic cause of war resides not in society but in our biological makeup. War, as they see it, is the genetic legacy of hundreds of thousands of years of natural selection during which our hominid ancestors were able to survive, and eventually to flourish, primarily because of their skill as predators and hunter-gatherers. From this perspective, warfare is rooted in such innate human tendencies as aggression, territoriality, group bonding, and xenophobia, with the particular causal mix hinging on the particular author's views at the moment. In short, people, not society, are to blame for war. If this is so, purely structural reforms would not seem to offer a very promising line of attack.

A Concluding Note

To what extent have ethology and sociobiology provided satisfactory answers to these long-standing questions? Since this is the topic to which most of the other chapters are addressed, I will deal with it quite briefly here. I would then like to touch on two related points that have increasingly concerned me.

I believe that ethology and sociobiology (if there is a significant substantive difference between the two) hold the promise of being able to answer the ultimate question: what is the nature of human nature. I also believe, however, that fulfillment of the promise is more likely to be anticipated for decades than for years. Both disciplines have a long way to go before they can provide an adequate explanation of behavior at the level of the lower primates, let alone that of *Homo sapiens*. Despite all that has been accomplished, both are still compelled to argue largely from analogy in dealing with humans. And, as the critical literature abundantly testifies, they have yet to persuade the skeptics that these analogies are valid or to devise research techniques that can obviate this difficulty.

But if a full answer still lies well in the future, in the short run ethology and sociobiology will certainly tell us a great deal more about our biological proclivities than we now know. We may not like what we find. A half million years of natural selection, occurring under rather exacting conditions, could have left a troublesome legacy. We may learn that, even when allowance is made for all other factors, there are behavioral differences among the "races"; that women do not manifest quite the same behavioral responses as men; or even that human nature, unless under firm social control, is not quite as noble as we would like it to be. Apart from our personal distaste for this kind of information, there is the further and more serious danger that it could, and likely will, be misused for a variety of political purposes. All too often, history has shown, "different from" is speedily converted into "worse than."

Second, ethology and sociobiology proceed on the explicit assumption that, methodological problems aside, we should study human beings just as we would any other species. However scientifically rewarding this may eventually be, a grave danger is latent in such an approach. With few exceptions, all schools of Western political thought concur in the proposition that people *are* different from all other living beings; that they stand in a very special relationship to God and/or nature; that, consequently, human beings constitute an end in themselves, with inherent rights, and cannot morally be treated simply as a means to some "higher" political end.

It is one thing to study ourselves as if we were just another species. It is altogether different to act as if this were actually true. The Gulag Archipelago, no less than Dachau and Buchenwald, illustrates what can happen when governments and societies violate this injunction. Should we lose sight of the unique human claim to special treatment, we would, like Faust, have purchased knowledge at a truly exhorbitant price.

Notes

1. "The root of political Aristotelianism is the belief that society grows from natural human impulses which, human nature being what it is, are inescapable and that the community thus formed provides all that a perfected human nature requires." (Sabine 1973, p. 247)

2. For a brief summary of recent "revisionist" assessments of Locke, see Winch (1978, pp. 28-33).

3. Nor were Voltaire and Encyclopedists, whose hostility to the established order was matched by their distaste for any notion of anything remotely approaching a system in which the masses might have a significant voice.

4. Although perhaps pride of place should be given to his countryman, William Godwin, Owen was undoubtedly the better known and the more influential.

5. It should be emphasized that not all utopians contemplate the abolition of private property or a society in which all are equal in material possessions. Comte, Fourier, and Hodgskin, to take only a few examples, built their "brave new worlds" around both private property and substantial differences in wealth between classes.

References

Ashcroft, R. 1968. "Locke's State of Nature: Historical Fact or Moral Fiction." *American Political Science Review* 62:898-915.

Dahl, R. 1965. "Cause and Effect in the Study of Politics." In *Cause and Effect*, edited by D. Lerner. New York: Free Press.

_____. 1979. "Pre-behavioralism in Political Science." *American Political Science Review* 73:24.

Owen, R. 1963. "Essays on the Formation of Character." In *A New View of Society and Other Writings*. London: Everyman and New York: Dutton, p. 16

Reynolds, V. 1976. *The Biology of Human Action*. San Francisco: W. H. Freman.

Sabine, G.H. 1973. *A History of Political Theory*. 4th ed., p. 247. Chicago: Dryden Press.

Wahlke, J. 1979. "Pre-behavioralism in Political Science", *American Political Science Review* 73:9-32.

Winch, D. 1978. *Adam Smith's Politics*, pp. 28-33. New York: Cambridge University Press.

6 Biological Determinism and Ideological Indeterminacy

Marvin Bressler

The major contention of social biology appeals to a paradox: if the proper study of mankind is man, he cannot be the sole object of his own inquiry. The traditional social disciplines have been content to escape the parochialisms of time and locale by insisting that general propositions about human behavior can be established only by recourse to history and cross-societal analysis. Social biologists are committed to the much more ambitious task of developing a unified science of all animate behavior, a grand-scale enterprise that requires a further expansion of orthodox perspectives to include nonhuman societies. Although Edward O. Wilson coined the term *sociobiology* to denote a new synthesis, its more enthusiastic votaries have sometimes implied that a latter-day Auguste Comte might prudently elect to substitute biology for sociology at the peak of the hierarchy of the sciences.

This radical proposal for the revision of the research agenda has predictably provoked intense controversy about the organization of knowledge, the university, and the curriculum. What are the permissible limits of inference in extrapolating the behavior of the "lower orders" to human populations? Which academic units shall exercise jurisdiction over an expanded research and instructional program? How can graduate training be structured to overcome the insular disinclination of specialists to cross disciplinary boundaries?

The debate on such vexing issues, for all their demonstrated capacity to create high emotion, has been relatively decorous compared to the fierce disputations as to whether the moral implications of social biology are malignant or benign. One active group of critics asserts that "biological determinism" generates theories that "operate as powerful forms of legitimation of past and present social institutions such as aggression, competition, domination of women by men, defense of national territory, individualism, and the appearance of a status and wealth hierarchy" (Sociobiology Study Group 1978, p. 280). In responding to this assault, E.O. Wilson has argued that the

> real significance of human sociobiology for political and social thought [is that] science is now in a position to approach . . . the very origin and meaning of human values, from which all ethical pronouncements and much of political practice flow. . . . All political proposals, radical and

181

otherwise, should be seriously received and debated. But whatever direction we choose to take in the future, social progress can only be enhanced, not impeded by the deeper investigation of the genetic constraints of human nature, which will steadily replace rumor and folklore with testable knowledge. [Wilson 1978, pp. 299, 302]

The polemic on the moral functions of social biology and the social responsibility of science is unlikely to subside. It is encouraging to note that although answers may differ, the protagonists nevertheless generally agree about the questions which must be resolved. What, in general, is the relationship between science and ideology? What social biological findings are "convenient" and "inconvenient" for particular ideologies? What are the range of available strategies in dealing with evidence that yields morally disconcerting implications? What standards should govern the choices among these alternatives?

Such questions are the proper concern of all thoughtful people, but they have a special salience for the producers and custodians of scientific knowledge. The assumptions, findings, and implications of the sciences may act as balm or abrasive to systems of belief about self and society. Thus the fundamental postulate that the physical universe exhibits discernible order is almost wholly reassuring. Nature loses its terror but not its grandeur; and as long as science does not presume to explain final causes, no one need be deprived of the consolations of faith. At the same time, even idea systems that are invented to deal with distant galaxies and remote events may shatter universal certainties and discomfit private convictions. It is enough to recall that people resisted the heliocentric hypothesis because Copernicus removed them from the center of the cosmos, and the theory of biological evolution because they preferred to think of themselves as a little lower than the angels rather than a little higher than the apes (see Bressler 1967, 1968; Bressler and Jaynes 1971). Any serious colloquy about the social responsibility of science must begin with the consciousness that discoveries in the natural sciences may be influential beyond their own domain and result in consequences that are disconcerting to their discoverers.

The social sciences, even in their "pure" form, have an even greater capacity to affect the *Zeitgeist* and influence the course of events. The evangelical impulse that drove colonial administrators to "enlighten" native populations, for example, was generated in part by the conviction that Western imperialism was a chosen instrument of historical necessity. After all, they had been repeatedly assured by nineteenth-century anthropologists that all cultures progress in preordained stages from "savagery" to "civilization." To cite an example from the opposite end of the political spectrum, the deepest yearnings of socialist ethics could be dismissed as fantasies in the presence of incontrovertible evidence of innate human depravity. For this reason, socialists are conspicuously more comfortable in the intellectual company of behaviorist psychologists than in that of orthodox psychoanalysts. A theory that locates the sources of action in the external environment, regards human nature as infinitely plastic, and contends that the transformation of personality can be readily achieved through the relatively simple mechanism of operant conditioning seems well attuned to dreams of a cooperative socialist commonwealth. By contrast, Freudian theory with its neo-Calvinist intimations of original sin contains the implicit message that the greedy, rapacious, and recalcitrant id would presumably assert its own imperious prerogatives against even the most benevolent society. Ideologues, then, whether of the left or the right, may be pleased or dismayed by factual propositions, including those that do not bear directly on their ultimate aims.

The ideological impact of social Darwinism, hitherto the most prominent sociobiological synthesis of the modern era, continues to haunt the living present and explains much of the suspicion that has greeted contemporary sociobiological research. No amount of close factual analysis demonstrating "what Darwin really meant," not even the recognition that Herbert Spencer was the author of the term "survival of the fittest," can wholly expunge the memory of past transgressions against social ethics committed in Darwin's name. Biology in general, and particularly evolutionary theory, only yesterday served too often as the first refuge of scoundrels. During the late nineteenth and early twentieth centuries a succession of pseudo-scholars such as the Comte de Gobineau, Houston Chamberlain, Madison Grant, Harry Laughlin, and a parade of less-celebrated elitists, sexists, and racists invoked "natural selection," "adaptability," and "fitness" on behalf of the "natural superiority" of winners in the ubiquitous struggle for power and privilege. Buchenwald represents the deranged extrapolation, beyond the pale of civilization, of the doctrine that biology is destiny.

Contemporary sociobiologists, however, should not be condemned for the trespasses of their predecessors. The past testifies against the present and the prospects of the future only if there is good reason to suppose that in any season biology is inherently, or at least probably, the ally of ethical primitives. The issue to be decided is whether intellectual gaucheries and moral offenses are intrinsic features of the biological perspective or only transient characteristics of an aberrant historical episode. Moreover, no discipline should be held accountable for the excesses of its exiled intellectual fringe. We do not rebuke astrophysicists because astrologers also presume to scan the heavens.

The immediate task, then, is to ascertain which claims, if any, of contemporary sociobiology are "convenient" and which "inconvenient" for specified ideological tendencies. An *ideology* may be defined as a comprehensive doctrine of secular salvation consisting of a more or less coherent

set of aspirations, explanations, and proscriptions that purport to render
the past intelligible and the future hospitable to a preferred state of individual and collective welfare. Ideologies command attention when they
include plausible connections between a powerful moral vision, on the one
hand, and established knowledge about the natural and social universe on
the other. The "facts" may be read as "mandatory" or, less peremptorily,
as "permissive," as laden with specific behavioral imperatives or merely as
free from insuperable constraints that necessarily inhibit the achievement of
a social goal. In any case, ideological conflict always rests in part on rival
empirical suppositions.

The heirs of the 1960s are unlikely to speak of an "end of ideology" in
the sense earlier employed by Daniel Bell (1960). Nevertheless, the standard
categories that once defined ideological loyalties—conservative, liberal
socialist, anarchist—are now beset by equivocal meaning, limited analytical
power, and a reduced capacity to stimulate political activity. Out of power,
conservatives employ their wistful rhetoric but, once elected, make no real
effort to dismantle the welfare state; liberals seem to have exhausted the intellectual dowry furnished by the New Deal; socialists have experienced an
efflorescence of Marxist scholarship but lack any semblance of a mass
political base; and anarchist impulses, strangely enough, are more prominent among "libertarian" reactionaries than among radicals. But if much
ideological dogma has been transmuted into mood, it is still possible to
identify competing systems of thought symbolized by such polarities as
"left-right," hard-soft," "tender-tough," and so forth. For our purposes it
is enough to cite such couplets as denoting change versus stability, equality
versus hierarchy, cooperation versus competition, *tabula rasa* versus human
depravity, internationalism versus nationalism, diversity versus homogeneity, experimental life-styles versus stable families—and the list could be
extended. The terms of these and similar paired opposites are elements of
conflicting value systems in the sense that a preference for any of the
polarities is ordinarily linked to other "soft" or "tough" sentiments.

The thoughtways of the left are expressed in the vocabulary of
possibilities, options, and alternatives; the right speaks of constraints,
limitations, and imperatives. The former is oriented to the possibilities of
the future, whereas the latter finds the present bearable but only the past
sublime. The left is accordingly wary of any implication that whatever is
must be "adaptive," whereas the right fears any tampering with the revealed wisdom incorporated in the "laws of nature." Their common bond
is the shared conviction that evolutionary theory and research is an ally of
the status quo and hostile to a more spacious moral vision.

The message of sociobiology is actually more difficult to decipher than
either side imagines. A relatively casual inspection of any of the recent texts
and compilations on sociobiology will yield a formidable list of analogs, in-

ferences, and obiter dicta that variously sustain the "leftist" or "rightist" sensibility and perhaps most often convey mixed ideological signals that are not susceptible to confident interpretation.

Sociobiology can be claimed as an ally by partisans of competing ideologies because, to begin with, prevailing standards of deriving permissible inferences for human populations from observations of nonhuman species are remarkably loose and casual. Accordingly, there are any number of preferred models of human behavior than can plausibly be linked to limited aspects of the rich and varied social repertoire of animal societies. Furthermore, even the most devout biological "determinists," no less than the "environmentalists," are prepared to concede that most of the variability in human behavior is attributable to social and cultural influences.

The expectation that social biology has *any* relevance for social philosophy, let alone in particular directions, rests on presumed connections between evolutionary universals, continuities, and "imperatives." The most secure evidence rests on the data of primate evolution. It is improbable that the reported characteristics of insects, fish, and fowl not manifested among primates can be reasonably applied to humans. Since human beings and the other primates have evolved from a common Oligocene ancestor, it is plausible to speculate that behavior that is universally present in both may be attributed to shared biological predispositions to act in analogous ways (for example, mating, rearing of infants, play, fighting). The relationship between a human universal and a trait that is observed only in some primates (for example, tools, facial signals, hierarchical groupings) or vice versa (nomadism) is much more problematic. Indeed, some of the more familiar claims of evolutionary continuity have been advanced on behalf of characteristics such as group fighting or territoriality that are neither human nor primate universals. Moreover, the study of animals has no discernible utility when one is dealing with universals that are unique to humans, such as language, adornment, music, marriage and burial ceremonies, dancing, hunting, artifical locomotion, or gift giving, since these probably evolved in hominids after they separated from the common primate stock.

Any thesis can be supported by ignoring the logical and empirical requirements of establishing evolutionary continuities and by substituting poetic metaphor for physical substrate and analogy for homology as principles of evidence. Thus the olfactory marking behavior that occupies so much of the time of lemurs has, as far as we know, no common nor even derived parallel in human behavior. It is possible, although surely strained, to extend marking behavior to include human activities such as raising flags, staking claims, building walls, protecting ghetto turf, or even waging war. But even if ideologues were more scrupulous in their use of evidence, genuine scientific problems would frustrate any effort to capture sociobiology for particular tendentious versions of the human condition to the exclusion of others. "Aggression, " for example, is doubtless a variform universal comprising a remarkably large repertoire of behavioral items, particularly in humans. This concept, with its intimation of robbery, homicide, and war, can be approached as if it were the biological counterpart of original sin or, more cheerfully, as an evolutionary mandate to wage unrelenting "war" on robbery, homicide, and armed conflict.

The admissibility of adopting one or another version of the meaning of aggression will vary with the task at hand and is further complicated by the recognition that almost all human social-behavioral universals are variform. Cultural anthropologists have amply documented the wide variation of response in human societies to generally similar social requisites, and no responsible sociobiologist now speaks of "imperatives" but rather of "opportunities" and "constraints." Biology is, and will perforce remain, a necessary but insufficient explanation of human behavior. It is a curious sort of determinism and reductionism that acknowledges that most "residual" variability falls outside its domain. Even on that distant and probably unattainable day when a mature sociobiology has solved the controversies surrounding transspecific inference, no reactionary, conservative, liberal, or radical need fear the necessity to retreat from cherished doctrine. And it is difficult to know in what way he or she would be harmed by knowing somewhat better the costs and benefits of achieving his aims.

Biology, in any event, is not uniquely vulnerable to accusations of ideological bias. It has not yet occurred to followers of either J.K. Galbraith or Milton Friedman that economics has any "intrinsic" ideological direction; but sociology, which has a widespread reputation as the refuge of bleeding hearts, has often been accused within the profession of supporting the status quo. A generation ago Robert K. Merton, in a classic essay, had occasion to defend sociology's dominant paradigm, functional analysis, from the imputation of charges strikingly similar to these now leveled at sociobiology. Merton noted that functionalists ordinarily accepted three interconnected postulates: the "functional unity of society," "universal functionalism," and the "indispensability" of all existing social and cultural items. The first resuscitates the organismic analogy and asserts that "all part of the social system work together with a sufficient degree of harmony or internal consistency, i.e., without producing persistent conflicts which can neither be resolved nor regulated (Merton 1957, p. 26); the second, which is directly analogous to the contention that all biological behavior is "adaptive," states that all "standardized social or cultural forms have positive functions" (p. 30); and the third, which is the sociological counterpart of biological "determinism," holds that not only must every society satisfy specified prerequisites but also that "certain cultural or social forms are indispensable for fulfilling much of these functions" (p. 33).[1]

These sociological postulates, if suitably amended, bear an uncanny resemblance to the underlying structure of some sociobiological thought and are equally objectionable and unnecessary to both disciplines. As Merton is able to show by appropriate empirical illustrations, societies, and for that matter biological organisms, are seldom fully "integrated"; some prevailing social patterns are "maladaptive," and the uniform functional requisites of any society may be satisfied by widely varied structures. In view of these and kindred considerations, some observers believe that functional analysis is inherently radical. Thus, for example, since "the patriarchal family system is collectively valuable *only if and to the extent* that it functions to the satisfaction of collective ends . . . as a social structure *it has no inherent value* since its functional value will vary from time to time and from place to place (Richard LaPiere, quoted in Merton 1957, p. 39). Merton properly notes that intellectual history knows of other instances in which various formulations were modified for doctrinaire purposes—Marx, for example, was obliged to "rescue" the dialectic from Hegelian "mystification"—and concludes that

> the fact that functional analysis can be seen by some as inherently conservative and by others as inherently radical suggests that it may be *inherently* neither one nor the other. It suggests that functional analysis may involve no intrinsic ideological commitment although, like other forms of sociological analysis, it can be infused with any one of a wide range of ideological values. [Merton 1957]

Sociobiology, then, is not the only arena in which ideological warfare is both fierce and indecisive. It is not at all clear that ideologues of whatever persuasion would be better served if biology were declared off limits to all combatants and the battle fought on other terrain. Indeed, liberals and radicals in particular have perhaps even less to fear from sociobiological findings than from other approaches, unless we can imagine that future research will confirm a series of propositions about human nature and social organization that are contrary to all existing social and genetic knowledge, namely:

1. The social behavior of "lower" animals is metaphorically and biologically unambiguous and may be directly extrapolated to human beings.
2. There exist a set of "autonomous," transspecific, morally vicious traits that cannot be prevented before they emerge, changed after they appear, or channeled for productive purposes; and these negate any possibility of creating and sustaining rational and compassionate human relationships at either the micro or macro level.
3. The determinants of social position are identical in all societies and in all historical circumstances.

4. At any given time, biological mechanisms account for all the interstratum variance in such determinants.
5. The salient biological characteristics of a stratum are transmitted intact to succeeding generations.

These propositions as stated would be disavowed by any serious sociobiologist and, like their equally extreme environmental counterparts, could not be sustained in the future by any conceivable body of new evidence. The "determinism" embraced by sociobiologists is a postulate in the philosophy of science, not a claim that the evolutionary approach exhausts the explanation of human behavior. It is unlikely, moreover, given the inherently problematic character of even very restrained sociobiological claims, that any dedicated ideologue would have insuperable difficulties in mounting an offensive against unsought and unanticipated findings. Every sophisticated belief system includes provisions for converting seeming embarrassments into triumphs. The incongruity of ubiquitous evil with a conception of a just and merciful Deity can be surmounted in the Judeo-Christian tradition by invoking God's mysterious ways and sinful human nature; the passivity of a designated revolutionary class can be explained away by Marxists as temporary proletarian "false consciousness"; and the perverse inclination of psychoanalytic patients to confound straightforward Freudian predictions can be attributed to "reaction formations" developed by recalcitrant analysands. To place the most cynical construction of the matter: it will always be possible to hail ideologically convenient findings as the work of pure genius and to discount contravening evidence as faulty, irrelevant (if sustained), and not crucial (if both demonstrated and pertinent). Over the years the choreography of biological dispute has assumed the predictable character of a gavotte, and its more accomplished devotees can be counted on to resist any invitation to a less-restrictive dance.

For the rest of us, it would be more prudent to acknowledge that ignorance is a treacherous ally of ethics, that biology is not a synonym for oppression, and that we cannot afford to spurn any intellectual resource that expands our understanding of who we are and what we might become. Those considerations are all the more compelling since conservative and radical interpretations of sociobiology are in important respects more consonant than either pretends. Thus, for example, each has a stake in the achievement of sexual, racial, and economic equality. This paradoxical convergence obtains because the significance of biological variation always depends on specific circumstance and should be interpreted in relation to social expectations, rewards, and sanctions. Indeed, it cannot be assessed at all unless all the actors are operating under the same opportunities and constraints. Accordingly, what is for liberals an abiding preference for egalitarian values can be endorsed by even the most conservative sociobiologist as an ineluctable methodological necessity.

Similarly, sociobiological implications for more general issues, such as the character of human nature and social change, are wholly compatible with yearnings for a radical transformation of society. Sociobiologists should not, and in the main do not, contend that evolutionary imperatives forbid human beings to create and adapt to social forms that so far exist only in the minds of visionaries. Biologists no less than others are aware that the concept of "human nature" has accommodated saints and scoundrels, and that the wider limits of biological adaptability can be ascertained only after men and women have fashioned social environments as yet undreamt of in their philosophies. The reflex reactions of some conservatives and liberals to sociobiology, then, surely obscure understandings that would become more obvious if polemic were to yield to reflection.

The joint function of the biological and social sciences is to make moral choices less problematic by rendering ends, means, and their relationships more intelligible. These sciences help people decide what goals to pursue, what actions make their attainment more probable, and what are the costs and benefits of success or failure. Moreover, since beauty is its own excuse for being, who would not welcome the emergence of a discipline that dares to affirm that the study of all living things will in time be subsumed in a unified science of behavior. To be sure, the process of discovery will entail the customary exhilaration or discomfiture that accompanies the collision of knowledge with the received wisdom. Sociobiology will neither demolish other disciplines nor lay waste to existing ideologies; but it may yield novel, disturbing, and confusing implications that will prove awkward to true believers of the left or right.

Individual scientists who are confronted by perceived conflicts between their craft and their *Weltanschauung* may react by adopting any of the orthodox strategies that remove the dissonance between rival loyalties. Some will declare for truth and ignore consequences, others will shelter belief by imposing extraordinary burdens on evidence, still others may compromise by electing to disseminate their findings only to professional audiences, to append morally relevant commentary, or—as in the case of some nuclear physicists—to participate in organizations that are devoted to achieving responsible social control over the products of their own scientific discoveries. A scientist who dares to work in any of the disciplines dealing with human behavior will surely have occasion to ponder his appropriate response to the interplay of knowledge, belief, and action; but sociobiology will not present him with uniquely troublesome agonies of choice.

Note

1. My colleague, Walter L. Wallace, is at work on a major theoretical treatise, which among other things, sets forth important linkages between

the biological and social sciences. It includes a more careful and systematic treatment of these relationships than currently exists in the literature. I am indebted to him for our discussion on these and other matters, including the nature of the differential assumptions underlying science and other thought systems.

References

Allee, W.C. 1978. "Where Angels Fear to Tread: A Contribution from General Sociology to Human Ethics." In *The Sociobiology Debate*, edited by A.L. Caplan, pp. 41-46. New York: Harper and Row.

Bell, D. 1960. *The End of Ideology*. Glencoe, Ill.: Free Press.

Bussler, M. 1967. "Sociology and Collegiate, General Education." In *The Uses of Sociology*, edited by P.F. Lazarsfeld, W.H. Sewell, and H.I. Wilensky, pp. 45-62. New York: Basic Books.

————. 1968. "Sociology, Biology and Ideology." In *Genetics*, edited by D.C. Glass, pp. 178-209. New York: Rockefeller University Press and Russell Sage Foundation.

Bussler, M., and Jaynes, J. 1971. "Evolutionary Universals, Continuities, and Alternatives." In *Man and Beast: Comparative Social Behavior*, edited by J.F. Eisenberg and W.S. Dillon, pp. 333-346. Washington, D.C.: Smithsonian Institution Press.

Eisenberg, L. 1978. "The 'Human' Nature of Human Nature." In *The Sociobiology Debate*, edited by A.L. Caplan, pp. 63-80.

Flew, A. 1978. "From is to Ought." In *The Sociobiology Debate*, edited by A.L. Caplan, pp. 142-162.

Hamilton, W.D. 1971. "Selection of Selfish and Altruistic Behavior in Some Extreme Models." In *Man and Beast*, edited by J.F. Eisenberg and W.S. Dillon.

Lorenz, K. 1978. "The Functional Limits of Morality." In *The Sociobiology Debate*, edited by A.L. Caplan, pp. 67-75.

Merton, R.K. 1957. *Social Theory and Social Structure*. Glencoe, Ill.: Free Press.

Miller, L.G. 1978. "Philosophy, Dichotomies, and Sociobiology." In *The Sociobiology Debate*, edited by A.L. Caplan, pp. 319-324.

Peterson, S.A., and Somit, A. 1978. "Sociobiology and Politics." In *The Sociobiology Debate*, edited by A.L. Caplan, pp. 449-461.

Sociobiology Study Group for the People. 1978. "Sociobiology—Another Biological Determinism. In *The Sociobiology Debate*, edited by A.L. Caplan, pp. 280-290.

Tiger, L. and Fox, R. 1978. "The Human Biogram." In *The Sociobiology Debate*, edited by A.L. Caplan, pp. 57-66.

Wilson, E.O. 1978a. "Academic Vigilantism and the Political Significance of Sociobiology." In *The Sociobiology Debate*, edited by A.L. Caplan, pp. 291-303.

_____ . 1978b. *On Human Nature*. Cambridge, Mass.: Harvard University Press.

Zajouc, R.B. 1971. "Attraction, Affiliation, and Attachment." In *Man and Beast*, edited by J.F. Eisenberg and W.S. Dillon.

7 The Sociobiology of Political Behavior

Glendon Schubert

This book grew out of a panel discussion organized around the responses of several political scientists and a political sociologist to Robert Trivers's elucidation of the relevance of sociobiological theory to human social behavior. The stated goal was to consider the implications, if any, of sociobiology for political behavior and the study of it.[1] That articulation between sociobiology and politics was handicapped, at least for the purpose of that discussion, by Trivers's avowed unfamiliarity with political science, not unlike his mentor Edward Wilson's evident innocence of the social sciences generally.[2] The inescapable consequence was that Trivers's remarks indicated nothing about which aspects of politics (or political science) might undergo change due to the putative revolutionary implications of sociobiological theory—or why this would happen, or how. This chapter will confront those unanswered questions.

As defined in Trivers's presentation, "sociobiological theory" re-introduces—albeit with a different false face—that familiar bogeyman of the social sciences, economic man, the specter of whose arid hyper-rationalism continues to haunt the predominant social and political ideologies of our own time, and their institutional embodiments—ideologies that have evolved culturally (while overlapping phenotypically) from Smith through Ricardo and Marx and Lenin to Friedman.[3] Thus it is entirely appropriate that Trivers should select a forebear from that lineage as his own tutor for a preliminary examination of the body politic.[4] As economic man's surrogate, hard-core sociobiology proposes the substitution of bionic man:[5] equally devoid of flesh,[6] single minded in his monotheism,[7] and unconcerned with the extent to which human behavior everywhere is embedded in a matrix of human culture.[8]

Because many critics confuse sociobiology with social biology, it is important to distinguish the theories of genetic determinism of behavior,[9] sponsored by a handful of evolutionary biologists and population geneticists,[10] from the mainstream of research in mammalian biology and especially in primatology. Inclusive fitness, kin selection, and altruistic behavior emerged during the mid-1970s as conspicuous subjects for popular discussion and public debate;[11] but the vastly larger and more important body of thought connected to sociobiology incorporates many other disciplines and new syntheses that *do* portend direct and important implicaions for the study of political behavior. (See Schubert 1979a,c; Schubert, forthcoming a,b,c; Hinde 1974; Reynolds 1976). This main body of relevant research includes the cross-disciplinary field of animal-behavior research, described by Hinde (1966) as a new synthesis of ethology and comparative psychology; primatology, representing an even broader cross-disciplinary synthesis; behavioral ecology; physiological psychology, including neurophysiology and what generally have come to be called the brain sciences; and behavioral genetics. All these fields are concerned with cross-species analysis of the social behavior of animals; some of them have also become involved in attempts to collect evidence bearing on certain aspects of hard-core sociobiological theory. On the other hand, Wilson (1975, p. 4) claims, "This book makes an attempt to codify sociobiology into a branch of evolutionary biology and particularly of modern population biology," just as he evidently has spoken often of sociobiology's mission to "cannibalize" the social sciences in general, and sociobiology in particular. But even he apportions to the hard-core theory only one chapter (chapter 5 on "group selection and altruism") and part of another (chapter 1, on "the morality of the gene"), of what has become the Koran of sociobiology; the remaining twenty-five and one-half chapters, including at least 95 percent of the text, are devoted to discussion of the field of animal social behavior, more broadly conceived. He is said to have adopted the watchword "sociobiology," from the title of the doctoral dissertation of one of his leading students.[12] As Mary Jane West Eberhard tells the story, in her review (1976) of the new Genesis:

> Once upon a time there was a small community of modest scholars called natural historians, who devoted their lives to philosophy and the contemplation of humble plants and animals. With the passage of time and the invention of Science they began to take on new names. Some called themselves Systematists; others Ecologists; and still others Population Biologists and Ethologists. Only their enemies called them natural historians. All of the new sciences grew and became rich. However, there was one small group without a name. They went about dressed in the castoff clothing of the titled sciences, and often failed to recognize each other, even when they hurried along the same paths. So they suffered greatly. Sometimes they had to learn to collect birds or identify ants in order to get jobs. Then one day there rose up a man among them. He had been called Entomologist, Ecologist, and even Biochemist. But that was not enough. All grew quiet as he raised his golden pen. "There shall be a new science," he said, "and it shall be called SOCIOBIOLOGY."

Hard-Core Theory

Although the roots go back much further, as any perusal of Sewall Wright's four-volume treastise (for example, 1968, 1977, 1978) makes abundantly clear, one issue of basic importance to the present discussion is whether genetic selection has (at least among humans) important effects in aggregations of breeding populations (demes) that transcend the individual and his closest blood relatives. Another issue concerns the relative importance to humans today of cultural as distinguished from genetic selection. Wynne-Edwards (1962) presented the prototype of the current revival of group-selection theory in a forceful book that argues several issues (such as genetically controlled population-reduction mechanisms in many types of social animals) with which we need not be further concerned here. His antagonist became William D. Hamilton (1964), who sponsored an alternative theory of "inclusive fitness," in which the concept of fitness was applied beyond the individual organism but was still limited to the individual and its closest lineal or collateral genetic relatives—hence the term "kin selection," as proposed by John Maynard-Smith (1964). Accordingly, an animal enhances its total genetic impact by behaving supportively so as to increase the survival prospects of conspecifics with which it is related, especially those that are closely related. Certainly a great deal of the empirical evidence concerning humans is consistent with the theory of kin selection; but there is also a fair amount of inconsistent evidence, given the high frequency with which assault, murder, and rape occur among nuclear-family members (to say nothing of the thefts, robberies, and other misappropriations that such persons make of each other's property).[13] It is also notable that there is extraordinary variance in the extent to which the rules of different cultures encourage or discourage behaviors that tend to reduce the fitness of family members, either phenotypic or genetic, with respect to each other. No single generalization can be made about the extent to which cultural norms either support or contradict the model of kin selection; but the very fact that many cultures (both past and present) establish norms that do contradict the model suggests that either (1) kin selection is an inappropriate model for human behavior generally, or (2) the model is appropriate, but the genetic norms are much weaker than, and are frequently overridden by, cultural norms that exert a much more direct and stronger influence on human behavior (see Richerson and Boyd 1978). Kin selection seems to be best supported by the ethnographic data for human primitive societies, and least well supported by the sociological data for contemporary urban industrialized societies.

Probably the most austere defense of hard-core theory is that of George Williams, who begins his book on group selection (1971, p. 2) with an appeal to dogma: "Darwin's great achievement was to show that both the mechanisms of self-preservation and those of reproduction are explained by a more basic principle of natural selection, the reproductive survival of the fittest." In an earlier statement, soon after those of Wynne-Edwards and Hamilton, Williams had said that:

> The essence of the genetical theory of natural selection is a statistical bias in the relative rates of survival of alternatives (genes, individuals, etc.). . . . If there is an ultimate indivisible fragment it is, by definition, "the gene" that is treated in the abstract discussions of population genetics. . . . [The] maximization of mean individual fitness is the most reliable phenotypic effect of selection at the genic level, but . . . a gene might be favorably selected, not because its phenotypic expression favors an individual's reproduction, but because it favors the reproduction of close relatives of that individual. . . . [T]he theoretically important kind of fitness is that which promotes ultimate reproductive survival. [1966, pp. 22, 24, 26]

Williams (1966, p. 19) invokes "the principle of parsimony" as the authority that compels him to sponsor this extreme form of biological reductionism: "it is my position," he says, "that adaptation need almost never be recognized at any level above that of a pair of parents and associated offspring."[14]

Curiously enough, it was Williams himself who in his next two books provided an argument that undermines much of the basis he had previously laid for the hypothesis of genetic control over individual animal altruism—at least among diploid sexually reproducing species such as humans. First he points out that "sexuality in evolution . . . greatly retards the final stages of multilocus adaptive change and severely limits the attainable precision of adaptation" (1975, p. 150). Moreover, "Sex generates recombinational load, and this largely annuls the effect of selection in each generation" (1975, pp. 150-151). Indeed, "there is near unanimity on the point that sexuality functions to facilitate long-range evolutionary adaptation, and that it is irrelevant and even *detrimental to the reproductive interests of an individual*" (1971, p. 12; emphasis added). With so many faults against sexuality, one can only echo Maynard-Smith's plaintive question, "What Use is Sex?" (1971).

An animal's inclusive fitness, which is to say its relative success in genetic competition, is in principle reckoned—it would be improper to say "measured" or "scored" for reasons that will be discussed later—by the total relative contribution that its genes make, in competition with conspecifics, to the sum of all genes for all animals of the species (the "gene pool"). As far as one can infer from the literature, this is true for as long as the species is recognized as such. I have seen no reference to logical positivism or other problems of the philosophy of science in the expositions of hard-core theory; and this may explain the apparent unconcern about the easy shifting back and forth that characterizes many of these discussion between inclusive fitness as an empirical statement about the consequences of genetic natural selection (under the assumptions of the relevance of only the Darwinian paradigm; of the classical gene; of the feasibility of measurement); and *normative assertions about animal behavior*. There is, of course, no objection to the latter as deductions from neo-Darwinian theory; but much of the discussion could profit immensely from a sharper discrimination between what are intended to be verbal translations of mathematical statements of relationships, and what purport to be empirical statements about observations of the genes as well as of the behavior of phenotypes. Consider, for example, Wilson's admission that "there [is] no rational calculus by which groups of [*sic:* or?] individuals can compute their inclusive fitness on a day-to-day basis and thus *know* the amount of conformity and zeal that is optimum for each act" (1978, p. 176). Putting aside for the moment the question of whether individual humans are in any better position to make such a calculation, it should be clear that Wilson is speaking here in a normative sense: to act rationally, people ought to behave according to the rules of inclusive fitness—if only they could figure the odds. Even more paradoxical, why should they worry about it at all? If inclusive fitness is under genetic control, then all they should have to do is whatever their genes tell them to do; there should be no need or even use for conscious thought, in order to maximize fitness.

In any case, the prospects for quantitative testing of inclusive-fitness theory seem remote indeed. Wright has observed that:

> Natural selection within a population necessarily operates directly on individuals and thus on genotypes as wholes rather than on allelic genes. The most significant "character" in this connection is by definition the "selective value" of the genotype. This, however, is an abstraction that is practically impossible to measure. It becomes necessary to focus on less comprehensive characters such as viability and fecundity or, still more narrowly, on specific internal adaptations such as the various aspects of metabolism, morphology of internal organs, homeostatic mechanisms or on specific adaptations to the external world such as instincts, intelligence, size and form appropriate to a particular niche, strength, speed, weapons, armor, concealing coloration. As analysis is carried down toward the immediate effects of gene replacements, the relation to selective value tends to become more remote and contingent. [1968, p. 55; compare Layzer 1978]

And West Eberhard notes that:

> The cost of altruism . . . is . . . clearly a function of the intensity of competition between donor and beneficiary. In general, we should find that *the greater the intensity of reproductive or ecological competition between two individuals, the less the probability of altruism between them.* The probability of altruism thus depends on such ecological parameters as the so-called carrying capacity of the environment, population size, and the population (or social) structure (since not all age or behavioral classes are equally competitive). This consideration immensely complicates the determination of K in nature. There is certainly no species for which the total ecological cost to conspecifics of adding another individual to the population (or subtracting one from it) is known. [1975, p. 13; emphasis added]

Even Williams admits that:

> Unfortunately, it is unlikely that really decisive evidence for choosing be-
> tween group selection and kin selection, either in general or even for
> specific examples, will be forthcoming in the near future. It is difficult to
> determine the degree to which nonbreeding social groups are made up of
> close relatives, and almost impossible to measure the cost of altruism to the
> donor or the benefit to the recipient. [1971, p.5]

On the preceding page he had claimed that "the most serious recent
thinking" was on his side; but our conclusion for present purposes must be
that if even the protagonists of hard-core theory do not know how to opera-
tionalize it, then no matter how hard or seriously they may think about it
there remains no persuasive evidence in support of the theory.

A related question concerns the concept of gene on which theory is
based. As Wright has remarked, "The question whether the genes . . . are
discrete entities or merely regions in a continuum is an old one" (Wright
1968, p. 22, chap. 3). And he makes his own position clear by pointing out
that "genes are merely regions of the chromosomes within which crossing
over or other breakage has so far not been observed to occur." Williams is
quite aware how simplistic the classic gene of Mendelian selection is from
the perspective of modern molecular genetics; and he does concede that
"[t]he genetic environment can be considered to be all the other genes in the
population, at the same and other loci" (1966, p. 38). Nevertheless, he concludes that "[t]he fact that this genetic environment is really made up of an
astronomical number of genetic subenvironments, in each of which the gene
may have a different selection coefficient, *can be ignored at the level of
general theory*" (1966, p. 60). Very much in the contrary, Lewontin concluded his book with the following emphasis:

> The fitness at a single locus ripped from its interactive context is about as
> relevant to real problems of evolutionary genetics as the study of the
> psychology of individuals isolated from their social context is to an
> understanding of man's sociopolitical evolution. In both cases context and
> interaction are not simply second-order effects to be superimposed on a
> primary monadic analysis. Context and interaction are of the essence.
> [1974, p. 218]

Indeed, Trivers himself (1978), speaking before an audience of professional
zoologists and comparative psychologists at the sociobiology panel at the
1978 annual meeting of the Animal Behavior Society, stated flatly that the
notion of "altruistic genes at alleles" is theosophy.

Trivers's best and most original work (1974) has been done on the
genetic basis for interest-behavioral conflict between reproducing animals
and their direct progeny, in sexually reproducing species; and his contribu-

tions there may be of considerable value to attachment theorists and others interested in child development. But very little of the transactions that take place between human parents and their children can have a direct impact on the practice of either politics or political science, at least as they are understood at present. Trivers's theory constitutes an extension of inclusive fitness and kin selection to the special circumstances of generational relationships between appropriate sets of consort males, breeding females, and their offspring (Trivers 1974, p. 249). The theory is developed mathematically with regard to parent-offspring conflict over the continuation of parental investment and its time course, and disagreement between the parents and the offspring themselves over the behavioral tendencies of offspring and their adult reproductive role.

Soft-Core Theory

Reciprocal altruism, the theory for which Trivers is perhaps better known, is quite another matter. Here Trivers presents a model of cooperative social behavior within and between animal populations; with the virtue, at least, of consistency, Trivers claims: "No concept of group advantage is necessary to explain the function of human altruistic behavior" (1971, p. 18).

The vocabulary that Trivers—not nature[15]—selected for the construction of the model is so fraught with morality and emotionality that even his abstract is apocryphal, being in many respects indistinguishable in content from what one might expect to find in an equivalent précis of any of several books of the Old Testament: "Specifically, friendship, dislike, moralistic aggression, gratitude, sympathy, trust, suspicion, trustworthiness, aspects of guilt, and some forms of dishonesty and hypocrisy can be explained as important adaptations to regulate the altruistic system" (Trivers 1971, p. 15). But the tone and level of the argument of the text is more reminiscent of that between Socrates and Glaucon, in a somewhat similar but older model of human nature and behavior (compare Masters 1978). For present purposes, we are less concerned with Trivers's use of his model to "explain" why certain big fish tolerate being groomed by certain little fish, and why some birds simultaneously advertise their own presence as well as that of predators. Whatever the merits of inclusive fitness as an explanation of interspecific symbioses, and of their own reciprocal (that is, interspecific predator-prey relationship), our concern must be with Trivers's application of his model to human behavior.

Trivers begins, appropriately enough, with an appeal to cultural rather than to genetic authority, by citing sociologist Alvin Gouldner (one of hundreds he might have selected) in support of the assertion that "reciprocal altruism in the human species takes place in a number of contexts and in all known cultures." This seems self-evident. He then offers as examples of such human reciprocity: helping in time of danger, food sharing, helping those who are temporarily or permanently physiologically impaired, tool sharing, and exchanging knowledge.[16] His discussion does not emphasize the equally universal antonyms of those behaviors: war and pillage, looting and robbery, the systematic starvation of most of the world's people by their ruling classes, capital growth and concentration, and the obligatory illiteracy of more contemporary humans than had ever lived up to a century or two ago. These latter phenomena are seen in moralistic terms as bad things that cheaters do for which they are—for genetic reasons—punished by their more righteous fellow reciprocals. Trivers's presentation therefore projects an aura of Puritanism that entitles it—whatever its merits as behavior-genetics theory—to a place in the ideological mainstream of American literature. If Vernon Parrington had survived to undertake a revision for the 1970s of his *Main Currents in American Thought*, Trivers's essay on reciprocal altruism would certainly be worthy of a footnote in it. It is, indeed, altogether appropriate that Trivers should have developed his theory in the same habitat that Hawthorne drew on for his *Scarlet Letter*, a work in the same tradition of preoccupation with moralistic aggression. But for these very reasons, Trivers's paper contains no new revelations about human behavior for readers already familiar with any of such diverse sources as the *American Sociological Review*, Shakespeare, the Bible, or Herodotus. The contributions of the humanities and social sciences to the practice and study of politics have been and remain the concerns of political science, entirely independently of Trivers's peroration. That alone would justify dropping the subject of reciprocal altruism for the present purpose.

First, however, it is important to note that Trivers's essay contains not a shred of evidence that would support a choice between his own innuendo— or muted assertion—that human reciprocal altruism today is genetically favored because of natural selection for reciprocal altruism per se that took place during the hunter-gatherer stage of human evolution;[17] and the alternative hypothesis that altruism (like cannibalism and infanticide) is a byproduct of cultural evolution in the context of specific biotic evolutionary (niche, habitat, ecological) pressures and constraints.[18] Cultural evolution in that sense certainly is based on the premise of the chicken-and-egg evolution of the neocortex and language; but at that level all human behavior today is "genetically determined."[19] Indeed, Trivers concedes that "There is no direct evidence regarding the degree of reciprocal altruism practiced during human evolution or its genetic basis today" (1971, p. 48). In the absence of such empirical evidence it seems prudent to continue to prefer the cultural hypothesis, for which there is a great deal of supporting evidence. Moreover, there are overriding technical grounds for *rejecting* altruism as an admissible extension of inclusive-fitness theory. As Eshel has pointed out:

> Social compensation may be granted in the form of . . . reciprocation . . . or discrimination against the selfish. Though these mechanisms undoubtedly account for many seemingly altruistic behavior patterns . . . patterns fully explained by social compensation are not truly altruistic by our definition, since *they do not reduce fitness*. [1972, p. 250; emphasis added]

Wilson admits that "the form and intensity of altruistic acts are to a large extent culturally determined" (1978, p. 153); but he argues that their motivational base remains genetic, because:

> "Soft-core" altruism . . . is ultimately selfish. The "altruist" expects reciprocation from society for himself and his closest relatives. His good behavior is calculating, often in a wholly conscious way, and his maneuvers are orchestrated by the excruciatingly intricate sanctions and demands of society. The capacity for soft-core altruism can be expected to have evolved primarily by selection of individuals and to be deeply influenced by the vagaries of cultural evolution. Its psychological vehicles are lying, pretense, and deceit, including self-deceit, because the actor is most convincing who believes that his performance is real. . . . [I]n human beings soft-core altruism has been carried to elaborate extremes. Reciprocation among distantly related or unrelated individuals is the key to human society. [1978, p. 156]

Campbell seems to agree, stating that:

> What I argue for in the present paper is an ambivalence between socially induced altruistic bravery and a genetically induced selfish cowardice. . . . The conclusion seems to me inevitable that man can have achieved his social-insect-like degree of complex social interdependence only through his social and cultural evolution, through the historical selection and cumulation of educational systems, intergroup sanctions, supernatural (superpersonal, superfamilial) purposes, etc. [1972, pp. 31-32][20]

On the broader question of cultural evolution in general, Wilson accepts the conventional position that:

> We can be fairly certain that most of the genetic evolution of human social behavior occurred over the five million years prior to civilization, when the species consisted of sparse, relatively immobile populations of hunter-gatherers. On the other hand, by far the greater part of cultural evolution has occurred since the origin of agriculture and cities approximately 10,000 years ago. Although genetic evolution of some kind continued during this latter, historical sprint, it cannot have fashioned more than a tiny fraction of the traits in human nature. Otherwise surviving hunter-gatherer people would differ genetically to a significant degree from people in advanced industrial nations, but this is demonstrably not the case. [1978, p. 34]

But his next statement, "It follows that human sociobiology can be most directly tested in studies of hunter-gatherer societies," patently does *not* follow, for two reasons. If there is no significant genetic difference between hunter-gatherers and the rest of the contemporary species, then it should not matter which people sociobiology draws as samples for its tests. Alternatively, as recent ethnographic reports of Bushmen, New Guinea highlanders, and Philippine mountain pygmies all make clear, there are no more hunter-gatherers living in a state of nature—or of Nature—uncontaminated by the press of civilization. Perhaps these groups should be studied, but not under the assumption that they are surrogates for mainstream conspecifics as those people lived ten thousand years ago.

It makes sense to assume that there was genetic evolution of the human brain, transactionally with the evolution of human language, which made possible the evolution of human culture.[21] But that genetic evolution was probably substantially completed several hundred thousand, not ten thousand, years ago. And the culture of human altruism is certainly very much older than the agricultural revolution, as Trivers agrees in his speculation that "one may wonder to what extent the importance of altruism in human evolution set up a selection pressure for psychological and cognitive powers which contributed to the large increase in hominid brain size during the Pleistocene." He evidently was thinking in terms of genetic altruism; but it may well have been cultural in substantial degree.

Wright postulates a combination of kin and interdeme selection as the genetic basis that made human culture possible.[22]

> The evolutionary advance since the beginnings of agriculture, and of the cities which made it possible, occurred only after some 96% of that after the origin of the species *Homo sapiens* began and 99% of that after the origin of the genus *Homo*. If any appreciable advance has occurred since, it has probably consisted more in the world-wide diffusion of the level attained by the most advanced peoples than in further progress of the latter. This is the last phase of the shifting balance process. . . . The mode of evolution of culture is analogous to that of the genetic system. Invention is the analog of mutation. Diffusion of culture is the analog of gene flow. Cultural variation is continually subject to selection on the basis of utility. There is random cultural drift, exemplified by the breaking up of languages into dialects. Finally, the most favorable conditions for cultural advance is local isolation, providing the basis for simultaneous trial and error among many variants and the diffusion of the more successful ones in analogy with the shifting balance process in biological evolution. . . . The state of the culture has been to a considerable extent an index of the rank of populations genetically in the distinctive human line of evolutionary advance, and reciprocally the demands of culture have been the primary selective agent in this advance in its later stages. Aspects of culture are continually being borrowed, but whether such borrowings are effectively integrated into the existent culture to form new peaks (as most conspicuously in the recent period in Japan), or are adopted only superficially and to the detriment of the previous culture, is also an index of genetic capability. [1978, pp. 455-455][23]

Soft Theory

Wilson's distinguished colleague, Richard C. Lewontin, has told us (in his Jessup Lectures, dedicated to Theodosius Dobzhansky and entitled *The Genetic Basis of Evolutionary Change* that:

> It is a common myth of science that scientists collect evidence about some issue and then by logic and "intuition" form what seems to them the most reasonable interpretation of the facts. As more facts accumulate, the logical and "intuitive" value of different interpretations changes and finally a consensus is reached about the truth of the matter. But this textbook myth has no congruence with reality. Long before there is any direct evidence, scientific workers have brought to the issue deep-seated prejudices; the more important the issue and the more ambiguous the evidence, the more important are the prejudices, and the greater the likelihood that two diametrically opposed and irreconcilable schools will appear. Even when seemingly incontrovertible evidence appears to decide the matter, the conflict is not necessarily resolved, for a slight redefinition of the issues results in a continuation of the struggle. It is part of the dialectic of science that the apparent solution of a problem usually reveals that we have not asked the right question in the first place, or that a much more difficult and intractable problem lies just below the surface that has been so triumphantly cleared away. And in the process of redefinition of the issues, the old parties remain, sometimes under new rubrics, but always with old points of view. This must be the case because schools of thought about unresolved problems do not derive from idiosyncratic intuitions but from deep ideological biases reflecting social and intellectual world views. *A priori* assumptions about the truth of particular unresolved questions are simply special cases of general prejudices.

> Attitudes about the kind and amount of genetic variation in populations, like all attitudes about unresolved scientific issues, reflect and are consistent with the intellectual histories of their proponents. . . . A scientist's present view of difficult questions is chiefly influenced by the history of his intellectual and ideological development up to the present moment. . . . [Lewontin 1974][24]

Such refreshing and perceptive candor serves to reinforce the biases about the process of scientific discovery that most social scientists have been socialized to accept. More generally, however, we ought to expect that even the most culturally empathetic biologists will tend to accept genetic-evolutionary explanations to a greater extent than the most biologically oriented persons who have been trained as social scientists, and vice versa with respect to cultural-evolutionary explanations. Indeed, such ideological differences undoubtedly cut within (as well as between) demes of scientists, so that a critical difference in the perspectives of biologists toward hard-core theory, altruism, and cultural evolution hinges on whether the animals with which they have had their predominant research experience are social insects or mammals. Five of the hardcore theorists (Alexander, Dawkins, Hamilton, Trivers, and Wilson) work with insects; Williams works with fish; Sewall Wright worked almost exclusively with mammals. (Unfortunately for the hypothesis, Lewontin also works with insects.)

The unconscious bias shows up in countless remarks, as exemplified by George Williams's assertion—in the introduction to a book on *group* selection—that "a territory, by definition, is an area that one individual defends against intrusion by other members of its species" (1971, p. 8). Of course, whether or not this is true depends on who is defining territoriality. Williams's statement certainly applies to sticklebacks and to many other species of fish and also of birds; but his assertion does not apply to most species of primates (which live in groups and defend group territories, to the extent that they defend any territory—as distinguished, of course, from the "personal space" that may accompany a primate wherever it goes). And Williams's definition most certainly is a half-truth that fails to include human warfare, which we shall discuss further later on. Similarly, Williams remarks in a different book that "a population cannot retreat to a marginal habitat to avoid being killed off by competition" (1966, p. 31)—and here he *is* speaking of mammals (house mice). But he clearly is not thinking of humans, who were doing so during the Pleistocene as well as at present.

Ideological bias shows up also in the penchant for teleological explanation that permeates Williams's writing, as exemplified by the selections that follow.[25] "The goal of the fox," he tells us, "is to contribute as heavily as possible to the next generation of a fox population" (1966, p. 68). And as with foxes, so with sexes: "The ultimate goal for both [males and females] is maximal genetic representation in the same population" (1975, p. 124). Indeed, "duck genes have chosen a life spent largely above the surface of the sea," whereas "tuna genes . . . have cast their fortune in submerged habitats" (1966, p. 69). More generally, "The succession of somatic machinery and selected niches are tools and tactics for *the strategy of the genes*" (1966, p. 70; emphasis added). And although what he may have intended to say is "to be increased," what he in fact assures us is that "it is possible for the donor *gene to increase its* frequency in the population" (1966, p. 196; emphasis added). Having spoken earlier of "the real goal of development" (1966, p. 44), he asks: "Do these processes show *an effective design* for maximizing the number of descendants of an individual?" (1966, p. 108; emphasis added). The clear implication seems to be that nature moves in mysterious ways, its wonders to perform.

Although there is every indication that he is *not* talking about humans,[26] Williams has ventured the observation that:

> At every moment in its game of life the masculine sex is playing for higher
> stakes. Its possible winnings, either in immediate reproduction or in an
> ultimate empire of wives and kin, are greater. So are its possibilities for im-
> mediate bankruptcy (death) or permanent insolvency from involuntary but
> unavoidable celibacy. [1975, p. 138)

We can take this as an example of patent anthropomorphism; and the hard-core theory is replete with anthropomorphic metaphors such as "altruism," "selfishness," "cheating," "moralistic aggression," "parental investment," and "kin" selection. In the English language from which they are taken, every one of these concepts implies ethical choice, which—as far as seems likely and as far as is presently known—only humans are capable of making, or else (as in the case of the latter two) they are peculiarly human intergenerational relationships among genetically related animals. It is a mistake to describe the interspecies predation of soldier ants as "altruism," when we believe that they have no choice but to respond as they do to chemical cues. Similarly, dogs and cats do not have mothers, fathers, sisters, or brothers—except in the minds of their human overlords, who only compound the confusion by attempting to cast themselves as surrogate parents to their pets. Dogs are not brothers to people, because to be a brother implies at least as much culturally as it does genetically; whatever the affective and subservient behaviors that some domesticated canids have been—artificially—selected to perform, a dog can share only in part physically, and very little cognitively, those aspects of human culture that define the reciprocal obligations of brothers to each other.

A recent sociobiological best seller entitled *The Selfish Gene* (Dawkins 1976) has been promoted in such a way as to suggest that the subject under discussion is human genes (or at least, one of them). Indeed, the title is knowingly deceptive, because the author is a sophisticated zoologist who understands only too well how extremely improbable it is that any set of behaviors as complex as "selfishness' could have evolved under the control of any single gene—and certainly not among humans.[27] In an interview in July 1978, Richard Dawkins explicitly denied that he had intended to emphasize in that book human selfishness or the sociobiology of human inclusive fitness. Many purchasers of the book must have expected otherwise; even in England, books about the population genetics of beetles rarely become best sellers. But if *The Selfish Gene* is not about humans, then Dawkins must answer to the charge that he is anthropomorphizing genetic control of the behavior of nonhuman animals.

If more sociobiologists were as well versed in metaphors and similes as they are in analogies and homologies, they might be more circumspect in their use of language. For example, the writings of Martin Landau (1972), a political theorist familiar with and much concerned with evolutionary theory, illustrate the perils of simplistic metaphorizing. Certainly it is simplistic to seek to bridge the gap between human behavior and that of other animals by trying to understand the other animals in terms—in *the* terms—of what are uniquely and idiosyncratically human abilities and relationships. Hard-core sociobiology will have to get beyond the Uncle

Remus stage before very many social scientists will take it seriously, let alone yield themselves to its purportedly masterful and prepossessing embrace.

The fundamental problem with the hard-core sociobiological approach to human behavior is its pious insistence that human social behavior is motivated by and explicable in terms of the competition among individual humans to maximize the contribution of each to a reified metaphor: the "gene pool." Most of the better-known spokespersons for hard-core sociobiology have asserted that human social behavior not only can be, but *must* be, explained in terms of inclusive fitness. Either in its moderate or its strong form, the postulate is pious because it rests on the act of faith that a nineteenth-century idea—Darwinian selection—must hold for all behavior of all animals, thereby assimilating the social and the cultural behavior of *Homo sapiens*, the species that has maximal genetic plasticity, to that of others (termites, for example) under much tighter genetic control. We should learn that, even in such physical sciences as astronomy and nuclear physics, theory appears invariant only during the stages of substantial ignorance about the phenomena under investigation. Contemporary, modern, recent, and medieval history alike—to say nothing of ancient history— are replete with instances of heathens plundered by missionaries and their secular acolytes. We may hope that zoologists will be dispassionate enough to recognize the possibility that they may be making a mistake in worshipping Darwinian selection as the exclusive deus ex machina for biotic change. But those of us who remain agnostics or even skeptics have an obligation to point out the fundamentally religious nature of the transactions implied by Wilson's call for the conversion of the social sciences.

Many commentators have proposed that genetically supported primate social structure, at least among such hominids as humans and Neanderthals during the past hundred thousand years, has been preadapted to hierarchical relationships to such an extent that the hero-god is an indispensable figure to serve as the leader of larger, as well as the largest, population aggregations (Tiger and Fox 1971; Odum 1971, chap. 8; and compare Willhoite 1977). Sometimes the hero-god (Mahatma Gandhi, Hitler, Mao) appears in the flesh to lead his worshippers; but the supernatural (or at least, sanctified) isomorphs (Christ, Jove, Buddha) exemplify one of the many advantages that cultural images enjoy in comparison with their biological phenotypes. Indeed, inclusive fitness—with its inexorable logic of the watering down, with each generation, of *any* individual's possible genetic contribution—proffers a pale ideal for immortality,[28] in contrast to the possibilities for growth offered by cultural immortality.[29] But if humans are preadapted to worship, then such an attitude must apply to scientists also, their socialization toward objectivity in more finite matters notwithstanding.

A scientific paradigm waxes or wanes in its authority as a consequence of sociocultural processes that we can document empirically; but to the extent that those sociocultural processes are influenced by underlying multiplex genetic determinants, both the putative genes and the interaction processes remain unknown and hence not amenable to empirical discussion at this time. The initial acceptance of any paradigm no doubt typically is based on what at the time appears, to the relevant population of practicing scientists, to be the clear preponderance of the evidence—or, at least, of the potential evidence (as in the case, for example, of Einsteinian relativity in twentieth-century astronomy and physics). But those scientists were members of an ancestral cohort (in terms of the evolution of scientific theory), limited to the information then available; and as Kuhn demonstrated almost a generation ago (Kuhn 1962), the persistence of the paradigm comes increasingly to depend for acceptance, by the rank and file of successor scientific cohorts, on faith rather than reason—indeed, on faith so strong and so passionate that it increases in fervor in direct proportion to the increasing failure of the paradigm to find support in the accumulation of new empirical information. The prophets of a new paradigm that threatens to displace the old orthodoxy are first ignored and then castigated (by the many stalwarts of the *ancien régime*) as fools, heretics, and knaves. The reasons for this are readily explained by contemporary social science, or by Shakespeare, or by any member of several generations of philosophers dwelling in Athens some two and one-half millennia ago. Of course, this is an evolutionary theory of paradigms; and it would be gratuitous to retell such a familiar story were it not for the zeal with which the failure of social scientists to embrace modern evolutionary theory is impugned, and the complacency with which the commitment of biologists to neo-Darwinism is taken for granted, in zoological writing generally—and hard-core sociobiological theory in particular—today (compare Corning, in press).

Lewontin has questioned the inarticulate major premise underlying the hard-core theory: that Darwinian natural selection is the only way, as well as the best way, to explain genetic evolution:

> For [some leading evolutionary geneticists] natural selection is vital in the divergence between isolated populations while for [others] natural selection is always primarily a cleansing agent, rejecting "inharmonious" gene combinations, and not necessarily the causative agent in the initial divergence between incipient species. Nor is this conflict of viewpoints yet resolved. During the last few years there has been a flowering of interest in evolution by purely random processes in which natural selection plays no role at all. Kimura and Ohta suggest, for example [in 1971], the *most* of the genetic divergence between species that is observable at the molecular level is nonselective, or, as proponents of this view term it, "non-Darwinian". . . . If the empirical fact should be that most of the genetic change in species formation is indeed of this non-Darwinian sort, then where is the revolution that Darwin made?

The answer is that the essential nature of the Darwinian revolution was neither the introduction of evolutionism as a world view (since historically this is not the case) nor the emphasis on natural selection as the main motive force in evolution (since empirically that may not be the case), but rather the replacement of a metaphysical view of variation among organisms by a materialistic view. . . . For Darwin, evolution was the conversion of the variation among individuals within an interbreeding group into variation between groups in space and time. [1974, p. 4; compare Caplan 1978b]

A much better-balanced and—in terms of relevance to human behavior—more useful perspective of evolutionary change is presented in the writings of Sewall Wright, the only surviving founder of the field of population genetics, whose own doctoral research at Harvard was completed before 1917. Wright remained a leading contributor to the mathematical theory of the genetics of evolutionary change for more than sixty years afterwards, and in the fourth volume of his treatise he remarks that:

If mutation pressures and random drift are rarely if ever controlling factors, we are left with only the two kinds of natural selection. Fisher and his followers, including recently Williams (1966), would also remove selective diffusion from consideration, leaving only mass selection, by invoking the principle of parsimony. . . . [Fisher would] be correct if there were only one mode of change of gene frequency, . . . selection in favor of specific modifiers of the heterozygotes. [But] degree of dominance is only one aspect of a complex interaction system (as I had found it to be in extensive experiments with guinea pigs [{in} 1916, 1917, 1927, and later]). . . . The occurrence of some sort of mass selection is no doubt more nearly universal than the occurrence of a population structure that favors selective diffusion and thus is to be adopted as the only factor under the parsimony principle. Yet where there is a suitable population structure, selective diffusion may be enormously more effective than mass selection. Where a wide stochastic variation is occurring simultaneously at thousands of nearby neutral loci and more or less independently in many demes . . . a virtually infinite field of potential variability from possible interaction effects is available without change of conditions. There is no such tendency towards exhaustion of additive genetic variance as under mass selection. The cost to the reproductive excess on which selection depends is also minimal. In general, the concept of shifting balance leads to very different conclusions than the parsimony principle. [1978, pp. 462, 463; table, p. 461; also see 1977, vol. 3, pp. 439, 453-455, 468, 560-562]

In further explicit contradiction of Williams, Wright summarizes the Wynne-Edwards thesis, and then remarks:

Elaborate behavior patterns . . . serve to establish a peck order or an allotment of territories in an orderly way, with a minimum of dangerous combat. . . . Under favorable conditions such behavior patterns tend to maximize reproductions by all individuals, but under unfavorable conditions they tend to allot adequate resources only to the fitter individuals at the expense of the others. Such patterns are much more easily accounted for by intergroup selection than by individual or familial selection. Since they exist, it would seem probable that intergroup selection is responsible. . . . [L]ocal populations that acquire modes of behavior that obviate overproduction of individuals before actual starvation or permanent destruction of food resources occur, would tend to replace neighboring populations in which individual selection pushes reproductive capacity to the limit under all conditions. It appears probable then that reproductivity under favorable conditions tends to be pushed as far as possible by individual (Fisher 1930) and familial selection (Hamilton 1963, 1964), but that intergroup selection (Wynne-Edwards) imposes behavior patterns that obviate disastrous overproduction under unfavorable conditions. [1978, p. 53]

With explicit respect to human evolution, Wright observes that:

During the 99% of species history while humans and their forebears of the genus *Homo* remained hunter-gatherers, no doubt there was a steady pressure of mass selection in favor of intelligence, but change of gene frequency according to the net effects of individual genes is a process that is not directed toward what matters most, the effects of interacting systems of genes, and it is subject to the severe cost imposed by selective replacement at one locus on replacement at other loci, especially severe in a species with the relatively low reproductive capacity of primitive man. . . . Simultaneous sampling drift at thousands of sufficiently neutral loci provides different material in innumerable localities without appreciable cost, material in innumerable localities without appreciable cost, material that can give the basis for effective interdeme selection. . . . The actual process of interdeme selection may take different forms. At one extreme, the local appearance of a superior genetic system is followed by expansion of its territory accompanied by complete elimination of its neighbors until it occupies the entire range of the species. At the other extreme there is merely . . . diffusion from the superior center. Neighboring populations are graded up until they reach the point (the crossing of a saddle in the surface of selective values) at which mass selection carries them autonomously to the new selective peak, or perhaps beyond, if they contribute something that improves on the latter. The location of the population with the highest selective peak may shift from place to place in the course of time, as a group of neighboring populations step each other up to heights well above the general level. [1978, pp. 452-453; 1977, vol. 3, pp. 471-473]

As for altruism:

The heroic virtues, including willingness to sacrifice one's own life for the good of the tribe, are traits that can hardly be developed (insofar as they have a genetic basis) by purely individual selection. They may to some extent arise as a by-product of familial selection in which close relatives with heredities strongly correlated with that of an individual who gives his own life to save them. . . . The importance of this sort of intergroup selection in evolution has been emphasized . . . by Hamilton. The increase frequency of traits deleterious in on the average to their possessors but beneficial to the deme may also, however, be increased by interdeme selection . . . if the benefit to the deme sufficiently outweighs the damage to the individual. [Wright 1978, p. 454]

Nowhere in the hard-core sociobiological literature of the past fifteen years do any of its protagonists undertake to explain why humans should be consciously motivated to attempt individually and competitively to maximize their respective personal genetic contributions. The steretyped rationale from evolutionary-biological theory is (as we know) based almost entirely on logical deduction and not on a systematic corpus of either naturalistic or experimental empirical observations. This rationale is as follows. Some animals breed more successfully than others of their species. The more successful breeders make relatively larger contributions to the "species gene pool" than do their less successful competitors. Whatever combinations and frequencies of genes are embodied by the successful breeders will tend to become more common, and the frequencies of the genes of the less-successful phenotypes will lose out. This does not presume any particular motivation on the part of individual animals, whether successful or not; genes that get reproduced (in any particular environment or set of environments) will become more common, whereas genes found in poor breeders will tend to disappear. So it is all a matter of stochastic processes—or almost. But the theory presumes also that the genes are *controlling* the behavior of the animals concerned. Genes for light-colored moths, once highly adaptive when these insects were roosting on their trunks of preindustrial birch trees, become displaced by the formerly rare genes for dark coloration once those same tree trunks became chronically coated with soot. As the trees gradually darkened, light-colored moths became relatively easier, and darker moths harder, for predator birds to perceive. To the extent that humans engage in equivalently stereotyped (that is, nonchoice) behavior that is equally highly correlated with human mortality, then the same arguments might apply—particularly if humans generally had no more cognitive discretion over behavioral choices than moths are deemed to exercise.

Unfortunately for inclusive-fitness theory, however, the most remarkable characteristic of our species, together with the brain structure and language behavior with which it is so conspicuously interrelated, is the plasticity of human behavior (Sagan 1977, p. 3). Even a wide range of infravisceral systems and functions, many of which used to be classified as "autonomic" and not subject to conscious control or influence, now are increasingly coming under the ambit of cognitive theory as teachable and learnable behaviors. A generation of human-evolutionary theorists has proclaimed that it is precisely this variability in behavior, this potentially extraordinarily broad range of adaptability to both natural and social ecologies, that the genes that distinguish our species have supported for half a million years or more. That range of choice, at least in genetic terms, includes whether or not to have children; when to have them (if at all); whether to nurture children begotten by others in preference to or in addition to one's own; whether or not to share resources with friends or with relatives or with complete strangers.

The metaphor of the "gene pool" is one that, through stereotyped overusage, has become hackneyed and hence misleading. The metaphor invokes the image of some pristine ocean, a maternal symbol by means of which all surviving genes at any particular time are aggregated (and in some sense summated). But the genes with which we are concerned here exist only in living organisms; the genes nurtured in laboratories for experimental purposes typically appertain to plants or to much simpler animals (at least, socially) than the social insects or the mammals with which sociobiological theory concerns itself. Hence genes are in fact aggregated only in units consisting of the organism characteristic of the species of interest, and then infrasomatically. The only conceivable way to "pool" the genes of any species would be to aggregate the entire species population, an entirely unnatural action that would certainly be lethal to the species (and therefore, to all the genes concerned) even if it could be performed. A gene pool is a purely imaginery hypothetical construct, one that bears no empirical relationship to the structure or the functioning of life in the real world. What is more, it is questionable whether any animal that has ever lived has intended either to make, or to fail to make, a contribution of its genes to the species gene pool—with the possible exception of a handful of hard-core sociobiological theorists. As far as we have any evidence (Griffin 1978), no nonhuman animal has any idea why it copulates, or to what end, or (in most instances, probably) with whom. Indeed, at least the first two-thirds of that statement could be asserted about most humans, until a very recent point in evolutionary time. Again, the substantial divorce between copulation and progenitation for the human species, as a consequence of the substitution of chronic for periodic and acute sexual availability among species females, is an idiosyncratic species characteristic; but it is another hallmark of behavioral plasticity that confounds prediction based on simplistic theories of genetic determinism. It if one thing to measure, in terms of ecological variables, the fitness of !Kung females as a function of their birth spacing, as Blurton Jones and R. Sibly (1978) have done using Devore and Lee's data; but it would be quite another matter to attempt a replication among human females living only a few hundred miles away on the other side of the Kalahari.

Campbell has pointed out that

> in Trivers's discussion of human reciprocal altruism, he makes use of
> learned individual tendencies as well as genetic ones, but he fails to give ex-
> plicit consideration to the social evolution of reward and punishment
> customs and tends to consider all personality and behavioral dispositions as
> genetically inherited. While he uses the mathematical models of evolu-
> tionary genetics, these are not developed for many of his most crucial
> speculations on human altruism. [1972, p. 30]

Trivers's trite example of "[O]ne human being saving another, who is not
closely related and is about to drown" (1971, p. 35), to which he applies the
cost-benefit-analysis jargon of inclusive fitness, provokes West Eberhard to
carry his reasoning to its logical conclusion:

> Theoretically, the most willing lifeguard should be a physically fit eunuch
> or post-reproductive individual (who has nothing to lose in terms of per-
> sonal fitness), and with few living relatives (little to lose in terms of future
> gains to inclusive fitness through aid to close kin). A good beneficiary is
> one with high reproductive value . . . such as a pregnant low-income
> Catholic teenager who is about to produce her first child. [1975, p. 81]

The winter of 1979 confirmed what we already knew: that several urban
adults could stand on a bridge over the Chicago River and watch a child
drown, with no more compulsion to intervene personally than if they were
spectators at yet another incident of urban arson. These people did not turn
to their pocket calculators for guidance in any decision as to whether or not
the odds of ultimate social reciprocity favored intervention. Living in
Chicago in the 1970s, they did not need to compute just how poor those
odds would be. It seems to me that thirty or more years ago, a group of
Chicagoans in a similar situation would have cooperated in trying to save
the child. It is disingenuous to argue that the change is due to changes in the
Chicago gene pool during that interval. Even for those Americans who
stayed put, a new generation was born and came of age after World War II;
we must keep in mind Williams's admonition that "in a heterogeneous and
fluctuating environment, each new generation may be regarded as colonists
entering new environments" (1975, p. 153).

There is a biological reformulation of the question of diminishing
altruism within a population that provides all alternative to the
sociocultural hypothesis just suggested. Clearly the issue is not confined to
Chicago, or to American megalopolises; it is a social disease—if altruism is
taken as good—that is endemic in industrial urbanization. To place the
biological hypothesis in context, we can turn to George Williams, who has
observed that "the phenomenon of fitness can be seen at all epigenetic
levels, from genic interactions to the ecological niche" (1966, p. 71).[30]

We must now transfer our thinking all the way from Trivers's postulated organic competition (which would be midpoint on Williams's scale) to biotic evolution, where competition is interspecific. The hard-core theorists tend to think of all kinds of fitness as a set of games being played against the nature that they typically reify; but our assumption is that "nature" is not trying to do anything in particular. The interspecific competition game is one at which humans have done extremely well, especially during the past thirty thousand years or so during which we eliminated or subsumed our only surviving competitors, the neanderthals, and virtually all the other large mammals of the Northern Hemisphere, a job that we are now in the process of completing for the Southern, while more recently we have turned our attention to the mammals of the sea. But in the process of getting rid of our competitors, improving our genetic fitness as a race (at least quantitatively), and exploiting both plant and physical resources at a logarithmic pace, we have also imposed important (and for ourselves, highly maladaptive) constraints on the range of variation left open to our only remaining antagonist—"nature"—and hence to the only biosphere available to us at present.

The mere mention of modern medicine, in the context of the acceleration of species population growth during this century, makes ludicrous the hypothesis that "natural selection" is shaping the future genetic composition of the human species, by the "mechanism" of having those *individuals* who are "best adapted" to their environment in the present generation leaving relatively more progeny, and thereby having the greater influence on the possible genetic combinations of future generations. Genetic competition today is waged among very much larger population aggregates than any individual (including his or her kin), and indeed between very much larger ones than the demes evidently envisaged by Wilson. The consistent trend of the past century has been for birth rates to drop to or below zero growth in maturing industrialized societies, while the countries that remain most traditional and most rural maintain the high population growth rates. If there is a global genetic competition for resources, it is taking place between Europe, North American, and Japan on the one hand, and the rest of the world on the other. Hard-core sociobiology makes no mention of such problems for the very good reason that it has nothing to offer toward either their comprehension or their solution. The reasons that, in general, members of the deme conglomerate of the industrialized West (including, for present purposes, Japan) do *not* undertake to maximize their individual (or collective) inclusive fitness—just as the reasons that most other humans outside the West *do* try to leave as many progeny as they can afford to raise, as successfully as they can—have very little to do with genetic determinism; they are instead the byproduct of human cultural differences.

There is a hypothesis—naive in both evolutionary and genetic theory—

that there is some sort of linear and unidirectional progress toward greater complexity and perfection ("up from the ape"), and that therefore the demes of industrialized societies are better adapted than those of the remaining agriculturalists of the third world, or that either type of deme is better adapted than the remnant hunter-gatherer bands whose existence, although "nasty, brutish, and short," has not yet been anthropologized. That sort of liberal optimism, which finds its soul mate in social-science environmentalism that postulates no limits to human perfectability beyond the imagination and creativeness of the perfectors (see Lasswell 1962, especially chap. 10), is increasingly contradicted by the facts of life in the twentieth century. Indeed, the converse hypothesis is much better supported: that hunting and gathering was a better adaptation for humans than agriculture, because the minimal demands made on the environment by hunting and gathering tended to ensure the persistence of the human niche for an indefinitely long future. Agriculture, on the other hand, in barely ten thousand years has had, and continues to exert, an accumulative, consistent, and malevolent effect on habitats that for millions of years were critical to the definition of the human niche. And industrialism, as we know only too well, has so accelerated the pace of habitat depletion that the species niche probably already has been irreversibly destroyed by processes already well advanced.

In this regard Williams has remarked that: "Extinction occurs not because an organism loses its adaptation to an ecological niche, but because its niche becomes untenable . . ." (1975, p. 147). "Sexual selection," he adds, "facilitates evolution indirectly by making extinction less likely . . ." (1975, p. 154). Nevertheless, "A population may even obliterate its own niche by becoming better adapted to it. All that is required is that increasing adaptation have a progressively adverse effect on total resources." As needed resources shrink, so does the population dependent on them, until the denouement is resolved when

> [e]xtinction occurs because there is no corrective feedback between dangerously low population size and the forces of evolution. The last pair of passenger pigeons to nest successfully had no way of knowing that they ought to take desperate actions. Approaching extinction evokes no emergency measures, but rather . . . the species doomed to extinction, innocently unconscious of its lack of "fitness," continues happily to perform its traditional rites. [Williams 1975, pp. 158-160]

When this will happen to humans—and evolutionary biologists generally are certain that it must—is not yet certain; nor can we be sure that the remnant humans, on the verge of species extinction, will be any more self-conscious about the matter than the passenger pigeons were, or than cetaceans are today. But if it is true that the principal social problem confronting our species today is the loss of altruism that had previously evolved—for whatever combination of cultural factors transactionally with genetic ones—in a niche that as then defined has now also been lost, then the principal objection to Trivers's theory of reciprocal altruism is that it is *trivial*, because it diverts attention to a side issue and away from what ought to be our central concern. Even if he were correct (and I am convinced that he is *not*) about the relative importance of genetic causation of human altruism, the human groups to which his theory properly applies are those of the hunter-gatherer epoch of more than ten thousand years ago, when people lived in face-to-face groups small enough so that all could know each other as individuals. Of course, his work would be less popular and not seem as "relevant" if it has been proffered—as I am arguing it should have been—as a contribution to human prehistory, rather than as advice about how and why people behave as they do today. Trivers's optimism about how our genes are going to keep churning out altruism now is a dangerous nostrum.

Population genetics has come up with a hypothesis that is helpful in elucidating the problem of altruism by focusing on its disappearance in the modern world, as Eshel has explained:

> Though it may be assumed that the development of a new altruistic trait requires a considerable span of time (see, for example, Simpson, 1945), the *extinction* of such a trait under a newly imposed condition of high mobility is a factor no doubt exclusive to human evolution. Thus, from a theoretical point of view, the quantitative understanding of the effects imposed by this factor on the selection of altruistic traits may add to our knowledge of human evolution.

> [Trivers (1971; and see also Campbell, 1966; Lee and DeVore, 1968) already has suggested that] the demographic conditions that prevailed in pre-Neolithic human populations were likely to favor the evolution of altruistic patterns. These patterns may in turn have been prerequisites for the subsequent development and maintenance of human societies. Yet because of the tremendous increase in human mobility during only the last ten thousand years or so, it may be that natural selection no longer favors such altruistic traits, however favorable for human society some of them may still be.

> A question repeatedly raised by ethologically oriented authors (Lorenz, 1963; Morris, 1967; and others) is to what extent the relatively short period of human civilization has been sufficient for man to adapt biologically to his new environment. Attempts have been made to explain the malfunctioning of modern society on the basis of the still-persisting "australopithecine" drives of man. But perhaps a more crucial question is whether human evolution is in fact headed toward a desirable social adaptation, i.e., whether present fertility selection necessarily favors traits that are beneficial to human society as presently constituted. The theoretical conclusion of this study suggests that the opposite may be true. It may be that some intrinsic human drives, altruistic in nature, that are fundamental for the establishment of any human civilization, could possibly evolve only under precivilization demographic conditions. And it is possible that just those selection forces imposed by civilization itself act to reduce the frequency of these fundamental drives within human population, thus leading it into the course of misadaptation. [Eshel 1972, p. 275]

Hamilton, whose earlier work on inclusive fitness inspired Trivers, has in fact already done what Trivers should have done, by focusing attention on the evolutionary genetics of cooperative social behavior in hunting-band humans. It is notable that Hamilton himself (1975, p. 150) cites Eshel with approval, and states as his conclusion that "civilization probably slowly reduces its altruism of all kinds, including the kinds needed for cultural creativity."[31]

Hardball Politics

Hard-core sociobiological theory offers little help in solving either the problems of hardball politics, or those of its "soft" template, political science. Individualism and associated notions of innate human selfishness have been a major component of political thought for at least three millennia, about as far back as the written evidence extends. Genetic theories of individual natural selection, such as Hamilton's concept of inclusive fitness, have nothing to say about political behavior today per se, because they are addressed to what for political behavior and political science is an inappropriate presocial level, characterized by Williams as "cybernetic abstraction." Kin selection is a step in the right direction, however, because it views human behavior as social behavior and as necessarily concerned with the group (population) context within which kin selection is hypothesized to occur.

Nepotism

We can imagine a set of postulates, deduced from the population-genetic model of kin selection, that would meet with considerable support by data drawn from, say, the State University of New York at Buffalo's Human Relations Area Files, in the reconstructions of hominid and human evolution by physical anthropologists. Nepotism is important in politics, and not only in the social structure of hunter-gatherer or primitive agricultural peoples. It remains a critical factor in political leadership, elite structure, and followership throughout the third world today—and in much of the second as well, as a sampling of world news headlines suggests. In India, the late Sanjay Gandhi was sentenced to prison for offenses committed under his mother's protection (and for which she was removed from office). The deposed Shah of Iran had exported from that country, in his own name and that of his extended family, a substantial fraction of Iran's liquid capital. These examples of nepotism come from two countries considered to have been "modernizing" during the past two decades. Nepotism is also characteristic of countries of the Arabian peninsula that have begun modernization, at least in certain economic respects, during the past ten years.

On the other hand, the trend in all the industrialized countries has been explicitly contrary to extended-family politics, for cultural reasons that have been well discussed by Max Weber, among many others. For Japan, China, the Soviet Union, Europe, and North America (at least north of Mexico), the surviving monarchies have been reduced to what are conventionally viewed by political scientists as vestigial political functions; Prince Charles's decision to sit with the cabinet, and the apparent involvement of Prince Bernhard as liaison with various international corporations, are recent exceptions that point in quite another direction. The reason for reexamining the political role of royal families is that political integration, of the subpopulations of consociational democracies, may be a much more important function that is recognized by the Bentlian, Dahlian, or Eastonian theories of interest-group conflict and organic-system components, with which post-World War II political science has been preoccupied, at least in the United States.

Similarly, the Kennedy brothers, who conspicuously were leaders of a family clan, became the most effective symbols of political integration within the United States during the past thirty years or so, with the possible exception of Martin Luther King—who also was eliminated by assassination. The conventional view is that the Kennedys and King all were the independent victims of random acts of political violence. But even if that is true, the possible presidency of yet another Kennedy brother argues for reconsideration of the relationship between family, politics, political integration, and political leadership, in republics as well as in monarchies.

From the point of view of public policy, antinepotism structures have been a byproduct of the past decade's overriding thrusts toward egalitarianism in sex, and to a much lesser extent in age; but certainly the theory of kin selection has implications for such questions. For example, the extension of kin selection to parent-offspring conflict and parental investment has an obvious bearing on political socialization, and consequently on political attitudes and participation. Such an inquiry is not entirely unprecendented, in view of Lasswell's well-known retrospection (1948, p. 69) about Judge X, in which the judge's political behavior on the bench was related to the pace of his toilet-training during infancy by the parental surrogate, a nurse. Lasswell's Freudian explanation never caught on; conceivably, more systematic data on weaning behavior, in relation to attachment theory (Alloway, Pliner, and Krames 1977) (of which Trivers's parent-offspring theory might be deemed a component) may have some relevance to various political behaviors.

Domestication

Genetic engineering has implications of a very different sort for political science. In the United States, local and federal governments have been competing with each other for several years over the regulation of genetic research. National Science Foundation (NSF) guidelines for research in reconstituted DNA constitute one widely publicized case in point. A related policy area of considerable interest and broad implications concerns the regulation of sperm banks. An Associated Press dispatch from London reports that "British hospitals are paying men to father babies by artificial insemination for women who cannot have children the normal way" (*Stars and Stripes* 1979). Payment became necessary because "insufficient numbers of suitable male donors could be found to give samples of their sperm under the state-run National Health Service program of artificial insemination." (Evidently, the word has not yet gotten around very widely, among the male half of the population in the country where the concept of "inclusive fitness" was spawned, about the virtually unlimited opportunities for genetic reproduction that await any enterprising young man in England.) From a technical point of view, a *single* (although not necessarily unmarried) male donor could, given appropriate care and distribution of his largess, inseminate every fecund female in the entire country. Given the diploid character of the species, this hardly amounts to cloning; yet it probably proffers the closest empirical analogy to generalized kin selection that even human ingenuity is likely to devise. It promises also to provide the route that would make the hard-core theoretical analogies between humans and certain of the social insects much more meaningful. Under the circumstances envisaged, genetic altruism ought to become a widespread consequence; but kin selection then would certainly constitute a major political problem because of its massive entailments.

To show how rapidly significant results could be expected, consider Sewall Wright's discussion of how bulls do it: one extraordinarily "fit" bull,

> Favourite, born in 1793, shows a random correlation of 0.55 with random Shorthorns of 1920 . . . [while] the breed (in which over 170,000 had been registered in Britain, over a million in the United States, and over 200,000 in Canada by 1921) was radically transformed in type by sires tracing to a single herd—that of Cruikshank, whose leading bull, Champion of England, born in 1859, shows a relation to the breed as a whole of 0.26 for 1850 but 0.46 by 1920. [1977, p. 533; see especially chaps. 3, 16]

It is true that Wright does point out elsewhere in his treatise that from the standpoint of biotic evolution, humans are a feral and not a domesticated species. But he was clearly thinking in terms of the past, not in terms of a future in which paternal surrogates would rival digital computers in their power of control over human behavior.

In the meantime, there are still problems of public policy, and therefore of politics, that will surely have to be confronted soon about the adjective glossed over so glibly by news reports. Who will be defined as a "suitable" donor, once donation becomes a buyer's instead of a seller's market? One presumes that, given the conservative character of the political leadership of the incumbent British government, the National Health Service is operating a laissez faire—to say nothing of a caveat emptor—policy, and is paying off any available donor who is free of obvious veneral disease and other apparent phenotypic (and putatively genetic) deficiencies. This is no doubt the easiest policy to administer, as well as the easiest for which to obtain initial political approval. Population geneticists, however, ought to advocate a policy of strict random sampling; this is because the rejection of even any of the readily diagnosed genetic diseases (many of which are semi-lethal and therefore do not prevent their male sufferers from achieving puberty) is fraught with the potentially greater risk of failing to prefer a complex of gene interactions that, although of no present or past value, might be critical to future species adaptation in environments that cannot be predicted with precision now. Surely some biologists, as well as many lay theorists will (as in the past) opt for a policy of eugenical choice that will blast Pandora's box open with a vengeance.[32] In the United States, the policy competitors of the eugenicists will surely include a host of special-interest advocates, from the American Nazi Party to, no doubt, the technical experts of the American Kennel Club. The problem is not beyond existing capabilities for either rational or political choice, but the controversy should be spectacular.

Once governments become heavily involved with sperm banks, the possibilities for policy expansion are promising. In the first place, it should be easy to establish rules to control the rationing of male donations to female recidivists; this could lead directly into a much broader program for population control, which obviously would have to be global, and administered perhaps by the United Nations Educational, Social, and Cultural Organization (UNESCO), to have optimal effectiveness. It would be a simple matter, once policy on suitability has become established and bureaucratized (see Frank 1947), to protect from the predictable black-market competition of freebooting male scabs, by arranging for the compulsory vasectomizing of all male infants at birth, instead of or perhaps together with circumcision, excepting only the ones earmarked during gestation as future drones. This will certainly be a very small minority, as sampling techniques improve in precision. Alternatively, compulsory vasectomies could be made a major feature of the puberty rites of the majority not elected to genetic immortality, thereby giving such neuters something to look forward to during their childhood.

Colonization

An intuitively plausible hypothesis that can be investigated is based on Williams's suggestion that each new generation can be viewed as colonists establishing themselves in terra incognita. Population geneticists have developed various models (Levins 1970; Boorman and Levitt 1972; Wilson 1975, pp. 107-117) to predict the adaptation of colonists to niches (novel to the colonists) that they exploit; and although this theory, which of course builds upon the work of Wright discussed previously, was developed to analyze lateral extensions of populations, moving through time together, it can also be employed (as Williams implies) to examine change in populations in relatively fixed places, with the habitats varying more according to time than to place. Or both time and place might be dynamics of equal importance, as seems to be true of internal U.S. demographic shifts over the past fifty years. The dependent variable would be change in political cultures and subcultures (Schubert 1979b). One emphasis in political gerontology (Cutler 1977) has been on differences in the political culture of generational cohorts, as exemplified by studies that show the lasting effects of the political culture of the time of their socialization on the subsequent beliefs and behaviors of political elites. (Schubert, forthcoming a). Thus the colonist hypothesis from evolutionary population genetics might contribute importantly to research in political change.

War

A promising contribution to the analysis of both public policy and political behavior is Wright's theory of interdeme selection, which is opposed by hard-core (individualistic) sociobiological theory as represented in the writings of Williams and, to a lesser extent, Wilson. Our premise here must be, therefore, that hard-core sociobiological theory has made an unwitting contribution to political analysis, having through its opposition directed attention to a component of more orthodox population-genetics theory that does promise to be useful in political analysis.

Physical and social anthropologists agree that hominid and human hunter-gatherers have been living in population groups of the size of Wright's postulated demes—from 50 to 500 individuals—for a very long time, probably since the differentiation of the genus up to six million years ago. Even after the shift to agriculture, most persons continued to live in or

near villages of the same size, notwithstanding the great political importance of the rise of a few cities, and subsequently city-states, beginning
perhaps six millennia ago. Even as recently as a hundred years ago in the
United States, a majority of Americans continued to live in demes of 500 or
less. In the middle of the nineteenth century there were only about eighty urban areas in the United States with populations of more than 1,000; of
these, fewer than half had more than 10,000 inhabitants. In terms of evolutionary time, humans have been crowded into megalopolises for only about
0.01 percent (10^{-4}) of their specific genetic experience.

A frequently suggested hypothesis is that at least until 10^4 B.P.,
neighboring demes were in genetic as well as phenotypic competition with
each other for the resources necessary to individual and group existence:
principally food, and within that category primarily animal protein (Ross
1978). Genetic punishment for too close inbreeding was so direct and so
highly probably that cultural norms to reinforce that learning doubtless
were invented independently in many times and places, and in any event dif-
fused rapidly (Bischof 1975; Demarest 1977), although, then as now, the
universality of their observance was another matter. The complement of incest norms is of course the systematic exchange of females between demes,
as Tiger and Fox (1971) and many others have proposed. Various
catastrophes, including but by no means restricted to those stemming directly from climate, always have been an important cause of the extinction
or absorption of particular demes. Much of the time contiguous demes—
and not necessarily any more "territorial" than the Lapps were fifty years
ago—were in direct competition for food; the exchange of females between
groups was probably more important as a medium for the reduction than
for the incitation of interdeme aggression. Consequently, chronic (although
by no means continuing) aggression between and among groups has been
adaptive for human demes for at least half a million years, not merely
during the few thousand years of recent history for which written and/or ar-
cheological evidence demonstrates indisputable that this has been true.

Two equivalent but apparently independently constructed analyses of
primitive warfare were published in 1975, both by population geneticists. In
one, William Hamilton, the godfather of hard-core sociobiological theory,
observes that:

> [E]ffective birth control (practices, including cannibalism] cut warfare at
> its demographic root. Unfortunately, it is possible that in doing so they also
> cut . . . the selection for intelligence. The rewards of the victors in warfare
> [include] tools, livestock, stores of food, luxury goods to be seized, and
> even a possibility for the victors to impose themselves for a long period as a
> parasitical upper class. . . . [I]t has to be remembered that to raise mean
> fitness in a group either new territory or outside mates have to be obtained
> somehow. The occurrence of quasi-warlike group interactions in various
> higher primates . . . strongly suggests that something like warfare may

have become adaptive far down in the hominid stock. . . . If the male war
party has been adaptive for as long as is surmised here, it is hardly surprising that a similar grouping often reappears spontaneously even in circumstances where its present adaptive value is low or negative, as in the
modern teenage gangs. . . .

It has been argued that warfare must be a pathological development in man
continually countered by natural selection and . . . must always endanger
the survival of a species [but] I see no likelihood for it as regards fighting of
individuals or of groups up to the level of small nations. . . . [F]or the
species as a whole, and in the short term, war is detrimental from the
biological demographic point of view, but . . . detriment to the species does
not mean that a genetical proclivity will not spread. . . . The gross inef-
ficiency of warfare may be just what is necessary, or at least an alternative
to birth control and infanticide, in order to spare a population's less
resilient resources from dangerous exploitation. Maybe if the mammoth-
hunters had attacked each other more and the mammoths less they could be
mammoth-hunters still. . . . Many examples in the living world [today]
show that a population can be very successful in spite of a surprising diversion of time and energy into aggressive displays, squabbling, and outright
fights. The examples range from bumble bees to European nations. [Never-
theless], it is hard in the modern world to see warfare as a stabilizing influence for man. . . . Pastoralists tend to be particularly warlike and the
histories of civilization are punctuated by their inroads. . . .[But] incur-
sions of barbaric pastoralists seem to do civilizations less harm in the long
run than one might expect . . . [because] certain genes or traditions of the
pastoralists revitalize the conquered people with an ingredient of progress
[*sic*] which tends to die out in a large panmictic population. . . . I have in
mind altruism itself, or the part of the altruism which is perhaps better
described as self-sacrificial daring. [1975, pp. 147-149][33]

Durham (1976, pp. 406-407) has proposed similarly that in primitive
warfare where competition is between relatively small, only distantly
related, hunting-band demes, an economical way to enhance the genetic
fitness of one group is to remove and subsequently display the heads of
members of the competing group. As he points out, eating one's (outgroup)
enemy is an effective means of eliminating competition for scarce protein,
while at the same time directly augmenting one's own supply. His empirical
example is not inconsistent with the prediction of inclusive-fitness theory;
but that is very far from a demonstration that the religious duty to eat one's
enemy—however common this may have been among humans of Neolithic
times—results or resulted from genetic control and not from cognitive
choice and learning. We certainly should expect cannibalism to be selected
against, in genetic evolution, under circumstances such as Durham
describes, where reciprocity is not only probable but (culturally) obligatory
and reinforced by kin selection.

Thus we are confronted with two problems. One the one hand, it is
essential to distinguish between the genetic and the cultural factors that

promote human war; and neither Hamilton nor Durham—nor, as far as I know, anyone else—has attempted to make such a distinction. And once that has been done successfully, it will be necessary to go considerably beyond the present level of metaphorical theory when neolithic is compared to nuclear (or even to napalm) warfare. The very facts about both demes and their environments that are used to support the explanation (whether genetic or cultural) of primitive war are conspicuously missing from the empirical structure of modern warfare. The hunting-band model may fit part of the data for the tactics and behavior of infantry platoons (possibly even of companies isolated in jungle fighting); but the hypothesis needs a great deal of work if it is to be of any help in modeling the possible triangular warfare between the United States, the Soviet Union, and the People's Republic of China. To be useful in political science—to say nothing of political practice—sociobiological theory will have to proffer a causal theory that explains and predicts warfare in, say, the Middle East, or in Southeast Asia, during the 1960s, 1970s, and 1980s. In view of many of its advance notices, hard-core theory ought to be demonstrated to do that at least as well as the presently available, admittedly woefully inadequate, theories produced so far by social scientists.

Among the relevant questions to be answered are:

Is war adaptive for the very much larger demes (countries) that now constitute the competing "groups" in international politics? for demes that compete within (and often, now, across) individual countries?

At the level of biotic evolution, is war adaptive for the human species?

Unreciprocal Altruism

There is a related hypothesis, cited with approval by such leading population geneticists as Eshel and Hamilton, that recent cultural selection has failed to halt the decline in cultural altruism that began with the rise of civilization and that is likely to continue at a progressive rate. If that is true, then clearly there are tremendous implications for public policy, politics, and political science. It will be recalled that the hypothesis assumes that cultural altruism was developed over an epoch to be measured in hundreds of thousands of years, and probably antedates the differentiation of our present species;[34] whereas it has been only some ten thousand years since the breakdown of the face-to-face interdependence of the hunting band resulted in a parallel breakdown in the rationality of reciprocal altruism. The denouement came with the shift from pastoralism to agriculture (and hence to cities, and eventually to the more efficient modes of stored-energy exploitation that characterize the past two centuries). The phenomenon of mass anomie is a familiar one (for example, Riesman, Glazea and Denny, 1951); so is the diagnosis of the underlying cause as the consequence of some regrettable aberrations in contemporary custom, amenable to alleviation by a new method of teaching reading, or of measuring intelligence. What is novel is the hypothesis that the basic cause is a product of cultural change so slow that it must be measured—like genetic change, although not to the same degree—on a scale of geological time.

This suggests that the likelihood is nil that any feasible kind of cultural change can succeed in reversing the trend toward diminishing altruism in general. The environmental conditions that supported the human niche during the Pleistocene are long gone. This would be true even if it were otherwise possible to cut the species population down to a fraction of 1 percent of its present size, and even if both the industrial and the agricultural ways of life could somehow be foregone. Obviously, worldwide nuclear warfare might produce such a consequence, but it is even likelier that its result would be straightforward and direct extinction for the species. This is a pessimistic conclusion, which if correct, implies that much greater emphasis should be placed on public policies consciously designed—culturally, of course—to attempt to rebuild human altruistic behavior at least on a selective basis. Conceivably, an immensely greater self-conscious effort, organized on something approaching a global basis, might bring about temporary stability and perhaps even some short-run increases in altruism. There is an even smaller chance that once such improvements in social altruism were established ("culturally fixed") in some critical mass of populations, then Wright's process of sampling drift would begin to operate through interdeme selection because the higher-altruism groups would prove to be better competitors than those of lower altruism. It is pleasing to contemplate such an ironic turning of the tables on inclusive fitness.

Addendum

The revision of Dr. Trivers's remarks, in the form in which they appear in this volume and beyond the transcript of his oral presentation in April 1977, did not reach me until June 1980—more than fifteen months after I had submitted the preceding chapter to the editor. These circumstances preclude the extensive revision that would be necessary to take into account all the new things that Trivers now has to say. But I do wish to point out that in its published form, Trivers's chapter still continues to evoke the question, not only from the average political scientist, but also from readers such as I who are in general highly sympathetic to a biological approach to the study of politics: what does anything he says have to do with politics? I must also point out that my failure to comment systematically in detail on what is now manifest in the Trivers's revised revision—a fault I presume will necessarily be shared by the other symposium participants for the same reason that constrains me—should not be construed as implying that Trivers's new remarks do not invite such detailed critique.

To take as an example a single page from his revised chapter manuscript: he asserts that "It makes all the difference in the world whether you believe that I am beating you up for the greater good of mankind or whether you believe that I am beating you up to further my own ends (ultimately, reproductive)." Why should it? Trivers would quickly learn, if he were to substitute empirical observation of human behavior for the abstract examples on which he typically relies in lieu of evidence, that if he were to attempt to beat me (and I venture to say, many other persons) up, it would be immaterial to his intended victims whether his claimed justification was that he was doing it for their own good, or to improve his sex life, or to enhance his genetic immortality. For a person trained as a biologist to spout such nonsense is itself testimony to the crying need for more social science in biological education. Two paragraphs later he remarks that when such a novel hypothesis as that of natural selection is modified by human culture to uphold "older patterns of thought," then, "Thus is progress impeded." Such an appreciation of cultural evolution as is implicit in Trivers's conception of "progress" evinces substantial ignorance of the nonphysical side of modern anthropology. Even at the more technical level of modern evolutionary theory, Trivers surely is incorrect when he says, in the very next sentence, that "in reality Darwin had discovered the exact, ongoing way in which organic creation is achieved"—unless he really meant to refer to Gregor Mendel. A little later we are treated to Trivers's extensive ruminations on the theme of male langur infanticide, a bestial fantasy of the slaughter of the innocents, which he made much of in his oral presentation in 1977 and which is now embellished in his written variations, based primarily on the doctoral thesis of his former student at Harvard, Sarah Hrdy (1974).[35] But for langurs there are at best a handful of direct empirical observations, of male-usurper infant killing, by professionally qualified ethologists (or primatologists) in support of the hypothesis; and there are no empirical studies (including those by Hrdy) that examine the available scanty evidence both quantitatively and systematically, and utilizing quasi-experimental controls, in relation to the indubitably high levels of infant mortality from *other* (nonsociobiological) causes, in groups of monkeys that have become confined to disappearing habitats where they are in intense competition with humans and other animals for life-supporting resources. Hrdy has reported, however, that

> Within the same species, infanticide may occur in some areas but not others, as evidenced by the variable expression of infanticidal behavior among Hanuman langurs. . . . At present, the chief candidate for determining behavioral differentiation between populations or groups of langurs are human disturbance and population density.

She herself favors the population-density explanation, but adds that "an association between infanticide and high population densities is equally compatible with explanations based on sexual selection or resource competition" (1979, pp. 13, 26, 29n). Any theory, sociobiological or otherwise, that has to rely on such shaky evidence as that which Trivers proffers to support langur male infanticide is in deep trouble—or, at least, would be so deemed among an audience of social scientists. (Vogel 1979; Eibl-Eibesfeldt 1980, p. 8; and Schubert forthcoming *e*) Nor is there a shred of evidence in support of the pressumption that langurs, or any other monkeys, can count up to six, or to seven; to say nothing of their being able to distinguish between the passing of six and of seven months.

For a final group of examples, I skip to the section on "deceit and self-deception" near the end of Trivers's chapter. In this section he speculates that "[a] portion of the brain devoted to verbal functions must become specialized for the manufacture and maintenance of falsehoods"—an assertion that runs directly counter to the emphasis on holism in contemporary neuroscience (Puccetti and Dykes 1978; White 1980). Trivers continues with the claim that "Of course it must be advantageous for the truth to be registered somewhere, so that mechanisms of self-deception must reside side by side with mechanisms for the correct apprehension of reality." This is naive neurobiology that typifies his penchant for mechanistic thought and analogies, which are misapplied to animals as plastic as humans; he merely compounds his problems with his very next sentence, that "the mind must be structured in a very complex fashion, repeatedly *split into public and private portions,* with complicated interactions between the subsections" (emphasis added). Trivers's speculations are in no sense acceptable as evidence supportive of his allegations about human morality. In the next section, on "the political attack on sociobiology," the third paragraph indulges in the gross oversimplification, characteristic of many sociobiological evangelists, of treating genes as though both polygenism and pleiotropism remain theories whose time has not yet come. But in the very next paragraph he vaults from behavior genetics to the sociological side of the fence, and postulates "an unfriendly section of the populace" whom hypocrites are misleading about sociobiology's true implications for institutional racism, especially with respect to imputed subpopulational differences in intelligence. It is puzzling to note that, in context, Trivers seems to equate the "unfriendly" population with black Americans; whereas the persons most agitated by the question that concerns him all seem to be white, well-educated elites, with social psychologists, cultural anthropologists, and sociologists constituting the unfriendly section of the populace, in confrontation with biometricians, most of whom are educational psychologists (with an occasional exception like Shockley.) In his concluding paragraph Trivers speaks of "Our [that is, sociobiologists'] destruction of group-selection thinking," a phrase that is both bombastic and untrue. The chances are that during the next two decades Trivers is going to experience a developing cultural evolution, in which the influence of C.H. Waddington and Sewell Wright will grow long after the current sociobiological fad has waned to its proper (and probably relatively miniscule) niche; this will be especially true to the extent that serious attempts are made to test with empirical data sociobiological theory applied to humans (see Schubert, in press; Schubert, forthcoming d).

Notes

1. On the more general question of the implications of biology for political analysis, see Ginsburg (1978) and Scott (1978). Also presented at the same Annual Meeting of the American Political Science Association, but since then published, is the Presidential Address of John C. Wahlke (1979). Schubert (1975, 1976); and (1975); Wiegele (1979).

2. Wilson, (1975), ch. 27. No great change in his knowledge, although perhaps some in his appreciation, of the social sciences is indicated in Wilson (1978).

3. Rooted in game theory and other econometrics, economic rationalism has reentered political science during the past two decades, in the guise of "positive theory." In that form it is no less, but certainly no more, in touch with empirical realism than the legal positivism that preceded it in political science. For a seminal work see Riker (1962); for a more recent example, see McKelvey and Ordeshook (1976).

4. When I pressed him to talk about what sociobiology implies for the study of politics, Trivers replied:

> I hope no one in here thinks I'm trying to communicate for your benefit. Any view of communication assumes that I'm trying to communicate for my benefit, and that may lead to different kinds of behavior than if I were really disinterestedly concerned with your own. . . . I've read a little bit about Marx and some of his work a year or so ago to try to keep up to date with what I was being accused of. [Transcript of recording of Symposium on Sociobiology and Politics, April 11, 1977, Temple University; made available by the chairperson, Elliott White, August 1977]

5. Credit for having suggested this term must go to Wilson, who writes:

> I have called . . . "hard-core" altruism, a set of responses relatively unaffected by social reward or punishment beyond childhood. Where such behavior exists, it is likely to have evolved through kin selection of natural selection operating on entire, competing family or tribal units. We would expect hard-core altruism to serve the altruist's closest relatives and to decline steeply in frequency and intensity as relationship becomes more distant [1978, p. 155]

He then further restricts the concept as applied to humans, by remarking that:

> Human altruism appears to be substantially hard-core when directed at closest relatives, *although still to a much lesser degree than in the case of the social insects and the colonial invertebrates.* The remainder of our altruism is essentially soft. [1978, p. 159; emphasis added]

According to this distinction, genetically determined altruism is "hard core"; culturally determined, "soft core."

6. George Williams says that

> In its ultimate essence the theory of natural selection deals with a cybernetic abstraction, the gene, and a statistical abstraction, mean phenotypic fitness. *Such a theory can be immensely interesting to those who have a liking and a facility for cybernetics and statistics.* [1966; emphasis added]

7. In his introduction to the same book, Williams has said that Darwinian

> "natural" selection is the sole creative force in evolution . . .[and] there is no escape from the conclusion that natural selection, as portrayed in elementary texts and in most of the technical contributions of population geneticists, can only produce adaptations for the genetic survival of individuals."

Unfortunately,

> Many biologists have recognized adaptations of a higher than individual
> level of organization. A few workers . . . have urged that the usual picture
> of natural selection, based on alternative alleles in populations, is not
> enough. They postulate that selection at the level of alternative populations
> must also be an important source of adaptation, and that such selection
> must be recognized to account for adaptations that work for the benefit of
> groups instead of individuals. . . . [But these] higher levels of selection are
> impotent and not an appreciable factor in the production and maintenance
> of adaptation. [1966, pp. 8-9]

8. "From the standpoint of the main issues treated in this book,"
Williams eventually concedes, "there is no more important phenomenon
that the organization of insect colonies" (1966, p. 197).

9. Wilson, for example, has stated that human marriage is based on
"genetic hardening" of the synapses (1978, p. 140). But his colleague
Lewontin makes infinitely more sense, in content knowledge of social
science as well as of population genetics (1977, pp. 6-20). Lewontin even has
a sense of humor, a saving grace not apparent in Wilson's pontifications.

10. A fair roundup of the principals would include Richard D. Alexander, Richard Dawkins, William D. Hamilton, Robert L. Trivers, George
C. Williams, and Edward O. Wilson—all zoologists. Indeed, the first four
appeared together in a panel discussion at the Annual Meeting of the
Animal Behavior Society in Seattle, June 22, 1978.

11. In addition to *Biology as a Social Weapon,* see vols. 7-9 (1975-1977)
of *Science for the People,* a bimonthly journal of social policy critique
which in more recent years has broadened its concerns considerably beyond
the paper tiger of hard-core sociobiology; Barlow and Silverberg (1980);
Caplan (1978a); and Sahlins (1976).

12. As remarked by Stuart A. Altmann, then president of the Animal
Behavior Society, in his discussion of the politics of sociobiology at the 1978
meeting of the society in Seattle; see Altmann (1962).

13. West Eberhard points out that

> The majority of social interactions, even among close kin, are probably
> competitive rather than beneficient in nature. Indeed, as Alexander (1974)
> has pointed out, an individual's closest relatives are his closest competitors
> because of their proximity and dependence on the same, often limited,
> resources. [1975, p. 30]

But this seems to contradict the very premises of kin-selection theory. See
Richerson and Boyd (1978).

14. But this is simplistic philosophy of science: Occam's razor is at best
a conventional, not an obligatory, criterion of relevance; and it is certainly
not the only index to the cutting edge for maximodeling empirical

knowledge. Here the parsimony argument makes sense only if we restrict our focus of interest and attention to the level of individual organic adaptation. But why *not* biotic adaptation? The world today is full of humans whose organic adaptability is being sacrificed on the altars of other people's notions of social policy that will be adaptive at levels ranging from the species to local communities. Even at the individual level, it is the biosphere that determines, among other things, the environment to which the individual adapts. It is the interaction between groups (at all levels) of individuals, and their respective environments, with which any viable theory of genetic influence on human behavior *must* be concerned, if it is to have any relevance to the concerns of political science.

15. It is notable that in his discussion of the views toward the biosphere of some of the major orthodox religions, Williams (1966, pp. 254-255) capitalizes "Nature" half a dozen times in less than a page and a half. Similarly, in one of his articles on the inclusive fitness of warfare, Durham (1976)—a student of Richard Alexander—consistently capitalizes "Selection." These authors convey the impression that they are thinking, as well as speaking, of some transcendental form of the deity, such as the "Holy Ghost."

16. For discussion of limited but definite reciprocal altruism (in Trives's use of the phrase) involving the sharing of food, implements, and knowledge—as well as the use of language—between nonhuman primates, see Savage-Rumbaugh, Rumbaugh, and Roysen (1978), and Schubert (1978). Ironically, Wilson has remarked that "On a few occasions, [Chimpanzee] males go so far as to tear off pieces of meat and hand them over to supplicants. This is a small gesture by the standards of human altruism . . ." (1978, p. 29). Should we infer that genetic control over reciprocal altruism is stronger in humans than in chimps?

17. His strongest claim is that "the above model for the natural selection of reciprocally altruistic behavior *can* readily explain the function of human altruistic behavior" (Trivers 1971, p. 48; emphasis added).

18. Campbell has wryly observed that

> The moralizing in the Old Tstament against onanism, homosexuality, and the temptation to sacrifice one's firstborn son . . . must be directed against socially produced dispositions, since these tendencies would be genetically self-eliminating. [1972, p. 34]

19. Trivers claims that "it is reasonable to assume that it has been an important factor in recent human evolution and that the underlying emotional dispositions affecting altruistic behavior have important genetic components" (1971, p. 48). No doubt arousal depends on human physiological functions that have evolved genetically; but Stanley Schacter and others have shown that the *meanings* associated with most human emotions

(perceived arousal) are almost entirely *learned* (culturally determined). See Schacter (1964); and Schacter and Singer (1962).

20. On the very last page of his book, Dawkins (1976, p. 215) manages to end in the same position as Campbell.

21. For an anthropologist's not very successful attempt to extend Williams's methodological individualism to cultural evolution, see Ruyle (1973); but a much better discussion of cultural evolution also given by an anthropologist, is included in Cloak (1975).

22. Wilson, of course, disagrees, asserting that "The sociobiological hypothesis [that is, genetic evolution] does not . . . account for differences among the societies" (1978, p. 154); in his view, cross-cultural differences must be due to cultural evolution exclusively.

23. Compare the remark of Mr. Justice Brandeis: "It is one of the happy accidents of the federal system that a single courageous State may, if its citizens choose, serve as a laboratory, and try novel social and economic experiments without risk to the rest of the country" (dissenting in *New State Ice Co.* v. *Liebmann,* 285 U.S. 262, 280-311 at 311 [1931]).

24. For an alternative commentary by a philosopher of science, see Burian (1978).

25. See Wright (1977, pp. 413-414) on Willis. In his incisive summary of the historical development of the theory of natural selection, Wright remarks that the postulation of "directed instead of accidental variation," which Darwin himself increasingly accepted as he grew older, implies the acceptance of "the inheritance of acquired characters" (1968, p. 7).

26. The preceding three sentences are: "In many species a typical adult female will enjoy something like the mean reproductive success. A male, especially in polygynous species, may not reproduce at all. Perhaps only the fittest 25% of the males will reproduce, and the top 1% may enjoy many times the mean reproductive success."

27. Evidently self-conscious about his hyperbolic choice of language, he offers this lame excuse: "To be strict, this book should be called not *The Selfish Cistron* nor *The Selfish Chromosome,* but *The slightly selfish big bit of chromosome and the even more selfish little bit of chromosome.* To say the least this is not a catchy title so . . ." (Dawkins 1976, p. 35). Apparently, he never considered an even simpler alternative: not to call it the selfish anything.

28. Williams says that "genes are potentially immortal" (1966, p. 24). More realistically, Alexander remarked, at the Animal Behavior Society's sociobiology panel on June 20, 1978, that genes do *not* survive forever—just considerably longer than populations and environments. But consider: inclusive fitness assumes a genetic value of 1 for each individual human, as a base for purposes of comparison. For each child the progenitor is assigned a score of 1/2; for each full sibling and each grandchild, 1/4; for full cousins and great-grandchildren, 1/8 each; and so on. At the end of only

nine successor generations—a bare moment in evolutionary time of two or three hundred years—after the progenitor's own phenotypic death, he or she may have hundreds of progeny; but his or her genetic contribution to any individual member of that ninth generation, a great-to-the-seventh-power grandchild, is less than 0.001, one-thousandth of its genetic constitution. And the progenitor's genetic influence is, of course, correspondingly attentuated. Immortality seems to be the wrong word to describe such genetic dissipation.

29. Christ (or, for that matter, Claudius I) is probably better known to more humans alive during the past hundred years than to all those of the preceding nineteen centuries combined. Certainly, Christ's cultural immortality must be deemed remarkable for a person whose reported inclusive fitness remains zero.

30. Indeed, there is a theory already two decades old, namely that competition between ecosystems is a fruitful level for analysis. It certainly is a level highly relevant to contemporary endeavors to redefine the human niche. See Dunbar (1960).

31. It is also notable that in his remarks at the sociobiology panel at the Animal Behavior Society's 1978 annual meeting, Hamilton took pains to pay homage to Sewall Wright, whom he claimed as his own intellectual ancestor.

32. The same Associated Press report concluded by noting that: "Colin Francome, a 34-year-old senior lecturer in sociology confirmed a report that he had urged his students at the Middlesex [sic] Polytechnic College near London to become donors" (*Stars and Stripes* 1979). More recently, the establishment of a sperm bank exclusively for Nobel Prize winners might be perceived as a step in the direction of a viable elite alternative to the British endeavor to bank for the masses—were it not for the American program's failure to exercise equivalent control over the choice of recipients. Conceivably, that omission may have been due to the paucity of premenopausal female Nobelists, which in turn suggests a possible defect in the very design of the experiment, as one more reminiscent of Aldous than Julian Huxley.

33. This is an odd caveat for Hamilton to interpose; much of the sociological data support the opposite finding, that teenage gang warfare is highly adaptive for most of its individual participants, whatever its impact on third parties (who are part of the environment, from the perspective of the youth warriors). For an ethological analysis of juvenile delinquency in the Netherlands, see van Dijk (1977).

34. Max Petterson has asked: "Will . . . the acceleration of human cultural change come to be regarded as a special case of a more general process? (1978, p. 205).

35. According to her:

I first learned of langurs accidentally, while satisfying a distribution requirement in one of Harvard's most popular undergraduate courses, primate behavior, starring Irven DeVore. A remark by the professor concerning the relation between crowding and the killing of infants in this exotic species of monkeys brought me back to Harvard a year after graduation to find out why the phenomenon occurred. My first paper in graduate school, entitled 'Infant-Biting and Deserting among Langurs," was a less than promising start. The course was meant to be on the evolution of sex differences, but I had attempted to slip in a topic related to my current obsession. According to the grader, an inspired teaching assistant named Robert L. Trivers, the paper had "nothing to do with sex." Later, while I worked under the guidance of [by then] Dr. Trivers, I was to learn how profound the relationship between langur infanticide and reproduction really is. [Hrdy 1977, p. vii]

References

Alloway, T.; Pliner, P.; and Krames, eds. 1977. *Attachment Behavior.* New York: Plenum.

Altmann, S.A. 1962. "A Field Study of the Sociobiology of Rhesus Monkeys, *Macaca Mulatta.*" *Annals of the New York Academy of Sciences* 102:338-435.

―――. 1978. "The Politics of Sociobiology." Paper presented at the Annual Meeting of the Animal Behavior Society, Seattle, Wash., June 1978.

Barlow, G.W., and Silverberg, J., eds. 1980. *Sociobiology: Beyond Nature/Nurture?* Boulder, Colo.: Westview Press.

Bischof, N., "Comparative Ethology of Incest Avoidance." In *Biosocial Anthropology,* edited by R. Fox, pp. 37-67. New York: Wiley, 1975.

Blurton Jones, N.G., and Sibly, R. 1978. "Testing Adaptiveness of Culturally Determined Behaviour: Do Bushman Women Maximize Their Reproductive Success by Spacing Births Widely and Foraging Seldom?" In *Human Behaviour and Adaptation,* edited by V. Reynolds and N. Blurton Jones, pp. 135-158. London: Taylor and Francis.

Boorman, S.A., and Levitt, P.R. 1972. "Group Selection on the Boundary of a Stable Population." *Proceedings of the National Academy of Sciences* 69:2711-2713.

Burian, R.M. 1978. "A Methodological Critique of Sociobiology." In *The Sociobiology Debate,* edited by A.L. Caplan, pp. 376-395. New York: Harper and Row.

Campbell, D.T. 1972. "On the Genetics of Altruism and the Counter Hedonic Components in Human Culture." *Journal of Social Issues* 28:21-37.

Caplan, A.L., ed. 1978a. *The Sociobiology Debate: Readings on Ethical and Scientific Issues.* New York: Harper and Row.

_____ . 1978b. "Testability, Disreputability, and the Structure of the Modern Synthetic Theory of Evolution." *Erkenntnis* 13:261-278.

Cloak, F.T., Jr. 1975. "Is Cultural Ethology Possible?" *Human Ecology* 3:161-182.

Corning, P.A. Forthcoming. *Politics and the Evolutionary Process.* New York: Harper and Row.

Cutler, N. 1977. "Demographic, Social-Psychological and Political Factors in the Politics of Aging: A Foundation for Research in Political Gerontology." *American Political Science Review* 71:1011-1025.

Dawkins, R. 1976. *The Selfish Gene.* Oxford: Oxford University Press.

Demarest, W.J. 1977. "Incest Avoidance among Human and Nonhuman Primates." In *Primate Bio-Social Development: Biological, Social, and Ecological determinants,* edited by S. Chevalier-Skolnikoff and F.E. Poirier, pp. 323-342. New York: Garland.

Dijk, J.J.M. van. 1977. *Dominantiegedrag en Geweld: Een Multidisciplinaire Visie op de Veroorzaking van Geweldmisdrijven.* Nijmegen: Dekker & van de Vegt.

Dunbar, M.J. 1960. "The Evolution of Stability in Marine Environments: Natural Selection at the Level of the Ecosystem." *American Naturalist* 94:129-136.

Durham, W.H. 1976. "Resource Competition and Human Aggression," p.1: "A Review of Primitive War." *Quarterly Review of Biology* 51:385-415.

Eibl-Eibesfeldt, I. 1980. "Too Many Jumping on the Bandwagon of Sociobiology." *Human Ethology Newsletter* no. 29, pp. 7-10.

Eshel, I. 1972. "On the Neighbor Effect and the Evolution of Altruistic Traits." *Theoretical Population Biology* 3:258-277.

Frank, P. 1947. *Mr. Adam.* London: Victor Gollancz.

Ginsburg, B.E. 1978. "What Will Students in Political Science Have to Know about Biology to Understand the New Dimension of Their Discipline and to Advance the Frontiers of Knowledge?" Paper presented at the Annual Meeting of the American Political Science Association, New York, September 1978.

Griffin, D.R. 1978. "Prospects for a Cognitive Ethology." *Behavioral and Brain Sciences* 1:527-538.

Hamilton, W.D. 1964. "The Genetical Evolution of Social Behavior." *Journal of Theoretical Biology:* 7:1-16 (p. 1), 7:17-52 (p. 2).

_____ . 1975. "Innate Social Aptitudes of Man: An Approach from Evolutionary Genetics." In *Biosocial Anthropology,* edited by R. Fox, pp. 133-155. New York: Wiley.

Hinde, R.A. 1966. *Animal Behavior: A Synthesis of Ethology and Comparative Psychology.* New York: McGraw-Hill.

_____ . 1974. *Biological Bases of Human Social Behavior*. New York: McGraw-Hill.

Hrdy, S.B. 1974. "Male-Male Competition and Infanticide among the Langurs (*Presbytis entellus*) of Abu, Rajasthan." *Folia Primatologica* 22:19-58.

_____ . 1977. *Tha Langurs of Abu*. Cambridge, Mass.: Harvard University Press.

_____ . 1979. "Infanticide Among Animals," *Ethology and Sociobiology* 1:13-40.

Kuhn, T.S. 1962. *The Structure of Scientific Revolutions*. Chicago: University of Chicago Press.

Landau, M. 1972. "On the Use of Metaphor in Political Analysis"; "Due Process of Inquiry"; "On the Use of Functional Analysis in American Political Science." Reprinted in *Political Theory and Political Science*, edited by M. Landau. New York: Macmillan.

Lasswell, H.D. 1948. *Power and Personality*. New York: W.W. Norton.

_____ . 1962. *The Future of Political Science*. New York: Atherton.

Layzer, D. 1978. "Altruism and Natural Selection." *Journal of Social and Biological Structures* 1:297-305.

Levins, R. 1970. "Extinction." In *Some Mathematical Questions in Biology*, edited by M. Gerstenhaber, pp. 77-107. Providence, R.I.: American Mathematical Society.

Lewontin, R.C. 1974. *The Genetic Basis of Evolutionary Change*. New York: Columbia University Press.

_____ . 1977. "Biological Determinism as a Social Weapon." In *Biology as a Social Weapon*, edited by the Ann Arbor Science for the People Editorial Collective, pp. 6-20. Minneapolis: Burgess Publishing Company.

Masters, R.D. 1978. "Classical Political Philosophy and Contemporary Biology." Paper presented at the Conference on Political Theory and the Question of Human Nature, Loyola University of Chicago, April 1978.

Maynard-Smith, J. 1964. "Group Selection and Kin Selection." *Nature* 201:1145-1147.

_____ . 1971. "What Use Is Sex?" *Journal of Theoretical Biology* 30:219-315.

McKelvey, R.D., and Ordeshook, P.C. 1976. "Symmetric Spatial Games Without Majority Rule Equilibria." *American Political Science Review* 70:1172-1184.

Odum, H.T. 1971. *Environment, Power, Society*, chap. 8. New York: Wiley.

Petterson, M. 1978. "Acceleration in Evolution, Before Human Times." *Journal of Social and Biological Structures* 1:201-206.

Puccetti, R., and Dykes, R.W., eds. 1978. "Sensory Cortex and the Mind-Brain Problem." *Behavioral and Brain Sciences* 1:337-376.

Reynolds, V. 1976. *The Biology of Human Action.* San Francisco: W.H. Freeman.

Richerson, P.J., and Boyd, R. 1978. "A Dual Inheritance Model of the Human Evolutionary Process," I: "Basic Postulates and a Simple Model." *Journal of Social and Biological Structures* 1:127-154.

Riesman, D. Glazer, M. and Denny, R. 1951. *The Lonely Crowd: A Study of the Changing American Character.* New Haven: Yale University Press.

Riker, W. 1962. *Theory of Political Coalitions.* New Haven: Yale University Press.

Ross, B. 1978. "Food Taboos, Diet, and Hunting Strategy: The Adaptation to Animals in Amazon Cultural Ecology." *Current Anthropology* 19:1-36.

Ruyle, E.E. 1973. "Genetic and Cultural Pools: Some Suggestions for a Unified Theory of Biocultural Evolution." *Human Ecology* 1:201-215.

Sagan, C. 1977. *The Dragons of Eden: Speculations on the Evolution of Human Intelligence.* New York: Random House.

Sahlins, M. 1976. *The Use and Abuse of Biology: An Anthropological Critique of Sociobiology.* Ann Arbor: University of Michigan Press.

Savage-Rumbaugh, E.S., Rumbaugh, D.M.; and Roysen, S. 1978. "Linguistically-Mediated Tool Use and Exchange by Chimpanzees." *Pan Troglogytes, Behavioral and Brain Sciences* 1:539-554.

Schacter, S. 1964. "The Interaction of Cognitive and Physiological Determinants of Emotional State." In *Advances in Experimental Social Psychology,* vol. 1., edited by L. Berkowitz, pp. 49-80. New York: Acadmic Press.

Schacter, S. and Singer, J.E. 1962. "Cognitive, Social and Physiological Determinants of Emotional States." *Psychological Review* 69:379-399.

Schubert, G. 1975. "Biopolitical Behavioral Theory." *Political Science Reviewer* 4:402-428.

———. 1976. "Politics as a Life Science: How and Why the Impact of Modern Biology Will Revolutionize the Study of Political Behavior. In *Biology and Politics: Recent Explorations,* edited by A. Somit, pp. 155-195. The Hague: Mouton.

———. 1978. "Cooperation, Cognition, and Communication." *Behavioral and Brain Sciences* 1:539-554, 597-600.

———. 1979a. "Ethology: A Primer for Political Scientists." *Center for Biopolitical Research Notes* 2, nos. 2, 3.

———. 1979b. "Subcultural Effects on Judician Behavior: A Comparative Analysis." Paper presented at a panel of the Section on Comparative Judicial Studies, International Political Science Association, Moscow, August 16, 1979.

_____ . 1979c. "Classical Ethology: Concepts and Implications for Human Ethology." *Behavioral and Brain Sciences* 2:44-46.

_____ . Forthcoming a. "A Biocultural Model of Activism and Restraint." In *Supreme Court Activism,* edited by C.M. Lamb and S.C. Halpern.

_____ . Forthcoming b. "Political Ethology." *Micropolitics* 1.

_____ . Forthcoming d. "Glaciers, Epigenesis, and Neoteny." Review of Valerius Geist, *Life Strategies, Human Evolution, Environmental Design: Toward a Biological Theory of Health* [New York: Springer-Verlag, 1978]. *Journal of Social and Biological Structures* 4.

_____ . Forthcoming c. "The Uses of Ethological Methods in Political Analysis." In *Biological Methods of Political Analysis,* edited by Meredith E. Watts.

_____ . Forthcoming e. "Infanticide by Usurper Hanuman Langur Males." Submitted for publication.

_____ . In Press. Review of "Kin Selection in the Japanese Monkey," by J.A. Kurland. In *Journal of Social and Biological Structures* 3.

Scott, J.P. 1978. "What Are the Expectations Regarding the Scope and Limits of Exploring the Biological Aspects of Political Behavior? Considerations of Methodology" Paper presented at the Annual Meeting of the American Political Science Association, New York, September 1978.

Somit, A. 1975. "Biopolitical Behavioral Theory." *Political Science Reviewer* 5:403-428.

Stars and Stripes, European edition, March 1, 1979, p. 18, col. 1.

Tiger, L., and Fox, R. 1971. *The Imperial Animal.* New York: Holt, Rinehart and Winston.

Trivers, R.L. 1971. "The Evolution of Reciprocal Altruism." *Quarterly Review of Biology* 46:35-37, 48.

_____ . 1974. "Parent-Offspring Conflict." *American Zoologist* 14:249-264.

_____ . 1978. "Remarks." Presented at the Sociobiology Panel at the Annual Meeting of the Animal Behavior Society, Seattle, Wash., June 1978.

Wahlke, J.C. 1979. "Pre-behavioralism in Political Science." *American Political Science Review* 73:9-31.

West Eberhard, M.J. 1975. "The Evolution of Social Behavior by Kin Selection." *Quarterly Review of Biology* 50:30.

_____ . 1976. "Born: Sociobiology." *Quarterly Review of Biology* 51:89-92.

White, E. 1980. "Clouds, Clocks, Brains and Political Learning." Paper presented at the 3rd Scientific Meeting of the International Society for Political Psychology, Boston, June 1980.

Wiegele, T.C. 1979. *Biopolitics Search for a More Human Political Science.* Boulder, Colo.: Westview Press.

Willhoite, F.H., Jr. 1977. "Evolution and Collective Intolerance." *Journal of Politics* 39:665-684.

Williams, G. 1966. *Adaptation and Natural Selection: A Critique of some Current Evolutionary Thought.* Princeton, N.J.: Princeton University Press.

Vogel, C. 1979. "The Hanuman-Langur (*Presbytis entellus*): A Key Example Regarding the Theoretical Concepts of Sociobiology?" *Verhandlungen der Deutschen Zoologischen Gesellschaft,* pp. 73-89. Stuttgart: G. Fischer.

———. 1971. *Group Selection.* Chicago: Aldine-Atherton.

———. 1975. *Sex and Evolution.* Princeton, N.J.: Princeton University Press.

Wilson, E.O. 1975. *Sociobiology: The New Synthesis.* Cambridge, Mass.: Harvard University Press, Belknap Press.

———. 1978. *On Human Nature.* Cambridge, Mass.: Harvard University Press.

Wright, S. 1968. *Genetic and Biometric Foundations.* Evolution and the Genetics of Populations: A Treatise in Four Volumes, vol. 1. Chicago: University of Chicago Press.

———. 1977. *Experimental Results and Evolutionary Deductions.* Evolution and the Genetics of Populations: A Treatise in Four Volumes, vol. 3. Chicago: University of Chicago Press.

———. 1978. *Variability Within and Among Natural Populations.* Evolution and the Genetics of Populations: A Treatise in Four Volumes, vol. 4. Chicago: University of Chicago Press.

Wynne-Edwards, V.C. 1962. *Animal Dispersion in Relation to Social Behavior.* New York: Hafner.

8

Rank and Reciprocity: Speculations on Human Emotions and Political Life

Fred H. Willhoite, Jr.

Cruelty of disposition; malice and ill-nature; that most antisocial and odious of all passions, envy; dissimulation and insincerity, irascibility on insufficient cause, and resentment disproportioned to the provocation; the love of domineering over others; the desire to engross more than one's share of advantages . . .; the pride which derives gratification from the abasement of others; the egotism which thinks self and its concerns more important than everything else, and decides all doubtful questions in its own favor—these are moral vices and constitute a bad and odious moral character.
—J.S. Mill, *On Liberty*

Political theorists should be grateful to sociobiologists for their insistence on the scientific legitimacy and necessity of taking the question of human nature seriously. This does not mean that any particular sociobiologist has "the" scientific answer to that question; for the most part they tend not to make such pretentious claims. But they do assert that we can hope to obtain a more nearly adequate understanding of our species only by learning about and trying to interpret properly its evolutionary history. They proceed in that effort by assuming that, because natural selection is a process of differential reproduction, individuals' behavior will normally be oriented toward maximizing the replication of their kinds of genes (both through personal reproduction and through assisting close genetic kin to reproduce and rear offspring).

That this Darwinian assumption applies to human behavior has been indignantly denied, on both social scientific and ideological grounds. The most sweeping and inclusive of such critiques is Marshall Sahlins's *The Use and Abuse of Biology: An Anthropological Critique of Sociobiology* (1976). Sahlins's scientific criticisms are directed primarily at "kin-selection" (or "inclusive-fitness") concepts as applied to human behavior. He maintains that there is no necessary correspondence between degrees of genetic kinship and how individuals classify and treat one another within the complex, culturally defined kinship systems of diverse societies. This fact is sufficient to falsify the basic premise of sociobiology and to exemplify the essential independence of the symbolically defined cultural realm from genetically shaped behavioral imperatives.

However, Richard Alexander (1978) has attempted to demonstrate that kin selection cannot be so readily dismissed. He contends that an adequate analysis of human societies must consider the use of kin designations to cement reciprocal relationships, the pressures for outbreeding, whether a marriage system is polygymous, and the degree of certainty of paternity. When these factors are taken carefully into account, he avers, close analysis of kinship systems does tend to support a genetic model for a diverse range of cultures. This debate is far from settled.

One of its beneficial effects has been to inspire evolutionary biologists to think seriously about human culture, as in Richerson and Boyd's (1978) "dual-inheritance" model of human evolution. They conceive of biological and cultural evolution as different processes, but with a complex interrelationship. Human kinship systems do tend to diverge somewhat from the sociobiological predictions that seem to hold true for nonhuman animals, demonstrating the independent influence of cultural norms and institutions. but across diverse societies, altruistic aid is, on the average, disproportionately directed toward genetic relatives, suggesting significant links between natural selection and kinship in the human species.

The ideological attack on sociobiology has been highly publicized and sometimes vicious. Fundamentally it rests on an argument of the "unmasking" or "demystifying" type, of which Sahlins's version is one of the clearest. He claims that sociobiologists typically interpret animal behavior in terms unconsciously derived from contemporary human societies—for example, competition, cost/benefit, reciprocity—and then assume that these categories constitute central principles of animals' social behavior and employ these allegedly "natural" principles to explain as evolutionarily "necessary" human behavior patterns that are in fact historically limited to societies shaped by modern capitalism. For example: " 'Reciprocal altruism' as Trivers views it is an economics of petty commercial exchange" (Sahlins 1976, p. 88). This is a circular process, which tells us a good deal about the theorists but nothing about the phenomena that they are claiming to interpret.

This argument, I believe, is fatally flawed. For one thing, the psychological or sociological origins of an idea do not determine its validity. Uncovering allegedly covert ideology is, in itself, nothing more than a form of ad hominem argument, one of the classic logical fallacies. Sahlins undermines his own argument by quoting from a letter in which Marx interpreted Darwinism as an ideological projection onto nature of central categories of English political economy (Sahlins 1976, pp. 101-102). That was probably quite correct, since Darwin made no secret of his indebtedness to the economic theory of Malthus. However, Marx did *not* claim that the source of inspiration for the concept of natural selection discredits it as a scientific theory. Indeed, this may well be a classic demonstration that exposing the ideological roots of a theory in no way suffices for evaluating its scientific fruits.

Furthermore, how *is* one to understand the field observations of intraspecies lethal violence among, for example, chimpanzees, gorillas, several types of monkeys, wolves, lions, hyenas, African wild dogs? Is it really "bourgeoismorphic" to interpret such behavior as competitive—for status, mates, or other resources—when the observed situation seems to make most sense in those terms? It seems entirely possible that ideological prejudice could prevent accurate understanding of *animal* behavior; the sword of "unmasking" cuts more than one way.

I am not implying that sociobiology is, or should be, immune from trenchant criticisms. Sociobiological theorists have sometimes given the impression that they consider the whole symbolic realm of human culture as a mere epiphenomenon expressing and partially masking genetic imperatives. This probably reflects an understandable lack of experience and naivete in dealing with human data, and anthropologists and other social scientists are well equipped to point out errors and mistaken assumptions on the part of evolutionary biologists. As I have indicated, some of the latter have begun to develop much more sophisticated conceptualizations of the evolution of human behavior, while continuing to insist that it must be interpreted within a fundamentally Darwinian framework.

It seems to me unwise at this time for political theorists to commit themselves unreservedly to one particular version of evolutionary theory. Biologists who mutually agree on the reality and fundamental significance of the evolutionary process still disagree on many important points of interpretation. However, I do regard it as perfectly legitimate to consider sociobiological speculations about human evolution and attempt to discern some of their potential implications, as long as the provisional and exploratory nature of this kind of thinking is clearly understood. If one desires to theorize within the boundaries of empirical science, there is no choice but to attempt to develop an evolutionary conception of human nature and politics, however fumbling, error prone, and interminable the effort may be.

As a student and teacher of the great political theorists of the Western tradition, I greatly admire the boldly speculative character of Robert Trivers's work. Starting from the fundamental assumption that the individual is the principal unit of selection within the evolutionary process, Trivers seeks to explore the implications of this assumption for our understanding of some of the most elementary social relationship—sor example, those between parents and offspring, or between siblings. I shall try to explore a few implications for political theory of one type of social interaction disussed by Trivers—"reciprocal altruism," exchanges of assistance or resources. This chapter represents my speculations, inspired by but not limited to Trivers's speculations. In no sense should he be held accountable for my extrapolations, nor did I present them in a spirit of dogmatic certainty.

Reciprocity

The bedrock importance of reciprocity within human societies is taken for granted by social scientists, and it is a very old theme in political theory. The first stage of Plato's imaginary polis in the *Republic* consists of exchanges of goods and services among diversely talented individuals; and the conception of political obligation as, in some sense, fundamentally reciprocal, runs like an unbroken thread through the whole great tradition of Western political thought.

Within the context of hominid evolution, the existence and significant role of within-group reciprocity is attested to by paleoanthropological evidence of extensive food sharing among East African "protohominids" living at least two million years ago (Isaac 1978). Glynn Isaac points out that humans belong to the only primate species within which food sharing is a normal behavior. With the exceptions of maternal nursing of offspring and the "tolerated scrounging" of meat among chimpanzees, nonhuman primate individuals obtain and consume all of their own foodstuffs. It seems highly probable that the reciprocal exchange of food items—for example, of wild fruits and vegetables gathered near the "home base" by females for some of the animal protein captured by male hunters—was one of the most important adaptations constributing to the unique characteristics of the genus *Homo*. Isaac speculates that forming and managing complex reciprocal ties would have called for an ability to calculate complex chains of contingencies reaching into the future. The selective advantages of an ability to plan and calculate must have been very significant in the evolution of the biological basis of human intellect—a point that echoes the conclusion of Trivers's noted article on reciprocal altruism (1971).

Concerning much more recent and complex societies, a sociological theorist has asserted: "A norm of reciprocity is, I suspect, no less universal and important an element of culture than the incest taboo, although, similarly, its concrete formulations may vary with time and place" (Gouldner 1960, p. 171). This norm minimally requires that individuals should help and also refrain from injuring those who have helped them. Even in present-day China, where the regime has made a massive effort to impose a uniform, ideologically based code of behavior, there is persuasive anecdotal, journalistic evidence for the widespread persistence of informal networks for exchanging scarce and highly valued goods and services (Butterfield 1977).

Given the phylogenetically ancient and continuing importance of reciprocity in human societies, Trivers argues that such behaviors originally evolved because in the long run they benefited (in "inclusive-fitness" terms) the individuals that performed them. This assumption has been challenged by Sahlins (1976, pp. 87-88), who contends that engaging in mutually beneficial reciprocity gives no individual a differential advantage in terms of natural selection; exchanges between unrelated individuals essentially involve helping one's genetic competitors as much as oneself. The evolution of such behaviors cannot therefore be explained on the basis of considering the individual as the prime unit of selection.

This is a serious criticism that requires detailed consideration by partisans of individual-level selection. At this point I would suggest only that one should consider group living to be a basic ecological parameter of species in the hominid line, probably extending much farther back into our primate past than does systematic reciprocity. Given group life as a species-specific adaptation—see Alexander (1974, 1975) for discussion of the costs and benefits of living in groups—it seems plausible that reciprocal altruism could have provided differential advantage to individuals within some groups as contrasted to less systematic reciprocators in other groups. As pointed out previously, food sharing is unique to hominids among the higher primates. Why and how it began is unknown, but it proved to be highly adaptive. Given its appearance and spread, any individual's alternative to participating in networks of reciprocity and thereby giving some aid to genetic competitors would have been nonadaptive exclusion from group life.

In short, "reciprocal altruism" should be thought of as a fantastically successful evolutionary compromise. As Trivers points out, it constitutes a dynamic and unstable system, which is what one would expect of a system incorporating a competitive component—both within and between distinctive groups. The ever present threat to a reciprocity system is the failure of inadequacy of reciprocation by individuals who have already received benefits—what Trivers calls the "cheating" problem. I suspect that this emphasis is what upsets many of Trivers's critics. He does not present a view of "mutual aid" as simply the most natural and life enhancing of biological phenomena; rather, it is analyzed within the Darwinian framework of inexorable competition.

The need for a regulatory system to cope with the cheating problem leads Trivers to speculate about the evolution of human psychological capacities and tendencies. Cognitive abilities promoted by reciprocity would include capacities to design methods of subtle "cheating" and to detect them in the behavior of others, to see the advantages of and design multiparty reciprocity systems, and to formulate and elaborate norms of reciprocity.

Trivers focuses more attention, however, on the evolution of emotional regulators of social interactions, which may well constitute the most promising area of evolutionary-behavioral research and speculation on the human species (Parker 1978, p. 854; McShea 1978). Trivers explains clearly why he suspects that reciprocal altruism promoted the evolution of gratitude, sympathy, guilt feelings, trust, distrust, suspicion, and a tendency to feel friendly toward altruists. I shall be concerned primarily, however, with exploring the character and implications of an emotional reaction that Trivers considers centrally important as a regulator of reciprocity: "moralistic aggression and indignation."

This is a strong feeling aroused by a perception of injustice, unfairness, and lack of reciprocity. Against the alleged cheater it may well trigger verbal or even physical violence that appears to be an overreaction to the supposed offense. "But since small inequities repeated many times over a lifetime may exact a heavy toll in relative fitness, selection may favor a strong show of aggression when the cheating tendency is discovered" (Trivers 1971, p. 49).

I shall try to bring more concreteness to this consideration of reciprocity patterns and their emotional regulators by discussing the !Kung San (formerly called Bushmen), an African hunter-gatherer people who live in the Kalahari Desert. Since the members of our species and its predecessors lived as hunter-gatherers for hundreds of millennia, we may indirectly gain some clues to human-behavioral evolution by seeking commonalities in the cultures of the few remaining hunter-gatherers. Such evidence can be suggestive but never conclusive with respect to human behavioral evolution, because all living hominids are members of a single subspecies, *Homo sapiens sapiens.*

When we turn to the !Kung for illustrative particulars, we find that kinship and reciprocity are centrally important in their societies. The basic local community is a camp, comprising people who live and move around together for months at a time. The core members of each camp group are several siblings or cousins of both sexes, who are acknowledged to be hereditary owners of the nearby water hole (Lee 1976, p. 77). Within a camp, huts are constructed along the circumference of a circle. Each hut is usually occupied by a nuclear family, and huts belonging to members of an extended family are contiguous (Yellen 1976, pp. 61-63).

The resource-laden area around the water hole belongs to the resident group—but not exclusively. Anyone who has a relative in the camp may enter the area and hunt or gather food. There is a good deal of moving around, and the composition of any single group seldom remains the same for very long. One clear pattern is that groups that own the most reliable water holes spend most of the year moving about to enjoy the seasonally available food resources of their neighbors, who in turn receive access during the dry season or prolonged droughts to the relative bounty of those who can always count on having water. Reciprocal access to vital resources obviously benefits the members of all groups involved in these exchanges, and explicit rules govern this pattern of reciprocity. In basic respects, they are very similar to land-use rules found among many other hunting-gathering peoples (Lee 1976, pp. 78-91).

Of the ubiquitous sharing among the !Kung, Lorna Marshall remarks: "Altruism, kindness, sympathy, or genuine generosity were not qualities that I observed often in their behavior. However, these qualities were not entirely lacking, especially between parents and offspring, between siblings, and between spouses" (Marshall 1976, p. 350).

Sharing and giving among the !Kung are to a great extent reciprocal. (Note Trivers's view that reciprocal altruism is likely even between close relatives, in addition to the nepotistic altruism favored by kin selection [Trivers 1971, p. 46]. This simply follows from the nonidentity of relatives' reproductive "interests.") Individuals frequently give away objects such as arrows, tools, or meat; but the recipient has an iron-clad obligation to return a gift to the giver in the near future. In fact, it is perfectly acceptable to ask for a gift from a recipient whose giving one considers overdue. Among the !Kung, the motives for gift giving seem to be "to measure up to what is expected of them, to make friendly gestures, to win favor, to repay past favors and obligations, and to enmesh others in future obligations" (Marshall 1976, pp. 352, 369, 361).

On the basis of her long experience with the !Kung, Marshall has concluded that there is yet another motive for their extensive reciprocal gift giving: "Even more specifically in my opinion, they mitigate jealousy and envy, to which the !Kung are prone, by passing on to others objects that might be coveted" (1976, p. 368). The !Kung are far from unique in this respect. In fact, I should like to explore the possibility that envy is an evolved emotional reaction in humans, which functions, in part, as an important regulator of reciprocal relationships involving whatever things or qualities people value—wealth, beauty, love, power, prestige, position. I suspect that envy is very much involved in the psychology of Trivers's "moralistic aggression and indignation."

Envy is a term that we often confound with *jealousy*, but in this discussion it will mean a strong, aggressive, potentially destructive emotion that "stems from the desire to acquire something possessed by another person, jealousy is rooted in the fear of losing something already possessed . . . an envier is not envious of the thing he would like to have; he is envious of the person who is fortunate enough to have it" (Foster 1972, p. 168). It is even possible that the envier cannot really imagine himself with the envy-provoking trait or possession of the envied person, yet the latter becomes the target of the envier's destructive resentment (Schoeck 1970, p. 19).

On the basis of surveying a broad variety of cultures, George Foster concludes that envy is "a pan-human phenomenon, abundantly present in every society, and present to a greater or lesser extent in every human being" (1972, p. 165). Envy tends to be considered an extremely dangerous emotion because it implies aggressive hostility and the possibility of destructive violence. Therefore, every culture incorporates symbolic and institutional devices for controlling the effects and mitigating the fear of envy.

Helmut Schoeck likewise stresses the ubiquity of envy and the fear it provokes in all human societies. But he also contends that envy has a definite phylogenetic basis—innate aggressive drives as shaped, channeled, and frustrated within the context of sibling rivalry. The lengthy period of immaturity in our species leaves a lasting mark on our reactions to all interpersonal comparative situations, although individuals differ greatly in the strength of their aggressiveness and thus in the degree of envy that they are likely to feel (Schoeck 1970, pp. 62-64).

Robert Trivers's analysis of intrafamily conflict implies that rivalry is phylogenetically more basic than aggression, which is essentially a competitive device. Since the ideas he presented in another landmark article (Trivers 1974) are discussed elsewhere in this books, I will mention here only his view that some degree of conflict between parents and offspring and between siblings is to be expected because the strategies through which even highly related individuals can maximize their inclusive fitnesses are not wholly compatible.

One of Trivers's main examples of parent-offspring conflict that has been observed in diverse species is "weaning conflict." A striking instance of such conflict has been related by a !Kung woman, and it seems that the difficulties of the weaning period commonly give rise to sibling rivalry among the !Kung (Shostak 1976; see also Konner 1976). In this connection it is appropriate to recall Marshall's belief that envy is omnipresent within their societies and that fear of its effects is an important motive for gift giving.

The possibly critical role of the "envy complex" (in which I include envy, fear of the envious, and guilt induced by such fear) in regulating reciprocal exchanges among the !Kung suggests that it may have significant effects even within large-scale, very complex societies. Schoeck claims that "the mutual and spontaneous supervision exercised by human beings over each other—in other words, social control—owes its effectiveness to the envy latent in all of us" (Schoeck 1970, p. 87). That is, one motive for our usual tendency to conform to established social norms is fear of arousing the aggressive envy of others should we do or achieve something that violates prevailing expectations. Schoeck's interpretation seems more persuasive to me if one views envy as an evolved psychological weapon used to protect individuals against "cheaters" within their recipocal relationships.

A tendency toward suspicion of nonconformists would then be entirely comprehensible.

A symbolically extended and generalized expression of envious feelings is what Schoeck calls indignation-envy. This is manifested as a "visceral" sense of outrage at what we consider unjust treatment—not merely toward ourselves but also toward others. Without the widespread existence of this kind of emotional reaction among members of a society, a criminal-justice system probably cannot receive enough support to function effectively. also, "vulgar envy" of individuals who are perceived as getting away with violations of law undoubtedly plays an important part in deterring potential law breakers and in inspiring unofficial assistance in apprehending some who do commit illegal acts (Schoeck 1970, pp. 233, 248, 253).

It seems to me that Schoeck's "indignation-envy" is very similar to Trivers's "moralistic aggression and indignation." Also, Trivers proposes that guilt has evolved to motivate "cheaters" to make reparations in order to avoid their exclusion from all reciprocity. Both Schoeck and Foster interpret guilt as one reaction to the fear of being envied—that is, of being considered the beneficiary of an "undeserved" quality or possession (Trivers 1971, p. 50; Foster 1972, p. 171; Scoeck 1970, pp. 244-226). I would therefore suggest that the emotions that may have evolved as regulators of the competitive and cooperative relationships involved in networks of reciprocal altruism stem from and are mediated by the psychological mechanisms of the envy complex.

Because envy is a self-serving emotional "weapon," the extent and intensity of its expression will not necessarily correlate significantly with what an individual actually deserves, as judged by neutral, uninvolved observers in terms of the reciprocity norms professed by the envious individual himself. As Trivers points out, "selection may favor feeling genuine moralistic aggression even when one has not been wronged if so doing leads another to reparative altruism" (Trivers 1971, p. 50).

Ubiquitous fear of the envious can also restrict individual development or achievement. For example, Marshall notes that the !Kung are very thin and often express anxiety about getting food. Most of their nourishment comes from wild plants, which are usually available in relative abundance. But as a rule !Kung women, who do most of the gathering, spend only two or three hours per day on that effort. Marshall suggests that if a woman gathered more than her family needed at a given time, she might attract the envious attention of others in the camp and be blamed for not sharing her surplus—even though the !Kung have no norm that requires extrafamilial sharing of foods other than meat (Marshall 1968, p. 94).

Schoeck argues that limiting the effects of envy and the fear and guilt it provokes is an essential preconditon for significant social innovation. A society tends to "stagnate" when fear of being envied is permitted to function as a potent inhibitor of individual achievement. This effect can be discerned even in modern, change-oriented societies. Studies of working-class young people in Europe have shown that many who have scored well enough on qualifying examinations to enter high-status secondary schools fail to do so because they fear envious reactions from parents and peers (Schoeck 1970, pp. 179-180, 243-244). Perhaps "class consciousness" does not stem solely from rational self-interest and fraternal affection.

Within some societies envy-based inhibitors of personal achievement and social innovation have been overcome, with the assistance (possibly fortuitous) of belief systems that justify and rationalize unequal attainments and rewards. The ancient Greeks believed that a very well-off—and especially prideful—individual would almost certainly run up against the limits of Nemesis and meet with misfortune. But individuals could still strive for fame, wealth, or glory, because Fortune was believed to be wholly impersonal. The threat of Nemisis—even if it represented a symbolic projection of generalized envy—proved much less of a damper on individuals' striving than would have been the case if the envy of their actual neighbors had been legitimized. Vulgarized Calvinism seems to have functioned similarly in the early modern age, insofar as it justified the prosperity of the "elect." The popularized nineteenth-century American belief in the legitimacy of enormously unequal rewards for hard work, shrewdness, and good luck almost certainly limited the sociopolitical effects of envy (Schoeck 1970, pp. 122-124, 285, 352-353, 131-132).

In sum, I consider it entirely possible that the envy complex evolved in our species as a crude but powerful emotional regulator of reciprocity. It may even be indispensable to the functioning of society—but only if it is individually sublimated and its effects corporately limited. In practice, it will often be extremely difficult to differentiate between wholly legitimate "indignation-envy" and circumstantially unjustified "moralistic aggression," since the latter may be expressed with as much sincerity as, or more than, the former. I am not implying, however, that we should not make every conceivable rational effort to make this distinction.

Rank

More briefly I shall consider hierarchy-related behaviors. Elsewhere (Willhoite 1976) I have argued that we may well have inherited a tendency—widespread in the primate order—to form dominance-deference hierarchies. That still seems likely to me, but I would not give somewhat greater stress to the variability of hierarchy-related behaviors and structures. From a sociobiological perspective, both dominance and deference are behavioral strategies evolved within the competitive context of differential reproduction.

Flexibility in their degree and modes of expression would allow for adaptive responses by individuals to a considerable range of social environments. In general, it appears that the more overt and continuous the competitive interactions within and between human groups, the more likely it is that within-group social organization will be overtly hierarchical.

Studies of hunting-gathering societies generally do not discover what we would ordinarily call political hierarchies. They do disclose hierarchical status and authority differences in the various sets of parent-child, older-younger, male-female relationship. But, at least in Aristotelian terms, these are essentially domestic rather than political relationships, the latter involving the concerns of the larger community (Service 1975, p. 49).

Yet differential influence and even leadership exist in hunter-gatherer societies. There seems to be general recognition within the group of the distinctive traits or abilities of particular individuals, perhaps outstanding hunting skills or persuasiveness in performing magical rites. Such leadership is purely charismatic, and is in no sense an institution or office. Mediation of disputes is usually performed ad hoc by a kinsman who is equidistant in his relationship to the quarreling parties (Service 1975, pp. 50-57).

Compared with large-scale societies, then, hunter-gatherer societies are politically egalitarian. But they also incorporate the hierarchical authority principle—within families. Among the !Kung, for instance, a father has authority over his sons and sons-in-law and can expect them to obey if he asks them to go hunting. When he goes with them, he is in formal command of the hunting party (Marshall 1976, pp. 357-358). It seems reasonable to assume that hunting-gathering bands in the Pleistocene were organized along similar lines.

If so, it seems almost certain that elaborate, steeply graded hierarchical political structures originated through the cultural evolution that stemmed from a settled, agriculture-based way of life. Farming began to develop on a widespread basis about eight thousand years ago and inexorably spread to cover most of the inhabited territory on earth. This radically new ecological adaptation was made possible, of course, by the previously evolved high intelligence and behavioral flexibility of our species. But, I continue to assume, this flexibility was limited by learning propensities and emotional reactions evolved as adaptations to the preagricultural way of life.

Growing and storing food made it possible to support populations much larger than those of hunting-gathering societies, and the need for farm labor may have provided a strong incentive for increasing family size. Agriculture also required that people settle and remain—often for a lifetime—in a single location. This necessity probably led to a significant increase in social tension and conflict. Among the !Kung, for example, serious quarrels tend to be resolved without fighting when one of the families involved migrates to another camp (Lee 1976, p. 91). People who live by working the land cannot so readily use this technique; these circumstances led to the development of institutionalized means of adjudicating disputes and regulating the expression and effects of hostility.

Here I find it necessary to discuss in a highly truncated and schematic way the evolution of the state. I realize that there is much controversy on this subject among anthropologists and prehistorians—see, for example, the varied arguments in Cohen and Service (1977)—but for present purposes those complexities will remain largely unexplored.

At some prehistoric point in the neolithic, "chiefdoms"—small-scale monarchies incorporating a few villages—began to develop. The first chiefs were probably charismatic—men generally recognized for their outstanding personal abilities, most likely as leaders in warfare between villages or between villagers and nomadic marauders. But chiefs subsequently assumed additional functions. For example, Sahlins (1972, pp. 130-148) has interpreted chiefdoms in Polynesia as political differentiations of a kinship order that incorporates fundamental norms of reciprocity. The chief's obligation to redistribute the economic product of society—through storing surpluses for times of general scarcity or by providing lavish celebratory feasts—often served as a basis and justification for inequalities in political authority. Hawiian chiefs' conceptions of their rights to command the labor and products of others tended to expand until, in some cases, they were met by violent popular resistance. Much evidence drawn from contemporary preliterate societies indicates that "inheritance of status by primogeniture must be a nearly universal feature of chiefdoms." That is, it is "natural" for a chief to attempt to pass on his authority to his oldest son (Service 1975, pp. 72-74). Within the course of cultural evolution, societies with well-established and generally accepted systems of hereditary authority would have had the advantages of stability, cohesion, and coordination in military competition with simpler societies. Successful chiefdoms must have been the building blocks of the first institutionalized, large-scale states, which originated within the past five or six thousand years in a half dozen separate areas of the world.

According to one anthropological theory (Carneiro 1970), the first states all emerged within a distinctive type of environment—populations pressing on the limits of agricultural land that was bounded by geographic limits such as deserts, mountains, and oceans. Under these conditions, rivalries between chiefdoms led to wars of conquest, with successful rulers enlarging their domains. Continuing over a period of centuries, this process produced the first imperial-scale states. The families of the successful monarch-chiefs, their priests, and their leading warriors became the nucleus of an upper class controlling and profiting from the labor of subjugated peoples. Some of the latter became serfs or slaves; others who had become landless flocked to administrative-religious centers, which developed into the first cities. Here they became laborers, craftsmen, and merchants, who were paid for their goods and services by the agricultural surpluses squeezed out of the peasants by upper-class landowners. Thus was born steeply hierarchical political and social stratification—and also what we call civilization. The rest is history.

In the absence of patterns of conquest, overt, institutionalized political rank orders presumably would never have developed. Does conquest, which features force, fraud, and fear, provide an adequate basis for sustaining complex hierarchical systems? Fear of coercion seems to be a necessary but certainly not sufficient condition for producing a stable, long-lived system; an additional necessity is the symbolic process we call legitimacy. As Tiger and Fox point out, this is one of the ways in which we are a very distinctive primate—"one who creates out of the stuff of a local hierarchy the basis of an imperial apparatus. By the use of symbol wedded to underlying propensity, we strive to control huge areas of land and large groups of people" (Tiger and Fox 1971, p. 33).

During most of recorded history, legitimations of absolute monarchy have tended to be patriarchal—the ruler as "father" of his people—possibly a symbolic expansion of the family-based hierarchical component of politically egalitarian small-scale societies. In addition, kings and emperors always claimed to embody divine authority—either as gods themselves or as divinely authorized to rule (Service 1975, pp. 92, 296-297). This may represent a symbolic projection of the "Alpha" position in a linear rank order.

It seems a bit puzzling to me that hierarchy-rationalizing legitimacy systems have so often (although by no means always) proved effective if our species is phylogenetically adapted to living in politically egalitarian small-scale societies. Could the change of social scale trigger "regression" to a baboon-like pattern of linear dominance simply because of the plasticity of our type of primate hierarchy-forming capacity? Perhaps, but I should like at least to suggest that the tendency to develop semiautomatic obedience to authority figures could have been a highly adaptive trait within the selective context of human prehistory.

Several of the most eminent sociobiological theorists concur in the hypothesis that intergroup combat was probably the most distinctive and powerful selective force in hominid evolution—the critical influence on the evolution of the human brain: "No hunt needs quite so much forethought or ability to communicate complex instructions as does a war, nor do such drastic demographic consequences hinge on the outcome" (Hamilton 1975, p. 148; see also Alexander 1971; Bigelow 1972; Wilson 1975, pp. 573-574). Military success requires that combatants have effective capacities to command and obey, behaviors that are basic to hierarchies. Selection favoring the manifestation of such behaviors under conditions of perceived threat to

group integrity could partially account for the ease with which we learn
them and with which they persist, even apart from realistic threats of coer-
cive sanctions (Milgram 1974).

Anthropologists tend not to accept this view of human evolution, principally because of the relative lack of political hierarchies and of intergroup
fighting among surviving hunting-gathering peoples. But violent conflict
may be rare between such groups mainly because they live in a social environment that differs drastically from a world comprising solely hunter-
gatherers. Peoples living in that way are now very few. They have long since
been subordinated by crop-growing and pastoral peoples and pushed into
extremely marginal lands that differ greatly from the habitats of most
prehistoric hunter-gatherers. There is probably no way for us ever to be very
sure of how peaceful or bellicose intergroup relations were in prehistory;
but basic Darwinian theory would imply that, in significant ways, hominid
life has always been intraspecifically competitive.

Dilemmas of Rank and Reciprocity within Large-Scale Societies

In this concluding section I shall raise some questions and suggest some
ways of thinking about them. Although the questions are not new, they
have received little or no consideration from a sociobiological perspective.
This is a very tentative and extremely speculative attempt to begin doing so.

It is highly probable that reciprocal altruism and the whole complex of
emotions and abilities that govern it evolved within and between small
bands of individuals who usually knew each other personally: ". . . the
hunting band is a face-to-face economy in which one is locked into a system
of personal obligations" (Tiger and Fox 1971, p. 124). In reading about
reciprocity among the !Kung, I was struck by how carefully each person
"keeps score" of gifts he has given and received and how important it seems
to each individual that a satisfactory equivalence of exchanges be maintained.

The enormous change of scale from face-to-face societies to societies
millions of times more populous, in which social ties among most individuals are anonymous and formally symbolic, has affected human
behavior profoundly. But it seems reasonable to assume that we are just as
much concerned about being "cheated" or "exploited" in our exchanges of
goods and services as are the !Kung or, presumably, our common
prehistoric ancestors, and that phylogenetically deep-seated emotional
responses can be triggered by our involvements in processes of exchange.

An obvious problem within large-scale, complex societies is that it is
much harder for us than for the !Kung to "keep score." Although it may be
true that "[money] is a quantification of reciprocal altruism" (Wilson

1975, p. 553), as merely a symbolic medium of exchange it may heighten rather than alleviate anxiety about the "real" balance between parties engaged in economic transactions. Of course, as Garrett Hardin (1977, p. 19) points out, money use can also liberate individuals' time and attention for more productive purposes than "score keeping.") Aristotle's condemnation of charging interest on loans may reflect an ancient fear that money will facilitate "unnatural" exchanges—dealings in which reciprocity is violated. To allow money to breed more money could be viewed as contradicting a profound expectation of substantive, not merely symbolic, reciprocity in the cooperative exchange of goods and services on which the life of the polis depends.

An apt example of this attitude toward money is presented by Sahlins (1972, pp. 257-258). A European explorer in the nineteenth century tried to explain the nature of money to a Tonga chief. The latter thoroughly disapproved of it, because money is essentially useless for any physical purpose. Trading excess yams for bark cloth makes sense because it is obviously of mutual benefit, but since money is not even made of iron it cannot be converted into something practical such as a knife or an ax. Although money is handy, since it will not spoil, this trait enables people to hoard rather than share their wealth as a chief is obliged to do. The Tonga leader concluded: "I understand now very well what it is that makes the [Europeans] so selfish—it is this money!"

It is widely believed that money-based economies, whether agricultural or industrial, do make "cheating"—one-sidedness or exploitation in exchanges—much more likely and much harder to prevent than in face-to-face economies. Money-based economies function within societies characterized by a significant degree of stratification; and Durkheim, for example, maintained that disparities in power between social classes constrain to an unequal exchange of goods and services across class boundaries. This exploitation of less by more dominant classes creates a socially destabilizing sense of injustice, because it leads many members of society to believe that a fundamental *norm*—the expectation of reciprocity—is being persistently violated (Gouldner 1960, p. 167).

Concern and anxiety about breaches of the reciprocity norm give rise to "moralistic aggression," "moral indignation," "indignation-envy," and envy-induced fear and guilt on a massive scale. It seems likely that the more complex and remote from personal experience and control the economic system becomes, the more such emotions and attitudes flourish.

Even the objective, long-run outcomes of the economic system may not decisively affect the persistence of emotions stemming from "reciprocity anxiety" (although the consequent attitudes will probably be much more common in times of economic adversity). In this connection, Joseph Schumpeter predicted the demise of capitalism, even though he contended that it was the most productive type of economic system and, over time, would spread a higher level of well-being to a larger proportion of mankind than would otherwise be possible. He thought that critical intellectuals would undercut moral support for the capitalist system by using the rationalistic type of argumentation originally fostered by the matter-of-fact economic rationalism intrinsic to capitalism itself. Counterarguments defending capitalism, however empirically and logically sound, would not persuade the critics: "Such refutation may tear the rational garb of the attack but can never reach the extra-rational driving power that always lurks behind it" (Schumpeter 1950, p. 144). My concern here is not to assess Schumpeter's defense of capitalism but to suggest that his "extrarational driving power" could well consist of emotional reactions to "reciprocity anxiety." In particular, I mean the "envy complex," which includes strong feelings of fear and guilt.

The major type of political rank structure today is the government of the sovereign nation-state, and all governments are deeply enmeshed in the economies of their societies. As indicated previously, ethnographic evidence suggests that the earliest governments—chiefdoms—took responsibility for redistributing the social product, that is, supervising the reciprocity system at a somewhat more complex level of organization than that of the hunting-gathering band. Highly stratified sociopolitical systems have always been rationalized at least partially in reciprocal terms—the people's taxes and tribute in exchange for the divine ruler's magical guarantees of fertility, the vassal's military service and the serf's labor in exchange for the noble lord's armed protection, the workers' quiescence in exchange for guaranteed employment and the privilege of riding the wave of the future. Whatever the degree of fraudulence—no doubt considerable—in these kinds of claims (see Sahlins 1972, p. 134), they do point up the force and persistence of the reciprocity ideal.

In the modern age, social-contract theories have all been premised on the fundamental necessity and justice of reciprocity in political relationships. Perhaps Locke even unconsciously returned to a phylogenetic "state of nature" in opposing divine-right patriarchy, the type of symbol complex that had served historically as the principal justification for severely hierarchical authority systems. During the seventeenth and eighteenth centuries, social-contract ideas served as potent weapons in the ideological armory of antiabsolutist movements that were fueled affectively by bourgeois "indignation-envy" of the allegedly parasitical and exploitative hereditary nobility.

Schematically speaking, these ideas and emotions were significant components of the complex developments that gave rise to modern constitutional democracy. This seems to me the least unsatisfactory governmental system that cultural evolution has thus far produced for alleviating the harshness and severity of hierarchical differentiation within the structure of large-scale states. (That is simply a more cumbersome but evolutionary version of Churchill's famous remark that democracy is the worst form of government—except for all the others.) That result is accomplished—to a degree, at least—by institutionalizing competiton for governmental authority, which the victors temporarily exercise in return for not grossly displeasing a majority of the adult populace. These devices can function to provide at least some rough equivalent of reciprocity in relationships between governors and the governed.

But concern and anxiety about reciprocity in economic life create very difficult problems for this type of government. As Tiger and Fox point out, governments have resumed a deliberately redistributive function in reaction to the perceived shortcomings of unregulated economic competition (Tiger and Fox 1971, p. 133). In all modern societies with democratic political systems, movements fueled by "indignation-envy" and envy-induced guilt have contributed—along with real circumstances of economic breakdown, insecurity, and distress—to creating the present-day "mixed economy." This compromise seems to satisfy neither the partisans of self-interest-based competition nor the champions of absolute "fairness," "social justice," or "equality."

I would suggest that as genetically distinct but necessarily interdependent and cooperative beings, conditioned by a culture that stresses the worth of the individual and by living in complex, stratified, rapidly changing societies, we tend to place a high value on personal freedom but also feel anxiety and guilt about exploitation. Historical experience has shown that all-out, unregulated economic freedom cannot persist. It has been unavoidably necessary for governments to become involved to an increasing degree in redistributive activities. A difficult and troubling question with which this trend confronts us is whether, and in what ways, its indefinite continuation would undermine the socioeconomic preconditions of personal and political freedom.

Governments that do attempt to control and regulate nearly all exchanges of goods and services, with their controllers claiming that they guarantee total economic justice—truly *reciprocal* altruism—are hostile to personal freedom. Furthermore, their rigid, elaborately graded, and unresponsible hierarchies represent cultural-evolutionary regression to the governmental system of theocratic empires—without providing the psychological consolations of the supernatural. And, as far as I know, there is no persuasive evidence that these political systems are in practice any less economically exploitative than the mixed economies associated with constitutional democracies.

According to Tiger and Fox (1971, pp. 238-239), the only possible utopian system would be a return to the hunting-gathering type of society to which we are evolutionarily most explicit adapted. As we have seen, within that kind of social structure, extrafamilial dominance is mild and sporadic and reciprocity is policed by each individual for himself and his family. Envy functions to ensure social control and a considerable degree of equality among peers.

Most of us, no doubt, have been so "corrupted" by the arts and sciences and by civilization generally that we would shun such a "utopia." But, of course, it is "possible" only in the sense that it might (in the presumed absence of the fatal Tree of Knowledge) provide a relatively good psychological fit between human nature and social structure—not in the sense of being a conceivable way of life for more than a handful of people today. Within the complex societies that we have created and that are essential for life itself in a crowded world, we can only hope to gain further understanding and some rational mastery of our anciently evolved emotions. That might help us to calculate more realistically the economic, political, and moral costs and benefits of their embodiment in public policy.

References

Alexander, R.D. 1971. "The Search for an Evolutionary Philosophy of Man." *Proceedings of the Royal Society of Victoria* 84:99-120.

———. 1974. "The Evolution of Social Behavior." *Annual Review of Ecology and Systematics* 5:325-383.

———. 1975. "The Search for a General Theory of Behavior." *Behavioral Science* 20:77-100.

———. 1978. "Natural Selection and the Analysis of Human Sociality." In *Morals, Science, and Society*, edited by T. Englehardt and D. Callahan, Hastings-on-Hudson, N.Y.: Hastings Center.

Bigelow, R. 1972. "The Evolution of Cooperation, Aggression and Self-Control." In *Nebraska Symposium on Motivation,* edited by J.K. Cole and D.D. Jensen, pp. 1-57. Lincoln: University of Nebraska Press.

Butterfield, F. 1977. "In China Austerity Is Less Austere if One Has Friends in Right Places." *New York Times,* December 11, pp. 1, 14.

Carneiro, R.L. 1970. "A Theory of the Origin of the State." *Science* 169:733-738.

Cohen, R., and Service, E.R., eds. 1977. *Origins of the State: The Anthropology of Political Evolution.* Philadelphia, Pa.: Institute for the Study of Human Issues.

Foster, G.M. 1972. "The Anatomy of Envy: A Study in Symbolic Behavior." *Current Anthropology* 13:165-202.

Gouldner, A.W. 1960. "The Norm of Reciprocity: A Preliminary Statement." *American Sociological Review* 25:161-178.

Hamilton, W.D. 1975. "Innate Social Aptitudes of Man: An Approach from Evolutionary Genetics." In *Biosocial Anthropology*, edited by R. Fox, pp. 133-155. New York: Wiley.

Hardin, G. 1977. *The Limits of Altruism: An Ecologist's View of Survival.* Bloomington: Indiana University Press.

Isaac, C. 1978. "The Food-Sharing Behavior of Proto-hominids." *Scientific American* 106:90-108.

Konner, M.J. 1976. "Maternal Care, Infant Behavior and Development among the !Kung. In *Kalahari Hunter-Gatherers: Studies of the !Kung San and Their Neighbors,* edited by R.B. Lee and I. DeVore, pp. 218-245. Cambridge, Mass.: Harvard University Press.

Lee, R.B. 1976. "!Kung Spatial Organization: An Ecological and Historical Perspective." In *Kalahari Hunter-Gatherers,* edited by R.B. Lee and I. DeVore, pp. 73-97.

McShea, R.J. 1978. "Human Nature Theory and Political Philosophy." *American Journal of Political Science* 22:656-679.

Marshall, L. 1968. "Discussion." In *Man the Hunter,* edited by R.B. Lee and I. DeVore, p. 94. Chicago: Aldine.

_____. 1976. "Sharing, Talking and Giving: Relief of Social Tensions among the !Kung." In *Kalahari Hunter-Gatherers,* edited by R.B. Lee and I. DeVore, pp. 349-371.

Milgram, S.W. 1974. *Obedience to Authority.* New York: Harper and Row.

Parker, G.A. 1978 "Selfish Genes, Evolutionary Games, and the Adaptiveness of Behavior."*Nature* 274:849-855.

Richerson, D.J., and Boyd, R. 1978. "A Dual Inheritance Model of the Human Evolutionary Process. I. Basic Postulates and a Simple Model." *Journal of Social and Biological Structures* 1:127-154.

Sahlins, M. 1972. *Stone Age Economics.* Chicago and New York: Aldine-Atherton.

_____. 1976. *The Use and Abuse of Biology: An Anthropological Critique of Sociobiology.* Ann Arbor: University of Michigan Press.

Schoeck, H. 1970. *Envy: A Theory of Social Behaviour,* translated by M. Glenny and B. Ross. New York: Harcourt, Brace and World.

Schumpeter J. 1950. *Capitalism, Socialism and Democracy,* 3d ed. New York: Harper and Row.

Service, E.R. 1975. *Origins of the State and Civilization: The Process of Cultural Evolution.* New York: W.W. Norton.

Shostak, M. 1976. "A !Kung woman's memories of childhood." In *Kalahari Hunter-Gatherers,* edited by R.B. Lee and I. DeVore, pp. 246-277.

Tiger, L., and Fox, R. 1971. *The Imperial Animal.* New York: Holt, Rinehart and Winston.

Trivers, R.L. 1971. "The Evolution of Reciprocal Altruism." *Quarterly Review of Biology* 46:35-57.

———. 1974. "Parent-Offspring Conflict." *American Zoologist* 14:249-264.

Willhoite, F.H., Jr. 1976. "Primates and Political Authority: A Biobehavioral Perspective." *American Political Science Review* 70:1110-1126.

Wilson, E.O. 1975. *Sociobiology: The New Synthesis.* Cambridge, Mass.: Harvard University Press.

Yellen, J.E. 1976. "Settlement Patterns of the !Kung: An Archaelogical Perspective. In *Kalahari Hunter-Gatherers,* edited by R.B. Lee and I. DeVore, pp. 47-72.

9 Political Socialization from the Perspective of Generational and Evolutionary Change

Elliott White

"Political socialization" has been defined in a wide variety of ways. . . . The most conventional definition implies society's molding of the child *to some a priori model, usually one perpetuating the status quo. Such terms as "indoctrination," "acculturation," "civilizing," "cultural transmission," and "adopting cultural norms" are common synonyms for this usage. Langton (1969, p. 4) puts it this way: "Political socialization, in the broadest sense, refers to the way society transmits its political culture from generation to generation."* —David O. Sears, "Political Socialization"

Your dearest wish is for our state structure and our ideological system never to change, to remain as they are for centuries. But history is not like that. Every system either finds a way to develop or else collapses.
—Aleksandr I. Solzhenitsyn, *Letter to Soviet Leaders*

Each generation differs uniquely from the preceeding one; and each new generation brings with it important and irreversible changes in the art, economics, and politics of society. This truth, at once simple and universal, yet evades the canons still dominant within the social sciences.

From the perspective of contemporary social science, each individual is the product of external environmental forces beginning with birth. Childhood consequently becomes identified with a process of socialization whose function, and end product, is the creation of adults who conform to the norms and attitudes set down by the previous generation. The effective functioning of the socialization process in theory ensures the continuity and stability of the major institutions in society. Generational conflict has no place in this perspective.

An evolutionary framework that allows for the genetic diversity of all populations and hence all generations alters such a static view. In this chaper I wish, first, to elaborate the biological basis for generational change and conflict, with special emphasis on sociobiological theory; second, to explore the implications of such a basis for the study of political socialization in particular and political behavior in general, with a focus on issues that relate to the philosophy of science; and, third, to indicate in general terms the

picture of generational change that emerges from the application of this
biological perspective, with special attention to political socialization.

The Biological Basis for Generational Change
and Conflict

> Let copulation thrive, for Gloucester's bastard son
> Was kinder to his father than my daughters
> Got 'tween the lawful sheets. [Shakespeare, *King Lear,* act IV, scene 6.]

> Underneath the surface of cooperative unity and absolute propriety that
> the Rockefellers would manage to preserve even at times when tensions
> were high between them, there was conflict and a struggle for precedence
> among the sons, and a chafing desire to be free of their father's authority.
> [Peter Collier and David Horowitz, *The Rockefellers: An American Dynasty*]

Contemporary evolutionary theory implies uniquely important and irreversible generational change; and this is true independently of
sociobiological theory. Trivers (1974) asserts, in the very opening lines of
his classic paper on "Parent-Offspring Conflict," that, "In classical evolutionary theory, parent-offspring relations are viewed from the standpoint of
the parent" and hence "offspring are implicitly assumed to be passive
vessels into which parents pour the appropriate care." What Trivers asserts
certainly applies to the contemporary behavioral sciences and to their view
of the socialization process, but his critical remarks present more problems
with respect to evolutionary theory. There is no question that
sociobiological analysis as Trivers has formulated it in his pioneer paper
emphasizes the presence and persistence of parent-offspring conflict and
that such an emphasis can nowhere be explicitly found in prior evolutionary
thinking; but what I wish to indicate is that contemporary evolutionary
thinking does, in a larger sense, imply the genetic individuality and thus independent behavior of human beings—embracing, therefore, both parents
and children and suggesting the necessity of generational change and conflict. In support of this contention, an elucidation of some of the major
features of the evolutionary process will be necessary, drawing especially on
the work of three of the most prominent evolutionists of the past generation—Ernst Mayr, George Gaylord Simpson, and Theodosius Dobzhansky.

I do not equate generational conflict and change, for the one need not
imply the other (a point to which I will return in the following section).
Basically, I argue that human evolution encompasses such an array of
behavioral (phenotypic) characteristics as necessarily to give rise to both.
(In the case of generational (and other) conflict in particular, an analog with
automobile accidents might be instructive. With millions of automobile

drivers with differing temperaments driving under a myriad of conditions, some collisions are bound to occur, although any one accident, rather than being predetermined, must be examined in the light of its unique antecedents.

The evolutionary process, first of all, presupposes both genetic and environmental diversity; for if neither the genetic composition of life nor the environmental circumstances surrounding it were ever to vary and change, then no evolution of life would occur. The fact of environmental diversity and change encourages the development of genetic diversity, for life that is genetically homogeneous may find it difficult to adapt successfully to changing circumstances. It is the impact of these circumstances that provides the mechanism of natural selection in the evolutionary process.

Trivers himself (in Davis and Flaherty 1976, p. 62) observed in a 1973 conference devoted to the causes and social significance of human diversity one year before the publication of his paper on parent-offspring conflict—that "the genetic system not only produces the genetic variability that natural selection works on but is itself a consequence of natural selection; all the complicated mechanisms that affect variability of offspring are themselves under the influence of natural selection."[1]

The "genetic system" in life does indeed produce genetic variability. In populations of all sexually reproducing forms of life, including humans, each organism is unique. As Dobzhansky has written of the human species:

> Every human being has, then, his own nature, individual and nonrepeatable. The nature of man as a species resolves itself into a great multitude of human natures. Everybody is born with a nature that is absolutely new in the universe; and that will never appear again (identical twins and other identical multiple births, of course, excepted). [1966, p. 57]

If each human being is genetically unique, then it follows that each generation of humans is unique—uniquely different from the preceding as well as the following generation. Each generation, after all, plays its small part in the larger evolutionary process. The advent of human culture, even the arrival of a postindustrial society with a life science that includes genetic engineering, has not halted the human evolutionary process. The title of Dobzhansky's seminal work, *Mankind Evolving,* is still apt, as is his contention within it that, in the long term, the evolutionary process is irreversible—that "as evolution proceeds more and more genes are altered," so that "gene alterations" become "so numerous that the probability of retracing all the genetic steps in reverse becomes negligible" (1970, p. 178).

Each generation does its bit to guarantee the irreversibility of the evolutionary process. Each generation represents an additional attempt on the part of the population to adapt to changing circumstances. The existence of generations is itself, in other words, a mechanism of adaptation.

Generations exist because individuals reproduce and die. If individuals lived forever—and ceased reproduction to avoid the risk of being replaced by their offspring—then there would no longer be either any generations or any evolutionary process. Presumably, however, the survival of the species would also be endangered; with its genetic variability thereby restricted, so also would its adaptability in the face of changing environmental conditions.[2]

The uniqueness of each generation becomes significant in behavioral terms if one recalls the admonishment that Ernst Mayr directed toward any student of human behavior well over a decade ago. Mayr asserted that he would be "bound to make grave mistakes if he ignores these two great truths of population zoology: (1) no two individuals are alike, and (2) both environmental and genetic endowment make a contribution to nearly every trait (1963, p. 650).[3]

Behavioral diversity becomes a necessary end result of both genetic and environmental diversity; and one should keep in mind, with respect to the latter factor, B.F. Skinner's acknowledgment that the environment is never the same for any two individuals (1965, p. 424). Each individual, then, with his or her own unique genetic endowment, central nervous system, and set of environmental circumstances, must to some extent arrive at different opinions, even from his or her close neighbors or, more to the point, own family members. As James Madison long ago contended in *Federalist Paper* no. 10, the seeds of faction are sown in the nature of man.

This individualization of behavior, according to George Gaylord Simpson, has within the human species been carried "to altogether new heights" and "is a prerequisite for the human type of socialization," paradoxically finding here the "opportunity for its greatest possible development" (1971, p. 236). Such a perspective hardly stresses the conformity of children to parental standards. Dobzhansky's emphasis on human genetic variability (1970, p. 101) leads him as well to reject the behaviorism of J.B. Watson wherein a dozen babies may be made into any type of adult desired. Genetic diversity characterizes families as well as larger populations and guarantees both behavioral diversity and the possibility of conflict. It is noteworthy that identical twins are significantly more cooperative and less competitive than fraternals (see Koch 1966), although there may of course be a good sociobiological explanation for this fact as well.

The developmental process in the young adds to the probability of parent-offspring conflict. Again, differences are sure to emerge on the phenotypic or behavioral level. The limited cognitive functioning of young children described by Piaget is enough to ensure that parent and child will not always see eye to eye. The hormonal changes that accompany adolescence, affecting behavior and increasing family difficulties, are well known. Recent research increasingly emphasizes the individuality and independence of behavior in early childhood beginning from birth (see Westman 1973; Thomas 1976; and Jackson and Jackson 1978).

The evolutionary position taken here, however, goes beyond the view that generational conflict is rooted in the nature of the developmental process of the young—that, for example, the *sturm und drang* of adolescence guarantees resistance to parental (and other) authority. In fact, this position is compatible as well with an opposing emphasis on the developmental process as one in which children are unusually malleable and susceptible to parental guidance. Some biologists indeed stress this point: J.P. Scott (1963), for example, generalizes from puppies to children in assigning to both a "critical period" during which basic social attachments are readily formed; C.H. Waddington (1960) speaks of children as being naturally "authority acceptors", and E.O. Wilson (1975, p. 562) refers to the "absurdly" easy "indoctrinability" of humans. Although the persistent occurrence of conflict between parents and their children appears as a matter of common experience, we must note further that generational conflict need not cease once children have matured.

Generational conflict will occur because of behavioral diversity between generations, both within families and without. Even the most devoted young disciple will necessarily, because of a different genetic endowment, different brain, and different set of environmental conditions, alter in some fashion the teachings of the older master. The alterations may, in fact, become so crude and vulgar as to lead the master to disavow these corruptions of his doctrine, as when Marx denied that he was a Marxist. As Dawkins acknowledges with respect to his concept of the "meme," the cultural analog of the gene and unit of cultural transmission, memes may not be "high-fidelity replicators at all": "Every time a scientist hears an idea and passes it on to somebody else, he is likely to change it somewhat" (1976, p. 209). Since all of human culture is susceptible to such alteration—which in theory is inevitable, given human diversity—the opening sentence of this chapter should now make sense within an evolutionary framework: "Each generation differs uniquely from the preceding one; and each new generation brings with it important and irreversible changes in the art, economics, and politics of society." Memes, like genes, are sure to mutate.

To the extent that it is valid, sociobiological theory further ensures generational conflict. If each individual acts so as to perpetuate his own genes and if each individual starts life with his own unique set of genes, then conflict is inherent in social life even on the level of the family, wherein parents and children will share only half their genes (or at least chromosomes) (see chapter 4 by Masters in this book). Twins and "supertwins" will constitute the only partial exception, that is, only in their social relationship with each other. Since they will share the same genetic

inheritance, they will also possess, in theory, the same underlying motivation for social behavior vis-à-vis each other. In other words, because they
have identical genetic interests, their behavior ought to be unusually
cooperative rather than competitive toward each other, as indeed appears to
be the case.

Identical multiple births aside, however, sexually reproducing life is
destined, in sociobiological terms, to produce competition and conflict. As
Barash has written:

> A world in which virtually every individual is genetically distinct is one in
> which substantial disagreements between individuals would be expected,
> with each selected for maximization of its *own* inclusive fitness. Therefore
> real possibilities exist for conflicts of interest between individuals of the
> same sex (males versus males and females versus females), between mates
> (male versus female), and even between parents and offspring. [1977, p.
> 172, emphasis in the original]

Thus this inherent potential for social conflict—for Madisonian fac-
tional strife—is universal, including even genetically related individuals or
kin and therefore extending to sibling relations (that is, it implies "sibling
rivalry") and to parent-offspring relations. As Trivers notes, the latter relationship, following W.P. Hamilton (1964), "is merely a special case of relations between any set of genetically related individuals" (Trivers 1974, p.
250).

The major theoretical contribution of Trivers's parent-offspring
analysis lies in emphasizing the role of the child as an independent actor on
his own vis-à-vis the parents and thus in emphasizing the natural and continuing basis for generational conflict. Such conflict might be implicit in
prior evolutionary theory, but it is not explicit. And as Trivers (1974, p. 26)
rightly observes, such conflict has no basis at all in behavioral theory. A
Freudian view, of course, does stress an innate and persistent generational
conflict, but on theoretical grounds that are problematical though still very
much open to debate.[4]

Trivers's analysis is inadequate, however, in treating the full range of
possible conflict (and the basis for it) that may exist within families. We
may see this inadequacy in Trivers's remarks concerning possible conflict
between parents and offspring even when their genetic interests overlap.
Circumstances change, and as Trivers (1974, p. 262) observes, it is the
parent who is most likely to discover such changing circumstances as a
result of his or her greater experience. Trivers does indeed extend his
genetically based analysis here by pointing to the independently important
role of experience. But he simply stops short of a full discussion of additional factors that may also importantly and differentially affect the perceptions of parent and offspring.

Trivers's reference to experience is, ironically, made within an implicitly behaviorist context. That is, the parent, merely by virtue of greater age and life history, has the greater experience. This sounds like a truism unless one reflects that mere exposure to a multitude of environmental circumstances does not necessarily ensure the attainment of experience in the full sense of that word—that is, the greater capacity to adapt to changing circumstances. In short, Trivers appears to adopt here the behaviorist premise that external environmental circumstances by themselves are responsible for learning (see also chapter 2 of this book, by William Etkin).

Variable environmental conditions do indeed have to be taken into account beyond genetic factors, but in conjunction with two additional factors: (1) biological development and (2) biological individuality. In the case of the former, a Piagetian genetic epistomology reminds us that children are not, biologically speaking, minature adults and that adults are not matured homunculi. If adults persisted in viewing the world with the same brain that they had as two-year-olds, then clearly little experience would be gained. This differential capacity between parent and child for gaining experience must presumably add to their potential conflict, quite apart from changes in environmental conditions. Parent and child are simply going to view the world differently, even when they share the same interests.

Biological individuality further complicates the picture. Because of an underlying genetic diversity, all parents as well as all children will, with their unique brains, view the world differently. Thus what one parent may learn from experience, another will fail to learn. Children, too, will vary in their learning capacities; in an extreme case a precocious child might even surpass a slower parent in responding to a changing circumstance. Trivers, in ironic company with the behaviorists, fails to treat adequately the profound implications of human biological variability.

Trivers, in other words, in focusing on genetic relatedness, slights the dynamic and continuing interplay of diverse genetic factors with environmental ones, which constitutes the developmental process and produces for each individual a set of constantly changing phenotypic traits and for an entire population a wide range of individual traits that are in turn undergoing changes on the individual level (for an emphasis on the independent significance of phenotypic variance, see chapter 3 of this book, by Canton). Such a varied and dynamic picture will likely include a broader range for conflict (both within families and without) than a strict adherence to a sociobiological position.

To return to the preceding example of automobile accidents, sociobiological theory may have to move to a considerably more probabilistic mode of analysis. Parent-offspring conflict, rather than being a universal constant, may—like auto collisions—potentially exist but erupt only at certain times under certain conditions. The actual form of the conflict might vary considerably from families experiencing "violent colli-sions" on the one hand, to those escaping throughout a lifetime with only a number of "minor scratches," on the other. Such a picture would appear to conform to the historical reality, although clearly much more scientific in-vestigation is in order.

There is, furthermore, in the sociobiological obsession with degrees of genetic relatedness the dubious assumption of the rough equality of genes. It seems not to matter in sociobiological analysis precisely which genes are held in common. Thus there exists precisely the same basis for conflict be-tween all parents and all children insofar as the proportion of the genes that they share is the same.

Might it not, however, make a difference precisely which genes are shared? Might there not exist a qualitative difference in genes with respect to their implications for social behavior? Certainly genes that affect physical traits such as stature, skin color, and the size of one's nose may also affect behavior; but on the whole, would not those genes that influence aptitudes and interests that may be shared in common turn out to be the most critical of all in any analysis on intrafamily conflict?[5] Would not parents and children who turn out to share key psychological traits be less predisposed to conflict than those who shared less psychologically relevant ones, independently of the overall proportion of genes held in common?

These questions will have to await future research. But the next several generations of scientific inquiry into the developmental process, with par-ticular emphasis on the central nervous system, should tell us much more when these findings are related to social behavior. A broadening of sociobiological theory in anticipation of the complexity of such findings might nevertheless be in order (see White 1979).

The Implications of Parent-Offspring Conflict for the Study of Political Behavior

> In place of the social scientist's favorite myth of the second coming (of Newton), we should recognize the reality of the already-arrived (Darwin); the paradigm of the explanatory but nonpredictive scientist. [Michael Scriven, "Explanations, Predictions and Laws."]

Sociobiological theory is caught between two largely incompatible goals: on the one hand, the desire to build a systematic, comprehensive science emphasizing the discovery of universal generalizations applying, in some cases, from termites to man; and, on the other, an effort to explicate a biological reality that in the very nature of things is rich, myriad, and fluid. Trivers's analysis of parent-offspring conflict provides an especially perti-nent case in point.

Trivers's biology is populational, but his theoretical framework tends to be typological. This way of posing the incompatibility owes its terminology to Ernst Mayr. According to Mayr

> The assumptions of population thinking are diametrically opposed to those of the typologist. The populationist stresses the uniqueness of everything in the organic world. What is true for the human species of animals and plants. . . . All organisms and organic phenomena are composed of unique features and can be described collectively only in statistical terms. Individuals, or any kind of organic entities, form populations of which we can determine the arithmetic mean and the statistics of variation. Averages are merely statistical abstractions; only the individuals of which the populations are composed have reality. The ultimate conclusions of the population thinker and of the typologist are precisely the opposite. For the typologist, the type (eidos) is real and the variation an illusion, while for the populationist the type (average) is an abstraction and only the variation is real. No two ways of looking at nature could be more different. [1963, p. 5]

Trivers is populational in his explicit recognition of important individual differences even within families. His theory of parent-offspring conflict is, of course, postulated precisely on such intrafamily genetic variation. The behaviors of parent and child will diverge because of differing genetic endowments and hence genetic survival interests.

In this view conflict between parent and offspring becomes inevitable. It also becomes constant and universal for Trivers, but only by virtue of his typological theoretical bent. It becomes constant and universal for any given sexually reproducing species, not in the sense that the conflict between parent and offspring takes precisely the same form in each case—for clearly it makes a difference whether one is talking about, for example, a first or last born in relation to the mother—but rather that the same pattern obtains across the board for a particular species. This emphasis on the general, the typological, is indicated in Trivers's constant use of the phrases "the mother" and "the offspring" in his analysis, as if he were constructing archetypal roles.

An emphasis on the constancy and universality of parent-offspring conflict implies generational conflict, but not necessarily generational change. Insofar as parent-offspring conflict is constant, it recurs in generally the same form over generations. It is simply based on the recurring fact that in each generation the very same set of genetic relationships characterizes parents and their offspring.

The problem that arises here is that Trivers implicitly ties behavioral diversity mechanically to an organism's degree of relatedness. If, however, the unique genetic endowment of each organism, through the developmental process, also results in a unique behavioral pattern, then a much more profound behavioral diversity will characterize any sexually reproducing population.

Such a behavioral diversity should, therefore, also characterize parent-offspring conflict. Perhaps partly because Jane Goodall has, in her own words, "always been interested in the *differences* between individuals" (1971, p. 47; emphasis in the original), in her description of mother-child relationships among chimpanzees, she reports a wide variation in behavior—even for the relationship between mothers and their adolescent daughters, where she was able to observe only two cases. In contrast to the generally easygoing and mutually protective relations between Flo and her daughter Fifi, the other relationship (whose members remain unnamed) "seemed very different: in feeding situations she was obviously afraid of her mother, and we never saw either of them show concern if the other was threatened or attacked" (Goodall 1971, p. 185).

No doubt an observer of the human family could also readily report a broad variety of behavior in parent-child relationships. To repeat the conclusion of the first section, the wide range of genetic and environmental factors would seem to ensure a wide range of phenotypic and hence behavioral diversity, both within and beyond the family. By stressing genetic diversity only as a function of differing degrees of genetic relatedness, Trivers's analysis takes on an overly one-dimensional quality.

Yet even Trivers's limited recognition of genetic diversity importantly qualifies the sociobiological search for universals. For it acknowledges that even within a family behavior will vary as a result of varying genetic endowments. In other words, as against Wilson's search for a species-specific biogram—a set of transcultural behaviors—and his willingness to write off cultural and group variations in behavior to environmental causes, Trivers's approach indicates that even intrafamily behavioral variation may have a genetic basis. Thus intracultural variation may also rest on some genetic basis.

Both Trivers and Wilson are, of course, entirely aware of human genetic variability. We have already alluded to Trivers's observation that the mechanism by which genetic diversity materializes has itself been selected for through the evolutionary process. But sociobiological theory, with its emphasis on universals, finds it difficult to acknowledge the full behavioral ramifications of the presence of genetic diversity. For to do so would suggest an important theoretical qualification; it would mean the recognition, following Simpson, that the life (and hence social) sciences are historical in nature, as opposed to nonhistorical (as is the case with physics and chemistry). As Simpson explains, "The chemical reactions and physical processes in cells are indefinitely repeatable, unchanging in character, and non-historical," whereas "each real, individual organism at a given time is unique and changes through time to other unique, non-recurrent configurations. Those individual configurations are historical, while the physical and chemical properties and processes by which they change are not" (1964, p. 122).

To refer to the life and social sciences as historical, as Simpson does, is to adopt a contextual as opposed to a deductive philosophy of sciences.[7] The deductivists hold that the main goal and practice of scientific inquiry (at least in its pure preprobabilistic form) revolves around the subsumption of individual empirical events within general laws; these laws in turn govern the occurrences of all such events in the present and the past (entailing "explanation") and imply, given the necessary specified initial conditions, their occurrence in the future (entailing "prediction"). The contextualist—who may allow that deductivistic explanation and prediction are in principle possible—holds that in practice the complexity of the concrete interrelationships of events within the social universe implies constantly changing and significantly unique configurations that defy any general ordering—and that, moreover, to insist on abstracting such an ordering will result only in the formulation of static, ahistorical, and empty formalistic laws.

Certainly there is continuity and universality in life as well as change and diversity. But both of the former imply the latter. The genes now carried by all living things trace their origins to the beginning of life and are characterized by the same molecular composition, DNA. Yet the continuity of heredity is inevitably also characterized by change or mutation. And the universal operation of what Trivers referred to as the genetic system is such as to ensure genetic variability. Insofar as phenotypic and hence behavioral characteristics are necessarily vitally affected by such change and diversity, the observer of human behavior must come to grips with this reality. (see Almond and Genco 1977)

Nothing in current evolutionary science in general or in sociobiological research in particular contradicts such a populational view of life and behavior, especially for humans. Yet a young imperialistic frontier science, as it were, is impatient with subtlety, ambiguity, and qualification; and just as the behavioral sciences over a generation ran roughshod over the more complex aspects of human behavior, a sociobiological approach promises to do the same. Insofar as sociobiology constitutes an "antidiscipline" in relationship to the behavioral sciences, furthermore, its role, following Wilson (1977a), is to explain cultural phenomena by reference to their lower or biological basis. Hence sociobiology necessarily tends to be reductionistic in nature.

A certain inevitability may be inherent in this prospect. A bold new theory, however one-dimensional, must be worked through; and new insights will no doubt emerge in the process. But there is no point in denying the distortions and simplifications of the pioneering effort, for they all will have to be faced and corrected in time.

Political Socialization in the Light of Generational
and Evolutionary Change

> As seen in the model, the society, itself moving through time, is the com-
> posite of the several unique cohorts—at varying stages of their journey,
> and often traveling divergent paths. Only by understanding this fact can we
> comprehend the sources of tension and pressure for change inherent in the
> differing rhythms of individual aging and societal change. Each individual
> must endure continual tension throughout his lifetime because, as he learns
> new roles and relinquishes others, he must adjust to shifting, often un-
> predictable and seemingly capricious, societal demands. And difficulties
> can beset the society because each new cohort that is born—characterized
> by its own size, sex composition, distribution of genetic traits and family
> backgrounds—requires continual allocation and socialization for the se-
> quence of roles it must encounter within the prevailing social structure.
> Small wonder, then, that there can be no fixed process of aging! [Matilda
> White Riley, "Aging, Social Change, and the Power of Ideas"]

The picture of generational change that emerges from the foregoing
discussion, then, is one in which such change becomes viewed as inevitable,
irreversible, and unique for each generation—indeed, for each family and
for each individual. Current studies in political socialization clearly do not
operate on such a premise. In this section I wish to indicate how even Mannheim's dynamic analysis of generational change fails to conform to this picture fully and thereby also fails to indicate how political-socialization
studies reflect this inadequacy.

In his classic paper on "The Problem of Generations," Karl Mannheim
(1932) argued that a new generation was always in the process of emerging
and making "fresh contact" with "the accumulated heritage" of the
culture. Hence the experience of each generation was novel, and generational change was inevitable.

Mannheim's historical approach warns against overgeneralization
based on the experience of one generation; that is, if each generational experience is unique, then one such experience cannot be applied wholesale to
other generations. Yet, as Matilda White Riley argues, many analyses do
precisely this; even the sophisticated and influential work of Erik Erikson and
Lawrence Kolberg may be guilty of what Riley calls "cohort-centrism." As
she cautions, "one generation's folklore and 'common sense' about the life
course may no longer make sense to a later generation" (1978).

Political-socialization studies may also share this problem. Thus Cutler
points out that findings that relate chronological age to differing political attitudes may be historically bound: "Why should it be assumed," he asks,
"that the difference between 10 and 15 year-olds in 1960 will be descriptive of
differences between youngsters who will be 10 and 15 years of age in 1980?"
(1977, p. 300). As Cutler might have added, we have already witnessed

noticeable changes in the attitudes of American children toward political authority, in the form of the president, from the days of Eisenhower and Kennedy to those of Nixon during Watergate (see Easton and Hess 1962; Arterton 1974). And such attitudes will, no doubt, continue to shift in the future.

Ironically, socialization studies that tend to overgeneralize their findings and hence to take a static view by assuming generational continuity also are typically environmentalist in their approach. As Mannheim has indicated, on environmentalist grounds alone, generations will necessarily change in unique ways. Nothing is more fluid and certain to change than environmental conditions. To attempt to build a hard deductivist science on environmentalist foundations is to build on quicksand.

Interestingly, the only theoretical grounds for a systematic science that generalizes over time and therefore stresses generational continuity would be a genetic determinism that operated on an asexually reproducing species. In other words, a human species of clones, which in turn reproduced itself by cloning and whose behavior was wholly genetically determined, would be characterized by a uniform process of socialization and the absence of generational change, indeed of politics itself—unless, of course, each clone nonetheless underwent a developmental process that involved elements of rebellious or otherwise independent behavior.

As it is, such continuity as exists between generations probably has a biological basis. Mannheim may overstate when he writes that the biological principles underlying generations operate "with the uniformity of a natural law" (1932, p. 319), but he does thereby point to certain biological constraints and constants. Even if the onset of puberty can and has shifted over recent generations, for example, there are nonetheless some biological parameters that govern the maturational process and ultimately limit the variation and change that is possible, thereby making the process generally comparable over the generations. The sociobiological quest for species-specific behavior that is universal and grounded in evolution is not, after all, totally unjustified. It is the human biogram that directs the process of maturation and ensures some degree of uniformity and continuity for each generation, at least in the evolutionary short run. It is this elemental human nature that also guards against an excessive historicism (see chapter 4 of this book, by Masters; White 1979).

Yet Mannheim's historicist perspective does not go far enough in two key respects: It fails to take into account the reality of human genetic variability and of the dynamic interactional character of the developmental process. Both these factors importantly qualify his generational analysis.

First of all, Mannheim tends to view a generation as a uniform entity: Belonging to the same generation endows the individuals involved "with a common location in the social and historical process, and thereby limit [5] them to a specific range of potential experience, predisposing them for a certain characteristic mode of thought and experience, and a characteristic type of historically relevant action'' (1932, p. 319).

If we recall B.F. Skinner's acknowledgment that the environment differs for each individual, then we must qualify Mannheim's typological view of each generation on environmental grounds alone. As Rintala noted over a decade ago, ''Each generation speaks out with more than one voice—there is conflict within each generation as well as among generations'' (1968, p. 43).

Needless to say, we must also insist on the impact of human genetic variability. As a result, each generation, far from being monolithic, will include genetically unique individuals, all of whom are responding to the ''same'' historical events in their own unique way. To what extent members of the same generation may share historical experiences will thus always remain problematical.

The preceding observation applies with equal force to intragenerational factors. S.N. Eisenstadt's discussion (1956, 1965) of the youth groups that have emerged in modern culture, for example, must also be placed within a populational framework. Young people remain genetically and hence biologically unique during the developmental process; and this fact implies that even the most cohesive peer group will be characterized by individual variation.

The proposition that such individual variation might be, in part, genetically based is still generally rejected within the contemporary behavioral sciences, including the field of political socialization. Thus, for the social scientist, behavioral diversity is the exclusive result of environmental diversity. If biological factors are at all acknowledged, they serve only as a necessary basis for human culture and a virtually infinite variety of cultural practices. S.L. Washburn sums up this viewpoint well:

> The social sciences assume basic human biology and are concerned with the extraordinary variety of behaviors that may be learned. Human biology is primarily concerned with understanding the common biological base. The biological differences between individuals may be important in medicine and psychiatry or in achievement, but individual biological difference is rarely important to the social sciences. [1978, p. 412]

Just why the study of human behavior—in contrast to the areas of human medicine, psychiatry, and achievement—should be exempt from individual genetic influences is not made clear by Washburn, who, however, prefaces his remarks with the following example. Humans swim because there is an underlying biological capacity, but the particular manner in which an individual swims is a matter of learning and not of heredity; thus just as people swim in different ways that are unrelated to biological differences, so people behave in different ways solely by virtue of different learning experiences. Yet Washburn concedes that human achievement may be influenced by genetic factors; is it not possible, therefore, for one individual to swim appreciably better than another in part for genetic reasons, for example, genes that produce an exceptionally lithe body? Similarly, might not individuals be born with differing potentials and talents, with profound implications for social organization? This is not to say that each individual realizes his or her full potential, but rather that genetic factors may act as independently important causal agents on an individual basis. An overachiever and an underachiever may be found, for example, in the same academic environment; although both conditions may be environmentally influenced, they may also be genetically influenced as well. That a biologically literate cultural anthropologist such as S.L. Washburn should discount the behavioral implications of human genetic variability well illustrates the extent of the resistance within the contemporary social sciences to the full acknowledgment of such an impact.

A second difficulty with Mannheim's approach is its failure to see intra- as well as intergenerational change as real and dynamic also. Mannheim tends to view each generational perspective not only in typological but in static terms as well. Once a generational perspective becomes formed by early adulthood, it is presumed to persist through time. As Rintala writes, "Implicit in a generation's approach to politics is the assumption that an individual's political attitudes do not undergo substantial changes during the courses of his adult lifetime" (1968, p. 94).

Recent studies in political socialization cast doubt on such an assumption (see Sigel and Hoskin 1977); but since none of these studies are able to separate maturational and generational factors, the explicitly biological basis for change remains unexplored. It is at least theoretically plausible that insofar as one of the defining characteristics of the phenotype is constant and irreversible change,[8] then attitudinal and behavioral change is inevitable and rooted in the maturational process. If one grants this possibility, then Mannheim's emphasis on the uniformity of biological processes through time becomes misplaced and his analysis becomes even more dynamic than he might have wished.

The dynamic model of social change that Riley describes (at the beginning of this section) reasonably well accounts for the complexity of the process. Students of political socialization should accordingly take note. Nonetheless, there is one fairly important question raised by the Riley model that invites special examination by those interested in the political socialization process. This question concerns the part played by that process in social change. Riley correctly points to the difficulties that beset society because each new cohort "requires continual allocation and socialization for the sequence of roles it must encounter" and because therefore each individual "must adjust to shifting, often unpredictable and seemingly capricious, societal demands." What is missing in this formulation, however, is precisely the emphasis provided by Trivers's parent-offspring analysis, wherein all parents and all children have their own individual genetic interests and therefore, in theory at least, can be expected to assert them actively—even if these run counter to parental or other social authority (in the case of the children). In short, the aims of the socialization process and the actual outcomes may turn out to be very different; and the process of socialization thus becomes as dynamic as the model Riley proposes for social change. Indeed, if one reflects on it, one can see that the two processes are intimately related.

If behavioral theory is clearly too often guilty of viewing the socialization process in passive static and unidirectional terms, sociobiological theory is itself somewhat schizoid in this matter. Wilson writes, after all, that "[h]uman beings are absurdly easy to indoctrinate—they *seek* it" (1975, (1975, p. 562; emphasis in the original). Although a high degree of genetic relatedness characterizes parent-offspring relations and therefore suggests cooperation as well as conflict, acceptance as well as resistance, nonetheless Wilson's statement would appear to go well beyond the mixed and ambiguous nature of a relationship implied by a 50-percent sharing of genes. Of course it may well be that young children are in particular unusually receptive to adult direction, that they both seek and need it, although even here important individual differences may well be present. Future scientific inquiry must attempt some clarification of this point.

There is of course the possibility that at least some apparent instances of indoctrination are successful only on the surface, that outward conformity does not always imply inner acceptance. In other words, children (or for that matter, adults) may be deceitful in their relations with authority. For instance: a graduate student in political science, who as a youth had escaped from Hungary during the 1956 revolution, once told me of his participation in the rites marking the death of Stalin in 1953. It seems that he and his adolescent peers marched in this ostensibly solemn ceremony, but privately wisecracked among themselves; and although apparently it was all they could do to keep from "cracking up," they nonetheless managed to appear properly respectful to an outsider. Thus from a distance, order and decorum were preserved; but a closer look discovered an irreverence that, while camouflaged for obvious reasons, nevertheless proved to be quite real, as the revolutionary events of 1956 were to show. "True believers" surely exist, but not every member of a youth group (or other organization) matches outward conformity with inward belief.

The Russian futurist poet Mayakovsky enjoined the Soviet leadership to consider the komsomol, to look over their ranks, and to ask whether all were really komsomols or whether they were just pretending to be. (cited in Solzhenitsyn 1974a, p. 42)

The possibility that an individual's inner beliefs and outer behavior may diverge speaks to the need in political-socialization research to supplement mass-survey research projects with intimate in-depth studies. The latter may not effectively resolve this question, but the former clearly will not. One should note that Trivers's emphasis on the possibility of deceit as a strategy of behavior, especially as it might be placed within a conscious or intentional framework that would begin to apply to adolescence, suggests that not all the findings of political-socialization (or any other) research can be taken at face value.

Two points remain to be raised as guides to future research in the area of political socialization. The first is to reiterate the necessity of placing political-socialization studies fully within the context of genetic and environmental diversity, that is, to recognize the biological and historical paremeters that limit each study and thus to warn against generalizing beyond them.

Both a behavioral and a narrow sociobiological approach share this propensity for overgeneralization. A narrow as distinguished from a broad sociobiological approach, as I have written elsewhere (1978, p. 283), tends to focus unduly on inclusive-fitness theory as the basis for all behavior, whereas a broad approach leaves rather tentative and open the basis for behavior as it attempts a synthesis of the continuing scientific research undertaken in such socially relevant fields as ethology, population genetics, and neurobiology.

The so-called generation gap provides a case in point. Trivers's analysis implies constant conflict between the generations, but does not concern itself with cultural and historical factors that might significantly affect the nature of that conflict. Margaret Mead (1970), on the other hand, sees a qualitative progression from *postfigurative*, through *cofigurative*, to *prefigurative* cultures. In the former, "children learn primarily from their forebears"; in the intermediate, "both children and adults learn from their peers"; and in the latter, "adults learn also from their children."[9]

"Postfigurative cultures," writes Mead "in which the elders cannot conceive of change and so can only convey to their descendants this sense of unchanging continuity, have been, on the basis of present evidence, characteristic of human societies for millennia or up to the beginning of civilization" (1970, p. 2). Mead notes, however, that, "Intergenerational relationships within a post-figurative society are not necessarily smooth" (1970, p. 15). Certainly parent-offspring conflict of the type Trivers describes is not incompatible with this model.

Prefigurative culture, on the one hand, is the result of irreversible changes that have taken place since the beginning of the industrial revolution. "The primary evidence that our present situation is unique, without any parallel in the past," Mead asserts, "is that the generation gap is world wide" (1970, p. 18). Yet Joseph Adelson concludes (writing of the 1960s, which formed the backdrop for Mead's work): "There was, in fact, no generation gap, at least no more so than in any other historical period, so far as one can tell from the evidence" (1979, p. 33).

These divergent views have been raised, not in any attempt to resolve them, but rather in order to indicate the problems that arise when a historical finding is overgeneralized. Mead, for example, may have overstated the extent of youth rebellion based on the student protest movement of the 1960s. Adelson rightly points to the likelihood that atypical adolescents, such as those involved in student protest movements, monopolize both scholarly and popular attention, with the result that their behavior becomes overgeneralized to encompass an entire generation. Yet Adelson, too, may be overgeneralizing in stressing the similarity of intergenerational relationships over historical time. Mead's argument for qualitatively irreversible changes is compelling; and as she herself has noted (1964), such irreversible cultural evolution is the analog of evolutionary change.

If cultural change is, in fact, irreversible (as was also argued in the first section of this chapter), then both a narrow sociobiology and a deductivist social science need to be corrected in order to place their findings within a unique historical and evolutionary context. Empirical findings, however valid, may constitute no more than a snapshot of what is otherwise part of a unique and dynamic process; and longitudinal studies, unless perhaps continued indefinitely, provide no definitive solution of this problem. Continuous longitudinal studies, moreover, are premature at this point, since for obvious reasons they should not be undertaken before the social sciences have accepted a theoretical approach that can, with some reasonable assurance, be projected into the more distant future. Neo-Darwinian evolution has served its purpose for biology for over a century and promises to do so indefinitely into the future, albeit with qualification. Now such a perspective is quite likely to be extended to the social sciences as well, not so much in the manner that a narrow sociobiology might envision, but rather, as Simpson has argued, to join the life and social sciences together as historical studies. This development would ensure that both social scientists and sociobiologists would cease chopping up a complex and dynamic reality to fit a procrustean theoretical emphasis on uniformity and predictability.

Our final point concerns the more immediate matter of the directly political implications of generational conflict. Suppose in particular that, however qualified and elaborated, Trivers's parent-offspring analysis retains some central core of substance. What, then, follows in general terms for the study of political socialization? The most basic implication lies in the assumption that the child is an independently important actor in his or her own right and that therefore the political-socialization process should not be viewed as a unidirectional one—passing from adult authority figures to passively accepting children. Indeed, at times, Margaret Mead's prefigurative model may apply with some force; that is, the views of youth may influence adult politics.

Yet once again, a warning to avoid typological formulations is in order. The student activists behind Eugene McCarthy's 1968 anti-Vietnam War presidential campaign clearly had a national impact; yet, as Adelson reminds us, they were also clearly a small, atypical minority. Similarly, Triver's view of the child as an independent actor may be too broadly formulated. Are all children in fact equally resistant to parental (and other adult) authority? Elsewhere (1969) I have suggested that although the child must in general be viewed as an independent actor in the socialization process, important individual differences may exist, in part on the basis of differing processes of learning that can be in turn related to differing levels of cognitive ability.

Given a populational outlook, the following observation of Rintala makes sense: "There is undoubtedly much personal conflict between fathers and sons, but most of this conflict has no direct political significance" (1968, p. 93). As Lane (1962) has shown in his study of "damaged" father-son relationships in working-class, lower-middle-class families, no political implications follow, inasmuch as politics is simply not of salient concern.

Parent-offspring conflict should have direct political implications, however, for families in which politics is in fact salient. The most obvious case would involve families that have been prominent in positions of political leadership. Striking modern examples that come to mind include the following: Queen Victoria, who lent her name to the puritanical era of her reign and who, with Prince Albert, designed the most exacting moral and intellectual upbringing for her oldest son, Edward—who, in turn, became a far-from-intellectual playboy and a subsequent disappointment to his mother; Joseph Stalin, who as a most durable totalitarian ruler, ran the Soviet Union with an iron and ruthless hand, but who ultimately could not control the thought and action of his own daughter, Svetlana—who came to spurn both Marxist ideology and Soviet Russia; and David Rockefeller, the epitome of Western capitalism, whose daughter, Abbey, became an avowed Marxist and bankrolled protest demonstrations aimed against her own family name.

Clearly, many questions are raised in these examples. Why did the children in question, and not any of their siblings, become (political) rebels? What individual characteristics and environmental circumstances seem to be most critical in fostering rebellion, especially of a political character? Finally, why have other leading political families managed to avoid such dramatic instances of generational conflict (if in fact they have)? Some of these families, such as the Roosevelts, the Churchills, and the Kennedys, clearly afford additional fascinating case histories of their own. Future research (one might also usefully refer to Schubert and Willhoite, chapters 7 and 8, respectively, in this book) in applying the analysis of parent-offspring conflict to political socialization might well start here.

Notes

1. Trivers's observation was not novel, however; a similar point, for example, was made by Theodosius Dobzhansky (1970, p. 303). See Dobzhansky (1966, p. 57; 1970, p. 178).

2. See E.O. Wilson et al. (1977, pp. 109, 372-373). Whether or not genetic variability is adaptive on a group or an individual level poses an especially interesting question. Dawkins rejects completely any group-selectionist basis for individual death. See Dawkins (1976, pp. 42-45). See also Roger Masters, chapter 4 of this book.

3. My own attempt to apply Mayr's "two great truths of population zoology" to political behavior can be found in White (1972, pp. 1203-1242).

4. For Freud's view of generational conflict, see Freud (1931). For a more recent neo-Freudian statement on generational conflict, see Feuer (1969).

5. Interestingly, the American composer, Richard Rodgers, in effect touches on this point in his autobiography, *Musical Stages*:

> Most people have a strong desire for continuity. One way we continue ourselves is through our work; what we create or accomplish is our method of reaching out and becoming part of others [see Dawkins 1976, chap. 11]. But the most basic way we manifest our desire for continuity is by having children. This is biological continuation, but it can also be a form of creative continuation when one's children become involved in the same field that we are. [1975, p. 248]

Rodgers goes on to observe that both his daughters "have many traits and characteristics that are to be found" in his wife and himself, "but from a purely selfish point of view, it is especially gratifying to me that not only do they have a strong love of music, they also have been gifted with the ability to perform and compose."

Rodgers further indicates that only one of five of his grandchildren show comparable musical aptitude, although, like their grandmother, they demonstrate talent in the visual arts; although Rodgers prefaces this observation with the clause "[g]enticists may note . . . ," it is revealing that both professional geneticists and lay parents (and grandparents) are especially concerned about a relative handful of traits, that is, those intellectual and personality traits that particularly matter to people.

6. See, for example, Wilson (1977). Wilson is somewhat inconsistent in his *On Human Nature* on the question of whether human behavioral variation may be genetically influenced. As Schubert (in this book, chapter 7) points out, Wilson's view assumes no genetic influence on cross-cultural differences; but Wilson does, however, explicitly recognize a genetic basis for intracultural behavioral variation.

7. Contextualist philosophers of science include Michael Polyani, (1958); Stephen Toulmin (1972); and Michael Schriven (1962). However, I do not agree with the relativistic conclusions of contextualist philosophers of science. See, for example, my critique of Toulmin (White 1979).

8. In White (1972) I explicitly urge that an interactional approach be applied to political socialization. Some movement in this direction can be seen in S.A. Renshon (1977), and J.C. Davies (1977).

9. See C.H. Waddington's contention that "[t]he most fundamental and basic characteristic of phenotypes" is "that they change over time" (1968, p. 9).

10. Mead's (1978) revision does not alter substantively her (1970) empirical analysis, but she does alter and extend her more philosophical interpretation of that analysis.

References

Adelson, J.Y. "Adolescence and the Generation Gap." *Psychology Today* 12:33-37.
Almond, G., and Genco, S. 1977. "Clouds, Clocks, and The Study of Politics." *World Politics* 29:489-523.
Arterton, C.F. 1974. "The Impact of Watergate on Children's Attitudes toward Political Authority." *Political Science Quarterly* 89:259-288.
Barash, D.P. 1977. *Sociobiology and Behavior*. New York: Elsevier.
Collier, P. and Horowitz, D. 1976. *The Rockefellers: An American Dynasty*. New York: Harper and Row.
Cutler, N. 1977. "Political Socialization Research as Generational Analysis: The Cohort Approach Versus the Lineage Approach." In *Handbook of Political Socialization*, edited by S.A. Renshon, pp. 294-328. New York: Free Press.
Davies, J.C. 1977. "Political Socialization: From Womb to Childhood." In *Handbook of Political Socialization*, edited by S.A. Renshon.
Davis, B., and Flaherty, P., eds. 1976. *Human Diversity: Its Causes and Social Significance*. Cambridge, Mass.: Ballinger.
Dawkins, R. 1976. *The Selfish Gene*. New York: Oxford University Press.
Dobzhansky, T. 1966. *Heredity and the Nature of Man*. New York: Signet.
_____ . 1970. *Mankind Evolving*. New York: Bantam.
Easton, D., and Hess, R. 1962. "The Children's Political World." *Midwest Journal of Political Science* 6:229-246.
Eisenstadt, S.N. 1956. "Archetypal Patterns of Youth." In *From Generation to Generation*, edited by E. Erikson, pp. 29-50. Chicago: Free Press.
_____ . 1965. "Archetypal Patterns of Youth." In *The Challenge of Youth*, edited by Erik Erikson, pp. 29-50. New York: Anchor.

Feuer, L. 1969. *The Conflict of Generations*. New York: Basic.

Freud, S. 1931. *Totem and Taboo*. New York: New Republic.

Goodall, J. 1971. *In the Shadow of Man*. New York: Dell.

Hamilton, W.D. 1964. "The Genetical Evolution of Social Behavior." I, II. *Journal of Theoretical Biology* 7:1-16, 17-51.

Jackson, J.F., and Jackson, J.H. 1978. *Infant Culture*. New York: Doubleday.

Kaplan, A.R., ed. 1976. *Human Behavior Genetics*. Springfield, Ill.: Charles C. Thomas.

Koch, H.L. 1966. *Twins and Twin Relations*. Chicago: University of Chicago Press.

Lane, R. 1962. *Political Ideology*. New York: Free Press.

Mannheim, K. 1932. "The Problem of Generations." In his *Essays on the Sociology of Knowledge*, edited by P. Kecskemeti, pp. 276-321. New York: Oxford University Press.

Mayr, E. 1963. *Animal Species and Evolution*. Cambridge, Mass.: Harvard University Press.

Mead, M. 1964. *Continuities in Cultural Evolution*. New Haven: Yale University Press.

———. 1970. *Cultural and Commitment: A Study of the Generation Gap*. New York: Doubleday.

———. 1978. *Cultural and Commitment: A Study of the Generation Gap*. Revised ed. New York: Doubleday.

Polyani, M. 1958. *Personal Knowledge*. London: Routledge.

Renshon, S.A. 1977. "Assumptive Frameworks in Political Socialization Theory." In *Handbook of Political Socialization*, edited by S.A. Renshon, 3-44.

Riley, M.W. 1978. "Aging, Social Change, and the Power of Ideas." *Daedalus* 107:39-53.

Rintala, M. 1968. "Generations: Political Generations." In *International Encyclopedia of the Social Sciences*, edited by D. Sills, pp. 42-46.

Rodgers, R. 1975. *Musical Stages*. New York: Random House.

Scriven, M. 1962. "Explanations, Predictions and Laws." In Minnesota Studies of the Philosophy of Science, edited by H. Feigl and G. Maxwell, pp. 173-190. Minneapolis: University of Minnesota Press.

Scott, J.P. 1963. "The Process of Primary Socialization in Canine and Human Infants." *Monographs of the Society for Research in Child Development* 28, no. 1.

Sears, D.O. 1975. "Political Socialization." In *Handbook of Political Socialization*, edited by Greenstein and Polsby. Reading, Mass.: Addison-Wesley.

Sigel, R.A., and Hoskin, M.B. "Perspectives on Adult Political Socialization—Areas of Research." In *Handbook of Political Socialization*, edited by S.A. Renshon, pp. 259-293.

Simpson, G.G. 1964. *This View of Life: The World of an Evolutionist*. New York: Harcourt, Brace and World.

_____. 1971. *The Meaning of Evolution*. New York: Bantam.

Skinner, B.F. 1965. *Science and Human Behavior*. New York: Free Press.

Solzhenitsyn, A.I. 1974*a*. *The Gulag Archipelago, 1918-1956*, pt. I. New York: Harper and Row.

_____. 1974*b*. *Letter to Soviet Leaders*. New York: Harper and Row.

Tanner, J.M. 1971. "Sequence, Tempo, and Individual Variation in the Growth and Development of Boys and Girls Aged Twelve to Sixteen." *Daedalus* 100:907-930.

Thomas, A. 1976. "Behavioral Individuality in Childhood." In *Human Behavior Genetics*, edited by A.R. Kaplan.

Toulmin, S. 1972. *Human Understanding*. Princeton, N.J.: Princeton University Press.

Trivers, R. 1974. "Parent-Offspring Conflict." *American Zoologist* 14: 249-264.

Waddington, C.H. 1960. *The Ethical Animal*. London: Allen and Unwin.

_____. 1968. "The Basic Ideas of Biology." In *Towards a Theoretical Biology*, edited by C.H. Waddington, pp. 1-31. Chicago: Aldine.

Washburn, S.L. 1978. "Human Behavior and the Behavior of Other Animals." *American Psychologist* 33:405-418.

Westman, J., ed. 1973. *Individual Differences in Children*. New York: Wiley.

White, E. 1969. "Intelligence, Individual Differences and Learning: An Approach to Political Socialization." *British Journal of Sociology* 20:50-68.

_____. 1972. "Genetic Diversity and Political Life: Toward a Populational-Interaction Paradigm. *Journal of Politics* 34:1203-1242.

_____. 1979. "Genetic Diversity and Democratic Theory." In *Through the Looking Glass: Epistomology and the Study of Political Inquiry*, edited by H. Falco, pp. 311-328. New York: University Press of America.

Williams, G.C., ed. 1971. *Group Selection*. Chicago: Aldine.

Wilson, E.O. 1975. *Sociobiology*. Cambridge, Mass.: Harvard University Press, Belknap Press.

_____. 1977*a*. "Biology and the Social Sciences." *Daedalus* 106:127-140.

_____. 1977*b*. Foreword. In *Sociobiology and Behavior*, edited by D.P. Barash, pp. xiii-xv.

_____. 1978. *On Human Nature*. Cambridge, Mass.: Harvard University Press.

Wilson, E.O. et al. 1977. *Life, Cells, Organisms, Populations*. Sunderland, Mass.: Sinauer Associates.

Index

About the Contributors

Marvin Bressler is Roger Williams Straus Professor and chairman of the Sociology Department at Princeton University. His interest in the ideological consequences of sociobiology antedates E.O. Wilson's "new synthesis," and he has contributed several earlier pieces on this subject at symposia under the auspices of the Smithsonian Institution and Rockefeller University.

Hiram Caton is professor of humanities, Griffith University, Brisbane, Australia. He did his undergraduate work at the University of Chicago and received the Ph.D. in philosophy from Yale University. He was assistant professor in philosophy at Penn State University before receiving a five-year appointment in the Research School of Social Sciences at the Australian National University. He has published articles in a wide range of topics concerning the social sciences, his particular interest being experimental social science based on behavioral biology. He is presently at work on a study entitled "Politics of Progress."

William Etkin is professor and chairman of the Department of Biology at Touro College. He received the Ph.D. in zoology from the University of Chicago. He has been professor of biology at The City College of New York and professor of anatomy at Albert Einstein College of Medicine. Dr. Etkin is the author of *Social Behavior and Organization among Vertebrates* and *Metamorphosis: A Problem in Animal Development*. His research interests include neuroendocrinology of amphibian development, human evolution, and the philosophy of science.

Roger D. Masters came to the study of evolutionary biology and human politics from the field of political philosophy. After receiving the Ph.D. from the University of Chicago, he taught in the Department of Political Science at Yale University. Since 1967, he has been in the Department of Government at Dartmouth College, where he is a John Sloan Dickey Third Century Professor. Among his publications are *The Nation Is Burdened: American Foreign Policy in a Changing World* (1967), *The Political Philosophy of Rousseau* (1968), editions of Rousseau's *First and Second Discourses* (1964) and *Social Contract* (1978), and numerous scholarly and journalistic articles.

Glendon Schubert is university professor at the University of Hawaii at Manoa, where he teaches the biology of political behavior. In recent years he has been a Fellow of the Netherlands Institute for Advanced Study in the Humanities and Social Sciences; a National Science Foundation Faculty Fellow in Science Applied to Societal Problems; and a Fulbright-Hays Senior Research Scholar at the Zoological Laboratory of the Biology Center of the University of Groningen, The Netherlands. His publications include a monograph on the biology of primate sociopolitical behavior and articles on political ethology, ethological methods in political analysis, nonverbal communication as political behavior, infanticide by usurper Hanuman langur males, and the structure of attention.

Albert Somit is currently president and professor of political science at Southern Illinois University at Carbondale. Some of his publications include *Biology and Politics* and, with Professor Joseph Tanenhaus, *American Political Science: From Burgess to Behavioralism.*

Robert Trivers, formerly of Harvard University, is professor of biology at the University of California at Santa Cruz. One of the foremost socio-biological theorists, Trivers has contributed a number of classic papers to the literature. Several of these (key selections of which are reprinted here) received special interest from social scientists. He is currently working on a book on sociobiological theory.

Fred H. Willhoite, Jr., received the Ph.D. in political theory from Duke University. He has published articles on political theory and biopolitical topics and a book on the political ideas of Albert Camus. He is professor and chairman of political science and coordinator of the Biosocial Science Program at Coe College.

About the Editor

Elliott White is professor of political science at Temple University. He received the Ph.D. in political science from the University of Chicago. Dr. White has published articles on biology and politics in several journals, including *The Journal of Politics* and *Political Science Reviewer*. His current research interest is the relationship between neurobiology and the social sciences.

DATE DUE

OCT 3 0 1985			

GAYLORD   PRINTED IN U.S.A.